FOR REFERENCE

Do Not Take From This Room

SUPPLY CHAIN AND TRANSPORTATION DICTIONARY
4TH EDITION

SUPPLY CHAIN AND TRANSPORTATION DICTIONARY
4TH EDITION

BY JOSEPH L. CAVINATO

KLUWER ACADEMIC PUBLISHERS

Distributors for North, Central and South America:
Kluwer Academic Publishers
101 Philip Drive
Assinippi Park
Norwell, Massachusetts 02061 USA
Telephone (781) 871-6600
Fax (781) 871-6528
E-Mail <kluwer@wkap.com>

Distributors for all other countries:
Kluwer Academic Publishers Group
Distribution Centre
Post Office Box 322
3300 AH Dordrecht, THE NETHERLANDS
Telephone 31 78 6392 392
Fax 31 78 6546 474
E-Mail <orderdept@wkap.nl>

 Electronic Services <http://www.wkap.nl>

Library of Congress Cataloging-in-Publication Data

Cavinato, Joseph L.
  Supply chain and transportation dictionary / by Joseph L. Cavinato.—4th ed.
    p. cm
  Enlarged ed. of: Transportation-logistics dictionary / Joseph L. Cavinato, ed. 3rd ed. 1989.
  1. Shipment of goods—Dictionaries. 2. Physical distribution of goods—Dictionaries.
  3. Transportation—Dictionaries. I. Title: Transportation-logistics dictionary. II. Title.

HF5761.C36 2000
388'.044'03—dc21   99-088173

Printed on acid-free paper.

Printed in the United States of America

CONTENTS

PREFACE

This book is a moving target. The supply chain and transportation fields are evolving at an accelerated pace. Since the last edition in 1989, entitled *Transportation—Logistics Dictionary*, this book has grown from 3,500 to over 5,000 entries. In this brief ten year period there has been the reduction of transportation regulations and related agencies in many nations. On the other hand, new technologies are coming about in the field. Too, both freight transportation and logistics have grown into concepts of supply-, value-, and enterprise chains. Coupled with this is the recent development of eBusiness applications and the Internet.

The compilation of terms and their common usage is a complex task. This book reflects terms found in most frequent everyday use by transportation, logistics, materials management, and supply chain managers. While many of the terms in this book might seem distant from pure transportation or logistics ones, it was developed around the terms and concepts that effective managers in these fields know and apply in the effective conduct of their work.

No book is written without the aid and encouragement of many other people. A special thank you is extended to Jack Barry, eTime Capital; Dr. Richard R. Young, The Pennsylvania State University and the Acquisition Research & Development Center; Janet L. Cavinato, BP-Amoco; and, Joseph L. (Josh) Cavinato, III at Computer Sciences Corporation for their contributions. Finally, a warm thank you to Mary Ann Cavinato for her encouragement.

AAAA

A1   In transportation, a first-class vessel. The letter "A" specifies the class in which the hull is scheduled, and the numeral "1" refers to the stores and equipment. In Lloyd's Register, vessels are rated A1, A2, and so on down. In the American system, the registry descends from A by fractions—A1, A1 1/4, A1 1/2, and so forth.

AAR   1) Insurance. Against all risks. 2) Industry Association. Association of American Railroads.

ABAFT   Refers to a location near the stern of the vessel.

ABANDONMENT   Term has different meanings in different modes. 1) Rail. The permanent discontinuation by a carrier of service over a line. 2) Water. Constructive total loss. The insurer may treat such a loss as a partial loss, or abandon the vessel to the insurer and treat it as a total loss. 3) Air. Same as rail.

ABANDONMENT   General terms for direct computer to computer links between firms for order entry and processing and possibly for transmitting directions for shipping, checking on inventories and lead times, and billing.

ABATEMENT   A discount allowed for damage or overcharge in the payment of a bill is termed abatement. The extent of the abatement is usually designated before the bill is due. The amount of the abatement is deducted from the bill. The term abatement also refers to a suspension of proceedings.

AB INITIO   From the beginning.

ABOVE THE RAIL COSTS   Method of cost determination in the rail industry whereby only those costs of the train and train operations are included. Thus, anything related to the rail, rail bed, track maintenance, etc. are not included.

A-BURTON   A stowage term used in designating cargo stowed athwart ship instead of fore and aft.

ABC COSTING   Activity based costing.

ABC MANAGEMENT   Application of Pareto's Law or the 80/20 rule, the ABC classifications are determined by descending rank order of all products according to each as a percentage of the total. "A" products are the most important or the highest in volume, "C" are the least. Ranking can be performed in terms of volume, dollars, pounds, tons, etc.

ABOARD   A nautical word on or in a ship; also applied to railroad cars and other vehicles.

ABSOLUTE ADVANTAGE   Economic term used when relating two countries, firms, or other entities. It signifies that one of them enjoys an advantage that the other does not. This might be from possessing a patent or resources that are found in one but not in the other. It poses a barrier to entry for the one not possessing the item.

ABSOLUTE LIABILITY   A condition in which the carrier is responsible for all liability and is not exempted from the normal exemptions found in bill of lading or common law liability.

ABSORPTION COSTING   System of attaching variable and some fixed costs to units of inventory as they travel through the company.

ABSORPTION   1)Carrier rates: Carrier absorbs the cost of special service or privileges and does not include the freight charge, it is called absorption. The special charges may be for switching, lighterage, or wharfage. 2) Purchasing: practice of seller paying for some of the freight charges so as to equalize freight costs with that of a competitor firms for order entry and processing and possibly for transmitting directions for shipping, checking on inventories and lead times, and billing.

ABSTRACT   An abridgment of evidence omitting unessentials.

ACCEPTABLE QUALITY LEVEL   A quality control and inspection term for the limit of item characteristics that can be accepted (includes tolerances, ranges).

ACCEPTANCE   1) International. A time draft (bill of exchange) payable at a fixed or determinable future date. The acceptance of a draft is accomplished by stamping or writing the word "accepted" on the face of the draft, followed by the date and signature of the acceptor who must be the drawee. All the acceptances carry an unconditional obligation of the drawee to pay the face amount at maturity. 2) Purchasing. The second half of a contract formation (offer and acceptance). Typically, buyer sends offer (to buy) to seller who responds with a statement agreeing to sell. Upon acceptance, with no major exceptions, a contract is formed.

ACCEPTANCE, BANKER'S   A time or date draft drawn on and accepted by a banking institution. This signifies that bank's commitment to pay the face amount at maturity to a bona-fide holder.

ACCEPTANCE CHARGES   A charge generally made by a Foreign Bank for presenting drafts for acceptance if the drafts are not left with them for collection.

ACCEPTANCE, DOCUMENTS AGAINST(D/A)   An indication on a draft that the documents attached are to be released to the drawee only upon acceptance of the drawer.

ACCEPTANCE NUMBER   A quality control and inspection term for a number of faulty items in a lot that can be accepted while not rejecting the entire lot.

ACCEPTANCE OF HONORS   A term expressing a third party's acceptance of a bill of exchange to save the honor of the drawee when the drawee fails to carry out his obligation to accept it.

ACCEPTANCE SUPRA PROTEST   An agreement to pay a bill of exchange after it has been protested, to save the credit and honor of the drawer or endorser.

ACCEPTANCE, TRADE   A time or a date draft which has been accepted by the buyer (the drawee) for payment at maturity. Trade acceptances, unlike banker's acceptances, are drawn on the buyer, carry only the buyer's obligation to pay, and cannot become bankers' acceptances or be guaranteed by a bank.

ACCEPTOR   One who, by his signature, makes acceptance of an order draft or bill of exchange.

ACCESS   Modern purchasing and supply term for the act of linking with another firm to gain use of its technology or other beneficial resource. Thus, if the first firm can not develop the advantage itself, it will seek to access it from the other. It is the act of acquiring something that the firm can not develop on its own.

ACCESS AISLE   Passageway which allows access to storage areas.

ACCESS TIME   This term is used in data processing. It is the time required to link up to and begin an information flow.

ACCESSORIAL CHARGES   A wide variety of services and privileges that are made available in connection with the transportation of goods are assessed accessorial charges. Examples would be charges for switching, loading, unloading, weighing, pickup, delivery, transit stop-off, storage, inspection, grading, repackaging, billing and fabrication. A demurrage charge is likewise thought of as an accessorial charge.

ACCESSORIAL SERVICE   A service rendered by a carrier in addition to a transportation service, such as assorting, packing, precooling, heating, storage, substitution of tonnage, etc.

ACCIDENT REPORT ACT (MAY 6, 1910)   Amended on August 26, 1937, this act requires monthly reports of railway accidents. The Department of Transportation is authorized to conduct the investigation of the accidents.

ACCOMMODATION BILL (OR PAPER)   Sometimes known as a wind mill or kite, is a bill of exchange drawn, endorsed, or accepted without value being given for it, and for which no party is liable until value or consideration is given. The parties involved are known as accommodation parties.

ACCOUNT   The general category of customer service as listed on the company books.

ACCOUNTING, CONNECTING-LINE   Accounting for the movement of traffic on a through rate from point of origin to destination when two or more carriers participate in the haul. Each carrier receives a predetermined percentage of the revenue.

ACCOUNTING COST   Any cost that is captured and reported in the accounting system. Typically based upon past transactions or accrual updates. See ECONOMIC COST, OPPORTUNITY COST.

ACCOUNT PARTY   The purchasing party, the importer, the buyer in any transaction. Also "accountee."

ACCOUNTS AUDITED   To check the procedures and inventory of a customer account for accuracy.

ACCOUNT STATED   An agreed balance of account.

ACCREDITED CUSTOMER LIST   A list of accounts authorized to draw directly upon the stock in the warehouse. Generally furnished by the owner of the goods or his designated agent.

ACCRUALS   The accounts maintained for services rendered. The sum of the amount due.

ACID TANKER   This specially constructed tanker is acid-resistant. When applied to motor transportation, it usually involves a considerably smaller trailer.

ACID TEST   One measure of financial strength of a firm. It is the ratio of liquid assets to current liabilities. The liquid assets include cash, securities, etc. The higher the resulting number the stronger the ability to cover current liabilities.

ACKNOWLEDGEMENT   A voluntary declaration of the execution of an instrument before a proper officer.

ACOUSTIC CLOUDS   The levels of the atmosphere which impede sound. It is said that this is responsible for the erratic pattern of fog signals and other sounds.

ACQUIESCENCE   When a bill of lading is accepted or signed by a shipper or his agent without protest as to the conditions which appear thereon, he is said to acquiesce in the terms, giving a silent appearance of consent.

ACQUISITION   The transfer of title of one company to another through a purchase.

ACQUITTANCE   A written receipt in full, in discharge from all claims.

ACRONYM   Term signifying that a name for something consists of the first letter or letters of a series of names applying to the item; example is COLA for cost of living adjustments.

ACROSS THE BOARD INCREASE   An upward adjustment of all rates charged by a carrier on all commodities handled by it, with the exception of some that are subject to "hold down."

ACT   1) Regulation. A statue passed by legislature. 2) Law. The effect of the exertion of power, such as the Act of God.

ACTION PLAN   The end result of a reengineering endeavor or business analysis that includes the implementation steps and timetable for accomplishing a change or pursuit.

ACTIVE INVENTORY   That lot of inventory that is available for picking and/or use. As opposed to RESERVE INVENTORY, which is often a larger lot used for safety and back-up stock. Active inventory is kept near the use and shipping are in order to minimize travel in picking and assembling.

ACTIVE TIME   This term applies to water transportation and involves the time a vessel spends loading and unloading at the dock.

ACTIVITY BASED COSTING   An accounting tool used to determine the cost of processes within an organization that is largely made up of overhead and functional costs. It is different than traditional accounting that collects and reports functional costs. Activity based costing (ABC) attempts to view costs across a process with the intent of reducing unnecessary costs.

ACT OF GOD   Accidents of nature beyond man's control, such as flood, lightning, hurricane, snow slide, etc., are usually referred to as acts of God. The carrier is not legally responsible under most circumstances for damage incurred from acts of God.

ACT OF HONOR   A term denoting the acceptance for honor of a bill of exchange.

ACT OF MAN   This term used in water transportation refers to the deliberate action of the master of the vessel in sacrificing cargo or otherwise for the purpose of making safe the vessel for the remaining cargo. Those sharing in the spared cargo proportionately cover the loss.

ACT OF PUBLIC AUTHORITY   One of the exemptions from carrier liability under bill of lading liability; covers delays from quarantines, court orders,

ACT OF SHIPPER NEGLIGENCE   One of the exemptions from bill of lading liability; it includes improper packaging, loading and misdescription of the goods.

ACT TO REGULATE COMMERCE (U.S.)   An act, now known as the Revised Interstate Commerce Act; originally came into being February 4, 1887, regulating carriers engaged in interstate traffic.

ACTION   In law, a lawsuit.

ACTIVE COMPETITION   Rivalry between two or more carriers, communities or commodities.

ACTIVE CORPORATION   An actively operating business with the facilities and organization required for administering and operating the business.

ACTUAL AUTHORITY   Authority to purchase given to a buyer in the form of express permission. Involves buying authority dollar limits.

ACTUAL BREACH   Situation whereby a supplier does not fulfill its part of a contract. Situations typical are late deliveries or deliveries of wrong specifications.

ACTUAL DISPLACEMENT   When a car is placed for loading or unloading at an available point other than on an industry track, due to inability of consignor or consignee to receive it, the carrier may, by leaving customary notice, consider it as being placed at the point usually employed or designated.

ACTUAL LOSS   The value of product loss and damage incurred by the shipper/consignee as distinct from the amount recovered or recoverable from the carrier.

ACTUAL PLACEMENT   The placing of a car on a designated site for loading or unloading.

ACTUAL VALUE RATE   A rate that carries with it the obligation for up to the full value of the goods in the event of loss and damage.

ADDED VALUE   A term implying that at each production and distribution function, products are having value added to them in the form of time place and form utilities from the various activities.

ADDITIONS AND BETTERMENTS   Railroad term for investments in improvements. Additions include all raw equipment, tracks, etc. Betterments refer to improvements in such assets.

ADDRESS   In data processing, this refers to a label name or number to designate a location in a computer.

ADHESIVE FACTOR   Also termed adhesion of drivers. A measurement of the extent force may be applied to rail wheels without slippage on the tracks. It is usually expressed as a percent of force to the weight on the drivers. This term was most commonly used for steam locomotives.

ADJACENT   Next to or bordering on. Mexico and Canada are known as adjacent foreign countries for they border on the United States.

ADJUSTMENT   Determining the amount of loss and liability; the settlement of claims.

ADJUSTMENT (OF RATES)   The authorized basis, either percentage or arbitrary, on which rates are considered.

ADMINISTERED PRICE   Situation in which the price is not determined by market forces nor are they negotiable. Typically whenever price is set by a regulatory agency or a cartel.

ADMINISTRATIVE FUNCTION   The act of administering a court or a regulative body. Providing for the actual work or carrying on of the court or the regulative body.

ADMINISTRATIVE LAW JUDGE   The official before whom cases are heard, or handled in many non-oral situations, at a regulatory agency.

ADMINISTRATIVE PROCEDURE ACT   An act passed by Congress on June 11, 1946, setting forth the manner of procedures before federal agencies.

ADMIRALTY   Jurisdiction over causes of action occurring in connection with contracts to transport by water, also other marine matters.

ADMIRALTY COURT   A court that has jurisdiction over legal disputes arising out of navigation on public waters, is called an admiralty court. The United States District Court is referred to as the court of original admiralty.

ADOPTION   When one carrier assumes the obligations and operations of another carrier it is called adoption. When this is undertaken, a legal document called an adoption notice must be filed with the Interstate Commerce Commission or the regulatory body in charge.

AD REFERENDUM   A form of contract in which some points are left open for settlement at a future time.

AD VALOREM (ACCORDING TO VALUE)   Customs duty that is based exclusively on the value of the goods that are subject to duty, irrespective of the quality, weight, or other considerations. Commonly, ad valorem rates of duty are presented in percentages of the value of the goods. This is normally ascertained from the specified amount of the invoice.

ADVANCE   When a partial payment is made by a merchant, broker, agent, etc., at the time of receiving the invoice and bill of lading it represents an advance. It is a process of paying part of the amount due on goods sent for

ADVANCE NOTICE   Notifies warehouse of rail car or truck en route, and the merchandise on the vehicles.

ADVANCED ARRANGEMENT   The mandatory advanced arrangement for the movement of some commodities by air carrier. Gold and other precious metals, live animals, and any other classes of shipment require such

ADVANCED CHARGE   The amount of freight or other charge on a shipment advanced by one transportation line to another, or to the shipper, to be collected from the consignee.

ADVANCED PLANNING AND SCHEDULING   Analysis of various alternatives with the implications of each one. Used in complex system analysis.

ADVANCED RATE   A rate that has been increased since a specified time.

ADVANCED SHIPPING NOTICE   Typically, a faxed, emailed, or courier delivered packing list of the details of what is included in a shipment made by a seller or shipper. The buyer or consignee receives it in advance of shipment delivery and thereby can plan the use or further disposition of the shipment. This avoids having to unload the goods for the initial purpose of counting, and verifying shipment contents. Also called ASN, it can greatly aid in the reduction of total inventory in a supply chain.

ADVANTAGE   In traffic work a factor often considered in determining the reasonableness of rates.

ADVANTAGE OF LOCATION   An advantage which one city or shipper has over another because of situation with respect to nearness to markets of consumption, sources of supply, or agencies of transportation.

ADVENTURE   Shipment of goods on shipper's own account. It is customary for exporters and merchants to keep a debit and credit account with each enterprise as Adventure to Buenos Aires. A Bill of Adventure is a document signed by the master of the ship which carries goods at the owner's risk.

ADVENTURE IN CO.   Adventure in Co. is a shipment of goods at the joint risk of consignor and consignee, to be sold on their joint account.

ADVISE NOTE   A letter telling the recipient that a particular business transaction has been completed, or is being undertaken on his behalf.

ADVISE ON SHIPMENT   A notice sent to a local or foreign buyer advising that shipment has been forwarded and contains details of packaging, routing, etc. A copy of the invoice is usually enclosed and sometimes, if desired, a copy of the bill of lading.

ADVISING BANK   The bank which advises the beneficiary that another bank has opened a letter of credit in his favor.

"A" END OF THE CAR   The end of the car opposite the hand brake.

AERIAL TRAMWAY   Urban transportation system, typically light rail, that is elevated in order to separate its movement from street traffic.

AERONAUTICAL RADIO, INC.   A non-profit radio communications facility owned by the certified route air carriers.

AFFIANT   One who makes the affidavit.

AFFIDAVIT   A written statement sworn before a Notary Public.

AFFINITY GROUP CHARTER   Airline charter that is based upon a group of people who are organized into one body, such as an alumni association, travel club, or company employees.

AFFREIGHT   To hire, as a ship, for the purpose of transporting freight.

AFFREIGHTMENT   A vessel chartering contract that provides for the movement of the merchandise.

AFFREIGHTMENT, CONTRACT OF   An obligation for a shipper to tender a specific quantity of goods over specified period of time to a ship.

A-FRAME   A metal hoist or support which is used to handle heavy objects from a rail car.

AGENCY   The term agency signifies relations existing between two parties by which one is authorized to perform or transact certain business for the others; also applies to the office of the agent.

AGENCY STATION   A railroad depot or station having a railroad agent would be termed an agency station. The term also applies to a motor truck point where carriers share a dock or warehouse facility.

AGENCY TARIFF   A tariff issued by a publishing agent for one or more transportation lines.

AGENT, BUYING   A person hired for the purpose of haggling prices with selling agents for the purchasing goods or services.

AGENT (ELEMENT OF LEGAL)   A person who acts on behalf of another, called the principal. It is the basis of the relationship of a buyer or purchasing person for their employer or employing company.

AGENT MIDDLEMEN   The agent middleman negotiates purchases and/or sales but does not take title. They receive revenue from commissions or fees which are paid by the buyer, or seller of the merchandise, but seldom both. The agent does not represent both the buyer and the seller in the same transaction. He may represent the seller and buyer in different transactions however. The classes of agent middlemen are: (1) broker; (2) commission merchant; (3) resident buyers; (4) manufacturer's agents; and (5) sales agents.

AGGLOMERATION   A term in location theory indicating that an area or locale contains certain economies of labor, skill or other cost factors because of the existence of a large firm or function there, this phenomenon serves to attract industries requiring the same inputs having the economies.

AGGREGATED SHIPMENT   When a shipment is made from different shippers to one consignee in a consolidated action, and treated as a single shipment, it is called an aggregated shipment.

AGGREGATE OF THE INTERMEDIATE RATES   Section 10726 of the Revised Interstate Commerce Act stated that common carriage by rail or water may not charge more for a through rate than the aggregate of the intermediates. No such provision existed in motor common carriage, but the Commission has held a joint rate which exceeds the aggregate of the intermediates to be unjust and unreasonable.

AGGREGATE PLANNING   A production scheduling term for the practice of intermediate term planning of work activity.

AGGREGATE SHIPMENTS   Those under which aggregate tender rates apply, included within a single motor carrier pick up move, the economies of the single consolidated pick up, and often part of the line haul, are passed on to the shipper in this lower rate.

AGGREGATE VOLUME   The total amount of goods or services to be purchased or shipped over a specified period of time. An aggregate volume contract is typically for a discount price or rate that is based upon a large quantity of purchased or shipped goods that will be transacted over a long time period. Distinct from an individual purchase lot price or shipped quantity rate.

AGREED CHARGES   A form of rail contract rate in which a reduced rate is applied in exchange for the shipper routing a certain percent of total movements over a certain carrier.

AGREED VALUATION   The value of a shipment agreed upon in order to secure a specific rating and/or liability.

AGREED WEIGHT   The weight which is prescribed for acceptance of a commodity shipped in specific containers or in a specific manner is the agreed weight. The agreement is between the shipper and the carrier.

AGRICULTURAL EXEMPTION   An exemption from route and rate regulation in motor carriage (and with some products on railroads) when the carrier is hauling such goods.

AIR BILL OF LADING   Domestic and international shipments by air move under a standardized air waybill. It is the basic airline document covering the movements of shipments on international and domestic air freight. The contents of the document provide information needed for dispatch and the proper handling at points of origin, en route and at destinations. It accompanies every shipment. Usually the air bill is prepared in sets of seven. They are respectively as follows: carrier's accounting copy, invoice, consignee memo, delivery receipt, original station copy, and destination station copy. The airline normally provides the shipper with individual forms in blank, and the shipper makes out the air bill before the shipment is turned over to the air carrier. The air carrier receives the second copy when a uniform domestic bill of lading is applied' but when an air bill of lading is used, the airline retains six copies, with the shipper receiving the original.

AIRBORNE SPEED   The method employed to measure the speed of aircraft. Computed by dividing the sum of the airport-to-airport distances by the flight hours. It is expressed in terms of great circle airport-to-airport distance.

AIR CARGO   An all-inclusive term used in referring to mail and property carried in air service. Air cargo includes: Airmail, International Airmail and First Class Mail, Air Parcel Post and International Air Parcel Post; Air Express; Airfreight and International Air Cargo; and Company Material.

AIR CARGO, INC.   This corporation was founded and is jointly owned by the scheduled air carriers of the United States. Its principal function is to execute contracts with the trucking companies that provide a connecting service.

AIR CARGO GUIDE   The official listing of all carriers serving cities in the United States and Canada. Provides information relative to schedules, equipment, customs, maximum acceptable weight, etc.

AIR CARRIER   A transportation carrier of cargo or passengers by air. The term means airline.

AIR COMMUTER   A class of airline that generally serves smaller market cities with airplanes ranging from four to about 30 seats, often same as air taxi.

AIR CONTAINER   The container used to facilitate air transportation of cargo.

AIRCRAFT MILES   The airport-to-airport distance for a flight.

AIRCRAFT PIRACY   This term refers to aircraft hijacking, or the taking over of an aircraft while it is in flight or awaiting flight. It involves the use of the threat of violence.

AIRFRAME   An aircraft, excluding its engine and accessories.

AIR FREIGHT   The movement of freight by air. In the past it meant only the movement by air carriers certified in the United States and Canada. Today it is a generic term for any movement of freight by air carrier.

AIR FREIGHT FORWARDER   Classified as a transportation carrier, the freight forwarder assembles and consolidates small shipments into larger shipments. Its rates approximate those of the small shipment, but it receives service from the carrier on the basis of the consolidated larger shipment. It operates pickup and delivery services, as well as line haul operations.

AIR FREIGHT RATES   These rates are simpler than those for other forms of transportation. The tariffs are put out by the Airline Tariff Publishers, Inc. as agents for the carriers. About six different tariffs are published. For example, SC 3 is a commodity rate tariff in charges per hundred pounds for minimum weights 100, 1000, 2000, 3000, 5000, and 10,000 pounds. Another example is CT 4 which is a container tariff It applies on general and specific commodities, and presents rates about one-third off of existing rates for all weights in a container that exceed a specified amount. Other tariffs cover service transportation to the airport, local and joint airport to airport movements, and a rules tariff.

AIRLINE   A commercial air transportation carrier, involving its equipment, personnel, and array of facilities.

AIRLINE EXCHANGE RAIL ORDER   An order drawn on the agents of rail carriers by airline companies to provide for passenger services as a result of grounded airline service. Sometimes it authorized cash for the grounded service.

AIRLINE TARIFF PUBLISHERS, INC.   This organization publishes airline tariffs, which present the station to station rates charged for the movement of cargo or personnel. Likewise published are the rules relative to air movement.

AIRLINE TERMINAL   The airport building, runways, aprons, and all facilities, including parking, for passenger services.

AIR MAIL   Airmail, Air Parcel Post and First Class Mail are carried in air Department. International Airmail and International Air Parcel Post are carried beyond the boundaries of the U.S. under contract to and through the agencies of the U.S. Post Office Department.

AIR PARCEL POST   The transportation by air of packages as air mail. Usually involves packages of five pounds or less. Packages cannot exceed seventy pounds in weight and 100 inches in combined length and girth.

AIRPORT   The complete land facilities required to service the landing and take-off of aircraft. Includes runways, aprons, hangars, terminal buildings, and all accommodations for passengers—including parking.

AIRPORT NOTICE   The statement of intent to serve a named point or points, authorized in the certificate. Filed with the Civil Aeronautics Board by the air carrier.

AIRSCAPE   Pictures taken from an airplane.

AIR SIDE   Airline industry term for that space in the terminal that is inside the security zone. Includes gates, hallways, lounges, and concessions that are within the "sterile" passenger screening area. Distinct from LAND SIDE.

AIR SLIDE   Type of covered hopper car that uses forced air to loosen the bulk lading along the slanted floor so as to facilitate unloading through bottom hatches.

AIRSTRIPS   Term for small airport runway.

AIR TAXI OPERATOR   An air carrier usually operating by charter only. Under former regulation the term meant a carrier limited to aircraft under a certain maximum takeoff weight. The distinction has passed in the United States with the elimination of the Civil Aeronautics Board.

AIR TRANSPORT BOARD   The regulatory authority for Canadian air transportation carriers. The counterpart of the United States Civil Aeronautics Board.

AIR TRANSPORTATION ASSOCIATION OF AMERICA   The AATA is the principal trade association for the certified, common air transportation carriers of the United States. It assembles statistics, serves as the spokesman, provides research, and performs numerous other functions for member carriers.

AIR WAYBILL   The document used for the shipment for air freight by the national and international air carriers. It states the commodities shipped, shipping instructions, shipping costs, etc.

AIR WAYBILLS (OF LADING)   A signed receipt and a contract to deliver goods by air. Such bills are non-negotiable and do not convey title to the goods as do "to order" bills of lading used by ocean and land carriers, the title passes to the party to whom the goods are consigned (the consignee).

AISLE   Any passageway within a storage area.

AKTIEBOLAGER A.P.   Term for Swedish stock company, or corporation.

AKTIEN-GESELLSCHAFT, A.G.   Term for German stock company.

AKTIESELSKABET   Term for stock companies based in Norway.

AKTIESELSKABET   A.S. Danish stock company

ALIGNMENT   General term indicating that the functions and processes of a firm are linked together and congruent with its overall strategic directions and thrusts of action.

ALIUNDE   From another course.

ALL-CARGO CARRIER   A class of air carrier operating for the movement of air freight as a common carrier. It carries air mail, express and freight, over specified routes on schedule. It may serve as a non-scheduled carrier and also carry passengers.

ALL-COMMODITY RATES   A freight rate usually based on a carload quantity, applying to a shipment which may include any combination of commodities, but subject to stated exceptions and conditions, is called an all commodity rate. It may also be called an all-freight rate.

ALL-CONTAINER SHIP   A ship fitted for container carriage in all available space. In van-container stowage, the ship is fitted with vertical cells for container placement. Some vans are carried additionally on deck. Longer containers are deck stowed. No provisions are available for cargo other than in container form.

ALLENGE   Attachment to bill of exchange for additional endorsements

ALLIANCE   Term to indicate that two or more firms have developed a relationship to be linked for the purpose of competing against another set of firms. The relationships can be focused upon presenting a common marketing face. Others are created for the purpose of developing and exploiting a technology. Airlines have created global alliances through scheduling and frequent flier programs in order for each of them in the alliance to extend their marketing and route influence without having to merge with the partner airlines.

ALLOCATION, OF EXPENSE   In transportation accounting, the apportionment of the expenditures and revenues to the respective divisions of the organizations, such as maintenance of way and structure costs being divided between freight and passenger service since they are used by both.

ALLOCATION, OVERHEAD   The act of financially dividing up overhead and spreading it across various products, lines of business, or other accounting units.

ALLOCATION, OF PURCHASES   Situation when suppliers do not have sufficient capacity to satisfy all demand. Customers are limited in the amount they may purchase in any given time period.

ALLOCATION OF RESOURCES   The use of the resources for different activities.

ALLOCATION, SALES   In times of short supply or capacity, sellers will assign specific quantities of product sales to specific customers. The actual quantities or percent of total production allocation schemes are usually based upon past loyalty and volumes that each customer has purchased from the firm over several years.

ALLONGE   A paper attached to a bill of exchange, on which additional endorsements may be placed when the back of the bill has already been filled with named.

ALLOTMENT TICKET   An order for payment of wages to seaman's family at set intervals during his absence on a voyage.

ALLOWANCE   A deduction made from the gross weight or value of goods or services. The Revised Interstate Commerce Act requires the carriers to furnish the service of carriage (haul) and also such facilities as are necessary to make the service of transporting a shipment as safe and complete as possible under conditions existing at time of movement. If the necessary equipment, such as dunnage, elevation, or private cars, furnished by the shipper and not by the carrier the carrier could under proper tariff authority' allow such costs. Mileage allowance is an allowance, based on distance, made by the railroads to private owners of freight cars. Lateral allowances are allowances for services performed granted by large rail lines to smaller connecting lines.

ALL PURPOSE AIR CARRIER   A carrier of passengers and cargo by air carrier

ALL-RAIL   An act of carriage exclusively by railroad transportation. The term includes those lines or that service using car ferries or lighters.

ALL-RISK CLAUSE   An insurance coverage in which all loss and damage to goods are insured unless caused by inherent deficiencies.

ALL-WATER   An act of carriage exclusively by water transportation.

ALOFT   Locations above the deck, such as an observer aloft, or cargo aloft on a derrick head.

ALONGSIDE   By the side of.

ALPHANUMERIC   This designates that the characters may be either letters or numeric symbols.

ALTERNATIVE CHANNELS   Paths of product distribution that are in addition to the ones traditionally used by a firm to get its products to market. Today, many brand manufacturers are exploring use of the Internet as an alternative channel to the traditional wholesaler and retailer network to reach ultimate consumers.

ALTERNATIVE or OPPORTUNITY COSTS   The cost of an option or commodity in terms of its alternative use. The value measured in terms of its foregone worth in an alternate usage.

ALTERNATIVE RATES   Two or more rates, of which the lowest charge is applicable.

ALTERNATIVE ROUTE   A motor carrier is authorized to perform regular service over a specified route under a permit or certificate. However, sometimes it is permitted to substitute an optional motor-carrier route instead of the specified route.

ALTERNATIVE TARIFF   A tariff containing two or more rates, from and to the same points, on the same goods, with the authority to use the one which provides the lowest charge.

AMBIENT   Term pertaining to the temperature of goods in a shipment. As contrasted with frozen, or chilled, ambient means room temperature or not having to protect against or provide for a specific temperature in transit and storage.

AMBIGUOUS   Susceptible of several interpretations.

AMENDED ITEM   An item that has been changed or modified by a succeeding publication, made necessary because of error or changed conditions, and showing item in its revised form.

AMENDMENT   An alteration, change or correction.

AMENDMENT   A written notice of change in the terms of a letter of credit, which becomes an integral part of the original letter of credit.

AMERICAN BUREAU OF SHIPPING   This organization is committed to the classification, specification, and examination of vessels for seaworthiness.

AMERICAN FLAG CARRIER   An air or water carrier operating in international transportation movements that is based in the United States. Such air carriers are approved for service by the President of the United States. Some carriers also perform domestic service.

AMERICAN NATIONAL STANDARDS INSTITUTE (ANSI)   Organization in the United States that served to develop standards for electronic data interchange protocols.

AMERICAN PRODUCTION AND INVENTORY CONTROL SOCIETY.   A professional organization with emphasis upon materials planning, production scheduling, shop floor control, and other factory-related inventory concepts.

AMERICAN SOCIETY OF TRANSPORTATION & LOGISTICS   A profes-
sional society in the field of transportation and logistics; has as its main form of
membership that of Certified Member. For Certified Members it requires passing
or waiving exams in the field and submitting a professional contribution in the
form of a paper, program, tape, or other form of quality communication. The
AST&L is based in Atlanta, Georgia; it has chapters throughout the United States,
and it publishes a journal called the TRANSPORTATION JOURNAL.

AMERICAN STANDARD ASSOCIATION MH-T COMMITTEE   A commit-
tee dedicated to the standardization of containers, container procedures and handling systems. It represents all segments of transportation carrier and shipper groups.

AMERICAN WITH DISABILITIES ACT (U.S.)   A law designed to provide access
by persons with alternate abilities to buildings, facilities, transport and workplaces.
It requires construction designs to comply with special standards.

AMERICAN TRUCKING ASSOCIATIONS   The trade association serving the
trucking industry. A composite of the state organizations of truckers operating in
the United States. Headquarters in Alexandria, VA.

AMERICAN WAREHOUSEMEN'S ASSOCIATION   Voluntary organization of
warehousemen established to assure high standards in the warehouse.

AMORTIZATION COST   The annual payment for expiring a debt according to
a contract or other agreement on a continuous basis 15 called the amortization
cost. Therefore, amortization cost is established when something is purchased from
borrowed funds, and the annual payment represents the gradual repayment of borrowed funds. In addition to the amortization cost, an interest on the unamortized
investment is likewise involved in the payment.

ANALOGOUS ARTICLE   Articles having similar characteristics. A term used in
determining the applicable rate among several commodity groupings in a tariff.

ANALOGY CLASSIFICATION BY   A term indicating that a product not specifically named in a tariff will be classified for rate billing purposes according to its
similarity in transportation characteristics and inherent nature with another product
that is specifically named in the tariff.

ANCHORAGE   A spot near shore where ships may be positioned for safety.

ANDERSON SCALE   The name given the mileage basis formally used by New
England (U.S.) carriers in a decision handed down by Commissioner Anderson of
the Interstate Commerce Commission in the years of regulation.

ANGLE STACKING   Placing stock in a storage area at a 45 degree angle to the
aisle.

ANKER   An international liquid measure, varying from nine to ten gallons.

ANNOUNCEMENT   A formal statement or notice given out by a regulatory authority or carrier with respect to its action or intent covering established practices or findings in a particular case situation.

ANNUAL REPORT TO THE INTERSTATE COMMERCE COMMISSION (U.S.)   Yearly reports to the Commission, summarizing its activities during the year and offering recommendations for legislative changes affecting interstate transportation. These are of historical interest by today's transportation economists and policy makers.

ANNUAL VOLUME RATE   A rate that is tied to a minimum annual tonnage volume by a shipper; a form of contract rate.

ANNUS   Year.

ANTE   Before.

ANTI   Against.

ANTICIPATORY BREACH   Situation whereby a buyer fears that a supplier will not act upon an agreed to future date. Buyer can take some action to determine if supplier will or will not perform. These actions or non-action may result in buyer safely assuming that seller will not perform in the future. This gives rise to an anticipatory breach.

ANTICIPATORY BUYING   Buying in advance of actual need or demand for the purpose of avoiding a shortage, stock-out, or price increase. A form of forward buying.

ANTI DUMPING DUTY   A tariff imposed for the purpose of preventing the sale of foreign goods in the country at levels below their standard price in the country of origin.

ANTITRUST LAWS   The legislation prohibiting acts that will cause or tend to cause monopolistic practices or price practices; includes the Sherman Antitrust Act in the U.S.

ANY-QUANTITY RATE   A per pound or per unit rate which is not determined by any weight minimum, and therefore is applicable to any quantity of freight tendered. This is a single rate which is applied regardless of the quantity shipped. There is no minimum weight on these rates. AQ rates are commonly used in cotton goods.

APEC   Short name for Asia-Pacific Economic Forum. A group of countries in this region that formed an economic cooperation block in 1989 for the purpose of increasing trade among them.

APPARENT AUTHORITY   Authority of a buying agent that is inferred by a seller. Apparent authority is generally perceived when similarly titled person in other firms have the same actual authority.

APPARENT GOOD ORDER   When freight appears to be free of damage and in proper condition so far as can be determined from a general survey, it is designated as apparent good order.

APPEAL   The transfer of a case from an inferior (lower) to a superior (higher) court.

APPELLATE JURISDICTION   Courts having power to review decisions of lower courts.

APPLET   A small Internet related program application that enhances a web page– calculator, etc.

APPLICATION   With rates, the points to, from, or between which the rates and routes named in a tariff apply; of tariffs, the points to, from, or between which the provisions of a tariff apply.

APPLICATION FOR CHANGE IN CLASSIFICATION   A form used in filing with a classification committee a request for change in the classification of a commodity.

APPORTIONMENT DISTRIBUTION   When rolling stock is distributed on a predetermined basis, or when the tonnage of several carriers is distributed without preference on a predetermined basis, it is usually referred to as apportionment distribution. The term is also applicable to passenger service. When the fares of an inter-line operation are distributed between carriers on a predetermined basis this term is also applied.

APPRAISE   To set a value on goods or property.

APPRAISEMENT   Ascertaining the value of goods or property.

APPRAISER   One who determines the value of goods.

APPRAISER'S STORES   The warehouse or public stores to which at least ten percent of imported goods are taken to be inspected, analyzed, weighed, etc., by examiners or appraisers.

APPROPRIATION   The allocation of funds for a specific purpose.

APPROVED PARTS LIST   Purchasing, materials management, and production term for those goods which were analyzed and are allowed for use in the system.

APPROVED SUPPLIER LIST   A listing of suppliers, vendors, which have been deemed to provide goods/services and deliveries in a satisfactory manner for the buying organization.

APPURTENANCES   As used in shipping, the term embraces whatever belongs to the owner on board a vessel or ship used for the object of a voyage.

APRON   An aircraft parking spot in front of a hangar, terminal, or aircraft shelter which is used primarily for loading and unloading of aircraft.

APRON TRACK   Railroad track along the apron of a pier designed for the direct transfer of cargo between the rail car and ship.

ARBITRAGE   The profiteering from the exchange of one country's currency for that of another to acquire the advantages in the exchange rate.

ARBITRARY   An added charge over a fixed rate to account for an added leg of a shipment. It amounts to the combination of a fixed rate with an added rate.

ARBITRATE   A less formal method of resolving disputes than would be necessary in a court of law. Both parties agree to the use of an arbitrator who will listen to the issues and make a statement toward a resolution.

ARBITRATION   A means of settling disputes (labor and loss and damage) with an objective outside party acting as a primary decision body.

ARBITRATION CLAUSE   An arrangement for settling disputes which is inserted in the sales contract.

ARBITRATION OF EXCHANGE   It is customary to calculate rates of exchange between two countries by a comparison of the currency of intermediate places to discover whether it is more profitable to forward money directly or indirectly. Simple arbitration involves the use of but one intermediate place and compound arbitration includes two or more intermediate places.

ARCH CONSTRUCTION   The arch construction of a vessel eliminates the need for lower beams in the vessel by making the deck beams of exceptional strength.

ARCHITECTURE   As used in supply chains today, this pertains to the designs of flow patterns, information systems, and financial settlements among a string of firms.

ARM'S LENGTH   Purchasing field term indicating that the extent of the buyer and seller's relationship is based upon price and delivery only.

ARM'S LENGTH RELATIONSHIP   See ARM'S LENGTH.

ARMED GUARD SERVICE   A service provided for in the tariffs which involves the surveillance of the shipment by armed guard. Extra charges are assessed for such service.

ARRIVED SHIP   When the following conditions prevail, the vessel is considered to be an arrived ship: (1) the vessel is ready to load or discharge cargo; (2) the vessel has arrived at the unloading berth according to the charger; (3) the shippers or consignees have been notified in writing.

ARRIVAL NOTICE   A notice, furnished to consignee, of the arrival of freight.

ARTICULATED   In railroad, bus, or ship transportation this is a vehicle consisting of two or more, full-sized attached units which can swivel or hinge.

ARTICULATED CAR   In railroad transportation, this is a rail car consisting of two or more attached units which can swivel.

ARTIFICIAL ADVANTAGE   An advantage which a locality of shipper has over another because of an action on the part of some transportation company or other agency. This differs from economic advantage which can arise due to an abundance of resources, capacity, or other benefit in an area.

ARTIFICIAL PERSON   A company, corporation, or other legal entity, considered in law or in commercial transactions. Distinct from a natural person.

AS-AT   Term placed on financial documents to indicate that the information contained therein was noted at a particular date. Example, balance sheet as-at December 31.

AS CUSTOMARY   A shortened form of "with all dispatch as customary." In a contract of affreightment, this refers to the usual manner of performing service, without specifically stipulating the period of time in which the work is to be performed.

AS FAST AS A STEAMER CAN DELIVER   A charter party clause providing for the discharge of a vessel's cargo with the utmost practical dispatch—port customs, facilities for delivery and other existing circumstances considered.

ASH PAN ACT (U.S.)   An Act of Congress requiring ash pans of certain specifications on all steam locomotives engaged in interstate or international commerce.

AS IS   Purchasing term for a price for something without any guarantees or warranties. Purchaser has no recourse to seller for quality or condition. Typical term in the sale of previously owned/used goods, machinery, equipment, or facilities.

AS PER ADVICE   A term used on a bill of exchange to indicate that notice of the drawing of the bill has already been sent to the drawee.

ASPIRATIONAL GOALS   Strategic term indicating certain accomplishments or capabilities that have been identified to be attained by a certain time. In supply chains, this might mean that a specific competitive advantage will result from implementing a certain information system.

ASRS   Acronym for automated stacker-retriever system; an automated form of materials handling that can perform put-away and picking with no or a minimum of human handling.

ASSEMBLING   The act of collecting many shipments at a certain point for consolidation in the line haul movement. This is a common foreign trade zone activity in East Asian countries for goods destined to European and North American retail store chains.

ASSEMBLY AND DISTRIBUTION RATES   When multiple shipments are assembled for shipment, or are terminated at a single point, they are less costly to handle than individual shipments originating from the business. Rates are lower due to the consolidated form of pickup or delivery at one end. In some cases a single document covers the "bulk" portion of the move. These rates service the industrial shipper who maintains a regular consolidation operation.

ASSEMBLY SERVICE   The process of a single carrier assembling many shipments en route to the same consignee.

ASSENT   An agreement between carriers for a publication by another carrier or agent relative to rates, etc.

ASSET   A property of tangible or intangible value owned by the business or individual.

ASSET RECOVERY   The act of refurbishment, repair, redisposition, or sale of existing assets for the purpose of capturing some value from them. This is typically a term used disposing of surplus inventories or old fixed assets.

ASSIGN   To transfer or make over to another party.

ASSIGNED RAIL CAR   A rail car that is only used by one shipper for a specific period of time. No other person may use this rail car without permission.

ASSIGNED SERVICE   Equipment or vehicles that are reserved for the service of a certain shipper or consignee, specifically equipped rail cars and contract carriage trucks are often assigned for loading only by the specific shipper.

ASSIGNED SIDING   A sidetrack owned by a transportation line, and assigned for the use of one or more firms, or individuals, in loading or unloading cars.

ASSIGNEE   One to whom a right or property is transferred.

ASSIGNMENT   1) Traffic: A term commonly used in connection with bills of lading, involves transfer of rights, title, and interest for the purpose of assigning goods. It authorizes a bank to pay the third party from the proceeds of the draft presented by the beneficiary. 2) Purchasing: A practice of taking an order from a customer and passing it along to another firm to produce or service the goods for delivery to the customer.

ASSIGNOR   One by whom a right or property is transferred.

ASSIST   In foreign trade, this is the act of the buying company in providing the selling firm with technologies, engineering help, or other tangible and intangible capabilities in order for them to manufacturer the goods that are to be imported from them.

ASSOCIATION   The union of a number of individuals or companies for a common purpose.

ASSOCIATION OF AMERICAN RAILROADS   The trade association of the railroads of the United States. It provides research, public relations, coordination, and numerous other functions. Headquartered in Washington, DC.

ASSOCIATION OF LOCAL TRANSPORT AIRLINES (U.S.)   A long standing trade association which served the interests of the local service, intra-Hawaiian and intra Alaskan air carriers.

ASSOCIATION OF PRACTITIONERS BEFORE THE INTERSTATE COMMERCE COMMISSION   An organization composed of persons admitted to practice before the I.C.C. It is today called the Association of Transportation Practitioners.

ASSOCIATION OF TRANSPORTATION PRACTITIONERS   Professional organization of concern with laws and regulations of federal and state regulatory agencies. Previously the Interstate Commerce Commission Practitioners Association.

ASSORTMENT   A collection of different SKU's.

ASSORTMENT PACK   A retail store term for units of inventory (packages) that contain two or more SKU items.

ASSUMPTION OF RISK   An expression of the assuming of all or part of the liability for loss and damage to a shipment.

A.S.T.M.   American Society for Testing and Materials.

ASTRAY FREIGHT   When less-than-truckload freight has been separated from the regular revenue manifest or waybill after it has been marked for destination, it is usually referred to as astray freight.

ATA—AMERICAN TRUCKING ASSOCIATIONS   The nationwide association of trucking companies in the United States is called the American Trucking Associations. It has headquarters in Alexandria, Virginia (U.S.).

ATHWART OR ATHWART SHIP   At right angles to the keel of the vessel.

AT SIGHT   A term used on a bill of exchange to indicate that the bill is payable on demand without any days grace.

AUDITING   The review of freight bills to determine errors is called auditing. An outside auditor or an inside rate person performs such auditing operations.

AUDITOR   An accountant who analyzes and passes upon the accuracy of accounts and procedures.

AUTHORITY LIMIT   Purchasing field term for the maximum financial commitment that a particular buyer may sign for in the purchase of goods and services.

AUTHORITY OF LAW   Where there is an exercise of the police powers of a state.

AUTHORITY TO NEGOTIATE   The advise of a bank to a local exporter, based on instructions from its foreign correspondent, to negotiate the exporter's drafts on a foreign buyer if the drafts are accompanied by certain specific documents.

AUTHORITY TO PAY   This document is not a letter of credit, but merely an advice of the place of payment which also specifies documents needed to obtain payment. It does not oblige any bank to pay. It is much less expensive than a letter of credit and has been largely superseded by "documents against payment" (D/P).

AUTHORITY TO PURCHASE   An authorization extended by the buyer's bank to an American bank, permitting the American bank to purchase the seller's time draft drawn on the buyer and payable to the issuing bank. This authority can be issued in a revocable or an irrevocable form. An irrevocable authority may be confirmed by the advising or paying bank, while the revocable authority is never confirmed. It also stipulates whether drafts are to be drawn with or without recourse to the seller. At the time of processing, the seller receives the face amount of the draft, and issuing bank's account is charged face value plus fees. An irrevocable authority without recourse credit. It differs from an irrevocable letter of credit in that the draft is drawn on the buyer, and thus neither bank can create a banker's acceptance. If the draft is drawn with recourse to the seller and the buyer fails to pay at maturity, the seller could be held responsible for refund. "Authority to purchase" exists only in Asian trade.

AUTO CARRIER   In motor transportation, this is a low slung trainer with ramps for the carrying of automobiles. This single axle, tandem wheeled trailer can sometimes be converted to a light capacity flatbed trailer.

AUTOMATED FARE PAYMENT SYSTEM   A rapid transit system whereby passengers can purchase and pay for their fares without the need for ticket sellers and fare collectors.

AUTOMATIC GUIDED VEHICLE   A form of materials handling that travels without human guidance or steering. It usually is controlled by electronic pathways and control systems.

AUTOMATED GUIDEWAY TRANSIT.   A rapid transit system that operates without the need for an operator.

AUTOMATIC ORDERING   A process of call-off or ordering by a buying company against a selling firm that is based upon a linkage that minimizes human intervention and avoids use of traditional requisition, purchase order, and other documentation. In some countries, beverage vending machines are equipped with sensing and transmitting devices that serve to automatically order replenishment quantities.

AUTOMATIC PASSENGER COUNTER.   A device that captures the number of passengers boarding a transport vehicle or passing a certain point.

AUTOMATIC VEHICLE LOCATOR SYSTEM (AVL)   A system that captures the location and disposition of buses, light rail, or other urban transport vehicles on a real time basis. Such systems are designed to manage and speed the flow of these vehicles.

AUTOMOBILE CAR   A rail car equipped with the facilities for the safe and proper handling of automobiles. These can be single, double, or triple tiered.

AUTONOMOUS DIAL-A-RIDE TRANSIT.   A full order entry and dispatching system on vehicles that is designed to minimize empty travel and maximize service to passengers seeking movement.

AUTO RACK CONTAINER   A container designed to store automobiles for shipment. It may be open or dosed sided.

AUTO SHIP   An ocean vessel specifically designed for the movement of automobiles. It typically has low ceilings and uses a maximum of the physical enclosed capacity of the ship.

AVAILABLE SEAT MILES   The product of the number of seats times the miles flown in a passenger transportation service. Applies primarily to air transportation, but seat miles could apply to any carrier mode. This measures is used to compute the percent of local demanded of the capacity of the carrier.

AVAILABLE STOCK   The amount of inventory on hand that can be sold or used.

AVAILABLE TON MILES   The product of the tonnage capacity carried and miles flown or traveled.

AVERAGE   This is a marine insurance term referring to the proportional distribution of a general loss. When a cargo must be jettisoned it is necessary to establish general average charges. The apportionment is usually prorated to the various cargo lots on the basis of value-in addition to the vessel itself and its freight earnings on the voyage. The shipment loss is collected from the insurance company and until this is paid the assessment of the loss constitutes a lien against the shipment. Even a shipper who is not protected by insurance can be made to pay a general contribution for a loss sustained from a jettison of other cargo. In order to validate general average it is necessary to establish the following: the action must be voluntary and for benefit of all; it must have come about as the result of the master's order, it must have been successful and necessary; and it must not have come about as a result of the fault of the party requesting the contribution.

AVERAGE BOND   A document signed by contractors to a general average adjustment under which they receive delivery of cargo upon agreeing to pay their proportion of general average contribution as soon as the amount is known.

AVERAGE CLAUSE   A clause inserted in marine insurance policies which specifies certain goods as free from average unless general average applies, or unless the loss is above a certain percentage.

AVERAGE DEMURRAGE AGREEMENT   An agreement made between a shipper and a railroad line whereby the shipper is debited for the time cars are held for loading and unloading beyond a certain period and credited charges are assessed by the transportation line at the end of the month, for any outstanding debits from cars held less than the free time allowed.

AVERAGE HAUL   The average distance in miles traversed by each ton of an aggregate number of tons, determined by dividing the number of ton-miles by the total number of tons.

AVERAGE INVENTORY   The average inventory level over a period of time. It is the average of the peak and base stock weighted for the amounts held at intermediate points in time.

AVERAGE WAREHOUSE COST   It is the cost of housing. When the industrial firm owns its own warehouse it computes the average warehouse cost by summing the cost of operation of the warehouse. This requires adding depreciation cost, warehouse utility cost, warehouse taxes, interest on investment in warehouse, and all other costs except for labor costs, obsolescence costs, stock out costs, and comparable thereto. Since labor costs is charged separately in a public warehouse, private warehouse labor is likewise treated separately. A distinction must be made between the warehouse rate, or storage rate, and the average warehouse cost. The average warehouse cost is comparable to the warehouse rate.

AVOIDABLE COSTS   The total set of costs that will disappear in the firm as a result of one unit reduction in output product or service; concept is applied in abandonment or plane discontinuance analyses.

AVOIRDUPOIS   The commercial standard of weight in the United States and Great Britain.

AXLE LOAD   This may refer either to an allowance or an existing weight carried on the axle of a motor vehicle. An axle limitation placed on a highway requires that the axle load weight cannot be exceeded by the heaviest axle. This is a crucial measure with regard to pavement and bridge weight limits.

AXLE WEIGHT   The gross weight of the heaviest axle of the motor truck.

BBBB

B2B   Term used in electronic business for that commerce and transactions between two or more businesses as opposed to consumer related business.

BACK DOOR BUYING   Purchasing term for situation whereby someone in the firm not authorized to purchase is in direct contact with a seller. Common examples are engineering, production and product development.

BACK DOOR SELLING   A purchasing field term for the situation in which a salesman goes around the purchasing manager to have a company engineer or manufacturing manager specify his/her firm's goods for the purchasing manager to order.

BACK HAUL   The traffic for the return movement of a vehicle which has already hauled traffic in an outbound direction. The term empty-back-haul infers that a payload has been achieved for the movement in one direction but a return payload is not available.

BACK HAUL RAIL CHARGES   Typically lower rates than normally charged on movements that are designed to fill return vehicles that would otherwise move empty. These are incentive rates that seek to fill vehicles with some revenue.

BACKING   A cushion made of paper cloth as a surface sheet, for protection.

BACKING WIRE   A piece of hardware (wire) used to take the strain of stopping and reversing of a barge when a towboat is backing. Located usually at the aft of the barge or towboat.

BACK LOG   1) The amount of work in a system, e.g., production, that is awaiting operation due to congestion from other work already in the system. 2) The volume of traffic left at a station after a scheduled flight, and which normally would have moved by that flight.

BACK ORDER   Items that have been ordered but can not be shipped due to stock out or some other reason. This is commonly used in association with the prime customer service goal of delivering OTIF (on time and in full).

BACK ROOM   General term for activities relating to the customer that the customer does not see. It generally includes all the administrative activities that start after receiving an order is received from a customer all the way through to billing and receiving payment. These activities are in addition to the customer interface activities such as sales, order entry, tracking/tracing, expediting, invoicing, etc.

BACKWARD INTEGRATION   The acquisition of firms in the supply chain that provide goods and services into the company. Loosely, it means buying a supplier firm or firms.

BAG   A flexible material used as a container.

BAGGAGE   Articles ordinarily carried by travelers.

BAGGAGE CHECK   A receipt given to a passenger by a carrier for baggage transported by it.

BAG TRUCK   A truck with two fixed wheels, having the framework of a pair of shafts and a shoe protection or blade.

BAIL   A container handle.

BAILEE   One to whom goods are entrusted.

BAILMENT   1) A delivery of goods by one party to another, to be held according to the purpose of the delivery and to be returned or delivered when that purpose is accomplished. 2) A transfer of possession without transfer of title.

BAILOR   One who entrusts goods to another.

BAIT BOX   Device with food or other attractant inside to lure rodents and trap them.

BAIT STATION   Area where poisoned food is placed to kill rodents.

BALANCE   An equality between the debit and credit sides of an account, and designated in balance. This term also represents the amount remaining after a lesser quantity or sum has been deducted from a larger—and known as balance due or balance on hand.

BALANCED SCORECARD   A relatively new term in the accounting field indicating that the firm is to perform well with a set of outcomes in addition to financial performance. Others may include customer service, social responsibility, safety, and innovation.

BALANCE OF PAYMENTS   A debit and credit system used by nations to account for payments made by residents to foreigners and payments made by foreigners to residents. When they're equal, there is a balance of payments.

BALANCE OF TRADE   The difference in value between total imports and exports of a country.

BALE   A unit of goods typically in bulk form that has been compressed and wrapped. Common in cotton and scrap textile movements.

BALE CUBIC CAPACITY   The number of bales, typically compressed cotton, that can be handled in a vehicle.

BALE SPACE   Expressed in cubic feet, it is a measure of cargo space under the deck.

BALLAST   A substance used to increase stability of a ship by placing a quantity of weighty substances (iron, stone, gravel, etc.) in the lower hold of a vessel to lower the center of gravity. In modern times, water tanks in the lower parts of a ship are used for this purpose.

BALLAST BONUS   Denotes a way that a charter can receive more of a payload.

BALLAST CAR   A special vehicle for carrying ballast and grading material for road-work.

BALLOON FREIGHT   Cargo that is light, bulky, and has low density.

BANANA BOAT   A ship specifically designed to move bananas. It includes special racking and handling equipment that can easily load and unload bananas.

BAND   Strapping of metal.

BANDING   Material used to wrap around the shipment to hold it in place and/or as a unit load. Material nailed to the sides of a car or trailer to hold merchandise in place.

BANK   A facility where transactions of loans, exchange of money, extension of credit take place.

BANK CREDIT   A term to denote the practice of a bank to increase the size of an account of a depositor to create credit; these purchases become assets of the bank.

BANK DRAFT   This is a negotiable instrument made out by a seller against the purchaser which directs the payment of a given amount of money through an intermediary bank. They are very similar to checks made on bank accounts.

BANKERS ACCEPTANCE   A term usually used in international trade, the bank pays specific bills for one of its customers.

BANKING SYSTEM   A financial institution that encourages credit that will create economic growth. The system has three primary functions: 1) lending money; 2) acceptance of funds on deposit; 3) creating and lending of its own credit.

BANK OF FLIGHTS   When an airline uses the hub and spoke system, this is the term for flights that are timed to arrive to offload and transfer passengers and freight to other flights that will depart for various destinations shortly thereafter. Thus, a bank of flights arrive in a short period and another depart soon after.

BANK RATE   A measure of interest for funds lent.

BANKRUPTCY ACT   An Act to accord relief to railroads and effect their reorgani-zation, approved March 3, 1933; often referred to as Section 77 Bankruptcy.

BAR CODE   A generic term for any system of digit or other character recognition reading, scanning, and tracking of units of goods or assets in a firm, retail outlet, or logistics system. Systems often provide speed and accuracy of reading and tracking.

BAR DRAFT   Maximum clearance for a ship to pass over the sand bar.

BAREBACK   The tractor alone—without its semi-trailer.

BARE BOAT CHARTER   A ship that is chartered without a crew. The person acquiring use of the ship for use must arrange manning and other services and goods that are normally performed by a ship operator. Typically used for long term charters.

BARGE   A flat-bottom boat used primarily in the transportation of such bulk cargo as coal, brick, grain, gravel, sand and lumber, etc., and employed in inland and coastwise water transportation movements. It may be pulled or pushed by a tugboat, or it may be self-propelled.

BARE POLE CHARTER   A ship without a crew that is chartered.

BARGAINING POWER OF A PURCHASING COMPANY   The ability of a buying firm to gain favorable price and other concessions in its negotiations and bidding from the supply market. In a monopolistic supply situation, this bargaining power is minimal. In a buyers' market, it can be almost complete.

BARGAINING POWER OF SUPPLIERS   The ability of selling firms to exact price and favorable concessions for themselves in selling situations. To the extreme it is called a sellers' market.

BARQUE (OR BARK)   A three-masted vessel carrying no square sails on the main mast.

BARRATRY   The willful act of officers or other members of a ship's crew in destroying, injuring, stealing, or otherwise performing a harmful act on a vessel or its cargo.

BARREL   Made of either wood, aluminum or steel, it is a container of cylindrical shape which is longer than it is wide and ends have equal diameters. In the oil industry, it is standardized at 55 U.S. gallons.

BARREL BARK   In freight measurement, five cubic feet.

BARRIER   A term to describe the separation of one element from another by a chemical or other agent.

BARRIER MATERIAL   Materials that can withstand water, oil, vapor and various other gases.

BARRIERS TO ENTRY   Hindrances facing a firm that seeks to enter a business or a market. In the airline industry it can be regulatory permission that is not forthcoming from a government body, or it can be the lack of landing slots at a busy airport at which it seeks to operate. In an economic setting, a barrier to entry might be a very high investment cost or a costly technology that is required for a firm to become an effective competitor in that market.

BARTER   A direct exchange of one commodity or service for another.

BARTERING   See BARTER

BASE   A term to denote either the container floor or home depot of container or equipment, or other transportation equipment.

BASE STOCK   An amount of inventory required to service an average amount of demand.

BASILOAD   Lift truck attachment designed to handle appliances with a handling flap on the carton.

BASIN   A basin is a dock for the berthing of ships along side of quays.

BASING POINT RATE   A designated geographic point which is the basis for constructing rates to or from the basing point to the designated destination is called a basing point rate. It is common practice to construct a rate by using the rate to the basing point plus a differential to a destination beyond.

BASING POINT   In a general geographic area, a particular point or city may be identified as representing the general area for rate making purposes. It may also be the point used in constructing through rates between other points. Sometimes it is the location specified in the sales contract for the purpose of making price determination.

BATCH (VS. REAL TIME)   Electronic system process whereby data and work is accumulated for processing at certain points in time rather than continuously (real time).

BATCH PICKING   Warehouse and materials handling term. Means picking each order or groups of orders at one time (in batches).

BATCH PROCESS   Any production or other process that is performed in a group at a specified point in time.

BATCH SIZES   The sizes of production or other work in terms of number of units.

BAUD   The speed at which modems can transmit/receive data from one computer to another. The higher the baud rate, the faster the transmission.

BAY   A designated area within a section of a storage area outlined by markings on columns, posts or floor. An inlet on the sea.

BAY STORAGE   The use of a large designated area for storing merchandise.

BAZAAR   A market or place of trade, and particularly applied to shops for sale of fancy articles.

BEAR MARKET   A general economic term for a soft economy that includes lowering of stock prices and overall economic activity.

BEATING THE FADE   Taking costs out of a product and business as it moves down the product life cycle of demand. By beating the fade a firm can take costs out of the business or product faster than the prices and revenues are dropping. Some firms can enjoy higher profits in this stage of a product life cycle than in the previous maturity stage of the market.

BED   A trailer or truck floor.

BEDDING (CHARGE)   At animal stock yards, it is a charge for straw sand hay or sawdust used on floors of cattle hauling cattle cars or trucks.

BELL BOOK   A book to record the time and signal of engine orders.

BELLY   A term applied to a jet aircraft which refers to its under floor cargo area. Each aircraft usually has fore and aft compartments which are generally heated and pressurized.

BELT DRIVEN   This applies to a tractor with tandem axles. Belts connected to powered front-axle transmit power to rear axle.

BELT LINE   An interchange rail carrier circumventing the city often serves the purpose of switching for a large commercial area. Belt railroads make it possible for a carrier approaching a major commercial area to circumvent the central area. This provides a great saving of time by avoiding transportation to the city center for a complex switching process.

BENCHMARK (ING)   The act of developing comparison data with which to analyze and use to improve an activity or function within the firm. It is also the act of gathering comparative prices paid in the market.

BENDING BOARD   A packaging term to denote a capability of withstanding a single fold through an arc of 180 degrees without damaging the plies in paper board.

"B" END OF THE CAR   The end of the rail car at which the hand brake is located.

BENEAPED   The term to denote a vessel run aground by the spring tides. These are generally the highest tides of the year.

BENEFICIARY   A person or a business entity to whom the money is payable. The entity in whose favor the letter of credit is issued.

BENELUX   A term for the original Belgium. Netherlands and Luxembourg custom union. Today, it is term used less often for these three countries. They are also referred to as the Low Countries.

BERANEK   The name of a guide used to determine the share of revenue for carriers in an interline.

BERMUDA CONVENTION   A series of agreements established after World War II to govern the growth of international commercial air transportation.

BERTH   The water area at the edge of a wharf or pier provided for a vessel for the purpose of discharging its passengers or cargo is called a berth. When a ship is on the berth it is in position to discharge its load or cargo.

BERTH CARGO   Freight a steamship does not normally solicit due to its poor shipping characteristics or low freight rates, but is often carried at low rates rather than sail the ship with water ballast; the berth cargo itself serves as a sort of ballast.

BERTH CHARTER, PORT CHARTER   A charter contract of affreightment for loading on berth.

BERTH RATES   In maritime, rates charged by regularly operating water lines on general cargo as distinguished from rates on full cargoes and chartered vessels.

BERTH (SLEEPING CAR)   The upper and lower beds in the passenger rail sleeping car.

BEYOND RIGHTS   The ability of an airline from country A that operates to country B to also pick up passengers and freight from B and carry them to country C.

BIBLE   The Golden Rule safe driving book for truck drivers.

BID ANALYSIS   The process of evaluating several bids with the goal of selecting the best supplier bid for the work. The bid analysis includes price and other factors.

BID BUYING   The act of selecting a supplier on the basis of requesting price bids from them and generally selecting the one offering the lowest price.

BID LIST   The listing of suppliers that have been previously approved in some fashion for sending requests for bids (RFB's).

BID, LOW   A bid that is at the low end of the group of bids received for work. It also pertains to the lowest bid among a set of them.

BID, LOW BALL   A bid from a supplier that is suspected to be lower than that supplier's normal offering. The fear in this situation is that the supplier might not be capable of performing the work for that price. Another fear is the creation of a dependency upon that supplier, once others leave the market, thereby creating a sellers' market by that supplier later in time.

BIG HAT   A state trooper or other police person.

BIG RIGGER   A driver who refuses to drive anything but big trucks.

BILATERAL AIR-TRANSPORTER AGREEMENT   Two nations exchanging air transport rights over specified routes in some type of an agreement.

BILATERALISM   The act of two countries exchanging goods and services to protect each country's consumer from international specialization.

BILGE AND CANTLINE   When barrels are stowed in a ship's hold, the bilge of the upper tier of the barrels fits into the cantline of the lower of the barrels to save space (a nesting principle). The bilges of the lower tier are normally raised off the floor by beds. The bilges are placed up to prevent leakage.

BILGE KNUCKLE   Denotes when the frame turns from the barge's vertical side to form the bottom of the barge.

BILL   1) A name given to statements in writing; as goods, a draft, a note, etc. 2) A law not enacted. 3) An exhibition of charges.

BILL AND NOTE BROKER   One who negotiates the purchases and sales of bills of exchange and promissory notes.

BILL ADVANCE   A bill used with a correction notice to denote a transfer of charges due to an error in billing a shipment.

BILL BOOK   A register of bills of exchange payable or receivable by a firm.

BILL DISCOUNTING   The act of raising money on a bill of exchange at interest before it matures.

BILLED WEIGHT   The weight shown in a waybill and freight bill for purposes of constructing the freight charges; may be different than actual weight in load.

BILLET CAR   A gondola car built entirely of steel for the purposes of transporting steel billets is referred to as a billet car.

BILLING   The process of sending a statement of charges to customers who have purchased goods/services on credit.

BILLING AND GUIDE BOOK   A schedule containing instructions for a waybill or the making out of a waybill.

BILLING MINIMUM   The smallest amount of money charged a customer regardless of activity.

BILL OF CREDIT   A letter of instructions issued by one person to another for a certain amount to a third person named therein and promising to reimburse the person making the advance requested.

BILL OF ENTRY   The statement of the nature and value of goods entering a customs house is detailed on the bill of entry. It is employed for statistical reference.

BILL OF EXCHANGE   A foreign bill of exchange is often used to obtain payment for an export shipment. When a signed order directs the addressee to pay a given amount of money to bearer on demand, or as of a given date, the document is called the bill of exchange. If it is payable in the country where made up, the bill of exchange is referred to as a domestic or inland bill of exchange.

BILL OF HEALTH   The authorities of a port make out a bill of health to a vessel operator which designates the state of the port with respect to public health at the time of sailing. A clean bill of health states that no plague or other contagious diseases exist at the time of sailing. A foul or touched bill of health confirms that a contagious disease exists, or is suspected, or anticipated.

BILL OF LADING   Both the straight non-negotiable and the order negotiable bill of lading document are contracts for transportation between the shipper and the carrier. The contents of the bill of lading were outlined originally in an act in the U.S. effective January 1, 1917 which codified the preparation, handling and negotiability of bills of lading in interstate commerce. The Uniform Commercial Code also covers topics pertinent to the bill of lading in Articles 2 and 7. There are numerous forms of bills of lading. Some are Clean Bills of Lading, On board Bills of Lading, Open Form Bills of Lading, Received for Shipment Bills of Lading, Short Form Bill of Lading, etc.

BILL OF LADING ACT   The United States Congress passed the Bills of Lading Act, January 1, 1917, which provided for the requirements necessary in the preparation of a bill of lading, and the character of the negotiability of the bill of lading. This has been further amended and codified-by the Uniform Commercial Code, Articles 2 and 7.

BILL OF LADING, CERTIFIED   When the consular officer endorses an ocean bill of lading, and specifies that the shipment meets certain requirements of their country for importation, a certified bill of lading is provided.

BILL OF LADING, CLEAN (OR CLEAR)   A clean bill of lading, or a carrier receipted bill of lading, is provided when a shipment is in good condition with no apparent loss or damage. Under these circumstances the bill of lading contains no exceptions and is a readily negotiable instrument.

BILL OF LADING, EXPORT (THROUGH)   In international joint land-water carrier movements, a through bill of lading is issued by the inland carrier to contract for the movement of goods from an interior point of origin to the ultimate foreign destination.

BILL OF LADING, NEGOTIABLE OR "TO ORDER"   A bill of lading consigned directly to the order of a party, usually, the shipper or a bank, whose endorsement is required to transfer the title to the merchandise. Title therefore passes to the holder or party to whom it is endorsed. The bill of lading must be surrendered to the steamship, railroad, or trucking company before the goods will be released.

BILL OF LADING, NON-NEGOTIABLE OR STRAIGHT   A bill of lading consigned directly to the consignee and therefore not negotiable. Goods will usually be delivered by the steamship, air carrier, truck, or railroad company without surrender of the bill of lading.

BILL OF LADING, "ORDER NOTIFY"   The same as negotiable or to order, except that the bill of lading contains an additional clause to the effect that a specified party, usually at the port of destination, is to be notified upon arrival of the merchandise. The insertion of this clause does not give the party to be notified title to the goods.

BILL OF LADING, THROUGH   A bill of lading issued by a shipping company or its agent covering more than one mode of transportation.

BILL OF MATERIAL   Listing of the components required in the manufacturing of an item. It is like a recipe for any manufactured good. A bill of material (B/M) is an essential element in materials requirements planning (MRP)

BILL OF MATERIALS   A term in Materials Requirements Planning; listing of all the components required for the manufacture of an item.

BILL OF PARCELS   A document containing a detailed account of goods sold and sometimes used for invoice; also knows as a *Fracture*.

BILL OF SALE   A contract for the sale of goods

BILL OF SIGHT   A customer house document, allowing the consignee to see goods before paying duties. Such inspection is made in the presence of a customer officer and is requested by an importer for the purpose of obtaining details which will enable them to prepare a correct Bill of Entry. This latter document must be completed within three days of Bill of Sight, otherwise goods are removed to government warehouses.

BILL OF STORES   A license to re-import dutiable British goods free within five years of the original date of exportation.

BILL OF SUFFERANCE.   When coastal vessels are given the authority to carry goods in bond, a document known as a bill of sufferance is provided.

BILL OF LADING ACT   The United States congress passed the Bills of Lading Act, January 1, 1917, which provided for the requirements necessary in the preparation of a bill of lading, and the character of negotiability of the bill of lading.

BILLS PAYABLE   Bills and notes issued in favor of other parties.

BILLS RECEIVABLE   Bills and notes made by others and payable to ourselves.

BINDER   A small payment that will cause an agreement to go into effect. Typically found at the end of a negotiation but prior to final contract creation and payment, or, upon purchasing of an insurance policy but prior to final price determination. A binder is a form of good faith payment.

BINDERS   Slang term for brakes.

BIN STORAGE   Storage in bins so that an item may be withdrawn without breaking open a package containing a number of such items.

BIRDYBACK   The intermodal operation of highway freight containers for a joint motor-air shipment.

BIT   A term in short for a binary digit.

BITTS   These are used for the purpose of securing mooring or working lines by the means of steel casts or wooden posts.

BLACK MARKET RATE   Terms for the currency exchange rate that is in effect between private individuals and/or firms. Rate is usually different than the official rate that might be in effect through required government exchange bodies. Typically found in soft currency nations.

BLANK   Shipping forms such as way bills, vouchers, bills of lading, export declarations and the like, are often referred to as blanks. In a more distinct sense a blank is a space left in a form to be filled in with the insertion of words necessary to complete the sense or to adapt the same to one particular case.

BLANK BILL   A bill of exchange from which the name of the payee is omitted.

BLANK CREDIT   This term signifies permission to draw money on account, no particular sum being specified.

BLANK ENDORSEMENT   The endorsement of a Bill of Exchange without specifying the name of the person or persons to whom it is given.

BLANKET AGREEMENT   An agreement between buyer and seller whereby certain goods will be purchased at prices established or by way of formula over a period of time. Such systems are used to reduce many small transactions that are processed by purchasing departments. These arrangements often allow user departments to order directly from vendors.

BLANKET BOND   Coverage of a group of people or properties through a bond.

BLANKET ORDERING   A system in which a firm agrees to buy a large quantity of goods from a supplier over time, each order in the blanket order is then handled in a simplified manner since the goods are all part of the overall agreement.

BLANKET POLICY   In marine insurance, a policy not on particular goods but on whatever there may be at a certain time or a varying quantity, such as on a stock of goods subject to sale and replenishing, or the cargo of a vessel on a particular voyage.

BLANKET RATES   A blanket rate is the extension of the group rate principal to geographic area that covers a large part of continental United States into a single group. Thus, a grouping of the area west of the Cascade Range might be considered a blanket rate grouping. It is believed that the most significant single causal factor for transcontinental group rates is competition between rail carriers and inter-coastal water carriers. A movement to or from any point in the blanket area to a given point takes the same rate.

BLANKET TARIFF SUPPLEMENT   A single publication containing additions to or changes in two or more tariffs.

BLANKET WAYBILL   A waybill covering two or more consignments of freight.

BLASTING AGENTS   A material designed for blasting which has been tested in accordance with DOT regulations and found to be so insensitive that there is very little probability of accidental initiation to explosion or of transition from deflagration to detonation while in transport.

BLIND CHECK   The tallying or checking of freight without access to records disclosing kind and amount of freight contained in the shipment. See BLIND TALLY.

BLIND CORNER   Intersection of an aisle or storage area where vision is blocked.

BLIND LABELING   Use of invisible ink to label packages moving through a supply chain. This practice is found with such high value goods as liquor, some pharmaceuticals, and computer equipment where theft would be a problem. Special reader equipment can read the SKU and other information that are not visible to the naked eye.

BLIND SIDE   The right side of a truck and trailer, or left side (in left side driving nations).

BLIND TALLY   Counting and recording inbound goods without package list or manifest indicating what might be on the load.

BLOCKADE   The act of besieging or blockading the passage of supplies by a hostile nation. The prevention of moving passengers or property to, through or from a specific point.

BLOCK DIRECTORY   A list of the principal points in rate blocks with a code showing the belt and tier to be used in determining the scale and mileage in computing the rate.

BLOCKED SPACE   A large volume shipper agreeing to ship a given minimum volume of freight between two cities over a given period of time. Provides the shipper a lower rate.

BLOCK (EXPRESS)   Groups of points considered together for the purpose of rate making in connection with express transportation.

BLOCKING   When pieces of wood or other material are used to prevent the movement of goods in a car, truck, ship, or container, it is referred to as blocking. It is used in the loading in order to prevent or reduce breaking and movement, bracing is a term which might be regarded as synonymous. Bracing is a term which might be regarded as synonymous.

BLOCK RATE   A rate applying between a point in one express block an entire entire region or area of points.

BLOCK SYSTEM   A system was devised for dividing railroad tracks into blocks of three or four miles in order to establish signal systems for safety purposes. Under the block system, a train cannot enter a block area until the preceding train has departed.

BLOCK TIME   A term to denote actual time from when the aircraft wheel blocks are removed prior to engine start and flight to when blocks are put in place at destination.

BLOCK TO BLOCK SPEED   A term to denote speed from the time an aircraft engine starts to the time of shutting off the engine at the destination.

BLUE LABEL   A term applied to radioactive cargo's warning label.

BLUEPRINTS   Specific drawings that include the dimensions and shapes of items. The purpose of these drawings is to transmit detailed information to the persons who will build them.

BOARD, FACE   Face of the box material.

BOARD FOOT   Measure in the lumber industry. An area one foot square by one inch thick.

BOARD, GREASEPROOF   Greaseproof paper or board made of such material as glassine, so it can be pasted to paper board, making the paper board grease and oil resistant.

BOARD, KRAFTLINEN   Sulphate pulp material in the top liner of the paper board, for exceptional strength.

BOARD, LAMINATED   Two processes for paper board: (1) combining two or more plies together; or (2) combining either side of a thin paper with specific properties.

BOARD OF TRADE   An association of business people or firms to regulate matters of trade and further their mutual interest; sometimes also called Chamber of Commerce, Merchants' Association, and the like.

BOARD, STENCIL   A product that is used to produce lettering and numbers. It is made of stiff oil kraft board.

BOARD, V.   Fiberboard made by U.S. government specifications.

BOB TAIL   A term for a tractor driven without its trailer; it can also refer to a straight truck.

BODY TRACK   Each of the parallel tracks of the yard, upon which cars are sorted or stored.

BOGEY   A term to denote a chassis that has two axes.

BOGIE TRUCK   Known as a restless dolly, it is a low skeleton platform mounted on two load carrying wheels, and fitted with either two or four stabilizing wheels.

BOILER INSPECTION ACT (U.S.)   A federal act was passed in 1911 requiring the inspection of boilers and steam generating facilities on locomotives in rail service.

BOILER PLATE TERMS   Specific terms and conditions a buyer firm wants to have included on purchase orders and purchase agreements. Because they are standard to most purchase documents, they are referred to as boiler plate terms. Typical terms included are FOB terms, payment periods, whether assignment is allowed, state in which any dispute would be handled, etc.

BOLL WEEVIL   An inexperienced truck driver.

BOLSTER   To block or hold a container on a trailer or rail car by a special device.

BOMB HOAX   False information of a bomb on the plane.

BONA FIDE   In good faith.

BOND   This term applies to a long term debt which is under contract, and has a specified interest rate and date due.

BONDED GOODS   Goods in charge of officers of customs and on which bonds instead of cash have been given for import duties.

BONDED WAREHOUSE   Goods which must be held until duties are paid or goods are otherwise properly released are normally put in a bonded warehouse. This warehouse must be approved by the a national government body, and it must be under bond or guarantee for compliance with the revenue laws.

BOND NOTE   A customs certificate showing that the bond has been given with reference to the regular acceptance of dutiable goods from a government or bonded warehouse.

BOND OF INDEMNITY   A bond of indemnity is a certificate filed with the carrier for the purpose of relieving it from liability or the payment of charges that might result from some action for which it might otherwise be liable a second time.

BONDSMAN   One who gives security for the performance of an act, payment of money or integrity of nature.

BOOKING   The act of making an arrangement for the movement of goods or persons. Can be the reservation of a space aboard a vessel, an airplane reservation, or the calling for a motor movement.

BOOKING NUMBER   An identity reference on bills; it is usually the number placed on a contract of affreightment.

BOOKING REQUEST FORM   The form often used by steamship companies on which shippers describe freight when seeking space on a certain sailing.

BOOKING SPACE   The act of contracting space aboard a vessel for cargo which is to be transported.

BOOK INVENTORY   A record of items on hand by type and number based on entries, additions, and deletions.

BOOK INVESTMENT   Recording in the accounts of carriers on how much their assets are worth.

BOOK VALUE   Property carried in the investment account of the general ledger of a carrier is valued at book value. It is also the amount carried in the general ledgers to record investments in securities, which could be a very different figure from the par value of the securities.

BOOM ATTACHMENT   Used to lift hollow objects, it is an attachment to a fork-lift truck.

BOOMERS   Devices used to tighten the chains holding the truck shipment.

BOOM IT DOWN   Tighten the chains holding the truck shipment.

BOTTLENECKS   Any goods or services that a firm purchases that present difficulty in their acquisition and use. These are items that pose problems in design, manufacturer, and delivery. They are the things that, if not delivered, can pose the threat of system shut down. Sometimes overly-specified items that are available from only one supplier are referred to as bottlenecks.

BOTTLERS BODY   A truck body designed for the movement of cased and bottled beverage

BOTTOM-UP ESTIMATING   A process of calculating all of the components of specific costs (labor, materials, etc.) for a proposed work and adding them up for a total estimated cost or price.

BOOT-TOPPING   Denoted usually by a red band of paint at the waterline.

BOTTOM DUMPS   Trailer that unloads through the use of bottom gates.

BOTTOM FREIGHT   Freight that carrier dock personnel perceive to be of such a condition that it can be loaded on the floor of a trailer or container with other freight being able to be loaded on top.

BOTTOMRY   The act of borrowing for the purposes of repair of a vessel, or the purchase of equipment for a vessel, is termed bottomry. When this is done the ship or its cargo is pledged as security for the loan.

BOTTOMRY BOND   The instrument or obligation generally executed in a foreign port in repayment of or as security for sums advanced to supply necessities for the ship, together with such interest as may be agreed upon. The bond creates a lien upon the ship, enforceable in Admiralty in case of safe arrival in port of destination, but becoming absolutely void m the event the vessel is lost before arrival at port. In order to make valid a bottomry bond against a ship, the following requisites are necessary: the repairs or supplies must be necessary, the master must have no apparent funds or credit available in the port, and the repairs or supplies must be such as would have been ordered by a prudent owner, had they been present.

BOW FENDER   A term to denote a device to protect the bow of a tugboat against damage; made of intertwined rope or rubber strips.

BOW THRUSTER   A device on the front of a ship, submerged in the water, that can assist in the steering of the ship sideways when docking and setting to sea.

BOX   Refers to a semi-trailer; also used to refer to the transmission of the tractor.

BOX BOARD DIMENSIONS   Dimensions of a box, where width is given first, then length.

BOX CAR   A closed railroad car with a roof and door in the sides and/or ends which is used for general service in railroad transportation.

BOX CERTIFICATE   A listing on packaging materials that indicates such things as package weight capacity, bursting strength, and other characteristics.

BOX CLEATED FIBERBOARD   A five or six cleated panel faces in a rigid container.

BOX CLEATED WOOD   A reinforced nailed wood box, inside or outside, with one or more sides and/or ends.

BOX CORRUGATED AND SOLID FIBER   A container made of either solid fiberboard or corrugated fiberboard. It is a rectangular and three dimensional shipping container.

BOX FOLDING PAPER   A carton made of bending grade paper board having a thickness of .016 or .045 inches, and suitable for packaging; not weighing more than ten pounds.

BOX LINERED END   A wire bound box, reinforced with liners, stapled across the grain.

BOX LOCK CORNER   Side and end members of a wooden box that are joined together by locks which interlock and are held together by glue. The ends are fastened by nails.

BOX PLAIN END   An unreinforced box.

BOX PLYWOOD   Made of single piece plywood. A box with a top, bottom, ends and sides which are nailed to cleats.

BOX SET-UP   A box made of paper and paper board that is three dimensional rigid in set up form, and has a specified dimensions.

BOX SET UP DROP-END   A two part, set up paper box, where the side of the base is made in two parts, which can be hinged together or an end is hinged to the bottom.

BOX SET UP FORM   A piece of box board which is loose or attached and placed within a base or lid.

BOX TELESCOPE   A container of two sections. The lid fits over the base.

BRACING   Protecting the contents of a car to prevent shifting and damage. Several methods of bracing are employed, such as center, crib, cross car, diagonal, K, knee, side, and top bracing. Bracing used inside a car is called bulkheading. See BLOCKING.

BRAKE VAN   European term for CABOOSE.

BRAND   The name of a manufacturer and/or line of products.

BRANDING   A method of putting addresses on wooden packages by means of hot irons; also used on cattle to denote ownership.

BRAND NAME   Purchasing term for the act of specifying goods according to the name of the manufacturer rather than using some other method of description.

BREACH (OF CONTRACT)   In purchasing, when a supplier delivered the wrong items, the wrong quantity, or items of quality/attributes other than what was originally contracted for. A violation or a breach of a contract or duty either by acting or by failing to act, as in the case of a carrier not delivering goods, which it has contracted to transport. See also Anticipatory Breach, Actual Breach.

BREADTH   A term measured by the distance between the outer faces of the frames is called the molded breadth. The registered breadth is measured between the outside of the shell plating.

BREAK-AWAY   Denotes the parts of a three piece trailer; the gooseneck, platform and rear axles.

BREAK BULK   1) When a large shipment is inbound to a distribution center, it is necessary to subdivide its many different component commodities for the purpose of scattered distribution. 2) Break bulk may also take the form of reducing a very large shipment of a single commodity to many small shipments to satisfy the need of dispersed buyers. 3) The splitting up of one consolidated shipment into smaller ones for ultimate delivery to consignees. 4) Term also applies to ocean shipping of packaged goods that are not containerized. Such ships, called break bulk ships, typically ply fixed routes according to a schedule. 5) Motor carrier industry term for intermediate handling of freight in order to attain long haul economies.

BREAK BULK BOAT   A ship that carries packaged, crated, bagged, etc., freight.

BREAK BULK POINT   A point at which a portion or all of the contents of a car are unloaded and distributed.

BREAKAGE   An allowance made by a shipper for loss caused by the destruction of merchandise.

BREAK EVEN CHART   A graph showing the break even points between a) a revenue/cost situation, or b) two or more alternative systems involving costs only (e.g., two different materials handling systems).

BREAK EVEN LOAD FACTOR   The minimum percentage of airplane seats or freight capacity on a run that must be filled in order to avoid a loss on the flight; the percent of seats necessary to be filled by revenue passengers in order to cover variable and direct fixed costs of the flight.

BREAK-EVEN POINT   A point where total cost equals total revenue at a certain production level. The point where revenue equals the sum of fixed and variable costs.

BREAKING DOORWAY   After the safe placement of the dock plate, unloading of the rail car can commence. If the load is dead piled, it will be necessary to place an empty pallet load. It will be necessary to off load enough product by this method until enough space is clear inside the rail car to place a pallet on the floor of the car.

BREAKING POINT   A point at which the rate is divided or at which rates are made.

BREAK THE UNIT   The process of uncoupling, or unhitching, the tractor from the trailer.

BREAKWATER   Denotes an embankment or bulkhead that provides shelter

BREAST WIRE   The attachment between two barges, or a barge and towboat that leads directly athwart ship at right angle to the reel.

BRENT CRUDE   An oil benchmark price based upon the North Sea crude oil market.

BRIDGE PLATE   A portable metal plate which is placed in the doorway of a railroad car to provide a ramp between two cars, or between a car and a platform.

BRIDGE TOLL   A charge made for transporting traffic over a bridge.

BRIEF   A written abstract of testimony and pleadings in a case and comments thereon.

BROACHING CARGO   A term to denote breaking into the ships cargo and stealing food, drink, and other articles for individual use.

BROADBAND   An internet term for the capability of transmitting and receiving content by way of graphics, video, audio, and other high speed output.

BROKEN STOWAGE   Denotes when space for storage is interfered with by parts of the ship that extend into the hold. Odds and ends of freight are used to fill the spaces.

BROKER   1. Person who owns equipment and leases it out 2. Person who arranges buying and selling of transportation or goods. 3. Ship agent who acts for the ship owner or charterer in arranging charters.

BROKERAGE LICENSE   Authority granted by a regulatory body in countries requiring it to persons engaged in the business of arranging for transportation of persons or property in interstate commerce.

BROWN FIELD   Construction of new manufacturing capacity at an existing site.

BROWNIE   An auxiliary transmission.

BROWSER   Internet related software that searches and presents web sites on a personal computer.

BUDGET   A formal financial plan for future income and expenditures.

BUDGETARY CONTROL   The actual performance under the planned budget of each department.

BUFFER STOCK   A certain level of inventory maintained on account of sales demand and lead time variations so as not to incur an out of stock situation.

BULBOUS BOW   An extended underwater protrusion at the front of a ship that makes its flow through the water more efficient than otherwise possible with traditional knife shaped bows.

BULL MARKET   An economic performance situation characterized with increasing activity and rising stock prices.

BULLWHIP EFFECT   A supply chain phenomenon revealing that gradual changes in consumer demand or shelf off-take increasingly cause larger variations in demand and activity farther back into distribution, production, materials, purchasing, and at suppliers. Also known as the Forrester Effect.

BULK DENSITY   Stated in pounds per cubic foot, this is the weight of a unit of volume of a given substance.

BULK (FREIGHT)   When a carload shipment is shipped loose or in mass, rather than being shipped in packages or containers, it is termed bulk-freight shipment. This commonly takes place in the movement of grain in a box car, sand in a hopper car, or in the transportation of sulfur in the hold of a ship.

BULKHEAD   An upright partition in a car, vehicle, or vessel which separates one part of it from another.

BULK HEADINGS   See BRACING.

BULK WAREHOUSES   Public warehouses providing tank storage of liquids and open or sheltered storage of dry products such as coal, sand, stone and chemicals.

BULK WEIGHT   This is the weight the carrier will show on a way bill or a freight bill for the purposes of assessing the charge.

BULKY   A term applied to freight taking up considerable space in comparison to its weight.

BULLETIN   A notice or an announcement officially published concerning matters of public importance.

BULL HAULER   A livestock mover.

BULLION   A commercial name for uncoined gold or silver.

BULL MARKET   A condition of rising prices of the most traded items, such as commodities, bonds, stocks, commodities, etc. in the market. See BEAR MARKET.

BUMBLE BEE   A two cycle engine.

BUMP   An airline term for a situation when a passenger who has a reservation and ticket for a particular flight is denied boarding, because of an over-sale of seats or the inability of the aircraft to take off due to weight and balance restrictions.

BUNCHING (CARS)   When rail cars are accumulated in excess of those ordered for the purpose of loading or unloading, or when cars are gathered in quantities that exceed the capacity of the tracks and unloading facilities, it creates a condition known as bunching. This is often done by the carrier in anticipation of future outbound shipments by the shipper, thereby avoiding the need for many car delivery runs.

BUNDLING   Term for situation whereby seller combines two or more products into one transaction for a single price. Computer hardware might be purchases "bundled" with certain software in a combined purchase.

BUNKER CHARGE   Coal loaded into the bunkers of a vessel for the use of the vessel is assessed a bunker charge for the loading operation. This does not include the cost of the coal itself.

BUNKER CLAUSE   A clause that charterers must replace and pay for the fuel and coal in the vessel's bunkers at port of delivery.

BUNKERING   The task of fueling a ship so that the greatest payload may be carried.

BUNKER (REFRIGERATOR)   The place where ice is stored in a refrigerator car.

BUNKERS   Denotes stowage space for fuel in a vessel.

BUOYS   Floats that give mariners information by their shape and color.

BURDEN OF PROOF   The party that must provide disputed facts which are at issue before a court or regulatory agency.

BURDEN VESSEL   A vessel that has to yield to an oncoming vessel.

BUREAU VERITAS   Classifications of ships by the French Society

BURTON FALL   A rope, cable, or whip which passes through a block set which is outboard above the wharf and beyond the gunwhale of the vessel for the purpose of lowering or hoisting goods to or from the hatch to the wharf

BUS   A motorized road and highway vehicle that carries many people.

BUSH FLYING   Flying in remote regions where there may be no airports or other navigable aids.

BUSHEL   A dry measure containing eight gallons or four pecks, 18 1/2 inches in diameter and 8 inches deep in size. Its capacity is 2,150.42 cubic inches.

BUSINESS   Any activity where commercial transactions and operations take place.

BUSINESS CLASS FARE   An airline service commonly found on long distance international routes with features that are between those of coach and first class. Typically, it includes larger seats than coach as well as other service amenities.

BUSINESS CYCLE   The cyclical changes that take place in an economy over time. The different stages are boom, contraction, recession, expansion. Contraction and recession are often referred to as bear markets, while expansion and boom are often called bull markets.

BUSINESS FLYING   A term to denote owner operated air transportation for the purpose of business.

BUSINESS INFRASTRUCTURE   A general term for the design of the firm's departments, processes, technologies, and linkages with suppliers and customers.

BUSINESS MODEL   A general term for how a firm designs its systems in order to offer its products and services to the market. Similar with BUSINESS INFRA-STRUCTURE. A web retailer's business model might include an ordering system and linkage with the actual manufacturers and logistics firms. A competing firm's business model might include its own manufacturing, because it produces what it sees as special advantages from doing so.

BUSINESS PROCESS REENGINEERING   The activity of examining all steps, functions, and processes in a firm or part of a firm for the purpose of removing redundancies, items that cause delay or those that present problems. The outcome of this practice is a lower cost, higher efficiency, or better customer service overall process.

BUSINESS-TO-BUSINESS   A commerce term indicating that transactions and relationships in a situation are between two businesses. Distinct from those that involve the consumer. See B2B.

BUSINESS UNIT COLLABORATION   A term found in multi-national or multidivisional firms whereby they coordinate a process, purchase, or use of a common activity. Thus, two European divisions of the same firm might collaborate with the use of a common third party logistics firm. The benefits can be lower logistics costs for both of them as well as the firm as a whole.

BUSTING STRENGTH   The actual strength (in weights) a package can withstand up to a point of breaking in a certain manner.

BUTTERWORTHING   Special ship tank cleaning processes and equipment.

BUTTON HER UP   The process of tying down the load on the trailer.

"BUY AMERICAN ACT"   Legislation requiring that certain military and government purchased or financed goods be purchased from U.S. suppliers only.

BUYER   One who orders goods/services and agrees to pay them.

BUYER'S MARKET   Market condition whereby demand is less than supply. Prices, terms, and conditions are usually driven more by the buyers m the market than they are by the sellers.

BUYER'S RIGHT TO ROUTE   The right of the buyer to designate the route of his/her shipment, when the seller doesn't pay freight charges. The seller is held responsible for the buyer's instructions. Routing is permitted for rail shipments, but not for motor shipments beyond the first carrier.

BUY-IN   A term indicating that persons, departments, groups, or other companies agree to cooperate with a certain initiative. Thus, the company's auditors might be said to have bought-in on the purchasing department's use of a five year contract rather than demand monthly bidding.

BUYING   The act of arranging for goods or services, including selecting a supplier, contacting that firm, and making a specific arrangement. Some follow-through activities include the subsequent paperwork leading to payment. Very narrow context of procurement today. Generally it applies only the tactical or executional part of acquiring goods by way of the transactions.

BUYING CONSORTIUM   When many independent firms gather to consolidate the purchases of goods and services that are used by all of them. The purpose of this practice is to lower purchased prices as well as overhead costs of the acquisition process.

BYLAW   Located in the constitution or in a fundamental law for the use of authority.

BY-PRODUCTS   An accessory product of some value resulting from some specific process or manufacture.

BY THE STERN   A term to denote that a vessel is deeper than normal at the stern, because of excess weight aft.

CCCC

CAB   The driver's operating compartment of a tractor on a truck or the locomotive of a rail engine.

C.A.B.   The Civil Aeronautics Board, formerly the economic regulatory authority for common carrier interstate air transportation in the U.S. The CAB was established under the Civil Aeronautics Act of 1938, but was called the Civil Aeronautics Authority until 1960. It ceased to exist on January 1, 1985 after phase out of air regulations stemming from 1977 and 1978 legislation.

CABOOSE   The car used by the brakeman and conductor which is placed at the rear of the freight train is called a caboose or cabin car. Sometimes referred to as the conductor's car or way car. In Europe, it is often called a brake van.

CABOTAGE   This water and air transportation term applies to shipments and passengers between points of a single nation. Most every nation has cabotage laws which require domestic owned vessels to perform domestic air and interport water transportation services.

CAB-OVER   A truck tractor unit that has the engine under the driver's cab and the front of the vehicle is flat; cab overs allow for longer trailers within the overall tractor-trailer length limitation.

C & F NAMED PORT   A selling term in international trade whereby the seller quotes a goods price that includes the freight charge to the named point of destination.

C & L   Canal and lake.

CALL AVOIDANCE   A customer service term for any web, printed manual, or instructional method that assists the customer in a way that reduces their having to call company personnel. With toll free number order entry, the alternative use of the web by the customer avoids calls that are more costly to process.

CALL CENTER   A site to which customers call for order entry, product/service information, or for technical problems.

CALL STATION   The pickup and delivery station presented by a carrier.

CANCELING DATE   The date agreed upon by the ship owner and charterer which the vessel must be ready for loading. Missing the loading date represents just cause for canceling the charter contract.

CAPABILITY   A strategic management term in use today. It relates to those actions and strengths that a firm, line-of-business, department, or person has that are strategically and competitively useful. For example, an air courier company's capability to predict arrival for a receiver might be of competitive use for certain high time demanding firms.

CAPACITY   The amount that can be carried in a vessel, truck, or car expressed in terms of weight or measurement, is its capacity.

CAPACITY AGREEMENT   An agreement among airlines to limit flights in certain origin-destination markets in order to conserve fuel, manage revenue, and other reasons.

CAPACITY CONTROL   Generally used in airlines and ocean shipping whereby agreements among governments and/or carriers limit the amount of carriage they provide on a route. The purpose is to protect those carriers and allow them greater volume and revenue than would otherwise be possible in a purely competitive situation.

CAPACITY PRICE   A general term for a high price that a firm would charge the next customer once it is already operating at capacity. At that high price, the firm would recover higher than normal profits. The firm's rationale is this situation is often a) to provide funds for further capacity expansion, b) to cover over-time and other extra costs of producing it, or c) to deter the customer.

CAPACITY UTILIZATION   The percent of a facility or equipment that is in actual revenue producing use as compared to the total capacity that is available. An example in the airline industry: a load factor of 68% indicates that the number of seats sold in revenue service is 68% of the total number of seats available in a given time period.

CAPACITY PLATE   Plate affixed to a forklift truck or forklift truck attachment indicating the maximum weight which can be raised or moved.

CAPITAL CHARGE   A budgetary charge made by a firm against assets employed in divisions, departments or subsidiaries; it reflects the opportunity cost of the firm's funds tied up in the fixed assets; example, 15% of asset per annum.

CAPITAL LEASE   A lease that is shown on the company's accounting statements as an asset as well as a future liability for the lease payments.

CAPITAL RATIONING   The process of allocating funds to capital budget requests; consists of the basic project accept/reject decision.

CAPSTAN   A mechanism used to raise and lower heavy weights, move objects, assist in the mooring of a vessel, and sometimes to move dead engines in a terminal area.

CAPTAIN'S PROTEST   A document prepared by the captain of a vessel on arriving at port, showing conditions encountered during voyage—generally for purpose of relieving ship owner of any loss to cargo, thus requiring cargo owners to look to the insurance company for reimbursement.

CAPTIVE SHIPPER   Rail industry term for a shipper that has no other railroad company option to ship to a destination other than the one serving the origin point. An expanded view includes no alternative feasible transportation (including water, pipe, or motor).

CAR DAY   One freight car on a railroad line held for a 24-hour period is a car day.

CARDEX FILE   System of cards used to report and keep track of inventory levels, inbound and outbound shipments.

CARETAKER   A person accompanying a shipment requiring special attention while en route.

CAR FLOAT   A flat-bottomed boat used to move rail cars. They are used primarily in harbor areas, and are equipped, of course, with track.

CARGO   The lading (contents) of a railroad car or trailer.

CARGO DATA INTERCHANGE SYSTEM (CARDIS)   A system providing for the movement of export/import and transportation information movement from one firm or organization to another.

CARGO TONNAGE   The weight in U.S. is 2000 lbs. or 2240 pounds. In British countries it is in the English long or gross ton of 2240 pounds. In the metric system the weight ton is 2204.62 pounds. The usual size measured ton is 40 cubic feet, but in some instances a larger number of cubic feet is taken as a weight ton.

CAR LINING   Materials placed on the walls of a car for the protection of the goods. Typically it is paper or plastic sheet lining.

CARLOAD   The weight requirement necessary to qualify for a carload rate is a carload; or, a car loaded to its total capacity may also be called a carload.

CARLOAD MINIMUM WEIGHT   The weight which must be transported or paid for to qualify for a carload rate.

CARLOAD, MIXED   A shipment consisting of two or more commodities which meet the requirements of having a total weight equal or greater than the minimum weight of the highest minimum weight commodity, and which is charged the rate of the highest rate commodity in the mixed carload shipment, qualifies as a mixed carload.

CARLOAD RATE   This is a rate that would apply to a quantity of freight qualifying for a minimum carload rate weight. It is applicable to rail movements. It should be distinguished from a per car rate. The carload rate is applicable to class rates. The carload quantity referred to on a carload rate has nothing to do with the quantity of that commodity that will be required to actually fill a rail car. The minimum weight specified to qualify for a lower class rate permits a carload rate.

CARLOAD TRAFFIC   A shipment of not less than 10,000 pounds of one commodity from one consignor to one consignee. Where mixed carload ratings are provided in classifications or tariffs a mixed carload is treated as a carload within the meaning of this paragraph, provided such shipment is from one consignor to one consignee at one destination or in the case of shipments upon which stopovers are permitted, from one consignor to two or more consignees each at a different destination, and provided the shipment is waybilled at and the charges are collected upon the basis of the carload rate applicable. In such cases, the shipment is treated as a carload of that commodity which forms the major portion of the shipment in weight.

CARMACK AMENDMENT (U.S.)   An amendment to the Interstate Commerce Act that presented the liability of the carrier and the requirements relative to the bill of lading forms and provisions.

CAR LOCATOR   A rail industry technology that captures the location of freight cars for the purposes of traffic flow and customer tracking/tracing.

CAR MILE   The movement of a car a distance of one mile. It may be subdivided into freight car miles, passenger car miles, loaded car miles, and empty car miles.

CARNET   A document and process that allows goods of value to be temporarily imported into a country and subsequently exported without having to pay customs duties. This is often found when goods are brought into a country for use at a trade show then returned to their home country. Carnets are also used in situations when goods pass through one country in-transit to the one finally importing them.

CAR POOLING   When car equipment is coordinated through the operation of a central control for the joint benefits of the owners and users of the cars, a pooling arrangement is established. This is performed for the benefit of the owners and users of all the cars controlled by the central agency involved in this type of service transportation.

CAR RENTAL   An amount which is paid for the use of private rail cars by carriers and others.

CARRIAGE   The actual movement of a consignment of goods from the point of origin after having been loaded and before being unloaded.

CARRIAGE AND INSURANCE PAID TO . . . (CIP)   An INCO 1990 international sales/shipping term that the seller has the obligation to arrange and pay for carriage of goods to a named destination along with the cargo insurance to that point.

CARRIAGE OF GOODS AT SEA ACT (U.S. and U.K.)   Legislation that covers to some degree ocean carrier loss and damage obligations.

CARRIAGE PAID TO . . . (CPT)   An INCO 1990 international sales/shipping term that the seller pays the freight for carriage of the goods to a named destination.

The shipper has no obligation to provide insurance. The buyer/receiver then takes over control of transport for the goods from the named destination (typically a port or city en route). They also typically arrange insurance for the entire origin-to-destination movement.

CARRIER   An individual, partnership or corporation engaged in the business of transporting goods and/or passengers.

CARRIER COMPETITION   Competition between one carrier and another serving the same points of origin and destination.

CARRIER, DELIVERING (OR DESTINATION)   The carrier that makes delivery to the consignee in either a joint or single movement is the delivering carrier.

CARRIER PERFORMANCE (METRIC)   The measurement means, or metrics, by which shippers and receivers evaluate the services and other attributes of specific carriers.

CARRIER, SETTLING   The carrier that actually comes to terms with the claimant; in the case of interline settlements, the carrier having a debit balance.

CARRIER'S LIEN   When a carrier is forced to retain the property it has transported for security for collection charges, the property (freight) becomes a carrier's lien.

CAR SCANNER   A trackside device used for car locator purposes.

CAR SEAL   A device fastened to the locks of the doors of cars; it will indicate if door has been opened.

CAR SERVICE   This is a general term which covers such services as car supply, handling and distribution. It usually becomes involved in matters of interchange, demurrage handling, settlements, per diem, allowances, etc.

CAR SERVICE RULE   A rule imposed by a regulatory agency so as to provide incentives or disincentives to certain practices in the national rail car fleet, includes powers over per diem, demurrage, car distribution and movement practices.

CARTAGE   The hauling and the transferring of goods by trucks, wagons, drays, etc. It is short haul and transfer in nature.

CARTAGE AGENT   Firm engaged in hauling freight on trucks, usually to and from ship piers, airports, and intermodal terminals.

CARTAGE, LOCAL   Service performed in local distribution by a common or contract carrier engaged in either local hauling or pickup and delivery service for over-the-road or line-haul carriers.

CARTAGE TO SHIP SIDE   The charge made for carting, draying or trucking freight alongside a vessel.

CARTEL   Any body of selling firms or organizations that collude to restrict capacity or fix prices in a market.

CARTING   The hauling of freight on carts, drays or trucks.

CARTON   A container constructed of solid or corrugated fiberboard or paperboard.

CARTON CLAMP   Type of fork truck that allows picking up lading by squeezing it from sides instead of lifting as with pallets or spreadsheets. Designed to handle unitized loads of cartons much like holding a box in between the palms of your hands.

CAR UTILIZATION FACTOR   1) The number of revenue trips per year a rail car handles. 2) The number of days per year in which a car is loaded with revenue moves. 3) The percentage of a car that is loaded in relation to its weight or cubic capacity.

CAR YIELD   A railroad management measure of rail car revenue producing experience, it is the total car revenue over a certain period divided by the number of loaded trips. If the car is in a consistent, assigned service, it is the carload revenue times the number of trips per month.

CASE   1) The subject matter of litigation or resolution before a regulatory body or court. 2) A consulting industry term for any project, whether it be for a client or a research endeavor.

CASH AGAINST DOCUMENTS   Payment for goods upon presentation of documents evidencing shipment.

CASH IN ADVANCE   A purchasing term that requires payment prior to shipping from seller's point of origin.

CASH EFFECT   As distinct from an accounting cost, the cash effect is the resulting cash outlays and receipts from an activity.

CASH SETTLEMENT PROCESS   The activities and steps required between the calculation and preparation of a customer invoice until making actual deposit of cash into the firm's checking account.

CASH TO CASH CYCLE   The time span from the moment a firm pays its suppliers for raw materials until it receives payment for the sale of the related finished goods. It is different than the physical cycle which measures the time spans of inventory receipts and outbound shipments.

CASH WITH ORDER   A purchasing term requiring payment with the initial order.

CASUAL LABOR   Temporary workers used by the warehouse or office to meet the workload.

CASUAL (OR OCCASIONAL) OPERATIONS   In freight or passenger train operations, seasonal service, maintenance, and/or operation, as distinguished from steady, or scheduled operations.

CASUS FORTUITUS   Contract of affreightment to protect vessel owner's liability in case of inevitable accident such as lighting and similar perils of the sea.

CATEGORY   The classification of goods. In fast moving consumer goods industries, these would be seen as the detergent category, canned soup category, etc.

CATEGORY MANAGEMENT   The management of a selection of related branded goods in a customer facility such as a supermarket. In modern supermarkets, Brand A might be chosen by the store to manage its products on the shelf along with Brand B and the store's own brand all together in the aisle.

CAVEAT EMPTOR   Let the purchaser beware.

CAVEAT VENDITOR   Let the seller beware.

C-CHECK   An airline maintenance term for a major overhaul and examination of an aircraft and its engines.

CE   Consumption Entry.

CEASE AND DESIST   A regulatory order to cease performance of a specific act which is usually in violation of the regulatory Act.

CELL MANUFACTURING   Method of production whereby related equipment is grouped in proximity with each other for the purpose of flexibly shifting from one type of work to another and increasing overall efficiency of operations.

CELLULAR FLOW   The term cellular flow is commonly applied in logistics to mean shipment volume. A cellular flow channel planning system involved the determination of the total logistics cost on the basis of the cost per shipment. Inbound and out-bound shipments to and from a factory take the form of single shipment of one or more commodities per shipment. Each shipment is a cell.

CENTER FLOW   A type of covered hopper car that has loading hatches longitudinally on the center top of the car; likewise, the internal walls direct the outflow toward a small hatch at the bottom center of the car rather than spilling over the rails as with conventional hoppers and covered hoppers.

CENTRAL EUROPEAN TIME ZONE   The time zone two hours east of Greenwich Mean Time.

CENTRALIZED PRODUCTION   When a manufacturer centralizes his production it locates all production facilities in the same general location. In its simplest form, this consists of a single large plant. Obviously, centralized production may consist of many plants located adjacent to one another that are complementary. Centralized production is to be distinguished from decentralized production only by the location of the production facilities, and not on the basis of the overall volume of output.

CENTRALIZED PURCHASING   The practice of purchasing from one location or group within a firm. Distinct from having the purchasing activity spread throughout various divisions of a firm.

CERTIFICATE OF ADMEASUREMENT   A document stating what portion of a vessel is excluded from gross tonnage.

CERTIFICATE OF ANALYSIS   Laboratory and other analytical certification as to the content and make up of products. Used as proof to the buyer that the goods they have ordered conform to their required specifications. Certificates of analysis are often conducted by organizations independent of the buyer and seller.

CERTIFICATE OF DAMAGE   A document or certificate issued by dock companies in regard to merchandise received or unloaded in a damaged condition.

CERTIFICATE OF INSPECTION   A survey of goods being shipped and attested to by an independent organization that they conform to the purchasing specifications. Often used in the clearance and export of goods involving a letter of credit.

CERTIFICATE OF INSURANCE   A document or certificate taking the place of a marine insurance policy.

CERTIFICATE OF MANUFACTURE   A document attesting to a) the method of manufacture of goods, and/or b) that the named manufacturer was the producer of the goods.

CERTIFICATE OF ORIGIN (COE)   This document is required on shipments to and from many countries. It is a certificate which specifies the country of origin, number of packages, number of packages/cases, weight, and description of goods. Some countries use this information to determine if shipment includes prohibited goods or if some have originated in nations not permitted to be trading with it. Most countries use it to determine product content and to assign specific customs duties.

CERTIFICATE OF PUBLIC CONVENIENCE AND NECESSITY (U.S.)   This is an operating right for a common motor carrier. It was a document issued by the regulatory agency of Congress which allowed the applicant to operate as a common carrier for a particular mode.

CERTIFICATE OF REGISTRY   A document issued by maritime authorities stating that a ship has been legally registered in a country.

CERTIFICATE OF SURVEY   A document prepared by an inspection and surveying firm attesting to the quantity and quality of the goods being shipped.

CERTIFICATE OF WEIGHT   An authoritative statement issued by the shipper as to the weight of a shipment.

CERTIFIED CHECK   A check that has been validated by a bank official upon which the check is drawn as evidence of its validity.

CERTIFIED INVENTORY REPORT   An inventory report signed by an officer of the company or designated responsible party to attest to the correctness of the report.

CERTIORARI   A legal term meaning "to be more fully informed." An original writ or action whereby a cause is removed from an inferior to a superior court for trial. The record of the proceedings is then transmitted to the superior court.

CESSER CLAUSE   This clause relieves the charter of the responsibility of the shipment from the time the cargo is shipped. It provides the owner with a lien on the cargo and assures the shipper's liability to pay the freight instead of paying the charterer.

CHAEBOLS   Groupings of manufacturing and service firms in Korea that are part of an overall corporate entity. Though not necessarily cross-owned, they operate within the umbrella of the overall firm that performs marketing and orchestration of work among the individual businesses.

CHAIN FALL   This contrivance is used to take off a demountable body from a truck chassis in a sling-like machine.

CHAMFER BLOCK   A wooden beam generally used on flat cars to prevent payload shifts while enroute. Short chamfer blocks are sometimes called chock blocks.

CHANGE ORDER   An amended purchase order.

CHANNEL   The means, in terms of ownership, by which product moves from the manufacturer to final user; includes brokers, wholesalers, company distribution centers, etc.

CHANNEL JUMPING   Situation when a firm by-passes a normal channel party to sell to a final user or buyer; example, large volume sales direct to user rather than through the regular wholesaler in the area.

CHANNEL OF DISTRIBUTION   The means by which a manufacturer distributes products from the plant to the ultimate user includes warehouses, brokers, wholesalers, retailers, etc. Approximately twelve distinct channels of distribution are in common use.

CHANNEL OF PROCUREMENT   The parties through which goods move inbound to a firm in the overall purchasing process. Concept is the mirror image of channel of marketing. Channel of procurement can include direct from supplier, through brokers, wholesalers, etc.

CHANNEL TUNNEL   The rail tunnel that links France and England under the English Channel.

CHAPS   Clearinghouse Automated Payment System. An interbank funds wire linkage.

CHARGE BACK   1) Term that is used when a supplier incurs a cost that is passed on to the buyer as an act of convenience to the buyer. Example is paying freight only for it to be billed to the buyer along with the invoice for the goods. 2) Term also used when a buyer deducts an amount from a due bill to a seller. Buying firms will often deduct charge backs for rework done that should have been performed by the seller.

CHARGE, CONTINUOUS   A shipment made through to destination without an interruption in transit for breaking bulk, transfer, or rebilling.

CHARGES (PAYMENT OF TRANSPORTATION CHARGES)   The specified amount of payment for transportation services rendered. Payment must precede the release of the goods. Credit may be extended up to specified days when adequate precautions for payment have been taken.

CHARTER   The contracts for the use of a vessel involve numerous types of charters. 1) The Bare Boat Charter is a lease which establishes that the charterer pays all the voyage and cargo expenses, pays crew costs, and covers the marine risk and repair services. 2) The Time Charter provides that the lessee is provided with the provision of ship, supplied with deck and engine room stores for a stated period, for a service within specified limits, to be operated over a given period of time, for a stated amount of money. 3) Under the Net Form Charter the ship is hired for a voyage and the freight may be charged at a specified rate on the dead-weight capacity or on a rate per unit—or even on a lump-sum basis. Under this type of charter the owner Days the operating expenses and the voyage and cargo expenses. 4) The Gross Form Charter establishes the owner pays all the regular expenses involved in a voyage from the time the ship is berthed until the cargo is unloaded.

CHARTERED RATES   Charterer agrees to pay a given price per tonnage on the cargo, when leasing a vessel or ship. Under a variety of conditions.

CHARTERED SHIP   A ship leased by its owner or agent for a stated time, voyage or voyages.

CHARTERER   One who leases a ship or part of its cargo space. A vessel charter may for round trip, or a stated period, under what is known as trip, or time, charter.

CHARTER PARTY   A marine contract between the ship owner and the one leasing the ship. A principal clause of every charter party refers to lay days, the time allowed the charterer for loading and or unloading. These lay days are usually calculated from 24 hours after charterers have been notified that vessel is ready to load. They may be either running days, i.e., consecutive days, or working days, i.e., those days usually devoted to work at the place where the vessel is loaded, omitting holidays and Sundays.

CHASING A MARKET DOWN   Those management activities a firm or line of business would engage in when taking costs out of a product that is declining in demand in the market or experiencing severe price pressure. The intent is to remove costs at a faster rate than the prices and demand are dropping.

CHECK, BLIND   The checking of freight in a given shipment by persons without them having access to records which show the kind and amount of freight contained in the shipment.

CHECKING (RATES)   Comparing rates assessed on a shipment with the tariff applicable or other authority to determine their correctness, considering rates in effect or proposed by representatives of the traffic department of carriers to determine their proper adjustment.

CHEP PALLET   A commercial pallet pooling firm and brand of pallets.

CHICANEUR   One who is shrewd, and lays claim to secure rebates and discounts to which they are not entitled.

CHILLED   Indicating the temperature of transporting and storing goods. Chilled is generally in the range of 35–55 degrees F.

CHINESE MENU   Anything indicating that a seller is offering a range of products and services that may be selected in various forms and sequences by buyers.

CHIPS   An electronic banking Clearinghouse Interbank Payment System that is based in New York.

CHOCKS   Blocks or stops which, when placed under the wheels of a rail car, trailer, or airplane wheels, prevent the vehicle from rolling while at rest.

CHUNNEL   See CHANNEL TUNNEL, colloquial term for it.

CHUTE   Inclined trough used to facilitate the flow movement of grain, livestock, etc.

CIF   A selling term in international trade whereby the seller quotes a goods price that includes freight charges to a destination point and marine insurance en route.

CIFCI   Cost, Insurance, Freight, Corrections Charges, and Interest. This is the basis of pricing commonly used in Asia.

CIFIE   Cost, insurance, freight, interest and exchange.

CIRCUITOUS ROUTE   Any indirect route that is longer than the shortest or fastest possible route. It had former significance in rail transportation in the allowance of certain rates along routes in maintaining a competitiveness against the more direct routes.

CIRCULAR NOTE   An issue of the bank for the accommodation of a traveler, calling upon its correspondence at different places to pay money on demand.

CIRCULARS   Publications issued by the carriers containing provisions for the handling of freight, distinguished from tariffs in that their provisions are general in character. Circular carriers are carriers that file brief circulars, showing only mileages and a few other facts.

CITATION   The record of a decided case, statute, decision or book of authority, to establish a basis of referral for future matters.

CITATION OF AN ADMINISTRATIVE REGULATION   Citation form of a regulation found within agency's administrative rulings, for example: U.S. Department of Transportation for domestic hazardous transportation regulations are in Title 49 of the Code of Federal Regulations.

CITATION OF DECISION   The reference made to the location of a decision or opinion rendered by a court or a regulatory commission.

CIVIL PENALTIES   A term to indicate that the legal penalty for a certain unlawful act includes fines and various decrees. Civil penalties typically are in the form of fines and other requirements.

C L & R   Canal, lake and rail.

CLAIM   When a document is submitted which shows evidence of a right to recover a loss by damage or overcharge it is referred to as a claim. It may require compensation to the owner for loss or damage of goods in transit. It may involve a request for refund by a carrier for charges in excess of the legal or tariff rate—which is called an overcharge claim. It may involve restitution for losses caused by applications of rates greater than the lawful rates. It may likewise involve a demand made by carriers on shippers for payment of undercharges.

CLAIM TRACER   A document seeking to determine the status of a claim which has been made, but not finalized.

CLAMP, BARREL   Lift truck attachment designed to handle drums and barrels.

CLAMP, PAPER ROLL   Lift truck attachment designed to handle rolled paper products.

CLARIFY REQUIREMENTS   The acts of either a) seeking from a buying company (customer) exactly what are needed in work to be performed, or b) within a firm, it is the process of standardizing complex specifications of products and services.

CLASS AND COMMODITY TARIFF   A tariff containing both class and commodity rates.

CLASSES   The various divisions or groups, designated by numbers and/or letters, into which articles offered for shipment are classified and to which rate schedules are adjusted.

CLASSES OF LEGAL SERVICE   Transportation carriers are classified in accordance with the character of the legal service offered in the following manner: (1) common carriers of property, (2) contract carriers of property; (3) private carriers of property; and (4) brokers of property.

CLASSIFICATION   In rate making, the ratings assigned to articles and commodities that relate to value, density, and value of service and other factors. These are contrasted to commodity rates. It is a book that groups commodities into classes for rate making purposes.

CLASSIFICATION OF CARRIERS BY COMMODITY   Transportation carriers are classified on the basis of the character of the commodities carried in the following way: (1) carriers of general freight; (2) carriers of household goods; and (3) carriers of special commodities.

CLASSIFICATION OF CARS (U.S.)   The designation of letters and the descriptive definitions adopted by the Association of American Railroads to cover various types of freight and passenger cars.

CLASSIFICATION (OF FREIGHT)   The grouping of articles that have similar transportation characteristics, for the purpose of simplification. Such factors as weight, risk in handling, bulk, value of article, competition, and cost of handling are considered in determining the class to which any article belongs for the purpose of applying class rates. Also, the class to which articles are assigned for the purpose of applying class rates.

CLASSIFICATION OF SHIPS   The process of gathering and correlating information concerning the seaworthiness of vessels which may be used by underwriters in providing an insurance. The registration assistants perform the operation of classification.

CLASSIFICATION RATING   The class to which an article is assigned for the purpose of applying class rates.

CLASSIFICATION SCHEDULE   A publication that contains the description and ratings of articles offered for shipment, together with the rules and regulations governing their preparation and handling.

CLASSIFICATION TERRITORY (U.S.)   The Classification Territory is a geographic area within which the classification of given freight applies. In the United States there are three classification territories. The Official Classification Territory involves the area north of the Ohio and Potomac Rivers and east of Lake Michigan, and a line drawn between St. Louis and Chicago. The Southern Classification Territory is the area south of the Official Classification Territory and East of the Mississippi River. The Western Classification Territory is the rest of the United States west of the Mississippi.

CLASSIFICATION YARD   The purpose of the railroad classification yard is to serve as a kind of break bulk station, but in this instance a break car station. It is generally seen as a rail yard for the purpose of sorting cars for long distance movement. A rail train will have its cars separated for movement in differing directions under separate trains in the classification yard. Trains approaching the Minot Burlington Northern Classification yard westbound, for example, would have their cars separated for new trains destined for varying points west, south, and north. One train may be made up for Seattle, another for Denver, and the third for a California destination. A transcontinental shipment may move through many classification yards.

CLASS RATE   A rate resulting from a rating provided in a classification. While commodity rates are available only on limited commodities with specific origins and destinations, a class rate can be found on practically any commodity between any two points. The rate in the class rate tariff is normally on class 100 commodities. To determine the class rate it is necessary to multiply the first class rate by a percentage figure applicable on its rating. In the uniform freight classification, the percentage of first class is automatically provided in tile classification. That is, a class 87 would mean approximately 87% of first class. Class rates were created to simplify the preceding process providing a specific rate on each commodity moved.

CLASS TARIFF   A tariff containing only class rates.

CLASS YARD   The railroad yard that is used to sort railroad cars for grouping into trains for specific destinations.

CLAYTON ACT (U.S.)   An anti-trust act of Congress making price discrimination unlawful. The Federal Trade Commission is empowered to enforce these prohibitions.

CLEAN BILL OF LADING   A bill of lading which the carrier has accepted without making notations relative to the Shippers Load and Count. It represents a clean acceptance of the freight in accordance with the content of the bill of lading.

CLEAN CREDIT   (See "Letters of credit").

CLEAN DOCUMENTS   International and transportation documentation that are complete and without mistakes.

CLEAN DRAFT   A sight or time draft (bill of exchange) to which no additional documents are attached (See "Documentary draft").

CLEANING IN TRANSIT   The stopping of articles, such as peanuts, etc., at a point located between the points of origin and destination to be cleaned.

CLEARANCE   A customhouse certificate stating that a ship is free to leave a port and that all legal requirements have been met.

CLEARANCE INWARD   A customhouse certificate stating the quantity of dutiable goods still remaining on a ship after the cargo has been discharged at a port and before taking on fresh cargo.

CLEARANCE LIMITS   The dimensions beyond which the size of, or projections on a shipment may not extend in order to clear obstructions along railway tracks, such as switchstands, platforms, tunnels, mail cranes, water tanks, third rails, low bridges, signal stands, etc.

CLEARANCE OUTWARD   A declaration made to the customs authorities by the ship's captain before preparing to leave a port stating that all legal requirements have been met.

CLEAR BLOCK   Railroad term indicating that a section of track between two points (or signals) is clear of any other train.

CLEAR DAYS   Business days free from weather, interference, strikes, or other problems.

CLEARING   1) Entering a ship at a custom house and obtaining clearance. 2) Exchange of checks and settling balances at the clearing house.

CLEARING A BILL   Receipt of money due on a bill of exchange.

CLEARINGHOUSE   A system whereby bankers in an area meet daily to clear checks among themselves so as to reduce float.

CLEAR RECORD   A record which shows that a shipment was handled without any loss or damage being sustained.

CLEAT   A strip of wood or metal used to afford additional strength; to prevent warping; to hold in position.

CLOSED CURRENCY   The currency of a nation that can only be exchanged through official banks or the government of that country.

CLOSED FLIGHT   A flight that is closed to any additional passengers or freight but that has not yet departed from the gate.

CLOUT   Term used in the purchasing field for when a firm has strong buying power relative to a supplier, or suppliers.

COASTING (COASTWISE) TRADE   Domestic maritime trade between points within a country as distinguished from trade between a point in one country and a point in another country.

COASTING VESSEL   Ships trading between ports of the same country.

COAST OFF   Airline flight term when a transoceanic flight leaves airspace over land and is starts flying over the ocean leg of the trip. The "coast-off" point of land often becomes a reference point in the flight. The Concorde is said to coast-off North America at Montauk Point, New York for its supersonic flight over the Atlantic.

CODE OF FEDERAL REGULATIONS (U.S.)   The U.S. Government Printing Office publications which contain the regulations various agencies have created and promulgated within their quasi-legislative powers; the DOT's rules are contained within Title 49 of the Code of Federal Regulation series.

CODE SHARE   Term used in the airline industry when two or more airlines use their individual flight numbers for one specific flight that is actually operated by only one of them. The purpose is to extend marketing reach for all the airlines doing it.

COD SHIPMENT   One in which the carrier is used by the shipper to collect the invoice value of the goods from the consignee prior to or at delivery; the amount is then remitted to the shipper less a service fee.

C.O.F.C.   Container-on-flatcar. Special C.O.F.C. tariffs were developed originally for a joint land/water movement for international shipments. Thus, a C.O.F.C. rate might be applicable on a movement between Salt Lake City and Seattle for a shipment destined for Japan. These rates were usually lower than other rail rates in order to encourage international shipments. This is a type of rail rate. Since trailers are a form of a container, some tariffs apply to both containers and trailers. Actually, the container car is a different type of car than a trailer flat car.

COGSA   Acronym for Carriage of Goods at Sea Act.

COG WHEEL RAILROAD   A railroad technology used in steep rail line areas whereby locomotive power turns a cog that meshes with the notches of a middle rail embedded between the tracks.

COLLABORATION   A general term for two or more firms in a supply chain that consciously agree to share information and resources for the purposes of competing against another set of firms.

COLLABORATIVE PLANNING, FORECASTING AND REPLENISHMENT SYSTEM   A collaborative supply chain integration process used by many fast moving consumer goods brand manufacturers and discount retailers for the purpose of making their collective supply chains more efficient and responsive.

COLLABORATIVE TECHNOLOGY   Electronic linkages between firms that typically involve sharing forecasts, production schedules, and sales plans. This type of activity is designed to smooth supply chain activities, remove costs, and gain competitive advantage.

COLLECT   Term that indicates that the receiver or purchasing party is to be billed for by the carrier and pay the freight charges. In a narrow sense it is the demand of payment for freight charges upon delivery.

COLLECTING BANK   A bank which acts as an agent to the seller's bank (the presenting bank). The bank's function is to surrender documents to the buyer that indicate proper actions by the seller. The bank will then seek payment or acceptance of the draft by the buyer. The collecting bank assumes no responsibility either for the documents or the merchandise. The collecting bank's risk for letters of credit; therefore, the service is less costly to the trading parties.

COLLECTION   A draft drawn on the buyer, usually accompanied by documents with complete instructions concerning processing for payment or acceptance (See Trade acceptances").

COLLECTION ON DELIVERY (C.O.D.)   The amount of the costs and charges on the shipment which are collected when the carrier delivers the goods to the consignee. The amount less a collection fee is then remitted by the carrier back to the shipper.

COLLECTION RATES   Rates for inbound movement of many shipments that were consolidated at an intermediate point for the inbound long haul; it is the reverse of Distribution Rates.

COLLECTIVE RATE MAKING   The activity of many carriers acting through the medium of a rate bureau to meet, discuss and establish rates.

COLLECTOR OF CUSTOMS   A representative of a government acting for it in connection with foreign traffic.

COLLECT SHIPMENT   A shipment on which the freight charges are to be paid by the consignee, receiver, or purchaser as opposed to the shipper, seller, or consignor. See Collect.

CO-LOAD   Transportation practice of moving two or more shipper's shipments in a single vehicle load.

CO-LOCATION, OF ENGINEERS, DESIGNERS, ETC.   A firm's practice in the product innovation process of having engineers, designers, and other product development resources located together so that the process can progress simultaneously. This differs from traditional sequential approaches in which each of these groups functioned individually and passed their results on to the next group in the overall process. Co-location speeds up the innovation process and generally produces better results.

COLUMNS   Beams used to support a building. May be placed vertically or horizontally.

CO-MANAGED INVENTORIES   Situation where both supplier and buyer firm are managing a single lot of inventory together, typically at the buyer's site.

COMBI   Aircraft that carries both freight and passenger on the main deck.

COMBINATION CARRIER   An airline that carries passengers and freight.

COMBINATION (OR COMBINING) CAR   A passenger train car divided into two or more compartments to accommodate different classes of traffic.

COMBINATION EQUIPMENT   Aircraft which carries both passengers and cargo.

COMBINATION RATE   A rate made by combining two rates published in different tariffs. That is, the total charges for Point A to C are computed by adding the separate charges for Points A to B to the separate charges of Points B to C.

COMBINATION THROUGH RATES   When more than one carrier is involved in providing through routes, but do not publish joint rates, a combination through rate would be effective. They are composed of any combination of local rates, joint rates, or a combination of local and joint proportional rates.

COMBUSTIBLE LIQUID   Any liquid having a flash point above 100° and below 200°F as determined in DOT tests.

COME-A-LONG   Chain and winch device used to open rail car doors.

COMMERCE CLAUSE (U.S.)   Article 1, Section 8, Clause 3 of the U.S. Constitution gives Congress the power to regulate commerce with foreign nations and between the several states.

COMMERCE COURT (U.S.)   A court created by Act of Congress (1909) to have jurisdiction in all cases for the enforcement of orders of the Federal regulatory agencies that adjudicate cases.

COMMERCE LAW   Varying and rather indefinite signification, includes legal rules for the usage of trade.

COMMERCIAL ATTACHE   A representative of a country who is located in a foreign country for the purpose of assisting and fostering the foreign trade of the home country.

COMMERCIAL AVIATION   Transportation of persons or property via air routes operated as a business enterprise.

COMMERCIAL GRADE   Specification term in purchasing. Means specifications that were created and are standard in particular industries (e.g., 16 inch centers in studs for house construction; Number 303 can holding 46 ounces of liquid in canning industry).

COMMERCIAL INVOICE   This is commonly referred to as the bill of statement. It specifies goods sold from one party to another. There are two forms of commercial invoices: 1) the Invoice and Certificate of Value; and 2) the Invoice and Declaration of Value. The commercial invoice is a term commonly applying to international exchanges.

COMMERCIAL TREATIES   Treaties between state regulating the commercial rights of the nationals of each in the territories of the other. They establish the condition under which debts due a foreign trader may be collected through the courts.

COMMERCIAL ZONE   Specified area within a city in which a trucking company may operate without being subject to economic regulation.

COMMINGLING   Whenever different shipments or goods are moved in one ship-ment; example is interstate goods moving along with others that are intrastate in a single movement.

COMMISSION   1) A fee paid to an outside sales person based upon the total reve-nue they produced through their efforts selling a firm's products and services. 2) The split of revenue paid by airlines and cruise ship firms to travel agencies for the bookings they produced with passengers on behalf of the carriers. 3) Slang for bribe given to a government official in order to speed up customs clearances or other needed activity.

COMMITTED INVENTORY   Inventory that is earmarked for a particular cus-tomer or use but has not yet moved from its storage spot in a warehouse.

COMMODITIES CLAUSE (U.S.)   This was a clause in the Hepburn Act of June 29, 1906 which provided that it was unlawful for a rail carrier to transport property for a company in which the carrier has ownership. Of course, this would not apply to commodities when the commodities are used for the common carrier's own purpose.

COMMODITY   1) A product that is traded on markets in the world, such as wheat, soybeans, gold, etc. 2) A popular term for any manufactured product or service that is widely available, standardized, and generally brings low margins to its pro-ducers. 3) A general business term for any product or service that the firm sells that is in the late mature stages of the product life cycle.

COMMODITY BUSINESS PLAN   Purchasing field term for analyzing and devel-oping a complete supply chain, market analysis, and company use of a product or service that is acquired by it for the purpose of more competitively acquiring and using it.

COMMODITY ITEM   Purchasing field term for any product or service that is widely available from many sources, is available in fairly standardized form, and for which price and delivery are the significant criteria when acquiring them. See also COMMODITY.

COMMODITY RATE   A rate on a specific commodity, or article, moving be-tween specific points, sometimes in a specific direction, and sometimes for a specific minimum quantity. The purpose of the commodity rate is generally to provide a lower rate to reflect lower costs resulting from large scale movement or otherwise. The commodity rate can be higher than a class rate, but it usually is not.

COMMODITY SWAP   Practice in some petroleum firm markets whereby points of demand at distant points by one firm are supplied by another firm, and vice versa. At the end of a time period, the balance outstanding is settled financially. The purpose is to minimize transportation costs by each firm.

COMMODITY TARIFF   A tariff containing only commodity rates.

COMMODITY WAREHOUSE　Cotton warehouses, wool warehouses, tobacco warehouses, other agricultural product facilities and grain elevators which are designed for optimum warehouse handling of specific products.

COMMON CARRIER　The most accepted characteristics of the common carrier are: a) availability of service to anyone seeking a transportation movement, b) the publication of rates in tariff form; c) provision of the service on schedule; d) service to designated points or a designated area; e) service of a given class of movement and commodity.

COMMON COST　A cost for a function, activity or staff necessary for two or more separate products or services, common costs are such that they can not rationally be traced to either one of the functions on any sound basis.

COMMON LAW　A legal finding which has long been accepted. The force of the law comes from consent, rather than written statute. The basis of contract law in the United States as codified into the Uniform Commercial Code (UCC).

COMMON LAW LIABILITY　Carrier is obligated for goods for all acts except those of God and public enemy.

COMMON POINT　A point reached by two or more transportation lines.

COMMON PRACTICE　The act of standardizing methods and procedures across a company or lines of businesses of a single company. Example would be contract administration that would be made similar in a multi-national petroleum firm's many divisions.

COMMON TARIFF　A tariff published by or for the account of two or more transportation lines as Issuing carriers.

COMMUNICATIONS ACT OF 1934 (U.S.)　An act of Congress regulating communication by wire or radio. Approved June 19, 1934.

COMMUTER (RAIL)　Rail transportation systems designed generally to move passengers to and from home and work.

COMPANY CAR　A rail car in operation on the line owned by the carrier. Sometimes the term is also applied to a car used by various departments of a carrier firm in the performance of construction work.

COMPARATIVE ADVANTAGE　1) Economics. An economic concept of opportunity that states that if two countries produce the same items (A & B), and one country produces A more efficiently than the B while the other country produces B more efficiently than A, then they should not produce and consume both items internally. Rather, the first country should produce A and export its surplus to the other, and the other nation should produce B and export its surplus to the first one. In this manner, each country can concentrate upon what it does best. 2) Firm to Firm. This same concept applies to firms whereby they identify their competitive advantages and have each one perform what it does best and serve the other with its surplus. It is the basic rationale behind sound outsourcing.

COMPARATIVE RATE SCHEDULE   A table of rates showing the differences in charges existing via two routes or through different modes of transportation; rail, motor, water, etc.

COMPARTMENTIZED CAR   A boxcar equipped with movable bulkheads, which can be used to divide the car into separate compartments.

COMPARTMENT TANK CAR   A tank car with compartments or separate tanks into which different kinds of grades of oil or other liquids may be transported.

COMPELLED RATES   A rate which is established lower than the general adjustment of its related rates usually as a result of downward competitive reasons. Competitive water routes is a common feature in rail transportation having the effect of rail rates being reduced to compete against the water rates.

COMPETENCY   An ability to perform certain things so well as to have that as a competitive advantage in the market. Thus, one firm might have a customer contact and data base system that is very detailed as compared with its competitors.

COMPETITION   Rivalry between interests in the securing of business or business advantages.

COMPETITIVE ADVANTAGE   An activity, process, access to resources, or organizational design such that it is better than those of competitors.

COMPETITIVE BIDDING   The act by a firm of soliciting two or more potential suppliers for what price and terms they would sell a needed product or service to it.

COMPETITIVE IMPERATIVE   A general term for the resources, strategic thrusts, and focus that a firm employs to compete in the market.

COMPETITIVE POINT   A point at which two or more transportation lines compete for the movement of traffic.

COMPETITIVE RATE   May be established for purposes of either carrier or market competition. When a rate is set on a particular level to offer competition with another line it is referred to as carrier competition. When a competitive rate is set sufficiently low to permit one producing area to compete with another producing area in a given market, it is called market competition.

COMPETITIVE TRAFFIC   Traffic in the movement of which two or more transportation lines compete.

COMPLAINANT   A person or party who makes a complaint.

COMPLAINT   A complaint filed with a regulatory agency alleging a violation of a statute and requesting it to be investigated and adjudicated by that agency.

COMPLEXITY A general term indicating the number and configuration of all activities and processes in a production operation, supply chain, or overall firm. Some firms are highly complex in organizational design and operations while others are fairly simple.

COMPONENT COSTS The costs of specific activities and processes within a firm.

COMPOSITE TRAILER A truck trailer that is divided into compartments for ambient, chilled, and frozen goods.

COMPOUND DUTY Customs duty that is assessed upon the basis of both a) a per unit charge, and b) a percentage of value.

COMPRADORE A native advisor or agent, employed by foreign establishments in China, to have charge of its native employees and act as an intermediary in transactions with natives.

COMPRESSED GAS Any material or mixture having in the container a pressure exceeding 40 pounds per square inch at 70°F, or pressure exceeding 104 psi at 130°F; or any liquid flammable material having a vapor pressure exceeding 40 psi at 100°F.

COMPRESSED TIME CYCLE A supply chain initiative for shrinking the time that goods require to pass through the entire system from raw material to finished goods. Within a firm, it often refers to the manufacturing time cycle which is the time from receipt of raw materials to the final packaging of them in finished goods form at the end of the production line.

COMPRESSION A term applying to cotton and meaning the compression of a bale of flat cotton to either standard density or high density.

COMPRESSION IN TRANSIT Shipment of uncompressed cotton tendered to the carrier and compressed by or at the expense of the carrier before delivery at destination. The cost of such compression in transit is included in the rate itself and is paid for by the carrier out of such rate.

COMPUTE (A BILL) Determine the maturity date for a bill of exchange.

CONCEALED DAMAGE When the consignee signs a Delivery Receipt not having seen obvious shipment damage, but later there is an discovered alleged damage, it is referred to as concealed damage. It may be either concealed damage or loss.

CONCEALED DISCOUNTING A situation in which a posted price remains high, but the supplier will begin to pay freight or provide other services for that same price thereby lowering the total landed cost to the buyer. A discount is thereby granted without having to change the posted price.

CONCEALED LOSS Alleged loss in spite of fact that consignee signed Delivery Receipt without exception.

CONCENTRATE   To bring to a common center; to gather into one body or force.

CONCENTRATION POINT   The geographical location where less–than-carload shipments are brought together to be combined for carload shipment.

CONCLUSIVE EVIDENCE   Evidence that cannot be contradicted by other evidence.

CONCURRENCE   When a carrier signs a document which verifies that it is participating in rates published in the tariff by a given agent, it is called concurrence.

CONDENSATION   The moisture given off from humidity or changes in temperature. This is an environmental problem in shipments of food and other key care products in supply chains.

CONDITIONAL SALE   A transaction in which the user is treated as the owner of the asset; the user acquires title to the asset upon payment of the final installment amount.

CONDITIONAL SALES CONTRACT   A method of purchasing a capital item whereby a contract is signed to pay certain amounts on a periodic basis; upon the last payment, title passes from the seller to the buyer.

CONDUCTOR'S TRAIN (OR WHEEL) REPORT   The conductor of a train makes out a report of the train's movement showing the equipment handled, the points between which all units are moved, etc. The numbers and names of all equipment are identified and initialed by the conductor. When freight cars are involved, the type of car, its contents, the origin and destination, the gross and net weight, etc., are also shown on most rail lines.

CONFERENCE   General term for a collective rate making body.

CONFERENCE RATE   Rates arrived at by conference of carriers applicable to transportation, generally water transportation.

CONFIGURE TO ORDER   A manufacturing and/or service system that creates specific configurations of product and service upon demand for customers in accordance to their orders.

CONFIRMED CREDIT   Credit that cannot be canceled without mutual consent of the buyer and seller.

CONFIRMING BANK   The bank that adds its confirmation to another bank's (the issuing bank's) letter of credit and promises to pay the beneficiary upon presentation of documents in compliance with the letter of credit (L/C). Confirmation is requested by the beneficiary when the issuing bank's ability to pay is in doubt.

CONNECTING CARRIER   A carrier which has a direct physical connection with another carrier for a through movement is called a connecting carrier. It may also refer more specifically to a carrier that provides a link between two other carriers.

CONNECTING LINES   All carriers which make up a through route are connecting lines.

CONSEQUENTIAL DAMAGES   Damages that result as a consequence of a failing or breach. Examples are lost production time, lost customer goodwill, or the cost of lost wages.

CONSIDERATION (IN A CONTRACT)   The benefit or service one party will provide for another; typically consideration is spelled out in terms of dollar payment.

CONSIGNED STOCK   The finished goods inventories in the hands of agents, dealers, or customers which are still the property of the manufacturing source by agreement.

CONSIGNEE   The receiver for a shipment of goods.

CONSIGNEE MARKS   The use of such symbols as a square, diamond, triangle, circle, a cross, etc. which is placed on packages for export and is used for the purpose of identifying the shipment for the consignee are termed consignee marks. These symbols are used with designated letters and numbers for identification purposes.

CONSIGNMENT   A movement of merchandise where the goods and the title remain with the shipper (the consignor) until the buyer (the consignee) sells the goods. Usually, the goods are stored in a warehouse by the shipper's agent until sold by the consignee.

CONSIGNMENT PURCHASING   A method of purchasing in which a vendor-maintains inventory on the premises of the buyer; the buyer's obligation to pay for the goods begins when he draws them from the stock for use.

CONSIGNOR   The shipper of a transportation movement.

CONSOLIDATE; CONSOLIDATION   1) Traffic Management. The act of combining many shipments into one for the purpose of attaining long haul rate economies. 2) Combining the logistics volume of one or more lines of business into one overall supply chain process. 3) Term that applies to a shrinking supply base as a result of some of them going out of business, merging, or acquisitions. 4) Act of consciously shrinking the base of suppliers from which a purchasing firm acquires goods or services.

CONSOLIDATED BILLING   1) Purchasing. Use of a single invoice from suppliers for situation where multiple purchases are made by a company. 2) Selling. Use of single invoice for all the purchases made by a customer and their divisions or business units over a period of time.

CONSOLIDATED CLASSIFICATION   Unifying minimum carload weights, number of classes, assignment of articles to classes, as well as descriptions of articles, and rules and regulations governing their preparation and handling.

CONSOLIDATING   Combining two or more small shipments in order to obtain reduced freight rates on higher volume shipments.

CONSOLIDATION   Practice of consolidating many less-than-carload or less-than-container load (L.C.L.) or less-than-truckload (L.T.L.) shipments in order to make carload or truckload movements is termed consolidation.

CONSOLIDATION POINT   When many small shipments—L.C.L. or L.T.L.—are combined for reshipment at a chosen location, the point is referred to as a consolidation point. Sometimes this is referred to as an assembly point.

CONSOLIDATION OF SHIPMENT   The process of combining a number of L.C.L./L.T.L. shipments into a carload, truckload, or container load shipment is consolidation.

CONSOLIDATIONS (OR MERGERS)   When two or more carriers or firms consolidate or merge and form one corporation for the purpose of management and operation, a consolidation or merger takes place. This should be distinguished from a joint acquisition, a lease, an acquisition, or an acquisition of control since it results in the legal unionization of the separate entities into a single corporate entity.

CONSOLIDATOR   A firm that combines separate shipments, usually piggy back, so as to realize cost savings and service improvement for what would otherwise be less than full load shipments.

CONSTANT COST   Those logistics costs which remain constant with an increase in the volume of activity or shipments are constant costs. Examples are rent on a warehouse, or depreciation on machinery used in the facility.

CONSTRUCTION DIFFERENTIAL SUBSIDY (U.S.)   The subsidy paid by the U.S. Maritime Administration for the extra cost of building certain U.S. flag ships in American shipyards rather than overseas at lower construction cost.

CONSTRUCTIVE MILEAGE   When a joint carrier movement is involved it is necessary to divide the joint rate. An arbitrary mileage is normally specified for each carrier on a mileage basis. This is termed constructive mileage, as distinct from the actual mileage incurred by each carrier.

CONSTRUCTIVE PLACEMENT   When a car is placed for loading and unloading at an available point other than on an industry track, due to inability of consignor or consignee to receive it at their site, carrier may, by giving customary notice, consider it as being placed at the point usually designated.

CONSTRUCTIVE PLACEMENT OF CARS   When a carrier cannot place cars on an industrial or private track due to conditions attributable to the consignee or consignor, and it is forced to place the cars elsewhere, it is termed constructive placement. Under these circumstances, the cars so placed are subject to the usual demurrage rules and charges.

CONSUL   A government official residing in a foreign country to care for the interests of his country.

CONSULAR INVOICE   THE This document is written in the language of the foreign country for which the goods are destined. It fully describes the goods to be exported and provides evidence of a shipper's Declaration of value of the shipment. The Consular Invoice is generally required by foreign countries for customs and statistical purposes.

CONSULAR REPORTS   Reports issued by consular officers regarding trade opportunities for specific classes of merchandise.

CONSULAR VISA   An official signature or seal affixed to certain documents by the consul of the country of destination.

CONSULATE   The office or position of a consul, also the premises occupied officially by a consul.

CONSUL FEES   Charges certifying and translating invoices.

CONSUMER COMMODITY (U.S.)   A hazardous transportation regulatory term that means a material that is packaged or distributed in a form intended and suitable for sale through retail purposes of personal care or household use. This term also includes drugs and medicines.

CONSUMER FOCUS   A sales, marketing, and supply chain focus of a producing firm upon the final consumer as opposed to the immediate customer (the retail store). In the increasing use of the Internet and web-commerce, many producers are attempting to link with the consumer as well as reach them through traditional retail stores.

CONSUMER SUPPLY REPLENISHMENT   An evolving supply chain and sales/marketing concept whereby a producer is linked with actual consumers in replenishing their homes when the inventory of those goods are low. See CUSTOMER REPLENISHMENT PROCESS.

CONSUMER VERSUS CUSTOMER   Recognition by a branded manufacturing firm of the distinction between the store (customer) and the consumer (the ultimate customer, the store's customer). Many brand manufacturers are investigating ways to reach the consumer directly via efficient supply chains and e-commerce linkages.

CONSUMPTION ENTRY   Customs term for processing the documentation related to imported goods where the intention is for those goods to be used and/or consumed in the country.

CONTAINER   Anything in which articles are packed.

CONTAINER CAR   In railroad transportation, an open flat-bed car used for the purpose of transporting steel freight containers is called a container car. Sometimes, the term container-type car is used to denote a flat-car equipped with a number of removable containers.

CONTAINER-TYPE CAR   A specially designed flat car equipped with a number of removal containers which may be lifted off and placed on another car or truck for transportation to any desired destination.

CONTAMINATION   The spread of physical qualities of one item to another so as to lessen the value or useful function of the second item; examples are odor in textiles, exposure of toxins to food, etc.

CONTENTS INSURANCE RATES   Rates assessed to the customer by their insurance company for protection of merchandise stored in a public warehouse. These rates vary according to the type of building and whether or not the building is sprinklered. The rates are expressed in terms of cents per one hundred dollars of inventory valuation.

CONTINUITY OF SUPPLY   One of the primary objectives or missions of modern purchasing management as practiced; it recognizes that an out of stock raw materials situation is more in cost than that of a higher price but more reliable source.

CONTINUOUS CARRIAGE   A shipment made through to destination without stoppage in transit for breaking bulk, transfer or rebilling.

CONTINUOUS IMPROVEMENT   A quality mind set in a firm whereby every product, process and activity are constantly under review for possible enhancement.

CONTINUOUS PROCESS   A manufacturing technology in which production takes place without interruption. Example: oil refining. It is distinct from batch process where specifically identified units of production are being produced in discrete production runs.

CONTINUOUS REPLENISHMENT PROCESS   The act by a supplier to constantly monitor their customer and deliver to them goods when needed or nearing stockout.

CONTINUOUS REVIEW   The inventory management practice of constantly monitoring the levels and demands/uses of the goods for the purpose of triggering reordering.

CONTINUOUS SEALS   A term denoting that the seals on a car remained intact during movement of the car from point of origin to destination; or, if broken in transit, that it was done by proper authority and without opportunity for loss to occur before new seals were applied.

CONTRA   Against.

CONTRABAND   Illegal or prohibited merchandise.

CONTRACT   An agreement between parties to do or to abstain from doing certain acts.

CONTRACT ADMINISTRATION   The post-purchase processes involving the monitoring and management of long term agreements that typically involve the delivery of goods or completion of work over a long period of time.

CONTRACT AMENDMENT   A documented change to a contract and its terms and conditions. Amendments must be mutually agreed to and documented as such.

CONTRACT CARRIER   The contract, carrier, whatever the mode, provides a service according to contractual agreement. The contract specifies charges to be applied, the character of the service, and the time of performance. There are no specified rates under regulation.

CONTRACT LOGISTICS   Term for the use of a firm using another one to perform warehousing, transportation, or other logistics services for it. It is often called third party logistics.

CONTRACT MANUFACTURER (ING)   A term for a firm that performs production for another.

CONTRACT MANUFACTURING   The practice of having another firm manufacture an item in place of it being produced in the firm's own facilities.

CONTRACT PRICE   Prevailing price that has been settled between sellers and buyers by means of long term contracts. These prices remain in effect market at any given time might be higher or lower than the contract prices m effect.

CONTRACT RATE   The rate charged by a contract carrier to its customer shippers and/or receivers as distinct from common carriage tariff rates.

CONTRACT WAREHOUSE   Warehouse operating under a formal agreement with a customer for a fixed amount of space and specifically defined value-added services.

CONTRIBUTION CIRCLE   A practice of assembling a multifunctional team of people for the purpose improving the quality of a good or service. See QUALITY CIRCLE.

CONTRIBUTION MARGIN   An accounting term for the residual left from revenue after direct variable and directly assignable fixed costs are deducted from revenue.

CONTROL CHART   Any graphical or numerical means of plotting the progress or conformance of an activity. One major application is in statistical process control. Common form: Gantt Chart.

CONVENTIONAL TARIFF   A tariff to contain and represent all the concessions provided for by the commercial treaties concluded by the particular country.

CONVERSION   1) Transportation. The process of appropriating all or part of a shipment by a carrier is called conversion. This is typically done to recoup unpaid freight charges. 2) Manufacturing Any manufacturing process. 3) Law. The taking by one person goods that belong to another for the purpose of selling and keeping the proceeds.

CONVEYANCE   Common application to the instrument or vehicle of transfer.

CONVEYOR   A mechanism which moves and transports freight by a revolving belt-like system for short distances.

COPACKER   Popular name for an outside firm that produces product for a brand name firm in place of that firm manufacturing it itself. The copacker packages the products in the name of the brand firm.

COOPERAGE   1) The process of reconditioning these types of facilities to make them suitable for safe transportation. 2) The price paid for putting hoops on casks or barrels.

COORDINATED SERVICE   A classification of transportation service whereby a) one form of service assists another in extending service into areas without sufficient traffic to support one service alone; b) one form of service is substituted for another for economical reasons; or c) two or more of the types of transportation are combined.

COPY   A reproduction of an original work.

COPYRIGHT   Exclusive rights of reproducing, by writing, printing or otherwise.

CORDAGE   The products of twine, cord and rope industry. More specifically, the rope of which the running rigging of a ship is made.

CORE CARRIER PROGRAM   A traffic management term for the special attention, contracting, and monitoring of the few carriers that were purposely selected for transporting the firm's products.

CORE PROCESS   A loose term for those activities and processes within a firm that it deems critical to the success of producing its output and competing in the market. It can be a highly technical manufacturing process, or it might be a highly focused customer service management team process.

CORNER GUARD   Plate used to protect merchandise from being hit by equipment.

CORNER POST   Upright guard post used to prevent equipment from hitting product or other equipment.

CORPORATE VOLUME RATE   A lower than normal rate charged to a shipper that has some arrangement with a carrier.

CORPORATION NAME   A name under which a corporation is authorized to do business and which must be used in filing complaints.

CORPUS JURIS   A body of law.

CORRECTION ACCOUNTS   The destination carrier may correct or adjust differences in the freight accounts which have been initiated by the forwarding or intermediate carrier. This process of auditing and correcting the interline freight account comes under the term of correction accounts.

CORRECTION NOTICE   In order to collect additional charges or to grant a refund, a form which presents a new billing, or which abstracts errors which have already been made on a carrier's record, may be made out. The correction notice is usually a copy of the freight bill as originally billed, with the refunds and corrections applied.

CORRESPONDENT BANK   A bank that maintains a link with another in the exchange of services, letters of credit and wire transfers are examples.

CORROSIVE MATERIAL   Any liquid or solid that causes visible destruction of human skin tissue or a liquid that has a severe corrosion rate on steel.

COST AND FREIGHT (CF OR C&F)   An international shipping and sales term (INCO) whereby goods are quoted at the outbound port with the seller arranging and paying for freight. The buyer must arrange for and pay for the cargo insurance.

COST BASED RATE INCREASE SYSTEM   This is a system for changing railroad rates to meet changes in costs. According to this system the percent of change of cost in the terminal and line haul areas would be separately computed. The extent of the rate change in each of these areas would be applied to that part of each tariff rate which involved respectively terminal and line haul costs.

COST AND FREIGHT (C & F OR CAF)   Same as CIF (Cost, insurance, and freight), except that the seller does not pay insurance costs.

COST CENTER   Term that applies to a warehouse or private fleet that recoups costs so as to break-even against a budgeted cost amount. Distinct from profit center or investment center.

COST CONTAINMENT   Purchasing term for a program with a vendor whereby vendor seeks to reduce or maintain costs at current levels.

COST DRIVER   A general term for those activities that cause certain costs in a business to behave in particular ways. Thus, labor is approximately a 50% variable cost driver in over the road trucking. Depreciation is a non-cash, time related cost driver.

COST INDEXING   The act of capturing and tracking costs of certain activities or commodity prices over time.

COST, INSURANCE, AND FREIGHT (CIF)   A basis for quotation by a seller which indicates that the seller will pay the insurance and freight charges to destination only.

COST, INSURANCE, FREIGHT, AND EXCHANGE (CIF&E)   An expression used in trade with British colonies, Australia, and South Africa; the element of exchange is added to the items of cost, insurance, and freight.

COST, INSURANCE AND FREIGHT (CIF)   An international shipping and sales term (INCO) whereby goods are quoted at the outbound port with the seller arranging and paying for freight and cargo insurance. In the event of a sailing loss, the buyer receives compensation from the insurance.

COST MODELING   A process of capturing all the costs of an activity or supplier for the purpose of determining if savings are possible to attain through further study. Some firms cost model suppliers to determine how much price negotiation leeway is possible to attain in an upcoming negotiation with them.

COST NEGOTIATIONS   Negotiations that target a supplier's specific costs rather than the overall price they seek to charge the buyer. These negotiations typically focus upon materials, then labor, then labor productivity, then logistics, etc. An overhead is further negotiated as is a margin for profit. Thus, the price is built up from negotiating the specific costs.

COST OF CAPITAL   The weighted average cost of all of a firm's debt and forms of equity and retained earnings. It is a measure against which its profits and capital expenditure projects are evaluated.

COST OF DOING BUSINESS   The sum of a firm's variable and fixed costs in addition to its costs of capital for certain activities or over a period of time.

COST PER CASE   A supply chain financial measure of the cost of producing and/or delivering each case of product.

COST PLUS   Arrangement whereby the price to be paid consists of the costs borne by the producer plus fee that includes profit.

COST PLUS FIXED FEE   Arrangement in a purchase situation in which buyer will pay for seller's costs plus a fixed fee that has been determined in advance. Fixed fee includes allowed overhead and profit for the work.

COST PLUS INCENTIVE   An extension of the cost plus fixed fee contract; the final payment will be for vendor costs incurred plus a fee that is greater for early completion or design improvement.

COST RATIO VENDOR RATING   A vendor evaluation scheme that uses percentage points for those attributes of the relationship that are important to the buyer. This percentage figure is then divided into the price quoted by the seller and the final result is seen as a surrogate figure of what the total cost would be to purchase from this vendor. Thus, a rating of 90% and a quote of $1.10 would result in a calculated estimated total cost of $1.22 from using that vendor.

COST REIMBURSABLE CONTRACT   Another term for a Cost Plus Fixed Fee-contract.

COST-TO-SERVE   A financial measure of what it costs a firm to sell to a particular customer. In many service firms, it is a measure of the cost of serving various customers or sets of customers.

COUNCIL OF LOGISTICS MANAGEMENT   An American based professional organization in the logistics and supply chain field. Based at 2803 Butterfield Road, Oak Brook, IL 60521.

COUNTER-PURCHASE   When one firm sells to another, a counter-purchase is the act of the first firm acquiring something else from the buying firm. In international sales situations, it can mean the buying country requirement that the seller agrees to also purchase items in that nation.

COUNTERTRADE   A term that applies to the requirement that a firm import something from a country to which it has sold something else. The imported goods need not necessarily be items that are included within the exported ones. Term for the requirement that a firm selling goods to a firm in another country must agree to acquire a certain amount of goods or services in return from that country.

COURSE OF EXCHANGE   The current price of bills of exchange existing between two places.

COVER NOTE   British form of a "binder" that will have the effect of establishing a commitment to a contract, transaction, or other arrangement prior to completion of final documentation.

COVIA   The name of one of the major airline reservation systems in the world.

C.P.M.   1) Certified Purchasing Manager. Professional designation by National Association of Purchasing Management for a person who has attained a certain position in the field as well as passed certification tests. 2) Critical Path Method. A system of planning complex project tasks.

CRANAGE   The price paid for the use of a wharf crane.

CRAZY EDDIE CLAUSE   Term often placed into a purchase contract whereby the buyer demands that the price of that contract will drop to meet any competitive price that might come into existence during the term of it.

CREDIT TERMS   The term in which a buying company must settle a due bill with any discount.

CREW LIST   The names and description of each member of the crew, place of birth, and residence.

CRIMINAL PENALTY   A legal penalty that could or will result in jail.

CRITICAL ITEM   A loose definition of any product or service that is important to the firm's overall competitiveness or cost structure.

CRITICAL MATERIALS   1) It is common in recent years to specify steel, copper, brass, bronze, aluminum, etc. as representing critical materials for national defense purposes. 2) Any goods which are critical to the smooth operation of to the provision of service to key customers and should almost never be out of stock.

CRITICAL PATH   That sequence of steps or operations in a complex process that would result in a delay in completion of the entire operation if a delay was to occur in any of them. Those steps along the critical path have no allowance for time over-runs.

CRITICAL PATH METHOD   An operations research tool that assists one in determining which sequence of tasks in a project will delay its completion if anyone of the individual components is delayed.

CRITICALS See CRITICAL ITEM   1) Purchasing. Those acquired products or services that are very important to the operations and profitability of the firm. 2) Sales and Marketing. Those finished goods or services that provide the firm with the highest returns to profit and involve its core competencies.

CROSS DOCKING   Fast through-put flow of material from inbound transportation to outbound delivery operations. It is generally a replacement to full warehouse receiving, storage, and outbound picking and shipping.

CROSS EXAMINATION   The inquiry by an opposing party in a case into points made by a specified person or item of evidence.

CROSS FUNCTIONAL TEAMS   Groups assembled within an organization composed of persons from many departments and groups who are all charged with solving a problem or accomplishing some outcome that requires input from all of them. This is common today in the planning and acquisition of complex product and service items as well as with customer service teams that are focused upon a major customer.

CROSS SUBSIDIZATION   The practice of charging price premiums on one or more forms of business in order to cover losses or less-than-full cost returns on others within the same firm. Thus, the one form of business helps to subsidize the other.

CROSS TRADER   1) Transportation. Ocean carrier that conducts business between countries in addition to outbound and inbound traffic of its own flag country. 2) Finance. Currency speculation involving currencies other than the trader's own national currency.

CROSS TRADES   Ocean trade term for a ship or traffic that is between nations other than the one in which the ship is domiciled.

CROWN   A highway design feature whereby the center of the road is peaked slightly higher than the sides thereby allowing rain/water run-off.

CTL   Professional designation of a person who has attained highest stature of membership in the American Society of Transportation and Logistics. Stands for Certified in Transportation and Logistics.

CUBE OUT   A transportation vehicle situation whereby when loaded with goods, its physical size capacity is filled while still having remaining weight load capacity available.

CUBE-PER-ORDER-INDEX   A mathematical technique that considers orders per-day and required–cubic-footage to determine a low cost stocking layout of a warehouse.

CUBE UTILIZATION   The percentage of cubic feet of space occupied compared to the total space available. An often used productivity measure of warehouse management and transportation.

CUBICAL CAPACITY   The carrying capacity of a car according to measurement in cubic feet.

CUBIC CARGO   Ocean shipping term for freight that is charged on the basis of its cubic size rather than on weight; usually light, bulky cargoes.

CUBIC CONTENTS   Solid or cubical contents of any package. When cubic restrictions are used they involve the length and breadth of the package. The product of these functions is a cubic dimension.

CUBIC FOOT   A cubic foot is 1728 cubic inches. It involves a cubic content of 12 inches $\times$ 12 inches $\times$ 12 inches.

CUBIC METER   Volume of space contained by three sides of one meter by one meter by one meter.

CUMMINS AMENDMENT (U.S.)   An amendment to the Act to Regulate Commerce relating to liability of transportation lines for loss of or damage to freight.

CURRENCY   Circulating medium by which debts are paid and business of the country transacted.

CURRENCY ADJUSTMENT FACTOR (CAF)   Surcharges on shippers of ocean freight charges paid in one particular currency to make up for losses or gains resulting from fluctuations in other world currencies.

CURRENCY EFFECT   Term that applies to the increase in cost or the decrease in cost from buying overseas when the change is due to shifts in exchange.

CURRENCY RISK   The risk in an international transaction that either the buyer or seller face in terms of a negative swing in currency value between the time of purchase/sale agreement and when payment will be made to the seller.

CURRENT OF TRAFFIC   Movement of trains on a main track, in one direction, specified by rules.

CURRENT RATIO   An accounting term; current liabilities divided by the sum of cash, securities, near term investment, accounts receivables and notes receivables.

CURVE FITTING   A mathematical process in which a series of data is described in terms of a formula that attempts to correspond to the actual data.

CUSHION UNDERFRAME   The spring' and shock absorbing mechanism built into some rail cars that act to reduce switching and train operating vibration and impacts upon the lading; a feature found mostly on specialized box cars.

CUSTOM CLEARANCE   An act of obtaining permission to import merchandise from another country. Typically performed upon landing the goods in the importing nation.

CUSTOM ENTRY   The act of submitting necessary paperwork for a custom clearance.

CUSTOMER COMPLEXITY   A term that applies to a large firm with many different groups and lines of businesses that all purchase from one firm in many different ways. The selling firm sees this customer as a complex one with which to do business.

CUSTOMER DRIVEN SUPPLY CHAIN   A supply chain that is focused upon delivery and response to customers or major customers. This differs from one that is designed to optimize internal operations costs.

CUSTOMER PICKUP   Merchandise picked up by a customer at the warehouse.

CUSTOMER RETENTION   Actions by sales, marketing, supply chain, and relationship management by a firm designed to keep and develop customer loyalty.

CUSTOMER RETURN   Merchandise sent back to the warehouse (after shipment) by a customer, because of error, damage, etc.

CUSTOMER SATISFACTION   The degree to which customers evaluate specific performance characteristics of a supplier against their preestablished expectations.

CUSTOMER SERVICE   Any supplier performance characteristics that a customer evaluates in addition to price and product. Major components of customer service are a) length of delivery time, b) variability of delivery time, c) ease of order entry, d) efficiency of problem resolution, etc.

CUSTOMER SERVICE TEAM   Typically, a multi-funtional team in a selling firm, consisting of sales, order entry, inventory management, supply chain, transportation, and other specialists, who all represent the firm with many capabilities to major customers. This is usually a single point of contact for the customer whereby any issue, problem, and service performance can be handled by this team.

CUSTOMER SERVICE LEVEL   The actual performance of a selling firm's customer service as measured by itself and/or its customers. Typical measures include percent of shipments received on time and in full, percent of shipments delivered on time, etc.

CUSTOMER SERVICE RATIO   A percentage figure that provides a measure of delivery performance. It measures the percentage of stock delivered when compared to the amount ordered.

CUSTOM HOUSE ENTRY   Making out a statement and paying the fees in the process of clearing a ship.

CUSTOM PALLETIZING   The act of using special pallets, pallet sizes, and/or unique stacking patterns for particular uses or customers.

CUSTOMS   The taxes, tolls, or other duties imposed on goods as they pass a frontier. It usually involves imported goods.

CUSTOMS BROKER   A person licensed by the U.S. Treasury department that acts on behalf of exporters and importers in clearing shipments for international moves.

CUSTOMS HOUSE BROKER   An agent whose functions are to expedite shipments by preparing the necessary import documents at the port of entry for subsequent movement through U.S. Customs and other regulatory agencies.

CUSTOMS INVOICE (U.S.)   A special invoice, prepared by the seller, on a form supplied by the U.S. Treasury, describing the imported goods. This invoice is presented to the U.S. Customs Bureau at the time import duties are paid.

CUSTOMIZATION   The act of producing the firm's products and services in such a way that they satisfy unique demands of specific customers. It might be as simple as painting a product different colors for each customer, or it might mean completely tailored service features for each customer.

CUSTOMS OF THE PORT   Charges, physical facilities, cargo transfer systems and methods, exchange, dues and general laws peculiar to a port.

CUSTOMS TARIFF   The government published schedule of charges assessed on the importing or exporting of goods. This is in the customs tariff.

CYCLE COUNTING   The counting and reconciliation of inventory frequently in order to maintain a close monitor on levels, instead of once a year purely for accounting valuation purposes; cycle counting is a valuable materials requirements planning element.

CYCLE STOCK   That part of the inventory which is depleted through sale or use, and is replenished through an order. Safety stock, the other main component of inventory, is not so replenished, and is not a part of cycle stock.

CYCLE TIME   The replenishment cycle represents a period of time required to order and make available the required stock. Consequently, cycle time is thought to be composed of two factors: a) order cycle; and b) replenishment cycle.

CYCLICAL INVENTORY COUNT   A continuously performed inventory count as contrasted to inventories taken periodically. A cycle inventory may be taken when the stock level reaches the reorder point, or when the stock ordered arrives.

DDDD

DAMAGE CLAIM   The formal claim for damaged freight made against the carrier by the shipper.

DAMAGE FREE RAIL CAR (DF)   A rail car that has internal bulkheads and other features that reduce the need for shipper dunnage and other bracing efforts and expenses.

DATA BASE   Data stored in a form that allows for ease of access and flexible sortation and report generation. Common applications are customer lists, routes, carrier selection maps, rate files, and inventory lists.

DATA CONTAMINATION   An electronic term indicating that a data base contains data that is not correct. Data contamination can occur when transferring information from one system to another and components of data change or disappear in the process.

DATA DENSE   A term indicating that a high degree of information is available about an activity or resource. A blood sample that is tested for thirty characteristics would be data dense in comparison to a check of the fuel level on a lawn mower. The lawn mower information contain no further insights as to its operating ability. Data density is a term applied that also applies to the amount of information that is possible to capture from transactions and activities.

DATA MINING   The act of analyzing a highly dense data base for the purposes of gaining insights for marketing or other uses.

DATA TERMINAL   Point for the sending and receiving of information via a computer.

DATA WAREHOUSING   The act of holding data in a system for purposes of maintaining its security and integrity while making it available for access and use. It is also a loose term for the central location of data that is used for real time access and use.

DEAD AXLE   Rear axle, tandem truck or trailer without power.

DEAD EYE AND BOLT   An eye at the end of a rope or wire that is used instead of a shackle.

DEAD HAULING   Without a load.

DEADHEAD   The movement of an unloaded vehicle on the line haul. It also refers to a non-paying crew passenger.

DEADLINE VEHICLE   When a vehicle is set aside for temporary repairs it is a deadline vehicle.

DEAD LOAD   The orders ahead which have not been released by a manufacturing, facility. They represent orders a departmental dispatcher has on hand. In air transportation, the term dead load applies to the power plant, fixed equipment, and structure of the aircraft.

DEAD PILE   Products received and shipped in other than unitized loads; require hand stacking.

DEAD SPACE   Unoccupied space.

DEAD STOCK   Inventory that is held on hand for which there is no sales nor revenue opportunity. This inventory is generally written off and disposed of.

DEAD STORAGE   Product which does not move in or out once it has been received.

DEAD-WEIGHT TONNAGE, DWT   The number of tons a vessel can transport of cargo, stores, and bunker fuel. In this concept, a ton equals 2,240 pounds. It is equal to the difference between the numbers of tons of water a vessel displaces when light, or empty, and the numbers of tons it displaces when submerged to the load line. The dead weight tonnage may also be termed the displacement tonnage.

DEALER OWN BRAND   A European term for private label; the act by a retailer of carrying goods with its own brand name on them.

DEBENTURE   A debenture is a certificate which entitles an exporter a refund on duties paid. It is a custom house certificate.

DEBENTURE STOCK   A form of preferred stock that provides for a specific return for a given period.

DE-BUNDLING   The act of selling a product or service in its component form as opposed to in complete form with full services. For example, less-than-truckload transportation typically is a bundled service with the driver loading, the carrier moving, and driver unloading the goods. This is all performed at a certain price. A de-bundled service might also be available at a lower price without the driver loading and unloading.

DECENTRALIZED PRODUCTION   Under decentralized production, rather than have production take place at one central location, production facilities are divided up among several locations and facilities. Decentralized production is deemed feasible for circumstances in which savings in logistics and/or marketing costs are sufficiently great to offset disadvantages in production costs on a per-unit basis. Beer and soda production is typically decentralized, because water makes up much of the total weight and that can be added at or near the final consuming market.

DECENTRALIZED PURCHASING   Purchasing that is spread out among various divisions or at different locations of the firm.

DECISION TREE   Quantitative analytical tool useful in evaluating outcomes of any number of possible events given various probabilities of each one occurring.

DECK   The floors of a vessel. A steamer will have a main deck and a raised forward section called a forecastle. The aft deck is called the poop deck. In larger vessels, the first deck above the tanks or hold is called the lower deck. Above this are the second, main, third, fourth and promenade decks.

DECLARATORY ORDER   A decision made by a regulatory agency that hopefully resolves an issue prior to a party committing a certain act rather than later it being found unlawful; a declaratory order is sought in advance of an activity.

DECLINING MARKET   A product or service market that is shrinking and has associated with it downward price pressure and lower profits.

DECOUPLING INVENTORY   A stock retained to make possible the independent control of two operations. It is sometimes called line-balancing stock.

DECREASING LOGISTICS COSTS   Those logistics costs which decreases with an increase in the volume of shipment are decreasing costs. It is the decrease in the per unit cost—as contrasted to total costs—which make these costs decreasing costs. Examples of decreasing logistics costs are ordering costs, the cost of carrier payment, the cost of purchase payment (not including purchase price), etc. These examples of decreasing logistics costs decrease per cwt. inversely and proportionally to the increase in the volume of shipment. For example, a five dollar ordering cost would cost five dollars per cwt. for a one hundredweight shipment, fifty cents per cwt. for a thousand weight shipment, and five cents per cwt. for a ten thousand pound shipment. Few decreasing logistics costs exist that do not decrease inversely and proportionately with an increase in the volume of shipment. However, one cost that may not decrease inversely and proportionately with an increase in the volume of shipment would be shipping and receiving cost. It may be found, that increasing volumes of shipment involve such completely different packaging and equipment usage that the per unit costs would decrease in something other than inversely and proportionately with an increase in the volume of shipment.

DEDICATED SERVICE   Transportation equipment and or crews that are assigned for the use of one particular shipper or client.

DEDICATED VEHICLE   See dedicated service.

DEDICATED STORAGE SPACE   That portion of occupiable storage space that is actually being used to store merchandise. Expressed as square footage.

DEEP TANK   The ballast tank amidships used to increase a vessel's draft and stability.

DE-ESCALATOR   As opposed to a contract escalator term that allows the supplier to raise its price during the term of the contract if it experiences certain cost increases, a de-escalator allows for price reductions if the supplier experiences certain cost decreases.

DEFECTIVE CAR   When a car is in the condition which makes it defective, and therefore liable to injure the contents of the shipment, it is designated as a defective car.

DEFENDANT   The party toward which a complaint is registered, or legal action of some form is taken.

DEFERRED AIR FREIGHT   A lower than normal air freight rate for slower service thus allowing the airline to use later flights that have greater capacity than earlier ones.

DEFERRED RATE   A rebate from carrier to shipper for having shipped a minimum volume or all tonnage via a certain carrier or set of carriers during a specified time period.

DEFERRED SHIPMENT RULE   A rule permitting shipments of cotton from points of origin to certain ports, moving on a through bill of lading, under instructions from the shipper. To be stopped in transit for compression or for consolidation with other shipments in order to aggregate the carload minimum. The through rate to prevail from origin on the weight reshipped from the transit station plus transit charge.

DEFICIT WEIGHT   When the actual weight of a shipment is less than the minimum weight for a particular route to apply, it is referred to as a deficit weight. The amount of the deficiency is the deficit weight.

DELAY   The amount of time in excess of the scheduled time for a departure, movement, or arrival.

DELIVERABLE   A sales and marketing term for those products and services that are considered as obligations to the customer in order for the arrangement to be fulfilled. A deliverable for a certain contract might consist of installing a machine, setting it up, testing it, and training employees for subsequent safe operations of it.

DELIVERED AT FRONTIER (DAF)   A 1990 INCO international shipping and transportation that requires the seller to produce and move goods to a named international border for title transfer and further control by the buyer.

DELIVERED EX SHIP (DES)   A 1990 INCO international shipping and transportation that requires the seller to produce and ship goods to a named destination port and unloaded from the ship for title transfer and further control by the buyer.

DELIVERED EX QUAY (DEQ)   A 1990 INCO international shipping and transportation that requires the seller to produce and ship goods to a named destination port, unload them from the ship, and pay for import duties for title transfer at that point and further control by the buyer.

DELIVERED DUTY PAID (DDP)   The seller must make all arrangements and be responsible for duties and insurances up to the point of final delivery to the customer at their final destination point.

DELIVERED DUTY UNPAID (DDU)   Same as DELIVERED EX QUAY (DEQ) except the responsibility for payment of import duties are upon the buyer, and the seller must arrange for the goods to be delivered to the ultimate destination.

DELIVERED DOMICILE   The country to which an exporter is responsible for complete delivery of its sale items.

DELIVERING CARRIER   The carrier that makes the delivery of the shipment to the consignee in a joint carrier movement is the delivering carrier.

DELIVERY   The act of transferring possession, such as the transfer of property from consignor to carrier, one carrier to another, or carrier to consignee.

DELIVERY CYCLE   The time from the receipt of an order to the time of the shipment of the product.

DELIVERY RECEIPT   This term is commonly used in transportation to indicate a document which names the commodities, the number of pieces, etc. for the purpose of permitting acknowledgement of a receipt of a shipment. When the consignee signs the delivery receipt with no exceptions noted, it means that the shipment is in good order, and the contract of carriage has been executed.

DELTA NU ALPHA   A professional education organization in the American transportation field.

DEMAND CHAIN   A supply chain term typically applied by a supplier for all those activities and processes employed from their production line to the customer. The customer, on the other hand, would see these same things as part of its supply chain. The driving concept in the demand chain is that the supplier is focused upon producing and delivering according to the demands of the customer.

DEMAND DRAFT   A bill which requires payment on presentation.

DEMAND DURING LEAD TIME   The amount of material required for sales or service during the lead time.

DEMAND, CROSS ELASTICITY   The degree to which the demand for one item is related to the demand for another. The demand for shoe polish is related in a cross-elastic manner with the demand for shoes over a period of time.

DEMAND, ELASTIC   A situation whereby a small change in price charged results in large changes in the quantity demanded. Elastic demand products are often said to be price sensitive.

DEMAND, INELASTIC   A situation whereby a large change in price charged results in small change in the quantity demanded. Elastic demand products are often said to be not price sensitive.

DEMAND SENSITIVE RATE   A rate designed to smooth out the peaks and valleys of seasonal product transportation demands; generally higher in peak season, sometimes lower in low season.

DEMAND VARIABILITY   The degree to which a firm's demands, or customer's orders, flux from day to day, week to week, month to month, etc.

DEMISE   This term is applied to the transfer of a ship to a charter for a limited period of time. Under these circumstances, while the ship is in use, the rights and obligations relative to the ship remain with the owner since the title stays with owner.

DEMOUNTABLE BODY   The body or box of a motor truck or trailer especially designed to be inter-changeable on railroad flat car equipment.

DEMURRAGE   The detention of a shipment beyond its specified time resulting in the payment for detention is termed demurrage. The basis for this charge is to recoup a rental fee for holding the equipment too long. The purpose is to prevent the use of freight cars for free storage. Two traditional plans have existed for demurrage: 1) straight demurrage, and 2) average or receiver for the first 48 hours after the first 7:00 am after placement of the equipment. After free time, the shipper/receiver must pay a daily fee. Under the average demurrage plan' the shipper/receiver receives credits for cars turned around faster than 48 hours, and these credits apply to those held longer than that time. Various other forms exist per contract between shippers/receivers and carriers.

DENSITY METER   An instrument to measure the density of a mixture.

DENSITY OF COMMODITY   The pounds per cubic foot, or other cubic measurement, represents the density of a commodity. Found by dividing the total weight by the number of cubic feet.

DENSITY RATE   A transportation rate that is generally lower per hundredweight for products that are dense (heavy per cubic foot) and vice versa.

DENSITY (VOLUME) OF TRAFFIC   The measurement of the volume of traffic per mile, or tons miles per period of time, indicates the density of the traffic.

DEPARTURE TRACKS (YARDS)   When cars leaving a classification yard from a receiving yard move to an arrangement of tracks for the purpose of switching, the connecting track is called a departure track.

DEPENDENT DEMAND   Situation in which the demand for a certain product is dependent upon certain other products or decisions.

DEPOSITION   A sworn statement of a witness taken down in writing to be used as evidence in lieu of the appearance of the witness.

DEPRECIATION COST   The allocation of the value of a fixed asset over its expected life period in the form of a cost for the purpose of determining allocated cost, per time period, is called depreciation cost. Under straight line depreciation costing systems, value or price / cost is divided by years of life to determine depreciation cost per year.

DERELICT   When a ship and its cargo are abandoned at sea the term derelict is applied.

DERRICK   This is a cargo boom with its foot at the base of the mast, and supported by a topping-lift tackle. It is controlled by guys or guy wires. It is employed to load and unload cargo.

DESPATCH (DISPATCH) LINES   Two or more carriers that operate through fast-freight schedules.

DESPATCHING FOREIGN SHIPMENTS IN BOND   Using the services of bonded carriers to avoid payment of internal-revenue tax on good which would be subject to this tax if sold in the countries. Bonded carriers may forward un-stamped goods and deliver aboard steamship in bond under customhouse inspection and certification. Goods imported into the United States are frequently carried in bonded warehouses without payment of dues until they are officially entered for consumption or re-exported.

DESPATCH MONEY   An agreement whereby the charterer received a fixed sum per day for each day saved in loading out of a number of lay days specified in the charter party.

DESTINATION   The place to which a shipment is consigned or passenger is traveling.

DESTINATION CARRIER   The line-haul carrier performing the delivery service at the destination. This does not include the destination local delivery service.

DESTRUCTIVE COMPETITION   Primarily a transportation term indicating one firm pricing below its costs temporarily with the intent of driving a competing firm out of the market.

DETENTION   The charge assessed on a motor vehicle held beyond the free time allowed. Assessed for the time required to load or unload beyond the free time.

DETENTION CHARGE (MOTOR CARRIER)   In the motor carrier industry the penalty assessed against shippers for delaying in releasing carrier equipment beyond the allowed free time is referred to as detention charge. In rail transportation this is called demurrage.

DETERIORATION   The value loss from spoilage during time in storage.

DETERIORATION COSTS   The quality of an article or commodity held in storage frequently diminishes through its inherent characteristics. Deterioration may be magnified if conditions of temperature, moisture content of the air, etc. are not proper.

DETERMINISTIC MODEL   A type of mathematical, computer or other analytical model that does not develop an optimal answer, rather provides an answer based upon information and data used within it; generally used to test "what if" type questions.

DETOURED FREIGHT   Shipments which due to washouts, wrecks, etc., are re-routed over the rails of another carrier for the convenience of the carrier on which the disability occurred.

DEVELOPING NATIONS   A general term for a previously undeveloped economy that is currently industrializing.

DEVIATION CLAUSE   A clause inserted in a charter party which authorizes a vessel to stop at ports other than the original port of discharge.

DEWAR   A tanker designed to transport gases in liquid form by holding them at low temperature. The temperature is kept under 100 degrees below zero by double-walled, vacuum-construction of the tank trailer. This was developed by a Scottish chemist named Sir John Dewar.

D.F.   When these letters are printed on the side of a rail car it means that the car is damage free. This means special equipment is installed in the car to eliminate damage to the merchandise en route.

D.F.B. CAR (DAMAGE FREE BULKHEAD CAR)   Rail car which is equipped with a cushioned under-frame, special blocking or bracing, and movable walls or bulkheads to hold merchandise in place.

DIAMETER, OUTSIDE–INSIDE   A measure of pipe. The outside diameter is that distance from one outer edge directly through the center to the opposite side outer edge. Inside diameter is from the inside of one edge to the inside of the opposite inner edge as measured through the center.

DIFFERENTIAL   1) lower than those of a more direct route applied in order to entice movements that would not normally travel over that route. Typically used to compensate for the longer time in transit of that route. 2) Part of the power unit that transfers energy from one component to another.

DIFFERENTIAL RATES   Differential rates are thought of as a reduced form of rate. The reduced rate is provided on an alternate less desirable routing. Frequently a combination of rail and water movements, in competition with an all rail rate, would receive a lower rate in order to encourage traffic. This lower rate is called a differential rate. The idea of the differential rate is to establish reduced rates for slower transportation and more handling of the freight. Sometimes differential rates are established in agreement between carriers to make rate concessions to less desirable ports.

DIFFERENTIAL ROUTE   Route for which there exists no published rate. The rate is obtained through existing published rates.

DIGITAL SIGNATURE An electronic transmission feature that provides for an authenticated and verifiable proof of a person's signature.

DIMENSIONAL WEIGHT SHIPMENT When the charges for a shipment are computed on the basis of volume rather than weight, it is referred to as dimensional weight shipment. If the tariff indicates a specific number of cubic inches per pound and the shipment exceeds this quantity, it will be charged on the basis of one pound for each of the specific number of cubic inches or fractions in excess.

DIRECT CONNECTOR A new term applying to joint line rate making now that some of the antitrust immunity of the rate bureaus has been repealed in the major U.S. legislative acts of 1980; only those railroads that directly connect on a through movement may jointly discuss rates on the through move.

DIRECT COSTS Costs that can be directly traced to a given product or service without overhead or common cost allocations.

DIRECT LOAD A warehouse practice of picking from a storage lot and moving the goods directly onto the transportation vehicle. This is distinct from stopping the goods at the outbound dock and staging them for later loading.

DIRECT FLIGHT The transportation movement without transfer of a shipment, on one or more transportation carriers. It may have any number of en route stops.

DIRECT FREIGHT CHARGES As applied to company material, specific freight charges paid to other railways and not included in the invoice.

DIRECTIONAL A term used to refer to rates which are reduced to encourage traffic in one direction to counter-balance traffic which is primarily in the other direction.

DIRECTIONAL IMBALANCES A transportation industry term for a situation when the traffic volume in one direction of a traffic lane is much larger or smaller than that in the opposite direction. Typical commuter operations experience an inbound morning imbalance into a city as compared to outbound traffic at that time of day.

DIRECT STORE DELIVERY The practice by a goods manufacturer to deliver directly to stores rather than distribute through the store company's own distribution centers.

DISCRETE LOT SIZING A production, shipping, order processing term indicating that goods are handled in certain size lots rather than m any range of quantities.

DISCRIMINATION In transportation this involves differences in rates not justified by differences in costs. This occurs when two commodities moving under essentially the same circumstances have completely different rates which cannot be justified by the cost of service.

DISCRIMINATORY FARES AND RATES Any form of rates or fares that unduly harm a particular commodity, region, or group of shippers to the extent of making it difficult for them to move their goods to their desired markets.

DISINTERMEDIATION   A term for the elimination of a sector in a channel of distribution. An example would be a channel that consists of a manufacturer, wholesaler, retailer, and consumer. Disintermediation would be the term for the wholesaler sector losing business to a trend of the manufacturer selling directly to the retailer. E-commerce has led to much disintermediation with branded manufacturing firms selling directly to the consumer.

DISPATCHED LINES   Sometimes this is spelled despatch. When two or more carriers operate on a through fast-freight schedule they are referred to as dispatched lines.

DISPATCHING   This is synonymous with expediting, or sending a shipment under a speeded up process. In the rail transport industry, the individual responsible for train movement is called a dispatcher.

DISPATCH MONEY   The payment on completion of the loading and / or discharging to the ship charterer. It is a payment for time saved on allotted lay days.

DISPLACEMENT, ACTUAL   In water transportation this refers to the loaded weight of the vessel for a particular voyage.

DISPLACEMENT, TONNAGE   In water transportation, the amount of water displaced by a vessel when afloat is its displacement tonnage. A cubic foot of water is calculated to weigh 64 pounds, or 1 / 35th of a ton (2,240 pounds). One may divide the cubic foot content of the vessel by 35 to determine its displacement tonnage. The term displacement weight means the weight of a merchant vessel when the crew and supplies are all on board. The term displacement loaded means the weight of the vessel when the full cargo, stores and passengers have also been taken on the vessel, and it is loaded to its maximum draft, or its deep load line.

DISPLACEMENT OF VESSEL   The weight in tons of water displaced by the capacity of the vessel and its cargo in tons of 2240 pounds. Displacement light is the weight of the vessel without stores, while displacement loaded is the weight of the vessel, cargo and stores.

DISTANCE RATE   The process of setting a rate on the basis of mileage. It is either a local or joint haul.

DISTRIBUTION   Traditionally viewed as all the activities and planning required to move product from the end of a production line to the final user. It is the post-production channel.

DISTRIBUTION CENTER   A warehouse of finished goods. Also applied to the facility from which wholesale and retail orders may be filled. A materials warehouse would also be a distribution center for the buyers of its stock.

DISTRIBUTION CHANNEL   The post-production channel. Not to be confused with the pre-production, or materials flow, channel.

DISTRIBUTION REQUIREMENTS PLANNING   A system of determining demands for inventory at distribution centers, consolidating the demand information backwards, and acting as input to the production and materials system.

DISTURBANCE OF ADJUSTMENTS   The situation that exists when the rate relationships or the authorized bases of rates are in jeopardy.

DITCH LIGHT   A spotlight aimed at the right-hand side of the right-of-way.

DIVERSION   Diversion is the process of changing the destination, while the shipment is en route. Both diversion and reconsignment must be done while the shipment is en route and not after the shipment has arrived at its original destination. While the terms diversion and reconsignment are not synonymous, the same rules prevail for both, and are published in the same carrier tariffs. In a diversion act, it is necessary to instruct the point of diversion before the car leaves that point.

DIVERSION OF TRAFFIC   A shift of traffic from one carrier to another, or one carrier mode to another. This diversion usually takes place as a result of rate differentials.

DIVERT   The process of changing the route of a shipment while it is in transit.

DIVISION   1) A managerial district on a railroad that is governed by a superintendent or general manager. 2) A division is a point at which crew changes take place. 3) The revenue split between carriers on joint rate moves.

DIVISIONAL NOTICE   Under Plan I piggyback movements, the tariff-like contract specifies for motor carriers the amount payable to the rail carrier.

DIVISION RATE   The proportion of a joint rate which is used to determine the revenue accruing to each carrier party to such rate for performing its part of the joint haul.

DOCK   The sorting or staging platform attached to where shipments are loaded or unloaded.

DOCK TO DOCK CYCLE   A time measure of the length of time required to move goods from one outbound dock to the destination inbound dock.

DOCKAGE   The charge assessed for the use of a dock.

DOCK AND WHARF BONDS   Bonds issued to provide funds for the construction and equipment of docks and wharves.

DOCKET   The official registration of a proceedings for a legal action.

DOCK PLATE   A movable ramp allowing access to a rail car or trailer.

DOCK RECEIPT   A document given to a shipper, or his representative, when goods are delivered to a dock or pier for an international shipment.

DOCK-WALLOPER   The person in charge of loading and unloading vehicles, also the handling of freight on the dock.

DOCTRINE OF THE LAST FAIR CHANCE   A rule that a person will do all in his power to avert, or lessen, a disaster that seems imminent.

DOCUMENTARY CREDIT   A letter of credit which requires the beneficiary to present a draft and specified documents. In practice, the documents must comply to the terms and conditions stated in the L/C before the draft can be paid (See "Clean credit").

DOCUMENTARY DRAFT   When a draft or order to pay has attached to it various documents of title, such papers as insurance certificate, etc., the draft and documents are referred to jointly as a documentary draft. The documentary draft is used in connection with export credit, or it may be required for clearance from a port, or to obtain entry abroad.

DOCUMENT CHARGE   The amount of money a customer pays for having a document (receipt or bill of lading) prepared.

DOCUMENTS AGAINST PAYMENT (DIP)   An indication on a draft that the documents attached are to be released to the drawee only on payment.

DOG   A truck which is not very powerful.

DOG TRACKS   A unit or straight truck which has run out of line.

DOLLAR   A unit of currency in mainly the United States, Canada, Singapore, and several other countries.

DOLLAR DENSITY   A logistics term indicating the value of a product per pound, determined by dividing pounds into item value; generally used to indicate modal split potential of various freight markets; high dollar density products can stand higher rate, premium services.

DOLLAR-FILL MEASURE OF   A customer service term indicating how much, in terms of dollars of orders, a facility was able to process during a given time period.

DOLLY   1) A trailer converter dolly—an auxiliary axle assembly having a fifth wheel used for the purpose of converting a semi-trailer to a full trailer; 2) A device with small platforms on rollers or wheels used for the handling of freight in a warehouse.

DOMESTIC CONTENT   A term used in import customs that pertains to what portion of a total product consists of parts produced in that country. This is an issue in the automobile industry where a foreign manufacturer imports parts for assembly into the complete automobile in the country of sale.

DOMESTIC OPERATIONS   Transportation operations within the territory of a single country.

DOMESTIC SHIP   When the owner of a ship resides in the country of reference, it is a domestic ship. A ship may be called either domestic or foreign, depending on the residence of the owner, rather than the nature of its enrollment.

DOMESTIC TRUNKS   Air transportation common carriers operating primarily in one country, and serving the principal gateway cities of time nation.

DOMINANT CHARACTERISTIC VENDOR RATING   A system of evaluating vendors that uses a plus, minus, or zero designation for the major attributes that a buyer sees as important. Examples might be price, quality, service, or responsiveness.

DONUTS   Truck tires.

DOODLE-BUG   A small tractor used to pull two-axle dollies in a warehouse.

DOUBLE BOTTOMS   1) Ocean Ships. Those vessels with a hull within a hull that would prevent spillage of oil and other liquid lading if the outer hull was pierced. 2) Motor Carriage. The hauling of two trailers by one tractor.

DOUBLE-CLUTCHING   The shifting of gears on a truck transmission without making them clash.

DOUBLE-DECK (STOCK CAR)   When a second floor is placed on a stock car for the purpose of increasing the capacity for carrying small livestock, it is referred to as a double-deck stock car.

DOUBLE STACK   A railroad method of carrying containers. It consists of a rail car with a depressed center between the wheel sets that holds a container. The wheel sets are shared by the cars, because they are positioned between them. This container is sufficiently low so as to allow for another one to be stacked on top of it for movement. This method of movement reduces the need for the actual rail car investment.

DOUBLE TRACK   A two-way rail track system to handle traffic moving in both directions.

DOWN IN THE CORNER   Creeper gear.

DOWNLOAD   A computer term for bringing data from another computer onto the one being operated at a particular site. If that same local site computer was to have data moved to another, it would be referred to as UPLOAD.

DOWNSTREAM   An oil industry term for all those activities involved starting at the refinery and outward toward the consumer. As distinct from UPSTREAM.

DOWN TIME   1) The amount of time an aircraft is not available for revenue service or other equipment is not available for use. This includes time required for maintenance, overhaul and other required services. 2) The time when production is not underway.

DRAFT (VESSEL)   The number of feet between the water line and the bottom of the vessel—or the depth beneath the water—is the draft.

DRAFT (BANK)   The draft is a written order transferring a certain amount of money from one person to another to be paid on a certain date. It provides a means of settling accounts in foreign trade. It is a negotiable evidence of a relative amount of indebtedness. This instrument affirms a buyer's obligation. The draft is also referred to as a bill of exchange.

DRAFT   An unconditional order in writing, addressed by one party (drawer) to another party (drawee), and requiring the drawee to pay at a fixed or determinable future date a specified sum in lawful currency (either in dollars or other currency) to the order of a specified person (the payee). A draft is a formal demand for payment. Also known as "bill of exchange."

DRAFT, CLEAN   A draft to which no documents are attached.

DRAFT, DATE   A draft so drawn as to mature on fixed date, irrespective of the time of acceptance, for example, 90 days after date.

DRAFT, DISCOUNTED   A time draft under an L/C which has been accepted and purchased by a bank at a discounted price. In practice, if the discount charges are payable by the beneficiary, the accepting bank pays a lesser amount than the face value to the beneficiary. If, on the other hand, the discount charges are payable by the buyer, the beneficiary receives the face amount of the draft.

DRAFT, DOCUMENTARY   See Documentary draft.

DRAFT, SIGHT   A draft so drawn as to be payable on demand upon presentation to the drawee.

DRAFT, TIME   A draft so drawn as to mature at a certain fixed or determinable time after presentation or acceptance. For example, 90 days A/S means draft will mature 90 days "after sight" from the date of acceptance by a bank or the buyer.

DRAG   The movement of one or several cars (usually without caboose or customary train make-up) within yard limits, or a transfer made at a junction or interchange point.

DRAG DOWN   Shift too slowly to lower gears.

DRAGLINE   A facility in a truck terminal which consists of carts drawn by a continuous cable, for transferring pickup to line haul operations or vice versa.

DRAWBACK   When a payment is made by the government to exporters for goods assessed as an import duty, the refund is called drawback. The amount of the drawback is almost the total extent of the original duties paid. In the U.S., it is 99% of the original import duties paid.

DRAWEE   Any party, such as an individual, a bank or a firm, on whom the draft is drawn and from whom the payment is expected. Under letters of credit the draft is drawn on a bank whose name usually appears on the left side of the draft.

DRAWEE BANK   The bank on whom the draft is drawn, also known as the "paying bank."

DRAWER   Any party who draws or signs the draft. Under an L/C, the beneficiary is the drawer of the draft, also called "the maker" of the draft.

DRAYAGE   The rate for the transportation of freight in trucks, drays, or carts. It involves local cartage movement.

DRAYAGE TO SHIP SIDE   The charge made for carting, draying or trucking freight to alongside a vessel.

DRILL   A local freight train that acts to pick up and deliver cars to shippers and consignees along a line.

DRILLING   The handling or switching of cars in freight yards or to and from industry tracks. Drill engine refers to the motive power used for such service.

DRIVE-IN RACK   Storage rack which allows high stacking and easy access of the same product.

DRIVERS   Drive wheels.

DRIVERS' DELIVERY TICKET   A receipt retained by the driver of a motor carrier for delivery of the shipment as proof that delivery did take place.

DRIVE THROUGH RACK   Storage rack which allows high stacking of products

DROMEDARY   A special type of vehicle that combines the truck and tractor, with a fifth wheel behind the body, and van at the rear of the unit.

DROP FRAME TRAILER   A low level trailer with minimum highway clearance.

DROP IT ON THE NOSE   Uncoupling the semi-trailer without lowering the landing gear to support the trailer.

DROP SHIP   Many specific definitions are in use for this term, but it generally means the multiple stops for delivery of goods to many sites from the same vehicle load.

DROP THE BODY   The process of unhooking the tractor from the semi-trailer.

DRP   See Distribution Requirements Planning.

DRUM   A shipping container of cylindrical shape and flat ends. They may be stored without crating or boxing.

DRUM FORKS   The forks used to lift drums, barrels or other cylindrical types of loads.

DRY DOCKAGE   A charge against a vessel that is placed in a dry dock for inspection and repair.

DRY LEASE   An aircraft leasing arrangement which provides for the lessor to lease only the aircraft. The lessee provides the personnel, provisions and fuel required in the operations.

DUAL RATE SYSTEM   Ocean conference rate practice in which a lower rate is charged to shippers that agree to move all of their breakbulk freight via member lines of the conference. Others pay a standard rate.

DUALS   A pair of tires mounted together.

DUAL SOURCING   Purchasing practice of acquiring the same item from two suppliers. This is generally done in order to maintain some competition between the two as well as to minimize the risk of one of them failing.

DUE BILL   The balance due, which usually involves additional charges as a result of error or otherwise, is the balance due bill. The due bill frequently has another meaning associated with a receipt signed for ocean bills of lading delivered with specific credit privileges.

DUE DATE   The date at which an order, part or otherwise should be completed.

DUMP BODY   A truck body that can be tilted to dump its load.

DUMP CAR   An open car that is equipped with automatic dumping devices for discharging its contents either through the doors or by tipping the total car body.

DUMPER   A mechanism for transferring bulk materials from open-top cars into the cargo space of vessels, used also at industrial plants for unloading materials into storage bins or onto piles, and at terminals for transferring materials from such equipment into other cars.

DUMPING   An import and customs term that generally means that the importing nation views the exporting nation as allowing the sale of goods at below the market costs of producing and the prices normally charged in selling them. This situation generally harms the competing industries in the importing nation. It would indicate that the selling country often subsidizes the manufacture and sale in order to maintain employment in that country.

DUNNAGE   This is lumber, wiring, or other material used for the purpose of stabilizing a shipment that has been placed on freight cars, vehicles, vessels, or other conveyances. It does not include the packaging.

DUPLICATE BILLING   Freight bill covering shipment(s) that has already been billed previously.

DUPLICATE PAYMENT   A double payment for the same shipment.

DUSTING   Driving on the shoulders of the road, creating dust.

DUTCH AUCTION   1) One form of it is a selling auction whereby the seller starts at a high price and gradually lowers it until a buyer comes forth. 2) Another is a buyer who states what they seek to buy and gives a price. It then asks sellers to come forth with prices that either meet or are less than that amount. Sometimes called a reverse auction.

DUTY   The charge assessed by the government on shipments imported or exported.

DYNAMITE ON THE BRAKES   Using every brake on the vehicle for a sudden stop

DYNAMOMETER CAR   A car specially equipped to measure the horsepower, draw bar pull, and other performance capabilities of a locomotive and the cars under operating circumstances.

EEEE

EARLY PURCHASING INVOLVEMENT   When purchasing is brought into a new project or product launch early in the design and development phases.

EARLY SUPPLIER INVOLVEMENT   When a supplier or suppliers are brought into a buying firm's new project or product launch early in the design and development phases.

EASTBOUND OR EASTWARD   The direction of train movement in which the distance by rail from a western point is increasing. Examples are San Francisco to Denver, USA or Lille, FR to Brussels, BE. A few exceptions have been established on branch lines where this rule would result in confusion because of so-called eastbound trains actually operating westbound or in another direction.

E-BUSINESS   A general term for an enterprise that extensively uses information systems for its purchases of goods, internal management, and selling of finished product.

E-COMMERCE   A general term for buying and selling using the Internet and various electronic linkages with suppliers and customers.

ECONOMIC COST   A logistics term for considering a cost that is not captured in the traditional accounting system. It is a surrogate cost. Best example is an opportunity cost of inventory. If company has 10,000 in inventory goods, then it might be seen as having an implicit cost at 10% of $1,000 per year.

ECONOMIC DEVELOPMENT   A general term the assistance of an industry by a local or national government. This typically consists of tax relief, low cost loans, or the training of employees. These are all designed to attract the new industry to the locale.

ECONOMIC REGULATION   Refers to the control given regulatory authorities over the economic activities of the carrier or business—including entry, rates, abandonment, the record system, financial requirements, service obligations, etc.

ECHELON CHANNEL   The post-production channel may be structured in many ways. The most complicated structure for the channel could take the form of moving goods from a manufacturer's facility through a series of echelon service facilities to the ultimate retailer. Under the echelon system, each echelon node would service the echelon node beyond it. Thus, a shipment from a manufacturing plant could consist of a truckload of kitchen ranges which would move to multi-regional warehouses. At the multi-regional warehouse a break-bulk operation would take place in which combinations of kitchen ranges, refrigerators, etc., would be made up for a regional echelon warehouse at a point beyond.

EDI   Acronym for Electronic Data Interchange. The electronic linking of firms typically between the order entry operation of one and the purchasing operation of another.

EFFECTIVE CAPACITY   A measure of asset utilization that is the product of actual capacity of the equipment combined with the rate of use or productivity. Two firms might have the same type of aircraft. One might be able to operate it for four trips per day while the other one is able to operate it for six trips. The second one would be seen as having an effective capacity that is fifty percent greater than the first one.

EFFICIENT CONSUMER RESPONSE (ECR)   A general term for the linkage of all the activities extending from the final consumer purchase of goods all the way back to the manufacturer of them. This is distinct from separate forecasting and operation of the individual links that connect in this chain. With ECR, all the components in the chain are linked directly from the consumer's purchase back to the manufacturing of the goods. Such systems can often operate with less total inventory than with traditional systems. Too, changes in demands, either upward or downward can more easily be responded to when linked in this fashion.

ELASTIC DEMAND   An economics term relating to the demand for goods or services whereby changes in price result in greater proportionate changes in the quantity demanded. Generally, elastic demand goods and services are very price sensitive.

ELASTICITY OF DEMAND   The ratio of change in demand for a change in price. A market is said to be elastic if a small percentage in price change results in greater percentages in demand and total revenue changes for the seller.

ELECTRONIC COMMERCE   See E-COMMERCE.

ELECTRONIC DATA INTERCHANGE   See EDI.

ELECTRONIC FARE PAYMENT SYSTEM   A transportation fare system that consists of the customer purchasing tickets or other proof of payment via electronic means as well as moving in the system using automatic collection means.

ELECTRONIC FUNDS TRANSFER   Payment of monies from one firm to another via wire or other electronic means, in place of writing checks and mailing them.

ELECTRONIC HAGGLING   A form of price auctioning on the web.

ELECTRONIC INVOICING   Transmitting an invoice for goods or services sold via electronic means in place of traditional mail systems.

ELECTRONIC POINT OF SALE (EPOS)   A general term for the cash register in a retail system that captures the details of the sale (the goods, quantities, other goods sold at the same time, often the person making the purchase, etc.). It can also be any scanner that acts to record a sale from an activity that constitutes a sale.

ELECTRONIC PROTECTION   A security system using electronic detection to notify a monitoring station if the building is broken into.

ELECTRONIC TICKETING   The sale and use of tickets in electronic form in place of paper based tickets. This is becoming a common feature with airline ticketing.

ELECTRONIC TRACKING   Capturing the movement or status of goods or services as they progress from one stage of activity to another. Electronic tracking systems have been in place for many years that capture rail car movements as trains speed by readers that subsequently transmit the event to shippers with ladings in the cars.

ELECTRONIC WALLET   A term for money that is placed on deposit at or is accessible by sellers involving Internet type transactions.

ELEVATING CHARGE (VESSEL)   A charge for services performed in connection with floating elevators; also charges for using grain elevators.

ELEVATOR   A hydraulic end-gate. Also the silo structure used to store grain.

ELKINS ACT   An act of U.S. Congress (1903), supplementing the Interstate Commerce Act, which made the giving of rebates and forms of personal discrimination unlawful and provides penalties for this and other violations of the Act.

ELQ   The most economic logistics quantity. Represents that quantity which will minimize total logistics costs in the shipment, or in the Cellular Flow. This means it must minimize whatever combination of purchasing costs, traffic costs and storage costs exist in the shipment.

EMAIL   Messages that are sent electronically.

E-MAIL   The sale of consumer goods, often by two or more branded firms, through the Internet. The concept of the "mail" arises from the consumer being able to view and purchase from several firms via the same site.

EMBARGO   A denial of entry of freight. It can be in the context of one country refusing to allow firms to sell to another country, or it can be a carrier in refusing to use a particular route or serve a specific point.

EMBARK   To board a vessel about to sail.

EMBAYED   Incapacity to enter a bay due to wind, current or sea.

EMBEDDED CHIP   A microchip that is contained within an appliance, equipment, or apparatus that is designed to perform certain preprogrammed functions.

EMERGENCY RATE   A rate established to meet some immediate and pressing need, and without due regard to the usual rate making factors.

EMERGENCY TEMPORARY AUTHORITY (ETA)   Government agency granted permission for carrier operations for short periods due to strikes, fires or other sudden problems.

EMERGING NATIONS   See DEVELOPING NATIONS

EMINENT DOMAIN   The right of a governmental power to take property required for a public use. This is a common governmental action when land needs to be acquired for highways, airports, ports, pipelines, and other public conveyances.

EMPTY BACK HAUL   A condition of low load factor which results from a greater volume of shipment in one direction than in the reverse direction is called empty back haul. Private carriage commonly results in empty back haul when deliveries are made and no return shipment is available. A general condition of a greater amount of volume moving regionally, internationally, or transcontinentally, than is true of the reverse direction.

EMPTY BACK-HAUL RATES   Rates that are set unusually low in order to provide some volume of traffic for vehicles that normally would move empty back to a required origin are called empty backhaul rates. Thus, the movement of industrial goods from Point A toward the Point B may create an abnormally large availability of shipping space for the return of the cars to Point A. In order to encourage some utilization of these cars when returning, a low rate on bulk commodities may be offered.

EMPTY CAR MILES   Freight car miles in the movement of empty cars.

ENABLER   A general term for any technology, system, or organization that acts as a catalyst or encourager of a value producing person, group, or activity. Data dense information systems that are easily accessible in data base form are seen as enablers of persons involved in customer service activities.

ENCRYPTION   Electronic security methods designed to prevent unauthorized reading and use of messages and data that are transmitted from one site to another.

ENDORSEE   One to whom a negotiable instrument is transferred by being endorsed or guaranteed by the signature of a third party.

ENDORSEMENT   A writing on the back of a negotiable instrument. Also, signature making the document a legal transfer of possession or other purpose.

END-TO-END COST   A general term for all of the costs incurred from the start of an activity until ultimate completion of it. Sometimes applied to the total life cost of acquiring and using an item up to the point of final disposal of it.

ENPLANEMENTS   Number of passengers boarding planes at certain points or on certain runs.

EN ROUTE   A shipment on its way, or involved on the route of movement is en route.

ENTERED   1) When the vessel has entered the port, and the master has gone to the customs authorities to declare the contents of the cargo. 2) A term for the placement of data or programs into a computer system.

ENTERPRISE CHAINS   The set of firms that are linked formally or informally from raw materials through to final sale. The collection of firms aligned in this manner are seen as a general enterprise that is competing against another set of firms for the same final customers.

ENTERPRISE RESOURCE PLANNING   Linkages between firms that includes, but is not limited to, forecasting, logistics, manufacturing, and planning.

ENTITY CHARTER   A charter specifying that the transportation costs will be borne by the chartering organization rather than the individual passengers.

ENTREPRENEUR   An independent business person. Engaged in a business of making, or trading products, or presenting a service for sale.

ENTREPOT   This is a place where goods are deposited without payment of duties while awaiting transportation elsewhere.

ENTRY   This term has two meanings. On one hand it refers to a right to operate. For example, the regulatory authorities control entry, or the right to operate. It also means the customs document required to clear a shipment which has been imported into the country.

ENTRY (CUSTOMS)   The process of registration of the ship's papers or goods with the customs authority is customs entry. The term entry inwards is used to apply to the statement filed on incoming ships or imported goods. When the shipment is outgoing, the statement made on goods under export is entry outward.

EOQ   A concept developed by Ford Harris of Westinghouse in 1915 which determines the most economic order quantity on the basis of ordering costs and carrying costs. When incremental ordering costs equal incremental carrying costs, the most economic order quantity exists. It does not optimize the order quantity, and thus the shipment quantity, on the basis of total logistics costs, but only ordering and carrying cost.

EPA   (U.S.) Environmental Protection Agency (U.S.); federal agency responsible for pollution by air, water, land, etc.

EQUALIZING RATE   A rate adjustment to make equal the rates charged to shippers of different localities. Typically, it means charging the same rate to and from points that are of different distances relative to a major city or port.

EQUIPMENT   The rolling stock of a railroad or motor carrier, the ships of a steamship line and the planes of an airline.

EQUIPMENT BOND   A loan secured by the carrier's equipment.

EQUITY   The net balance of a firm's assets over its liabilities. It consists of preferred stock, common stock, and retained earnings.

EQUITY INVESTMENT   1) Projects. When one firm invests capital in the form of stock purchase or acquisition of assets in another firm in the supply chain. In the oil patch, for example, one supply service firm might make an equity investment with the main oil firm in a well and enjoy a split of profits in the event of striking oil. This would have been in place of the firm simply being paid for performing services in the drilling of the well. 2) Ownership. When one firm buys the assets of another or acquires stock ownership of it.

EQUITY PARTICIPATION   See EQUITY INVESTMENT of projects

ERROR RATE, MEASURE OF   A percentage of total items picked and/or shipped in a distribution facility that are not specifically what were ordered by customers.

ESCALATION CLAUSE   A part of a purchase or rate contract that permits price increases during the term of the contract for cost factors beyond control of the supplier or carrier; usually for specific materials and fuel.

ESCALATOR   A term placed in a contractual arrangement that permits the seller to charge a higher price in the event that certain cost increases are incurred by them during the length of the contract. Opposite of DE-ESCALATOR that causes the price to drop in the event that the seller experiences price decreases.

ESCORT RATE   A rate charged with high, wide, heavy and otherwise specialized shipments for the person who accompanies the shipment to watch in the overall care of its movement.

ESCORT SERVICE   Found in high, wide and heavy shipments, owners or others having interest in shipment travel with it on train or in convoy.

ESTIMATED WEIGHT   When a weight is prescribed in a tariff for a commodity shipped in specific containers or in a specific manner, the prescribed weight is referred to as the estimated weight. For example, if a 4,700 cubic foot covered hopper car is filled to capacity with corn or wheat, it is estimated that it is 100 tons of product.

ESTOPPEL   A legal document that established liability for facts and obligations before a court of law.

ETA   Estimated time of arrival.

ETHICS   Certain accepted standards of conduct in business relationships.

ET CETERA   And other things; and so forth.

ETIOLOGIC AGENT   Hazardous transportation term for a viable micro-organism, or its toxin which causes or may cause human disease.

EURO   The name of the currency of the European Union.

EUROPEAN ARTICLE NUMBER (EAN)   Standard European coding system used for consumer goods so that the information related to them can be scanned, recorded, and further used in the supply chain and selling systems.

EUROPEAN COMMUNITY   The nations that have grouped together in Europe for purposes of having common customs and other trade and commerce features. Based in Brussels, Belgium.

EUROPEAN CURRENCY UNIT   See EURO

EUROPEAN ECONOMIC COMMUNITY   The nations of Europe that have entered into a common economic sphere involving customs, and movement among their respective nations.

EUROPEAN PALLET   A standard pallet used in Europe that is 800 by 1200 millimeters.

EUROPEAN UNION   See EUROPEAN COMMUNITY

EURO PRICES   A term that generally applies to the price of an item within a country that is stated in terms of the Euro rather than the currency of the country. This permits multi-country price comparisons of the same product in terms of the same currency.

EUROZONE CURRENCIES   Currencies of countries that have joined the EURO. These currencies will cease to exist in the year 2002.

EVERGREEN CLAUSE   A clause in a purchase or transportation contract that has the effect of making the contract continue without a specific termination date. Termination is possible upon specific act of either party, but the contract normally would automatically continue.

EVERGREEN CONTRACT   A contract that is designed to be in effect for a long period of time. It generally may be amended for specific changes in conditions and prices during its life.

EVERY DAY LOW PRICE (EDLP)   A policy of certain retailers and brand manufacturers that means that use of promotions will either not be used or will be minimized. Also referred to as EDLP, the intent of this practice is to smooth out fluctuations in supply chain activity thereby being lower in cost to both the producer, retailer, and consumer in the long run.

EX or X-OUT OF   The designation of a car whose contents have been transferred to another rail car.

EXAMINER   A person empowered by a government agency to inspect and clear shipments, or the name given to persons of regulatory agencies that oversee proceedings. Former title for such persons at the now defunct Interstate Commerce Commission (U.S.)

EXCELSIOR   A material made of shredded wood for cushioning.

EXCEPTIONS TO THE CLASSIFICATION   Ratings on class rates that differ and take precedence over those shipments known in the normally governing classification are called exceptions to the classification. While a commodity rate will give a reduced rate on a specific commodity moving between specific points, an exception to the class rating will give a reduced rate on a given commodity throughout the geographic area covered by it. The exceptions rating may be thought of as a change in the rating on a given commodity. The exceptions to the class rate are made available to all classification and tariff holders as they occur. The exceptions rating is frequently provided to distinguish one item in a general classification in order to provide a lower rating. Thus, a lower rating might be provided on men's jeans as compared to men's dress trousers.

EXCESS FREIGHT   When the amount of a shipment exceeds that shown on the original carrier's bill of lading, the amount in excess is referred to as excess freight.

EXCHANGE BILL OF LADING   One bill of lading exchanged for another bill of lading usually for a stop off operation.

EXCLUSIVE USE OF TRUCK   A provision in the bill of lading presenting a request by the shipper for exclusive use of the truck.

EXCURSION FARE   A reduced fare intended to encourage traffic in certain types of movements, at certain periods of time, or under other specified circumstances. Many airlines offer excursion fares across the Atlantic in coach seating during the low traffic months of January and February.

EX-DOCK   An F.O.B term that specifies that the title to the goods, and the responsibility for arranging the transportation movement, will change from seller to buyer when the seller places the shipment on their own dock ready for shipment at the originating point.

EXEMPT CARRIERS   Transportation carriers which carry certain products that are exempt from economic regulation.

EXEMPT COMMODITY   1) Commodities that are not subject to import duties. 2) Specific commodities which can be transported exempt of regulation of a government agency. No tariff rates or operating authority are required in this situation.

EXEMPTIONS   In order to encourage the importation of certain articles, duties are modified as they appear in the tariff. The articles for which the modification takes place are termed exempt articles.

EXEMPT TRANSPORTATION   A transportation service exempt from economic regulation by a regulatory authority.

EX-FACTORY   Under the F.O.B., Ex-Factory, both title and transportation cost responsibility transfer at the same point, which is at the seller's factory. The price quoted involves making the goods available for possession and transportation at the factory at a given date for the buyer. In an international shipment, all export taxes, transportation documents, etc., are the responsibility of the buyer.

EXHIBIT   A document or physical object introduced in evidence.

EX-LAKE   A term used to describe a commodity reaching the carrier by boat line plying on a lake.

EXPANDABLE   A flatbed trailer that is expandable for larger shipments.

EX PARTE   1) Transportation rates that are raised by a certain percent across all commodities and geographic points within a region. 2) This term was applied to investigations by the Interstate Commerce Commission, undertaken on its own initiative, for the purpose of determining general rate changes. This agency ceased to exist on January 1, 1997.

EXPEDITER   Refers to a personal tracer placed on goods or freight usually moving in carloads.

EXPEDITING   1) Purchasing. The act of contacting a supplier in the quest of speeding up the delivery date of an ordered lot of goods. 2) Traffic. The process of making arrangements for the transport of goods either prior to shipment or prior to arrival at a junction or transfer point in order to speed up the transportation movement.

EXPENSE BILL   A freight bill.

EXPENSES PER LOADED FREIGHT CAR MILE   The freight car total expense divided by the number of loaded freight car miles. This is a measure used to cost transportation movements.

EXPIRATION NOTICE   A date specified in a tariff for the expiration of the tariff, or some part of it.

EXPIRY DATE   The final date on which the draft and documents must be presented to the negotiating, accepting, paying, or issuing bank in order to effect payment. The issuing bank's obligation ceases on that date if the L/C is a "straight credit." If the L/C is a "negotiable credit," the issuing bank must honor the credit, provided the documents were submitted to the negotiating bank prior to the expiration (or expiry) date.

EXPLOIT, MARKET CYCLE   1) Purchasing. The practice of shifting toward hand-to-mouth buying when prices are dropping and negotiating long term contracts in the face of possible supply price increases or eminent shortages. 2) Selling. The practice of raising prices when demand increases.

EXPLOSION CHART   A pictorial illustration of an item with all its parts shown separately but in general relation with each other.

EXPLOSIVE   Hazardous transportation term for any chemical compound, mixture, or device the primary or common purpose of which is to function by explosion, i.e. with substantially instantaneous release of gas and heat.

EXPLOSIVE, CLASS A   A detonating or otherwise of maximum hazard.

EXPLOSIVE, CLASS B   In general, function by rapid combustion rather than detonation and include some explosive devices such as special fireworks, flash powders.

EXPLOSIVE, CLASS C   Certain types of manufactured articles containing Class A or Class B explosives, or both, as components but in restricted quantities, and certain types of fireworks.

EXPORT   To send goods to a foreign country.

EXPORT COMMISSION HOUSE   An agent for a foreign buyer in international trade.

EXPORT DECLARATION   This document is required by the United States government for all shipments destined to foreign countries. It is filed with the Customs House at the port of export. It provides a means for compiling statistics on international trade, and trade to territories of possession. The export declaration is approved by the Collector of Customs at the port, and is given a serial number and a validation stamp.

EXPORT INVOICE   A written account or itemized list, usually made out in triplicate, given to a foreign buyer. In addition to the customary commercial (domestic invoice items, it contains such significant facts for the buyer's information as steamer's name, insurance, marks, code words, and statement of inland freight, storage, cartage, and other charges.

EXPORT LICENSES   The U.S. Department of Commerce export licenses are of two categories: (1) general; and (2) validated. No application is required for the general license and no document is granted or issued. It is a document that is available to all persons and permits exportation within the provisions that are prescribed in the Export Regulations. The validated license specifies limitations for exportation of commodities. It is issued only on formal application accordant with procedures set forth in Schedule B. The export is presented to the Collector of Customs by the shipper before commodities are placed on the dock for loading on the carrier.

EXPORT RATES   Rates which reflect an export movement that are established on a lower basis than domestic traffic. These rates take precedence over other rates between the same points via the same route on export traffic.

EXPORT TRADING COMPANY   A firm or organization that provides financial assistance and/or coordinates various sellers in an effort to provide products for overseas sales.

EX POST FACTO   After that fact.

EXPRESS   Air transportation by the air express tariff.

EXPRESS BODY   An open box truck body.

EXPRESS MAIL U.S.   Postal Service line of service that provides overnight or second morning delivery. A premium service over first class.

EXPRESS TRAIN   A train that does not stop at all stations on the route, carrying express freight.

EXPRESS WARRANTY   A warranty in which a vendor makes a specific statement regarding condition, quality, or other attribute or performance of a product. Examples are length of life, speed of performance, etc.

EX SHIP   A term meaning that goods are available at a point of off loading from a ship. A related INCO 1990 international sales and transportation term relates to goods transfer at this point. See DELIVERED EX SHIP (DES).

EX WORKS (EXW)   An INCO transportation and selling term that requires the seller to produce the item for export and arrange all packaging and authorizations for exporting. They are to be made available at the plant for transfer of ownership and responsibility of the buyer for all other transportation arrangements.

EXTENDED SUPPLY CHAIN   A general term applied by a firm for all of its suppliers and suppliers' suppliers all the way through to the final user of its goods or services.

EXTENSION FORKS   Attachment placed on the forks of a forklift truck that permits longer reach and ladings to be handled.

EXTENSION OF PROTEST   Made out to support a Note of Protest. Endorsed by the officer, petty officer and two seamen. Reveals the circumstances of the voyage and actions taken to protect the shipment.

EXTERNAL ASSESSMENT   Examination of the market and environment for any factor that might be important to the strategy and success of a firm. It generally consists of a scan of emerging technologies, competition, and market opportunities.

EXTRA BOARD   The spot from which employees are called for work when they do not have sufficient seniority to bid for specific jobs.

EXTRANET   As distinct from the internet which relies upon an open web of linkages, an intranet is a fairly closed system among users but behaves in ways similar to an internet with email and web features.

EYE WIRE   A device used in barge operations, consisting of a rope or wire with a large eye or spliced loop on end.

FFFF

FAA   Free all average, Federal Aviation Administration.

FABRICATION-IN-TRANSIT RATE   A through rate plus an additional charge applied to a shipment stopped at some point between origin and destination for the purpose of fabrication.

FACILITATION   A system to increase the speed of international commerce through modernizing customs procedures, duty collection, agriculture inspection and other procedures.

FACILITY MANAGEMENT   Those activities and systems involved in the care and maintenance of office buildings, factories, and other operating structures.

FACTOR   An agent appointed to sell goods on commission.

FACTORY PACKAGE   The package that contains the actual product. Distinct from SECONDARY and TERTIARY PACKAGING.

FACTORING   A business operation which provides professional services for collection and credit.

FACTOR OF PRODUCTION   Land, labor or capital required for production.

FAILURE COSTS   Those costs incurred whenever a failure in product/service quality or processes occurs. This might be repair of breakage, safety incurred costs, downtime, or in customer service it might include premium transportation to replenish goods or lost goodwill with the customer.

FAIR OFFER   A general term for an offer to buy at a price that is deemed reasonable.

FALSE BILLING   When the shipping papers contain descriptions of commodities which fail to reflect the true contents of a shipment. It is referred to as a false billing.

FAMILY GROUPING   A term used in materials handling and stock layout indicating that different products of the same manufacturer or product lines are stored together.

FAMINE RELIEF   That transportation and other logistical support for the movement of food in an area experiencing drought and other causes of famine.

FAR   Federal Acquisition Regulations, the American government regulations governing purchase processes for the federal agencies.

FAR EAST   Western Coast of Pacific Ocean in vicinity of Japan, China, and Philippine Islands.

FAS (FREE ALONG SIDE)   A selling term in international trade whereby the selling party quotes a goods price including delivery of the goods along side the overseas vessel at the exporting port.

FAST-FREIGHT LINE   An organization of the carriers to promote dispatch of freight between certain points for specified traffic.

FAST FREIGHT TRAIN   A freight train which does not stop at all of the stations on its route.

FAST MOVING CONSUMER GOODS COMPANY   The general name for firms that manufacture, brand, and market products that are sold through super markets, discount stores, and other very competitive outlets.

FAX   Short term for facsimile transmission of an image, letter, or other document from one place to another.

FDA   Food and Drug Administration.

FEDERAL ACQUISITION REGULATIONS   The body of regulations that govern the processes of government agency purchasing.

FEDERAL AVIATION ACT   The federal legislation by the United States Congress which superseded the Civil Aeronautics Act of 1938 regulating air transportation. It was termed the Federal Aviation Act of 1958.

FEDERAL AVIATION ADMINISTRATION   The successor to the old Civil Aeronautics Administration. A federal agency which initiates and executes policy relative to the promotion of safety and efficiency in flight operations. It is now in the Department of Transportation (DOT) under a 1967 order.

FEDERAL MARITIME COMMISSION   Regulatory agency responsible for rates and practices of ocean traffic to and from U.S.

FEDERAL REGISTER   A publication produced by the U.S. government that provides information concerning notices and rules of the federal regulatory agencies. This was provided for under the Federal Register Act.

FEDERAL TRADE COMMISSION   Government body created for the purpose of overseeing business practices.

FEEDER   1) Air. Another term for air commuter company. 2) Ocean. Term for small ship that picks up at smaller ports for consolidated transfer to a larger ship at a central port, and vice versa. 3) Trucking. Term used in some companies for pick up and delivery operations, particularly those contracted or provided by another firm.

FEEDER LINES   Branches or short-line railroads traversing territory untouched by the trunk lines and interchanging traffic at connecting points.

FEEDER SERVICE   In motor transportation, short truck routes involved primarily in the collection and distribution of freight to and from main truck lines (for long hauls), usually from terminals.

FEEDER SHIPS   Ships that ply smaller ports in pick up and delivery like mode as a feed to larger trans-ocean ships.

FEEDING IN TRANSIT   The stopping of shipments of livestock, etc., at a point located between the points of origin and destination to be fed and watered.

FERRYBOAT   A ship specially designed for mass movement of passengers, automobiles, trucks, and sometimes rail cars for short and medium length water movements.

FERRY CAR   When a freight car is loaded with several L.C.L. shipments by a shipper to a railroad, or by a railroad to a receiver, it is termed a ferry car. It may also be called a trap car.

FERRY CHARTER RATE   The portion of the charter charged by the carrier to cover the necessary miles or hours of the aircraft to the point of origin of the charter, and the return of the charter aircraft to the destination of the carrier.

FERRY OPERATION   Operation of equipment from one point to another in non-revenue service for the purpose of positioning it for another revenue

FIBERBOARD   A shipping container material of heavy board 3 to 4 piles

FIELD   Computer term for an electronic space allowed by a program for the entry of variables or constants. Examples are the location to enter a person's name, address, etc.

FIELD ENTRY   A keyboarded entry of data into the field of a computer system.

FIELD WAREHOUSE   A warehouse provided by a public warehouse firm, located on the premises of a business.

FIFO   Inventory rotation, first in, first out.

FIFTH PARTY LOGISTICS   The outsourced form of logistics services that also includes management of the client firm's logistics operations as well as on-going analysis and consulting roles of how the client firm can change to improve its competitiveness.

FIFTH WHEEL   The device used to connect the semi-trailer and the tractor.

FIGHTING SHIP   When a shipping conference designates a particular ship to combat non conference competition, it is given the term fighting ship. This is executed by making the rates on the fighting ship so low that competition is forced out of business or required to reduce the rates to acceptable proportions. Fighting ships were declared illegal under the Shipping Act of 1916.

FINANCE DOCKET   The dockets of the Interstate Commerce Commission on which are listed for consideration and decision, questions relating to financing, extensions, abandonments, and consolidations of common carriers.

FINANCIAL ACCOUNTING STANDARDS BOARD, BULLETIN #13 (U.S.)   A statement from the accounting profession as to how leases are to be treated for accounting purposes; difference between handling them as leases or capitalizing them on the company balance sheet.

FINANCIAL HEALTH   The nature of a firm's financial strength with regard to cash liquidity, leverage, overall capitalization, ability to meet future debt payments, and the capability to invest in future resources and opportunities.

FINANCIAL LEASE   A lease in which the lessee makes payments and is responsible for the asset over its life. A lease that meets the requirements of a capital lease.

FINANCIAL STABILITY   See FINANCIAL HEALTH

FINANCIAL STATEMENT   A report of the liquidity, profitability, and solvency of a firm.

FINGER PIER   A long, enclosed walkway extending from airport terminal to the loading gate. Also a water carrier pier.

FINGER TERMINAL   The standard air terminal which has a central ticketing and general operations section, with projecting corridors for passenger facilitation.

FINISHED GOODS WRITEOFF   The accounting act of taking the value of obsolete, poor quality, or otherwise not needed goods out of the system by way of expensing them and removing them from the asset list of the firm.

FINK AWARD   A report issued in 1880 as to freight rate differential at Atlantic ports, when goods were, in addition to rail movement, water borne. Albert Fink was chairman.

FIRE, CLASS A   A fire involving combustible materials such as wood, packing materials, paper and cloth.

FIRE, CLASS B   Fires involving oil, gasoline, paint or grease.

FIRE, CLASS C   Fires involving wiring, fuse boxes, energized electrical equipment.

FIRE, CLASS D   Fires involving combustible metals.

FIRE CURTAIN   Large curtain made of a fire resistant material to prevent a fire from one side of the curtain to the other.

FIRE PALLET   Portable platform on which sits fire extinguishers and fire fighting equipment, to be moved to the scene of a fire.

FIREWALL   1) Warehouse. A wall, typically of cinder block, concrete, or other similar material that is designed to block the spread of a fire from one part of the building to another. 2) Electronic Systems. Protected mechanisms that are designed to prevent unauthorized entry from outside the organization.

FIRING POINT   The temperature required for the vapor from a liquid to be in sufficient quantity to provide a continuous flame. It is higher than the flash point.

FIRKIN   A capacity measurement equal to one-fourth of a barrel.

FIRM   A commercial establishment that provides goods or services.

FIRST CLASS SERVICE   Transport service for passengers where standard or premium quality service are provided.

FIRST MAIN TRACK   As applied to line-haul roads, a single track extending the entire distance between terminals, upon which the length of the road is based, used to effect a line-haul and therefore kept dear for the passage of trams.

FIRST PRICE SEALED BID   A purchasing method used in bidding whereby the buyers will only consider the best price of any of the bids without allowing further discussion by any of the bidders for submitting subsequent bids.

FIRST REFUSAL RIGHTS   An operating right situation in which a carrier has prior rights on charter or other special services in international transportation operations by air.

FIRST WORLD   A loose term for the major industrial nations of the world. Second world countries were those in the former communist bloc. Increasingly, today, the term second world countries applies to those nations that are newly industrializing. Third world nations are typically those without highly developed economies.

FISH BONE ANALYSIS   An method used to analyze complex processes in terms of the sequence of components, activities and steps required to complete an overall task. Each sub component activity is drawn on a diagonal line that feeds the prime center line in what becomes to look like a fish bone.

FISH BONE CHART   A graphic representation of a production process, wherein the backbone represents the production line flow and the rib bones are used to represent the critical factors feeding into the flow.

FISHYBACK   When highway trailers are transported aboard ships through a process of demounting the trailers, the shipment is referred to as fishyback.

FITNESS   A transportation regulation term pertaining to a transportation company's financial stature and responsibility.

FIVE FREEDOMS   1) Right to cross the territory of another country (by air), 2) right to land for technical, fueling or comparable necessities, 3) right to deplane traffic that was enplaned in the home country of the carrier; 4) right to enplane traffic bound for the home country of the carrier; and 5) right to enplane in one foreign country, en route to another foreign country. See also sixth-freedom traffic.

FIXED ASSETS   Non-consumable production facilities.

FIXED BASED OPERATOR   The selling of transportation and/or servicing of an aircraft, giving flying instructions, making charter flights, etc., all at an airport.

FIXED CHARGES   Those transportation costs which do not vary with the quantity shipped.

FIXED COSTS   Costs that do not change with a change in the volume of operations.

FIXED IMPROVEMENTS   Structures of permanent character.

FIXED INTERVAL SYSTEM   An inventory reordering rule in which goods are reordered at specified fixed time intervals, the size of the lot varies.

FIXED LOCATION SYSTEM   Location of a product in the warehouse—is in a specific place as indicated by a floor marking.

FIXED ORDER QUANTITY   An inventory reordering rule in which the lot size ordered each time remains the same, the length of time between orders varies.

FIXED PRICE   When price is not affected by demand. Contract term indicating that the price is a certain amount and not subject to escalation.

FIXED REORDER POINT SYSTEM   An inventory rule that calls for reordering at fixed time intervals.

FIXED ROUTE TRANSIT   Any transit system of moving people that plies rigid routes without deviation. They are typically scheduled.

FIXED WING AIRCRAFT   Aircraft having wings that are fixed to the airplane body.

FIXING LETTER   A document drawn to establish the conditions for a charter.

FIXTURE   A report of vessel charters that explains the basic elements of the charter.

FLAG STATION   A station at which trains stop only when signaled.

FLAMMABLE GAS   Any compressed gas meeting the requirements for lower flammability limit, flammability limit range, flame projection, or flame propagation criteria as specified in DOT regulations.

FLAMMABLE GOODS   Goods that give off vapors which become combustible at a certain temperature.

FLAMMABLE LIQUID   Any liquid having a flash point below 100°F as determined in DOT tests.

FLAMMABLE SOLID   Any solid material, other than an explosive, which is liable to cause fires through friction, retained heat from manufacturing or processing, or which can be ignited readily and when ignited burns so vigorously and persistently as to create a serious transportation hazard.

FLANGE   In rail transportation, the steel edge inside the rim of the wheels to provide guidance on the track.

FLASH POINT   A hazardous material transportation term that refers to the temperature at which a substance gives off a vapor or gas that can become ignited by a source of some form, such as a spark.

FLAT BED CAR   An open railroad car without sides or top.

FLAT BILL OF MATERIAL   A production chart and situation whereby a firm assembles subitems into a finished good in one step without having to perform subassembly steps prior to the final assembly.

FLAT BOTTOM   A flatbed truck or trailer without sides.

FLAT CAR   A freight car without ends, sides, or top, used principally for the transportation of lumber, machinery, and unusually bulky articles; often called a Platform car.

FLAT CHARGE   A single fee regardless of the freight on board.

FLAT FACE   A cab over engine type of vehicle.

FLAT PERCENTAGE RATE INCREASES   This is a system of changing rates to meet changes in costs of operations by means of changing all existing tariffs by a given flat percentage. This system may be criticized because it fails to take into consideration the difference in changes of costs of operations in the line-haul and terminal areas, respectively. It would be a coincidence if terminal and line-haul costs increased at the same rate, yet the flat percentage system assumes they do. The most common criticism applied to this method of rate increase has been that it results in a greater absolute increase to the long haul shipper. This is an erroneous criticism if the objective is to change rates to meet changes in costs. If the costs of transportation increase, it should be expected that long haul shipments will system a greater absolute increase in rates, since the distance is greater.

FLAT RATE   A local or joint rate applicable to all circumstances of shipment.

FLEXIBLE MANUFACTURING   A production system that is capable of producing either in a number of ways or various products with a minimum of switch over effort from one to another.

FLEXI-VAN   Truck trailers or containers that are loaded on specially constructed flat cars equipped with two turntables.

FLEXTIME   A worker scheduling system whereby they may set their own daily work times.

FLIGHT CORRIDOR   Air routes allowed by a country for aircraft from other countries. Noteworthy ones were the three that operated from West Germany into Berlin over East Germany from 1945 until 1991. Also, the corridors allowed American flag air carriers to fly across Cuba to reach southern destinations.

FLIGHT EQUIPMENT   The equipment facilities required for flight.

FLIGHT EQUIPMENT INTERCHANGE   Circumstances in which a single plane is used by more than one carrier on a route, and where the crew is changed to fly the routes of the carrier.

FLIGHT STAGE   The time from take-off to landing.

FLIMSEY   A train order to the crew indicating that certain action will be required by them or will otherwise affect their train.

FLOAT   1) Trucking. A flatbed semi-trailer. 2) Finance. The time in which a check is in transit and has not yet been deducted from the writer's account.

FLOATAGE   A charge for floating or transferring cars across water.

FLOAT BRIDGE   A drawbridge completing a connection between land, railroad tracks, and car floats, and affording an interchange of rolling stock.

FLOAT, CAR   A flat-bottomed craft without power, equipped with tracks, and accommodating from ten to twenty cars at a time. The cars are run from the land onto the float car by way of adjustable track that matches up the land tracks with the level of the car float tracks.

FLOATER   A driver who skips from job to job.

FLOATING CURRENCY   Any currency in which the value freely moves upward and downward based upon the supply and demand for it.

FLOATING RATE   Means that the exchange rate of a currency against others shifts upward and downward freely in response to market and economic conditions.

FLOATING THE GEARS   Changing gears without using the clutch.

FLOATS   Large single tires that are used instead of duals.

FLOOR LOAD   The range or maximum capacity of a car, in pounds per square foot.

FLOTSAM   Cargo swept from a vessel and found floating in the water. Since ownership o such property is not lost, flotsam is liable for salvage.

FLOWCHART   A diagram depicting the sequence of events that should take place in a complex set of tasks.

FLOW PROCESS CHART   Similar to a flow chart.

FLOW RACK   Metal rack which allows the stacking of product and easy access to product.

FLUTE   A zig zag rib, usually on the inside portion of corrugated fiberboard.

FLYER   A round trip run involving a trip to a distant terminal and the return trip without stop.

FLYING ORDERS   The instruction given the driver on the trip.

F.O.B.   Technically, it means "free on board." The F.O.B. terms go far beyond this concept and establish the contractual arrangement in which 1) title is transferred between seller and buyer and, 2) the point where transportation responsibility is shifted from seller to buyer. The F.O.B. abbreviation implies loading on a conveyance at the designated point. After these letters, it is usually designated where title and control of the goods pass to the buyer. In domestic settings, it does not necessarily indicate which party will pay the carrier for the freight charges.

F.O.B. COLLECT   Term indicating that the buyer will be billed for freight charges by the carrier. The term will usually have additional indications as to "origin" or "destination" passing of title.

F.O.B. DESTINATION   Free on board to the point of destination. Freight cost is paid to the point of destination. Title transfers at destination.

F.O.B. FACTORY   Under this term, cartage from the factory to the railroad head will be paid by the buyer. Both title to the goods and carrier responsibility terminates with the seller at the factory. If the factory has a railroad siding, the goods will be made available at the railroad siding.

F.O.B. (NAMED INLAND CARRIER AT NAMED INLAND POINT OF DEPARTURE)   Under this contractual term, the seller makes the goods available at an inland shipping point. Both title to the goods and responsibility for transportation are transferred at the named inland point for shipment. All transportation costs, export taxes, document costs, and responsibility for loss and damage transfer when possession of the goods is taken at the inland point of transfer. The seller places the goods in or on the conveyance for delivery to the inland carrier. The seller arranges for the loading of the goods on rail cars, trucks, etc. for transportation.

F.O.B. (NAMED INLAND CARRIER AT NAMED INLAND POINT OF DEPARTURE; FREIGHT ALLOWED TO NAMED POINT.)   Under this term, title transfers when the goods are placed on the inland carrier. A price is quoted which includes transportation charges from the factory in the country of sales to the destination. Thus, puce is the manufacturer's price, plus transportation costs to the consignee. The goods are sent freight collect, but the buyer is billed by the seller for the manufacturer's sales price, not including transportation. The seller arranges transportation, but he does not pay for it. The buyer has an opportunity to directly compare the total costs inclusive of transportation of all competing sellers. The buyer is responsible for all costs, including export costs, document expenses, etc. from the factory of the seller to the destination.

F.O.B. (NAMED INLAND CARRIER AT NAMED INLAND POINT OF DEPARTURE; FREIGHT PREPAID TO NAMED POINT OF EXPORTATION.)   Under this term, title transfers at the named inland point of departure for the initial inland carrier, but transportation is included in the seller's price all the way to the named point of exportation. The named inland point of departure obviously is not the same as the named point of exportation. The buyer is responsible for all export taxes, document costs, etc. necessary in the event of an export shipment.

F.O.B. (NAMED INLAND CARRIER TO NAMED INLAND POINT OF EXPORTATION.)   Under this F.O.B. term, a foreign buyer requests a price which includes invoice price, and the transport cost, to a common export point. Therefore, under the quoted price, purchase price and transportation cost may be directly compared. It permits the foreign buyer to control the international water routing, but puts the domestic routing from the named inland point to the export point in the hands of the seller.

F.O.B. PREPAID   Freight charges will be borne by the seller. This is typical in freight equalized selling. Term "origin" or "destination" further indicate where title will actually pass.

F.O.B. PREPAID AND CHARGED BACK   Title pass at either origin or destination (as indicated), but seller directly pays carrier and amount is passed on to buyer on invoice for goods.

F.O.B. VESSEL (NAMED PORT OF SHIPMENT)   Both title and transportation costs transfer after the goods are delivered on the vessel. Since they have not left the harbor, all export taxes and costs involved in documents for overseas shipments would be assessed to the buyer.

FOOD AND DRUG ADMINISTRATION   Agency of the U.S. federal government regulating activity concerning food and drugs. Inspects warehouses and factories.

FORBIDDEN (HAZARDOUS MATERIAL)   One that must not be offered or accepted for transportation.

FORECAST ACCURACY   The degree to which a forecast and actual sales or other physical activity correspond to each other. A highly accurate forecasting system can lead to a minimum of investment in unneeded safety stock.

FORECASTLE HEAD   The foremost part of the spar deck. It is the raised deck of most merchant ships, in the front of the vessel.

FORCED BILLING   When no bill can be located, the forced billing provides a means for delivery of freight. This is most common when the traffic is moving partly in the U.S. and partly in a foreign country, or involves an International movement.

FORCE MAJEURE   A term or condition typically found in purchasing, rail, motor, and water contracts that relieves either party from contract obligation if major unforeseen events beyond their control prevent compliance; typically the obligation is suspended for resumption at a later time.

FOREIGN AIR CARRIER PERMIT   A right to operate, issued by a government to a foreign carrier, authorizing it to operate between a foreign country and the home country that issued the permit.

FOREIGN CAR   In the railroad transportation business, rail cars move between lines and between nations. The car of one railroad used by another railroad line is termed a foreign car. It usually does not involve a foreign national car, but it can.

FOREIGN CORRUPT PRACTICES ACT   An American law that prohibits the use of graft and other inducements when dealing with business and political persons in other countries.

FOREIGN-FLAG AIR CARRIER   Foreign registered air carriers.

FOREIGN FREIGHT FORWARDER   A party that acts to arrange for foreign movement for shippers and consignees; distinct from domestic forwarders; foreign forwarders do not take on the same obligations.

FOREIGN TRADE ZONE   A site sanctioned by the Customs Service in which imported goods are exempted from customs duties until withdrawn for domestic sale or use; such zones are used for commercial warehouse or production plants.

FOREX   Shortened term for foreign exchange of currency.

FOR-HIRE AIR CARRIER   A common or contract transportation carrier.

FORKLIFT TRUCK   A machine which can raise and lower freight for stacking and move freight to different locations.

FORK POCKETS   Space under containers to facilitate the forks of a forklift truck.

FORMAL COMPLAINT   A complaint filed with the a regulatory commission alleging violation of the statute and to be investigated and adjudicated under formal procedure provided by the rules of that Commission.

FORMALITIES   A general European term for the processes that are necessary for immigration and customs clearances when entering a country.

FORRESTER EFFECT.   See BULLWHIP EFFECT.

FORWARD BUYING   The practice of purchasing in advance of needing specific goods. Typically done in advance of a price increase or product shortage.

FORWARDER, FREIGHT   One who accepts LCL shipments from shippers and attends to custom procedures and documents in connection with foreign shipments.

FORWARD INTEGRATION   The acquisition or development of firms downstream between the company and the final customers and consumers. Example: a metal producer purchasing a distributor; a brand manufacturer that acquires or develops distributors or retail outlets.

FOUL BILL OF LADING   A lading receipted by the agent of the carrier, indicating damage or a shortage when goods were shipped.

FOUND   Equipped, provided, or supplied; as, a ship was well found.

FOUNDER   To fill with water and sink; to cause (a ship) to founder.

FOUR BANGER   Four cycle engines.

FOUR BY FOUR   A vehicle with four speed transmission and four speed auxiliary transmission.

FOURTH PARTY LOGISTICS   An outside firm that operates typically transportation and warehousing services for a client in addition to providing the management and analytical processes of these functions.

FOURTH SECTION APPLICATION (U.S.)   When a rail carrier wished to publish rates which were in violation of the long and short haul principle. This stated that no rate may be higher to an intermediate point than to a farther point when the intermediate point was within the route between the origin and farther point.

FRAMES   On web pages, it is the placement of two or more pages that load on the same screen at the same time. Often, this one frame is useful as an index or table of contents that is always visible to guide the reader to all the sections of the web site.

FRANC   A unit of currency, mainly those of Switzerland and France.

FRANCO (DELIVERY)   When a delivery is made to the consignee's door, all charges have been paid, and all circumstances completed, it is called a franco delivery.

FRANK   To exempt mail express matter or telegraph messages from the usual charge.

FREE ALONG SIDE (FAS.) VESSEL   Under this F.A.S. term, the seller agrees to deliver the goods in proper condition along side the vessel. It may be delivered on a lighter or on a receiving pier. The buyer assumes all subsequent risk and expenses after delivery.

FREE ASTRAY   A term applied to freight which has been unloaded at the wrong terminal. It will be transferred to the correct terminal free of charge.

FREE BAGGAGE ALLOWANCE   The amount of baggage allowed to the passengers before an additional charge is made.

FREE CARRIER (FCA)   An INCO 1990 sales and shipping term that requires the seller to deliver goods ready for export to the carrier at the port or airport at which they will be exported. The buyer's responsibility begins at that point. It is similar to FOB Port of Export.

FREEDOMS   Long standing term in air industry pertaining to permission airlines have to serve other countries. First freedom: right to cross the territory of another country. Second freedom: right to land for technical fueling, or comparable necessities. Third freedom: right to deplane traffic that was enplaned in the home country of the carrier fourth freedom: right to enplane traffic bound for the home country of the carrier. Fifth freedom: right to enplane in one foreign country, en route to another foreign country. Sixth freedom: right to pick up in one country, transfer in home country, and deplane in third country (combination of third and fourth freedoms).

FREE ENTERPRISE   A national ownership system for production facilities. Prices are established through the supply and demand of the consumer and producer.

FREE (----) HARBOR   The delivery of goods to the port of entry named. The exporter assumes all expense connected with the movement of the goods, even to transshipment costs, should a vessel be forced, by accident or unseaworthiness, to discharge cargo at a port other than that named.

FREE LIGHTERAGE   When car lots are unloaded from cars, transferred to lighters, and transported to a restricted territory within a harbor with no additional charges attached beyond the rail head, this is referred to as free lighterage.

FREE MARKET   An economic situation in which price is the result of the supply of goods or services at different prices, and the demand for each price level.

FREE ON BOARD (FOB)   1) Export Side. An INCO international shipping and sales term that requires the seller to arrange and pay for all activities up to the goods coming to rest on the outbound ship. This includes obtaining an ocean bill of lading from the carrier. The buyer's responsibility is assumed from that point forward. This term would be named more specifically FOB Port of Export. 2) Import Side. A traditional shipping and sales term, FOB Port of Import, means that the terms of sale extended to the ship coming to rest at the destination port. If any heavy lift services were required to unload the freight, these would be the responsibility of the buyer. See DELIVERED EX SHIP.

FREE OF PARTICULAR AVERAGE (F.PA)   In maritime insurance, when goods are damaged by an accident of the vessel in which they are being conveyed but are not covered to the extent of minor damages, the term free of particular average is applied. If a shipment is free of particular average under 5%, it means that the insurance company will not allow a claim for partial loss or damage under F.P.A. conditions unless the actual damage and loss amounts to 5% or more of the amount for which the shipment had been insured. This is set forth in the policy.

FREE OF PARTICULAR AVERAGE UNDER 5 PERCENT   A term denoting that no claim under F.P.A. conditions will be allowed unless the actual damage or loss amounts to or exceeds 5% of the amount of the insurance policy.

FREE ON BOARD (F.O.B.)   In domestic trade, and when this term is used with no further attachments, it means delivery of the goods with all charges paid on board the cars at the point of manufacture.

FREE OVERSIDE (OVERBOARD)   Sold at a price to the buyer which does not include charges up to and including the unloading of a vessel.

FREE PORT   A port which permits the loading and unloading of ships without the payment of a duty.

FREEPORT LAW   A state law that exempts inventories held within the state from state inventory taxes as long as the inventory will eventually move on to customers or users out of that state; used as an industry attraction policy device; prime examples are Nevada and Georgia.

FREE TIME   The time allowed the shipper to load, or the receiver of the freight to unload before demurrage charges begin, is called free time. In LCL freight, free time is the time which would be allowed the consignee before storage charges begin to accrue. These conditions are spelled out in the Code of Car Demurrage Rules which govern rail carload freight.

FREE TRANSPORTATION   In Chapter 107 of the R.I.C.A., carriers are permitted to issue free passes only to their employees and persons engaged m certain pursuits.

FREEZABLE FREIGHT   Freight that cannot be frozen for shipment without damage.

FREIGHT   Goods being moved by transportation lines from one place to another; also, the transportation charge.

FREIGHT ALLOWED   This means that shipments will move freight collect and the extent of the transportation cost will be deducted from the total cost of the goods when the invoice is paid. This permits the seller to quote a price that does not include transportation charges, thus avoiding tying up his capital.

FREIGHT, ASTRAY (FREE ASTRAY)   When less-than–carload shipments become separated from the regular revenue waybill, even though it is marked for destination, it is termed freight astray.

FREIGHT BILL   The freight bill is the carrier's invoice. At the destination it is prepared from waybills or collect shipments, while at the point of origin it is prepared on the basis of prepaid shipments. An original and four copies of the freight bill are made out. While the original is known as the freight bill, the other copies are the arrival notice, delivery receipt, cashier's memorandum, and the station record.

FREIGHT CHARGE   The rate established for transporting freight.

FREIGHT CLAIM   A demand on a carrier for reimbursement as to overcharges, or loss, damage, delay, or other act of omission connected with the handling of freight.

FREIGHT CLAIM RATIO, FOR CARRIER   The percentage of revenues paid out in claims.

FREIGHT CLAIM RATIO, FOR SHIPPER   The percentage of shipments or value of shipments involved in claims.

FREIGHT CONSOLIDATION PLAN   Pool distribution in reverse. Consolidation of small orders at the warehouses into truckloads or carload quantities and thus gaining lower freight rates.

FREIGHT CONTRACT (STEAMSHIP)   The ocean carrier books cargo in advance of sailing. This permits the most efficient and maximum loading of the vessel. A contract is written which authorizes a shipper to deliver according to specific requirements. The freight contract contains the name of the ship, vessel, port, time for loading, cargo descriptions, etc. The carrier can cancel any part of the contract for circumstances such as strikes which are beyond the carrier's control. Freight contract bookings are entered on a booking sheet. Freight contracts are currently limited to bulk cargo.

FREIGHT, DEAD   When a charterer fails to provide a full cargo for the vessel he has engaged, the loss sustained by the ship owner must be made up by the shipper. The unused space is called dead freight. The term also applies to the unused space itself.

FREIGHT EQUALIZATION   Practice by sellers of paying some or all of the freight to some customers in order to have the various customers pay the same amounts for freight.

FREIGHTER   A vessel built and equipped for, and deriving its principal revenue from, the carriage of cargo.

FREIGHT FORWARDER   Designated as a common carrier under the Interstate Commerce Act, the freight forwarder is an individual or a company that accepts LCL shipments or LTL shipments from shippers and combines them into carload lots. Generally speaking, the freight forwarder charges the shipper on the basis of LCL size shipments, but pays the carrier on the basis of CL shipments and covers his costs, inclusive of fair return, on the difference between these rates.

FREIGHT FORWARDER   An agent whose functions are to help expedite shipments by preparing the necessary documents and making other arrangements for the outward movement of merchandise.

FREIGHT FORWARDER ACT   Originally Interstate Commerce Act, Part IV; now a Subchapter IV carrier in the Revised Interstate Commerce Act.

FREIGHT FORWARDER RATES   Freight forwarder tariffs are predominantly governed by the motor classification, since freight forwarders try to maintain rate levels that do not exceed those of motor carriers. Freight forwarder class and commodity tariffs present rates on both less than volume and volume shipments. It is because a freight forwarder pays carload or truckload charges that he is able to publish rates of his own to the public on any volume less than these quantities. Forwarder class rates are competitive with motor carrier rates down to Class 50 on less than volume shipments, and down to Class 35 on volume shipments.

FREIGHT HOUSE   The station facility of a transportation line for receiving and delivering freight.

FREIGHT, LUMP   Payment in one sum for the hire of a ship for a complete voyage or other purpose.

FREIGHT, MISSORTED   Freight which, through the carrier's error, is forwarded to the correct destination via a route with a higher rate than that applicable via the route specified by the shipper; also, freight for which the shopper has not specified route but which 15 forwarded via a route with a rate higher than is applicable via the cheapest available route.

FREIGHT PAK   A term applied to air freight customers.

FREIGHT RATE   Charge assessed for transporting freight.

FREIGHT REVENUE   The revenue received from freight, transit, stop, reconsignment and any other source required by the tariff.

FREIGHT TRAIN   A unit or a combination of units of equipment (exclusive of light locomotives) moving over tracks by self-contained motor equipment in connection with the transportation of revenue and company freight, whether loaded or empty.

FREIGHT TRAIN CAR   A freight-carrying car, caboose, or other train service equipment required in the operation o a freight train.

FREQUENT FLIER MILE   A unit of incentive employed by airlines as a means of capturing loyalty from customers. It is typically accumulated according to the number of miles flown on the carrier by the passenger.

FRICTION-FREE MARKETS   Financial and commercial markets that operate with a minimum of interference from government or other restrictive sources. It often means that transactions can take place freely and monetary settlements can quickly take place with a minimum of effort.

FROG   The section of a rail track which permits a cross-over to another track at an intersection.

FROZEN   Generally any item that is kept at a temperature of 32 degrees F or 0 degrees C or below.

FTC   Federal Trade Commission, regulatory agency responsible for administering a large part of the Robinson-Patman Act.

FUEL SURCHARGE   An extra charge on transportation movements to account for the increased fuel cost since the base rate was put into effect.

FUEL TAXES   Excise taxes on gasoline and other fuels.

FULFILLMENT   A term for mail order or telephone order systems that includes the picking and shipping of the items purchased by customers. Fulfillment systems often refers to companies that hold themselves out to perform this total service to branded clients in an outsource mode.

FULL EDI SET   An EDI system that is complete with the ability to handle orders, confirmations, shipping notices, invoices, and electronic funds transfer. Some also can handle routing email messaging as well.

FULL EMPLOYMENT   A situation in which unemployment is less than 4%.

FULL FREIGHT   A trailer with wheels on all corners, as contrasted to a semitrailer which requires the tractor to hold the front end.

FULL PAYMENT LEASE   One in which the lessor shall receive the full cost plus financing, overhead, and accepts a return on his investment.

FULL REACH AND BURDEN   Cargo space normally available, including deck.

FULL-SERVICE LEASE   The lessor can provide everything such as maintenance, insurance, taxes and other incidentals, this lease can be tailored to provide or eliminate any type of service or expense by the lessee.

FULL TRAILER   A trailer with wheels at both ends, rather than requiring a fifth wheel for support by the tractor.

FULLY ALLOCATED COST   A cost consisting of the variable cost per unit plus a prorata share of fixed costs, the latter term typically being total fixed costs divided by the expected number of units to be handled in the lot.

FUNCTIONAL MANAGEMENT   A term that indicates that an organization is designed around specific traditional or departmental structure functions such as manufacturing, purchasing, sales, etc. without close coordination of them except at senior levels of the firm.

FURNITURE CAR   A car equipped with facilities for safe and proper handling of furniture.

FUTURES MARKET   A sales opportunity for future delivery of commodities which may be bought and sold. This is an insurance against price fluctuations and avoids risks.

GGGG

GAGE (GAUGE) OF TRACK   The distance between the heads of the rails on a railroad measured at right angles thereto at a point 5/8 inches below the top of the rail. The standard gage is 4 feet 8 1/2 inches. Narrow gage is generally 3 feet. Broad gages range from 5 feet to 5 and one-half feet

GALE   A wind of from 35 to 65 miles per hour, of varying intensity.

GANGPLANK   A bridge of some sort from ship to shore.

GANGWAY   A platform used in conveying shipments from dock to vessel, platform to car, or car to car; also, the passageway by which passengers enter or depart from a ship.

GANTRY CRANE   A crane placed on track with the capacity to lift weights by a tackle.

GANTT CHART   A control chart which shows the relationship between planned performance and actual performance. It was named after Henry L. Gantt. One use is to measure loading performance, with one horizontal line representing capacity, and another to illustrate load compared to the capacity. Sometimes it is used to measure progress, with one horizontal line showing production schedule, and another showing performed progress.

GATEKEEPER   A loose term for any person or group that acts to control the application or selection of a decision. For example, though an engineering department might specify that a certain supplier by used for a purchase, the firm's purchasing department might still review and make the final approval of that supplier. In this way, purchasing is acting as a "gatekeeper."

GATEWAY   A point at which freight is interchanged between territories is normally thought of as a gateway. The term is commonly applied in air transportation to air terminals at which passengers may be transferred to other carriers. London Heathrow Airport is a major gateway as is New York's JFK Airport.

GAUNTLET   A railroad track set off from a regular high speed track that is used to bring trains close to an adjoining train platform for loading/unloading.

G.B.L.   Government bill of lading.

GEAR BONGER   Slang name applied to a driver who does not know how to shift gears.

GEAR JAMMER   Same as gear bonger—a driver who grinds the gears when shifting.

GENERAL AGREEMENT ON TRADE AND TARIFFS (GATT)   A former system of agreements among countries of the world designed to reduce tariffs and other trade barriers. It has been superseded by the World Trade Organization.

GENERAL AVERAGE   A contribution made by the owners of a ship and its cargo toward a loss sustained by one or more of their number whose property has been thrown overboard or sacrificed necessarily in order to save the ship and a part of its cargo.

GENERAL AVIATION   All civil aviation except common carrier service. It does not include the certificated common carriers, supplemental carriers, intrastate carriers or military movements. Business aircraft flights and contract flights represent the most common types.

GENERAL COMMODITIES   An operating right to carry all commodities except those specifically listed—such as iron and steel, brick, dry or liquid bulk

GENERAL COMMODITY AIR RATE   An air rate that applies to all commodities except special commodity rates. These rates are based on weight and distance. They are published for each combination of cities and air carrier serves.

GENERAL LICENSE (EXPORT)   Right to export without specific approval.

GENERAL RATE INCREASE   A term for a rate increase that applies generally to all or a broad set of commodities and traffic by a carrier; often called exparte increase.

GENERAL SHIP   A vessel, navigated by its owner, that receives and carries freight impartially for all who apply.

GENERIC ITEM   A purchasing field term for a product or service that is widely available, presenting low risk in purchasing and use, and for which brand name is not important to the buyer. Example in the purchasing realm: paper clips.

GENERICS   See GENERIC ITEM

GIS   Geographical information system; any related technology that uses satellite linkages to keep track of location of shipments, transport vehicles, etc.

GLAD HAND   A system to couple the braking system of the tractor with the brakes of the trailer.

GLOBAL POSITIONING SYSTEM   The satellite network that provides for GIS capabilities.

GLOBAL SOURCING   1) The act of seeking out and purchasing from suppliers regardless of where they are in the world. 2) Concerted acquisition of goods for all of a company's sites that are spread throughout the world.

GLOBAL SUPPLIER   A supplier that can supply goods and services to anywhere in the consuming world.

G.m.b.H.   Gesellschaft mit beschraenkter Haftung. A German limited liability company.

GOAT'N SHOAT MAN   A farm livestock truck driver.

GODOWN   A waterfront storehouse in East Asian ports.

GOH   Garment on hanger.

GOING CONCERN VALUE   A rate making term indicating that a rate that is over out of pocket costs will contribute to the overhead and profit of a firm, the covering of out of pocket costs and an addition to the firm's overhead is seen as contributing to what is needed for the firm to continue operating in the long term.

GON   Short term for gondola car.

GONDOLA CAR   An open car, with sides and ends but no top, used for hauling sand, gravel, coal, and similar commodities, and referred to as a gon.

GONDOLA CAR, DROP-BOTTOM   A gondola car having a level floor equipped with several drop doors for discharging the load.

GONDOLA CAR, DROP-END   A gondola car with the ends in the form of doors, which can be dropped to accommodate material whose length exceeds the length of one car.

GOODS   Merchandise in transportation.

GOODS-IN DEPARTMENT   A British term for "receiving"

GOVERNMENT BILL OF LADING   Special form of bill of lading used for U.S. Government and military traffic.

GOVERNMENT LICENSE   A document permitting goods to be shipped out of the country. Although basically a wartime measure, it is still required on some commodities shipped to certain foreign countries.

GRAB-ONE   The process of shifting to lower gears on a high grade.

GRAIN BODY   In highway transportation, an open flat body used to haul grain and other loose shipments. Low sides.

GRAIN DOOR   The partition across the door of a boxcar which prevents bulk loaded grain from leaking.

GRAIN ELEVATOR   A storehouse into which grain in bulk is carried upward by elevators and placed into bins arranged for the different grades of grain.

GRAIN TANKER   In motor transportation, a specialized grain carrying tank trailer. It is a low slung tank with grain trailer sides. The grain used in molasses production is carried on the top of the tank.

GRANDFATHER CLAUSE   When a carrier has been operating for some period of time and seeks an operating permit on the basis of its vested interest, it may be given a Grandfather Clause operating right. The Grandfather Clause of the U.S. Motor Carrier Act of 1935 permitted carriers to continue their operations upon implementation of regulation by simply establishing the extent of the operation prior to enactment of the new law.

GRANDMA   Has the same meaning as a creeper gear.

GRASS   The term for a rope used by a bargeman.

GRATUITIES AND GIFTS   Those items given to a person who is in position to assist someone who needs help from official sources. More stringently, a bribe.

GRAVITY CHUTE   A chute or trough used to load bulky commodities by gravity.

GRAY AREA   A transportation service which borders between the legal and illegal. These services are most subject to legal dispute.

GRAY MARKET   Situation whereby a retailer buys not from a brand manufacturer in the home country but rather buy from that same company out of a low cost production country in which they also produce the same goods. The retailer then imports the lower priced goods and sells them against the manufacturer's same goods in the higher cost country.

GREAT CIRCLE SAILING/FLYING   Sailing or flying along the great circle routes between ports or airports. The great circle route is the least mileage path between two points, versus single compass headings which are longer.

GREEN FIELD   Construction of new manufacturing capacity at a new site.

GREEN SEA   Name applied to solid water carried aboard.

GRID TECHNIQUE   A simple mathematical tool utilizing longitude and latitude scales with market and source tonnages to determine an ideal minimum total transportation cost location point for production or distribution.

GROCERY MANUFACTURERS ASSOCIATION   In the United States, it provides a suggested set of regulations for pallet sizes; often referred to as "GMA."

GROCERY PALLET COUNCIL   Provides a suggested set of regulations for pallet size and manufacture. Controls manufacture through licensing and stamps, which must be burned onto a pallet.

GROSS MARGIN   In the retail sector, this is the difference between the revenue received from a customer for a sold item and the price paid the supplier for it.

GROSS REQUIREMENT   The requirement for a particular component—not including any inventory of the component on hand.

GROSS TON (G.T.)   A long ton; the gross ton is 2,240 pounds.

GROSS TONNAGE   The term gross tonnage applies to the vessel and not to the cargo. The gross tonnage is determined by dividing the cubic feet of the vessel's closed m space by 100. Therefore, a vessel ton IS 100 cubic feet.

GROSS TON-MILE   The movement of a ton of transportation equipment and contents a distance of one mile.

GROSS TON-MILES PER TRAIN-MILE   The total gross ton-miles divided by the total train-miles, not including gross ton-miles of locomotive and tender unless so specified.

GROSS WAREHOUSE SPACE   Length times width of building—measured from outside wall to outside wall. Expressed as square footage.

GROSS WEIGHT   This is the weight of both the container and its contents, as well as the material that might be used for packing.

GROUND EFFECT MACHINE   This is more commonly known as air-cushion vehicle, hovercraft, etc. It travels on a cushion of air over land, water, swamp, mud, sand, etc., with only a few inches of elevation.

GROUND HANDLING SERVICE   Airline term for firms that offer services in and around an airport. Examples are companies that provide luggage handling, lounge management, plane provisioning, etc. for airlines. See HANDLING AGENT.

GROUNDING   A general order to stop flying. It may be a voluntary move, or an order from the Federal Aviation Agency. Usually the result of conviction of malfunctioning aircraft.

GROUND LEADER   Leader of a group or crew while working with them. Responsible for the details of assignments received from proper authority.

GROUND LEVEL DOOR   Overhead door which leads from the warehouse to the ground level outside the warehouse.

GROUND STORAGE   The storing of shipments on the ground. More commonly called outside storage.

GROUND SWELL   Undulations following the passage over shoaling water and proximity to the bottom.

GROUP   Several points considered together for rate-making purposes.

GROUPAGE   A consolidation service, putting small shipments into containers for shipment.

GROUP FARE   A reduced or promotional fare offered to a group of people that will fly together under certain conditions.

GROUP RATES   Group rates are established on two different patterns: 1) through the use of base points with distance scales determining different rate groups, and

2) under the commodity rate structures which group competitive producers and manufacturers in a geographic area which will receive the same rate. Under the second system, all salt fields throughout the country may be grouped together geographically, and a shipment from any salt mine to a destination would receive the same rate. Group rates tend to encourage dispersion of manufacturing facilities, and thus have long range beneficial environmental impact.

GUARANTEED LOAN   An aircraft purchase loan guaranteed by a sponsoring government agency.

GUARANTEED RATE   1) a contract carriage rate; 2) an annual volume rate.

GUIDE BOOK   A tariff containing instructions for waybilling and routing

GUILDER   Name of currency of the Netherlands.

GUM BALL MACHINE   Slang term for the rotating emergency light on a vehicle.

GUNTER'S SCALE   A two-foot ruler with logarithmic scale on one side and trigonometric functions on the other.

GUNWALE   The deck space between the outboard side of the hold and outside of the barge.

GYPSY   An unregulated trucking operation which consists of a self-owned vehicle, operated wherever traffic is available. It may take the form of a lease of the tractor, or tractor and trailer for single trips. Sometimes it takes the form of a buy and sell operation, under prearranged contracting.

HHHH

HAND CAR   The small maintenance car which is moved by hand power and employed in railroad track inspection and repair work.

HAND HELD TERMINAL   A data entry device that is small and can be carried and used in one hand. A movable scanner.

HANDICAPPED ACCESS   Architectural and facilities term indicating that persons with disabilities can access a facility or transportation equipment.

HANDLING AGENT   A firm that performs on behalf of a client firm, usually in the name of the client firm. Example: an airline based at its hub would perform services for another airline that has flights land at that airport once a day. As far as a passenger is concerned, the handling agent often has the appearance and uniforms of the airline upon which they will fly.

HANDLING AISLE   An aisle used to gain access from one area of the warehouse to another.

HANDLING CHARGE   A charge for ordinary labor and duties incidental to the final point, but not including unloading or loading of the cars, vehicles, etc.

HANDLING COSTS   The cost involved in transferring, preparing and otherwise accessing inventory.

HANDLING FIRM   See HANDLING AGENT

HAND-TO-MOUTH BUYING   The practice of making periodic purchases in lot sizes that are smaller than the usage or demand rate within the firm. Typically done in periods of dropping prices and/or when the firm seeks to work off inventories. Economic forecasters watch for increasing use of hand-to-mouth buying as a sign of a possible upcoming recession.

HARBOR   A place of security or haven for vessels.

HARBOR MASTER   An officer having charge of the berthing of ships.

HARD CURRENCY   A currency that is freely traded, widely circulated, and holds a value throughout the world. Traditionally the hardest of the hard currencies of the world are those of Germany, Japan, Switzerland, the United Kingdom and the United States.

HARDWARE   The equipment and physical components that comprise a computer system.

HARMONIZE/HARMONISE   The conscious act by a firm to reduce the number of similar items that it consumes or uses in its supply chain. An example would be a firm that produces a certain machine that requires 32 different fasteners (nuts, bolts, screws, etc.). By harmonization, it might reduce the total different number of them that are used to a lower number thereby providing purchasing economies and other efficiencies. Similar term: STANDARDIZATION.

HARMONIZED CUSTOMS CODES   Arrangements made between countries to standardize the descriptors used for the names of products that are imported. This is a great simplification benefit to the buying/selling and shipping communities.

HARMONIZED TARIFF SYSTEM   Also referred to as HTS, this is a standardized customs descriptor system that is being implemented between the United States and Mexico.

HARTER LAW   The Harter Law was passed in 1893 and established the rules for governing vehicles and their cargoes for clearing ports of the United States.

HATCH   The opening in the vessel's deck to enable merchandise to be lowered in the hold, or the opening through which grain may be placed in hopper cars or ice in refrigerator cars of railroads.

HAULAGE   British term for transportation of goods.

HAULIER   British term for transportation company of goods.

HAULING POST-HAULS   Driving an empty truck or trailer.

HAVEN   A place of shelter and safety. A sheltered anchorage for ships.

HAZARDOUS COMMODITY   Material that may be dangerous to move or to store. It may be subject to explosion, burning, or have damaging fumes. These commodities are subject to safety regulations while being transported. American regulations may be found in Title 49, Code of Federal Regulations, Parts 100–199.

HAZARDOUS MATERIALS   A substance or material which has been determined by a government body to be capable of posing an unreasonable risk to health, safety, and property when transported in commerce, and which has been so designated.

HEADACHE RACK   An extension of a holding rack over the cab from the trailer. Normally used for holding pipe or such freight.

HEADER BAR   A protective device placed at the front end of the flat bottom trailer which stops freight from inching forward.

HEADER RECORD   A record of constant, common, identifying or other information for data which will follow.

HEAP SYSTEM   An old term for a method of filing tariffs whereby schedules issued by various agents or carriers are segregated and kept in labeled boxes, drawers, or pigeonholes.

HEARING   The process by a regulatory authority which provides an opportunity for interested parties to present evidence concerning a particular case. This meeting and presentation is referred to as a hearing. A carrier rate conference may also conduct a hearing to receive evidence of interested parties. The regulatory authority will designate a time and a place for the hearing which will provide the sufficiency of evidence necessary for rendering a decision.

HEATED CAR SERVICE   Warming a car to keep perishable freight from freezing; sometimes performed by caretakers who accompany the shipment.

HEAVY LIFTS   When freight is too heavy to be handled by the ship's regular tackle, special equipment is used and a heavy-lift charge is assessed.

HEAVY RAIL   As distinct from LIGHT RAIL, or trolley transit, heavy rail is standard railroad transportation of people in commuter and transit systems. Heavy rail systems typically allow for higher speeds and larger quantities of passenger loads in any given train.

HEDGING   1) Purchasing. Purchasing goods in advance of known production needs so as to acquire them at today's low price in face of an expected price increase or commodity shortage. These goods are not earmarked for current use, but they are held as a price advantage or shortage cushion. 2) Finance. The act of committing to an international transaction for a specified price in the currency of another country and at the same time transacting a hedge contract for the currency of that country at or near the delivery date. The effect is to shield the buying firm (and selling firm, if performed by it) against shifts in currency values in the interim.

HELICOPTER VIEW   A general term for ascertaining the general idea of a concept. From the ability to see the macro-level of a complex situation.

HEURISTIC   The process of solving problems by evaluating each step in the process. A search for satisfactory, rather than optimal solutions. It restricts the number of alternatives to be considered by trial and error considerations.

HIDDEN COSTS   Those costs in logistics which are almost impossible to determine without a cost allocation process from the data available in conventional financial statements are commonly referred to as hidden costs. They are hidden because they are usually a part of a more general cost. Examples are manager's time, inventory opportunity costs, or interest costs over the period.

HIGH CUBE   A truck body with greater than average cubic space. It is usually constructed with thin walls and low floors.

HIGH CUBE CAR   A rail car with dimensions larger than a regular box car, such cars are either longer or higher enabling them to carry light bulky products or one more tier of palletized goods.

HIGH IRON   Mainline railroad track. Often named so due to the heaviest and strongest (and taller) rails being used on the mainlines where trains carry the heaviest and fastest movements.

HIGH OCCUPANCY VEHICLE Any car or van that carries two, three or more persons that are allowed to use special highway lanes as an encouragement of car pooling.

HIGH SEAS The unenclosed waters of the ocean outside the boundaries of any country.

HIGH STREET A general term for premium priced goods that are available through specialty and department stores.

HIGH TOUCH A customer service term indicating that a certain product or customer requires special and constant attention. This often requires a high cost of resource commitment by the seller firm.

HIGHWAYS A public road; a course or path on land or sea which everyone has the right to use, whether free access or by toll.

HOBO Tractor that is transferred from one terminal to another.

HOG LAW A law in the United States requiring train crews to leave the train after a maximum of 16 hours.

HOLD-DOWNS Those product or transportation rates on commodities that are not increased in a general rate increase.

HOLDER One in whose possession a bill or note may be.

HOLD ORDER A directive to interrupt or terminate certain operations, pending a change in the process.

HOLD POINTS A term applied to stocking points for semi-finished inventory.

HOLD TRACK It is common practice to place rail cars on a side track pending disposition. When orders are received from shippers or receivers, the car is moved from the hold track toward its originally intended destination.

HOLE A siding into which one train enters so that another may pass. Term often used, "in the hole."

HOME CAR A railroad car that belongs to another railroad as contrasted to a foreign car. A home car is a car operating on the track of its owner.

HOME DELIVERY Transportation term for shipments that are delivered to homes as opposed to businesses.

HOME LINE This term is used in connection with rail cars and has reference to the line owning the car.

HOME ROAD Used in connection with car service to denote the road that is owner or lessee of a car, or upon which the home of a private car is located.

HOME ROUTE   Railroad from which foreign freight car was originally received.

HOME SHOPPING   The term for home based ordering by the consumer and delivery directly to them by either retailers, brand manufacturers or others.

HONEYCOMBING   Any designated inventory holding area that has a current holding of goods that occupy less than its full capacity. An aspect of storage which from partial depletion of a lot results in the inability to utilize the entire cubic capacity of a given amount of floor area.

HOOD LIFTER   A mechanic.

HOPPER BODY   A freight carrying body that discharges through the bottom without need for tilting the entire trailer or rail car.

HOPPER CAR   A car which moves bulk dry freight and usually unloads through gravity by vents on the underside is termed a hopper car. Some hopper cars have an open top while others have closed tops.

HOPPER CAR, COVERED   A hopper car with a permanent roof and roof hatches, which has a bottom opening for unloading for the purpose of carrying cement or other bulky commodities.

HORIZONTAL INTEGRATION   The ownership under a single corporate entity of competing industrial operations on the same channel level. Usually this is thought of as involving ownership under a single company of competing producers. It may involve product or service producers. It is to be distinguished from vertical integration since it is common ownership of comparable business operations. The purpose of horizontal integration is control of the market, while the purpose of vertical integration is independence through control of producing institutions serving inbound and outbound movements.

HORSE   A power unit—one horse-power.

HORSE LIGHT   A spotlight placed on the hood or otherwise. It may be used to find open range livestock.

HORSEPOWER   The process of raising 33,000 pounds one foot per minute is one horsepower. Horsepower may also be measured by raising 550 pounds one foot per second. This is equivalent to 746 watts.

HORSE VAN BODY   A special vehicle used for transporting valuable horses or other livestock.

HOSE REEL   A portable carriage on which to store a fire hose.

HOSTLER   Truck terminal yard vehicle used to move trailers from one spot to another.

HOT LOAD   A rush shipment.

HOUSEHOLD GOODS   Furniture and house furnishings. When transported by transportation companies does not include such articles as silverware, valuable paintings, etc., except upon special contracts.

HOUSE TRACK   A track alongside or entering a freight house, and used for cars receiving or delivering freight at the house.

HTML   Hypertext Mark Up Language. The programming language of the internet that permits cross platform display of text and images.

HUB   A central transfer point in a transportation company's route structure; hubs are served by and serve spoke routes to outlying points.

HULL POLICY   An insurance policy covering the main hull and structure of a ship.

HULL SMOOTHNESS   The degree by which the hull of a ship is free of barnacles, etc. that obstruct flow of water and act against efficient ship movement through the water.

HUMP   This is a term applicable to a certain type of railroad classification yard. Cars are pushed up a hill and released one-by-one over the hump, and switches are set for their downhill gravity movement to selected outbound tracks. Each destination track contains a set of cars designated for subsequent outbound trains with different destinations. It is a gravity form of rail car sortation that obviates the need for locomotive powered sortation.

HUMP YARD   A switching yard with an elevated track or hump over which cars are pushed by a switching locomotive to travel by gravity to classification tracks or other designated points. See Retarder Yard.

HUNDRED MILE COFFEE   Strong coffee.

HUNDREDWEIGHT (CWT.)   In ocean-freight parlance the hundredweight is equivalent to 112 pounds, or $1/20$th of a ship's (long) ton of 2,240 pounds. In American rail and motor transportation, however, it is 100 pounds, or $1/20$th of a short ton.

HUSBANDAGE   The charge for attending the ship by an owner or agent for a commission is called husbandage.

HYPOTHECATE   In the shipping industry, the process of borrowing from the bank on the value of a consignment of goods by pledging the shipping documents as security.

IIII

ICE ALLOWANCE   Found in pulpwood rail moves and some coal, an allowance for the weight of ice/snow on the lading so that it is not counted as part of the product weight when computing freight charges.

ICE CLAUSE   A clause in ship chartering agreements that permits a captain to leave a harbor ahead of time if it is threatened by icing up.

ICING   This was a practice more commonly used in years gone by in which ice was placed in bunkers of a refrigerator car either prior to shipment or while in transit for the purpose of preserving the commodities.

IDLE-HOUR SYSTEM   A method of furnishing empty cars to coal mines whereby the allotment is reduced or increased depending on the state of idleness existing in comparison.

IDLER   This term is applied to a flat car which is used for the movement of commodities of a bulky nature that extend beyond the limits of the car. The article of shipment does not rest on the car but overhangs it.

IMMIGRATION PROCEDURES   Those official actions undertaken by a nation's immigration personnel in the checking and clearance of persons attempting to enter that nation.

IMMUNITY   Exemption from any duty, office or tax; freedom from natural or usual liability. Exempt from punishment for evidence rendered.

IMPLICIT COSTS   A term for considering a cost that is not captured in the traditional accounting system. It is a surrogate cost. The best example is an opportunity cost of inventory. If a company has $10,000 in inventory goods, then it might be seen as having an implicit cost at 10% of $1,000 per year.

IMPLIED WARRANTY OF FITNESS   A warranty that involves the buyer asking the seller for advice in the selection of a particular item. Upon the seller making the selection, the buyer can expect that the item purchased will fit their intended need.

IMPLIED WARRANTY OF MERCHANTABILITY   A warranty that states that the goods sold are fit for the ordinary purpose for which they are packaged, labeled, and sold. Example: a household light bulb would not have an implied warranty of merchantability for when it is used on the deck of an Arctic ice cutter.

IMPLIED WARRANTY OF TITLE   A warranty that states that the items sold possess legal title; buyer is entitled to acquire and use them without fear of patent infringement or any other encumbrance.

IMPORTANT MARINE RISKS   The possibility of loss in ocean trade from these possible contingencies: (a) Loss of vessel through standing, sinking, fire or collision; (b) loss or damage caused by shifting cargo, by seawater from bad weather, by fire or flood on shore before loading or after discharging, (c) theft or pilferage on board or while loading, or awaiting loading; (d) breakage from any cause; (e) war risks afloat or ashore.

IMPORT BROKER   A person who acts as an intermediary in the acquiring of goods overseas. The broker acts for a domestic buyer in the purchasing, movement, and landing of goods. The broker receives a fee for this service.

IMPORT CREDIT   A foreign buyer establishes credit in the country where a purchase is to be made in a bank in the country of purchase. The bank issues a letter of credit to the foreign shipper.

IMPORT MERCHANT   A person who acts for a domestic person who seeks to acquire goods from overseas. The merchant purchases the goods and imports them into the country. Once the goods have landed in the country, a transaction takes place between the import merchant and the buyer. The goods were always destined for the buyer.

IMPORT RATE   A specific domestic inland rate for traffic that has been imported.

IMPORT TRUST RECEIPT   An instrument executed by an importer, who wishes to dispose or use the goods during the interval of their arrival and maturity of the draft. It arrives the bank direct control of the goods or their proceeds, and enables the importer to effect final release of the consignment from the steamship company and custom house.

IMPOST   A tax on imported goods.

IMPROVEMENT PLANS   Any set of steps or actions that are designed to bring about an improvement in a process, activity, system, or firm.

IMPUTED COSTS   Similar to opportunity costs; often a charge levied in budgets against the fixed assets used by a division.

IN APPARENT GOOD ORDER   A shipment not showing any loss or damage, though subsequent examination might find some.

INBOUND LOGISTICS   Those activities involved with bringing goods and services to the firm for its subsequent manufacture or consumption. It generally includes purchasing, warehousing, materials, and incoming transportation.

INCENTIVE CONTRACT   A purchase agreement whereby the supplier is paid more for accomplishing some positive act within the terms of the contract. Examples are early completion or producing machinery with improved performance.

INCENTIVE PRICING   Any pricing scheme that is designed to encourage a customer to purchase more and/or to remain loyal to the supplier.

INCENTIVE PROGRAM   Any pricing and/or other actions that are designed to encourage a customer to purchase more and/or to remain loyal to the supplier.

INCENTIVE RATE   A general term for any low rate on lots heavier than the normal truckload or carload weight bracket so as to induce heavier loadings by shippers.

INCIDENTAL DAMAGES   Damages incurred other than to the physical loss or damage to goods involved; examples are overhead, lost cash opportunity employee tome, and filing costs that are not generally recouped in the claims process.

INCIDENTAL TO AIRCRAFT EXEMPTION   A motor carrier term signifying that pick up and/or delivery moves prior or subsequent to airline haul is exempt from ICC operating regulation; by 1980 all air freight moved in this manner is exempt while some passenger transportation prior or subsequent to air moves is subject to ICC jurisdiction.

INCLINE   An inland tract on a river bank at a protected landing place, with adjustable apron and cradle for connecting to the track on a car float for transfer of cars.

INCLINED PLANE   A transport mechanism designed to lift loads and passengers up steep sides of hills and mountains. It typically consists of a cable mechanism and a balancing of upward and downward vehicles.

INCO 1990 TERMS   International transportation and selling terms as developed by the International Chamber of Commerce in 1990. A listing of the terms is included in the Appendix.

INCREASING COST   The term increasing cost does not have exactly the same meaning as its usual economic definition. Whereas it usually is closely associated, if not synonymous with, variable cost it has a slightly different meaning when used in logistics management. Those costs which increase with an increase in the volume of shipment (as contrasted to volume of production) are increasing logistics costs. It is important to observe that increasing costs increase per unit—meaning per hundredweight. Obviously, practically all logistics costs increase with an increase in the volume of shipment (commonly referred to as the cellular flow) are inventory-in-storage and average warehouse costs. These costs increase directly and proportionately with an increase in the volume of shipment. Demurrage is also an increasing cost but it does not increase in a linear pattern, since the demurrage rate increases at an increasing rate for all time after 48 hours of free time.

INCREMENTAL COST   The extra costs incurred by the firm from additional units of output or service.

INDEMNITY   An indemnity is a guarantee against loss. It represents a compensation for the loss for damage which has been sustained.

INDENT   An indent is a comprehensive order transferred from a foreign buyer to a shipper, buying agent, commission house, etc. for the purpose of making a purchase. An open indent provides for the choice of the seller at the discretion of the house that handles the order. However, a closed indent would identify the firm with which the business must be transacted.

INDEPENDENT ACTION   A rate publication action by a carrier in rate bureau tariffs that takes place without the vote or discussion of the entire rate bureau; until 1980 independent action typically only occurred when a carrier rate proposal was turned down by the bureau membership and the carrier still wished to publish a rate on its own behalf.

INDEPENDENT DEMAND   An experience in sales or other demands in which one customer is independent of any other.

INDEPENDENT LINE   A line not dependent or supported by or governed by other lines.

INDEPENDENT PURCHASING ORGANIZATION (IPO)   An outside group from the firm or organization that performs purchasing services for it and others.

INDEPENDENT SYSTEM OPERATORS   Nonprofit controllers of electricity traffic from one utility to the next.

INDEX PRICING   Pricing that is set according to some industry pricing index of the products. Some prices are set as a percent off of that index price.

INDIFFERENCE VOLUME   Wherever a reduction in price is quoted for a minimum volume of purchase, transportation, or otherwise, an indifference volume may be computed. The indifference volume is that volume at which it is indifferent so far as total costs are concerned whether the total charge was computed on the basis of the less than quantity volume at the less than minimum volume price or at the volume price times the minimum volume. The computed indifference volume is the initial volume in the indifference volume zone.

INDIRECT COMPETITION   Rivalry between carriers, localities, commodities, etc. For example: A direct route between points in competition for a circuitous route.

INDIRECT SAVINGS   Any savings that might accrue in addition or in place of savings in price reductions from suppliers. One indirect savings might be less holding cost due to the supplier holding the inventory until needed by the firm.

INDUSTRIAL   Pertains to a productive industry. In transportation matters it signifies the difference between transportation companies and manufacturing industries.

INDUSTRIAL CARRIER   When a short railroad is owned or operated by one or more companies for their exclusive use, and does not serve as a common carrier, it is known as an industrial carrier. The industrial carrier has been known to serve likewise as a common carrier, however.

INDUSTRIAL MARKETING   Marketing and selling to or by primarily industrial manufacturing firms.

INDUSTRIAL TRACKS   Rail tracks which service mines, mills, or specific industries, and are not classified as branch lines, are called industrial tracks. The industrial track belongs to the industry and no rent can be charged for its use by a carrier.

INDUSTRY STANDARD SPECIFICATION   A specification that is based upon an industry standard such as the specification for egg sizes in the agricultural sector.

INELASTIC DEMAND   Demand for a good or service that is not very sensitive to the price charged.

INFESTATION   The spoilage of merchandise through the presence of rodents, birds or animal remains.

INFLUENCERS   Among a group of people or departments in a firm that is making a purchase decision, influencers are those who have some input into the final decision as to which supplier or set of specifications are selected.

INFORMAL COMPLAINT   A complaint made by letter or other writing to the I.C.C. protesting a violation of the Act.

INFORMATION INTEGRITY   The accuracy of information that is maintained when it is transmitted or converted. The process is said to maintain the integrity of the information.

INFORMATION NETWORK   Any information system, typically electronic, designed to link different groups.

INFORMATION RICH   A generic term for special bar codes and other data capturing devices that contain much data about the items it is measuring.

INFORMATION SHARING   A purchasing term for the process of sharing data with suppliers about the firm with the intent of having the supplier being capable of providing value added benefit to it.

INFORMATION STRUCTURE   Also referred to as information architecture, this term applies to generic system design. Up to the 1980s info structures were centralized, in the 1990s they were distributed, and from the late 1990s and on many are being built that are network centric.

INFOMEDIARIES   A firm in a web based network that acts to capture and disseminate information and contacts in an efficient manner for both the sellers and the buyers. These are web sites that are useful for finding mortgages, insurance, etc. In some cases they receive a part of the revenue of any transaction that might occur.

INFRASTRUCTURE   The generic term for the physical assets that are needed for economic activity to take place. In traditional ways, it is the ports, airports, telecommunications systems, highways, railroads, etc. that provide a means for production, trade, and commerce. In an electronic system, it is the networks, linkages, servers, and trunk lines.

INHERENT NATURE OF THE GOODS   A freight claim related term indicating that the goods involved have a potential problem of deteriorating while en route, particularly a problem with vegetables and fruits.

IN-HOUSE CONTRACT CARRIER   Term for a contract carrier that is subsidiary or division of a shipper firm. Many private carrier operations were turned into in-house contract carriers upon deregulation in the early 1980s.

IN HOUSE SUPPLIER   A supplier that is on the property performing functions for the firm in addition to providing its products and services.

INITIAL CARRIER   The carrier which receives the shipment and is first in a joint carrier operation is identified as the initial carrier.

INLAND BILL   A bill exchange or draft drawn upon a person in the same country.

INLAND CARRIER   The carrier performing the act of carriage on the domestic, export and import traffic between ports and inland points.

INLAND WATERWAYS CORPORATION ACT   This act was passed by the United States Congress on June 3, 1924. It provided for the creation of an inland waterway corporation. The purpose of the corporation was to operate government owned domestic waterway services. These services might involve canals, rivers, or coastal movements.

IN LINE DIGITAL IMAGING   A filling and packaging technology whereby product is specifically identified for filling into particular packages on a production line and the package then has printing applied for the customer and included contents. It is a form of flexible packaging and customer fulfillment.

INNOVATION CHAIN   A form of supply chain that is designed to attain innovation from suppliers and other input sources for the benefit of the firm's own innovation processes. This often consists of OPPORTUNITY SOURCING and long term relationships with suppliers.

INNOVATION FUNNEL   A general method for developing and evaluating innovation for a firm. It starts with the capturing of many ideas and the gradual filtering, elimination, and refinement of ideas until one or more innovated products, services, or enhancements are launched in the market.

INNOVATION PROCESS   The general term for the process a firm uses to identify, define, formulate, and launch innovative products and services.

INNOVATION RATE   The pace at which a firm innovates its products and services.

IN PLANT   A supplier employee who performs manufacturing or other processes on the firm's own site.

INSIDE MARGIN   A fast moving consumer goods industry term for the profit or margin a retailer obtains from exacting SLOTTING ALLOWANCE fees from the brand manufacturers. See also GROSS MARGIN.

INSOURCE   To bring a product, service, activity, process, or asset back into the firm's ownership and control from it being previously outsourced. This sometimes happens when the firm identifies that it is something that can provide competitive advantage and it seeks to control and develop it, or it will sometimes be seen when the outsource firms are no longer competitive in their service offering to the firm.

INSPECTION AND RATING OF A VESSEL   When marine insurance is place on a vessel, the extent of the risk must be assessed. The American Bureau of Shipping rates the vessel through inspection. A-1 for twenty years or A-1 for sixteen years, would be examples of a rating placed by the U.S. Steamship Bureau.

INSPECTION BUREAU   An organization maintained by the carriers for the purpose of seeing that commodities presented for shipment are properly packed and meet the requirements and rules of the governing classification or schedule.

INSPECTION CERTIFICATE   When the Department of Agriculture issues a document to exporters of meat products or livestock destined to various countries, it is called an inspection certificate. This is required by the customs regulations of the United States as well as by the foreign counselor's rules. A certificate issued by an independent agent or firm attesting the quality and/or quantity of the merchandise being shipped. Such a certificate is usually required in a L/C for commodity shipments.

INSTALLMENT SHIPMENTS   Successive shipments are permitted under letters of credit. Usually, they must take place within a given period of time. If not shipped within that period, the credit ceases to be available automatically unless otherwise authorized in the L/C.

INSTANTANEOUS REORDER   A system that places a reorder for an item once a current one is consumed or sold by the firm. This is an automatic replenishment by the supplier.

INSTRUMENTALITIES   Implements to carry out an activity. In transportation same includes boats, barges, cranes, elevators, etc.

INSULATED VAN BODY   A van body designed to protect from temperature changes and thereby used for moving commodities under controlled temperature.

INSURANCE   An insurance policy or certificate normally covers the shipments of merchandise from the time they leave the warehouse at the shipping point until they reach the destination point named in the policy or certificate. This type of coverage is called "warehouse to warehouse" and includes all modes of transportation necessary to deliver the goods to the point of destination. The insurance policy or certificate should be dated prior to, or on the same day as, the date shown on the shipping documents.

INSURANCE, ALL RISK   This type of insurance offers the shipper the broadest coverage available covering against all losses that may occur in transit. To establish a claim, it is not necessary for the assured to prove what caused shipped and that the loss was not due to any inherent vice of the goods. Exclusions: Losses arising from war, civil disturbances, and spoilage.

INSURANCE BROKER   One who negotiates insurance contracts between the insurer and the insured.

INSURANCE, FREE OF PARTICULAR OF AVERAGE   This type of insurance covers losses or damages arising only from marine perils: sinking, stranding, fire, or collision. It is the most limiting clause and is, thus, least expensive.

INSURANCE FREIGHT   Insurance that covers a shipment for damage en route.

INSURANCE, GENERAL AVERAGE   This clause covers damages or losses arising from maritime ventures for all parties shipping or owning. It covers partial losses resulting from voluntary sacrifice made on the part of ship or cargo to prevent the loss of lives, whole ship, or cargo. The voluntary sacrifice includes jettisoning, cutting away, or partial flooding of the holds. In one event, the master beached a sinking ship thinking it was sand but, in reality, it was mud. The loss incurred far exceeded the master's expectations and thus it was covered and shared by all parties.

INSURANCE POLICY   A contract between the insurer and the insured, to cover loss of life, injury to person or damage to property.

INSURANCE, WITH AVERAGE CLAUSE   This type of clause covers merchandise if the damage amounts to three percent or more of the insured value of the package or cargo. However, if the vessel burns, sinks, collides, or gets sunk, all losses, partial or otherwise, are fully covered. The word "average" in marine insurance is used to describe partial damage or partial loss.

INTACT SEALS   Seals that have not been broken or tampered with. (Car Seals)

INTANGIBLE ASSETS   Those assets of the firm that are not in physical or financial form. Example is goodwill, or the premium that an acquiring firm paid over and above the book value of an acquired firm.

INTEGRATE   A general term for the linkages and coordination that two or more groups undertake in their planning and operations.

INTEGRATED LOGISTICS MANAGEMENT   Management and control of logistics functions of a firm as a whole rather than optimization of each individual group (traffic, warehousing, inventory, etc.).

INTEGRATED SOFTWARE   A general term for software that links multiple management functions.

INTEGRATED SUPPLIER   An outside company that takes over an internal activity inside the firm. A common example is a former wholesaler of maintenance and/or office supplies that now operates this function inside a client firm.

INTEGRATED SUPPLY AGREEMENT (ISA)   The contract that applies to a relationship with an INTEGRATED SUPPLIER.

INTELLECTUAL PROPERTY   The ownership and rights to concepts, patents, software, music, visual content, copyrights and other information.

INTELLIGENT TRANSPORTATION   A general term for transportation systems that respond to demands rather than rote programmed route and schedule systems. An example would be scheduling according to real time demands.

INTER   (Latin) Between.

INTERCHANGE   The process of passing freight from one carrier to another between lines is called interchange.

INTERCHANGE POINT   When a joint movement involves more than one carrier, the location where transfer of freight between carriers takes place is known as the interchange point.

INTERCHANGE TRACK   A track on which cars are delivered or received as between railways.

INTERCOASTAL   As contrasted to coastal water operations, intercoastal refers to water transportation serviced between coasts, such as between the Atlantic and Pacific coasts.

INTERCORPORATE HAULING   Private truck operation whereby fleet handles movements for other subsidiaries of a parent company.

INTEREST CLAUSE   A clause in the face of a draft instructing a foreign bank as to either a) the party responsible for the goods at particular points in the movement, and/or b) responsible for financial charges.

INTEREST ON UNAMORTIZED INVESTMENT   The investment cost on the unpaid balance is the interest on unamortized investment. It is a contract debt that requires payment. It is computed on the basis of the contractual interest rate times the unpaid balance. It is not to be confused with the prorated payment of the loan.

INTERFACE   The contacts that exists when two or more systems or groups are placed in touch with each other. Example: two firms that form an alliance will have many interfaces in the form of their respective groups of innovation, logistics, purchasing/selling, accounting, etc.

INTERLINE   Between two or more transportation lines.

INTERLINE ACCOUNT   The process of reporting a settlement of a shipment and apportioning the revenue by the destination carrier to the other participating carriers on the basis of a published division of rates is referred to as an interline account.

INTERLINE DIVISIONS   The basis upon which the revenue derived from a through rate from origin-to-destination is divided between two or more carriers participating in the haul.

INTERLINE FORWARD   Railroad term for traffic that is originated by one railroad, interchanged to another for ultimate delivery to the consignee.

INTERLINE FREIGHT   Tonnage passing over the lines of two or more carriers. The interchange is termed an interline movement. Freight moving from point of origin to destination over the lines of two or more transportation lines.

INTERLINE RECEIVED   Term for shipments that are received by a railroad from another carrier for delivery to the consignee.

INTERLINE WAYBILL   A waybill covering the movement of freight over two or more transportation lines.

INTERMEDIATE CARRIER   The carrier that serves to bridge between two other carriers in a three carrier movement would be the intermediate carrier.

INTERMEDIATE CLAUSE   A provisional clause in a tariff for rates to points not listed therein but en route and intermediate to points that are listed.

INTERMEDIATE COMMERCE   The commerce of a country which passes through it.

INTERMEDIATE POINT   Any point that is located on the line of a carrier that is intermediate to the point of origin and destination would be an intermediate point.

INTERMEDIATE RATE   One of the factors used in making up a through combination rate.

INTERMODAL CONTAINERS   Containers designed to be carried by more than one mode of transportation.

INTERMODAL SERVICE   Through transportation movement involving more than one mode, e.g., rail-motor, motor-air, or rail-water.

INTERNET SERVICE PROVIDER (ISP)   A firm that holds itself out to be a linkage into the Internet for individuals and businesses.

INTERNAL ASSESSMENT   A purchasing term for determining and evaluating the needs and conditions of internal groups for which it will obtain goods and services.

INTERNAL CUSTOMER   A quality field term that views other departments in a flow linkage as customers for whom a group must serve as though it is an external customer. The intent of this focus is hopefully to improve the overall performance of the firm.

INTERNATIONAL SOURCING   A logistics term used by some European firms for the process of ordering and receiving goods from company factories for a sales and logistics group's further flow of them to company customers.

INTERNET   An electronic linkage of computers and servers in the world that is open for access to anyone with a connection to it.

INTERNET SERVICE PROVIDER   A local firm through which one can obtain a connection to the Internet.

INTER-PLANT SWITCHING   Industrial switching which involves rail carrier switching services within a plant or industry.

INTERNAL REVENUE   Government revenue derived from domestic sources.

INTERNATIONAL COMMERCE   The exchange of objects between buyers and sellers in two different countries.

INTERSTATE COMMERCE ACT, LATER, THE REVISED INTERSTATE COMMERCE ACT (U.S.)   An act of Congress (1887) which regulated the rates, rules, and practices of rail transportation lines engaged in interstate traffic (Part I; regulates motor vehicles for hire (Part II—referred to as the Motor Carrier Act of 1935); regulates common and contract water carriers operating in domestic trade (Part III); and regulates freight-forwarding companies (Part IV—referred to as the Freight Forwarders Act). It was recodified in 1978 to the Revised Interstate Commerce Act. The Interstate Commerce Commission is no longer in existence.

INTERSTATE COMMERCE COMMISSION   The agent of Congress of the United States designated to implement the Interstate Commerce Act. Consists of eleven members. The I.C.C. had considerable control over the economic actions of the common carriers under its jurisdiction. It was founded in 1887 and no longer is in existence.

INTERSTATE TRAFFIC   Traffic which moves across state lines in the course of a transportation movement from origin to destination is usually referred to as interstate traffic. By contrast, intrastate traffic has origin and destination within the same state.

INTER-TERMINAL (SWITCHING)   An interchange of cars, the movement of which is confined to the switching limits of the same station or switching district.

INTER-URBAN   The uniting of or belonging to two cities.

INTERVENE   To participate and take action in proceedings started by others. This takes the form of an intervening petition, and the one participating is an intervener.

IN THE CLEAR   A railroad term for a clear block ahead.

IN THE ROUGH   A term stating that an article is not in a state of complete manufacture. It is an unfinished product.

IN TRANSIT   En route between point of origin and destination.

IN TRANSIT PRIVILEGES   Changes in degree of manufacture, treatment and other accessional services provided for in the tariffs on commodities between points of origin and destination. Involves cleaning, dipping, elevation, fabrication, creosoting and milling.

IN TRANSIT RATES   Also referred to as transit rates. Ordinarily a local rate is charged into the transit point and the finished or semi-finished product which is forwarded to the ultimate destination is charged on the basis of the balance of the through rate applicable on the finished product from the point of origin to the point of destination. Because of the two moves and the cost of switching, billing, etc., many rail carriers started in the 1980s to discourage in transit services by offering better no-frill through rates from origin to destination.

INTRALINE TRANSFER   Transfer of freight or passenger between two vehicles and routes of a single carrier.

INTRAMODAL COMPETITION   Competition faced by a carrier from carriers of the same mode; e.g., motor-motor.

INTRANET   A closed net and email system, typically for an individual company.

INTRAPLANT SWITCHING   Switching performed within a plant of any industry.

INTRAPRENEURSHIP   Entrepreneurial behavior that a company person applies inside the firm.

INTRASTATE TRAFFIC   Traffic originating and terminating within a given state and not moving out of the state at any point is intrastate traffic.

INTRINSIC VALUE   The real value of an article. The same regardless of place or person.

INVENTORIED COST PER UNIT   This term is not to be confused with inventory-in-storage costs, which is the interest on the value of the goods stored for the time period they are in storage. Inventoried cost per unit represents the determination of the value for the products. Normally it includes the purchase price and the cost of inbound transportation. For products produced within the company, the standard manufacturing costs are used to establish the value of inventoried products. Since inventoried costs include transportation, the value for a given product at distribution centers will be greater than those at plants. In rare instances, inventoried costs are measured by the incremental value added to the product by moving it from a plant warehouse to a distribution center—but this is a rare interpretation of the term.

INVENTORY   The merchandise a customer has on hand at a warehouse, or a production process has on hand at one end or other of the production line.

INVENTORY CAPITAL COSTS   A component of holding inventory. Includes the value of the inventories assessed at a cost of capital for a period of time.

INVENTORY CARRYING COSTS   There are great variations in the definitions of carrying costs. Generally speaking, carrying costs involve all costs associated with holding goods in storage. As a minimum it should include inventory-in-storage, warehousing, obsolescence, deterioration or spoilage, and labor costs. The computation of the warehousing costs would also include property taxes, warehouse administrative costs, warehouse utility costs, depreciation on warehouse, and operating equipment depreciation, etc.

INVENTORY-IN-PRODUCTION   The capital costs of materials and parts in production (in assembly or manufacturing). Computed by applying the interest rate, times value, times the period of time (percentage of a year) in production.

INVENTORY-IN-STORAGE   The capital costs of materials, parts, supplies and finished products held in inventory for storage purposes in the pre-production, post-production, or in-production channels. Computed by multiplying the interest rate, times the value, times the period of time (percentage of a year) the goods are held in storage.

INVENTORY-IN-TRANSIT   The capital costs of materials, parts, supplies or finished goods en route aboard a transportation carrier (common, contract, or private). Computed by multiplying the interest rate, times the value, times the period of time (percentage of a year) the shipment is en route.

INVENTORY TAIL   When all stock keeping units of a portfolio of inventory is displayed in descending volume order, a typical phenomenon of a PARETO, or 80/20 situation will exist. That is most, or about 80%, of the total volume will be in, say 20% of the units. The remaining units will trail off to small amounts. The many stock keeping units (SKU's) that represent very low volume or demand are referred to as the tail of the inventory. This is the sector of the SKU portfolio that is examined for elimination.

INVENTORY TAX   A tax imposed by some state and local governments upon the value of inventory held on hand; usually consists of a determination of value of the inventory and an assessment of a percent of value.

INVITATION TO BID   When a buying firm sends out REQUESTS FOR BIDS or RFQ's, it is often referred to as an invitation to bid.

INVOICE COST   The computed total cost of receiving, processing and making payment for an invoice that is received from a supplier. This is an administrative costs that many firms are focusing attention upon in the overall quest of reducing the costs of business as well as lowering overhead.

ISDN   A form of high speed data linkage that is provided by telecommunications firms into businesses and homes.

ISO 9000   The primary quality system by the International Standards Organization for firms that produce goods. A 9000 series provides for detailed components of quality assessments that firms can follow in this accreditation process.

ISO 14000   The International Standards Organization quality assessment components involving environmental concerns and pollution control.

ISSUE ASSESSMENT   The basic macro-level assessment of a firm's needs for improvement. As practiced by consulting or quality/process improvement groups, this first assessment identifies the areas for further analysis and improvement.

ISSUING CARRIER   The carrier by which a tariff is published or bill of lading or other documents are issued.

ISSUING DATE   As applied to a tariff or other transportation schedule, the date it was issued, and shown on the title page.

ITEM POPULARITY   Materials handling term indicating how many times each stock keeping unit is demanded in a period.

ITEM SIZE   Materials handling term for cubic dimensions of each stock keeping unit.

IT VISION   The identification of the overall needs and directions for information technology and management that are needed by a firm. In today's practice, this first starts with a focus upon the firm's competitive needs and works back to what configuration of hardware, software, and linkages would best enable the firm to attain its competitive targets. This is distinct from former decades where investments in and changes to information systems were made according to an internal IT Department decision about new technologies that were being introduced by those suppliers.

JJJJ

JACKET   A cover placed over containers in the form of cans and bottles.

JACKING IT AROUND   The process of backing a semi-trailer around a sharp corner.

JELLY BEAN   A generic term for a low cost computer chip that performs simple tasks such as monitoring temperature.

JETSAM   Goods (generally refuse) thrown overboard which have sunk.

JETTISON   The process of throwing cargo overboard when the ship is in danger is an act of jettison. The division of the responsibility among the shippers and ship owner for an act of jettison which is done for the good of all shipments aboard is provided for in the maritime law and insurance.

JETWAY   A telescope-type structure that extends to connect an airline passenger terminal with jet aircraft; serves to protect passengers from weather as well as speed up loading and unloading process.

JIT   See JUST IN TIME.

JIT II   A practice developed by the Bose Corporation whereby duplicate activities between the firm and its suppliers were eliminated largely by having the supplier be an integrated part of the firm's internal supply chain.

JOBBER   A middleman who buys and sells merchandise for others.

JOINT AGENCY TARIFF   A tariff that is published on behalf of two or more transportation rate bureaus applying to traffic moving between the respective geographic jurisdictions.

JOINT AGENT   An official who acts as agent for two or more carriers.

JOINT BOARDS   In administrative regulatory law, when a case involves two or more jurisdictions, a joint board may be established with representatives of each to hear the case and make the decision.

JOINT COST   A cost in one area or function that arises automatically because another took place and cannot be rationally allocated to each one. Example: cost of backhaul in relation to cost of fronthaul. A true costs of each leg of the trip cannot be rationally calculated; it can only be allocated using arbitrary means.

JOINT METRICS   Application of common performance measures that are applied by two or more firms. The metrics might be related to customer service or financial measures.

JOINT RATE   A rate applicable from a point located on one transportation line to a point located on another transportation line. Such rates are made by agreement or arrangement between, and published in a single tariff under proper concurrence of all transportation lines over which the rate applies.

JOINT TARIFF   A tariff containing joint rates.

JOINT TRAFFIC   Freight that is transported by two or more carriers between origin and destination.

JOINT THROUGH RATES   When a transportation movement requires two or more carriers, and the carriers have agreed to a special joint through rate. A single rate is published to cover the interline movement. A distinction should be made between a joint rate and a through rate, however. A joint rate requires a specific written agreement between the carriers to be effective. A through rate is the result of an expressed or implied agreement. A through rate may be a joint rate or a combination of local or joint rates. It is a well established principle that a joint through rate is the only legal rate between the points where it is unconditionally established. It will take precedence over any combination of intermediate rates between the given points. However, a tariff may provide that the aggregate of the intermediate rate is applicable. Under these circumstances, if a combination of several intermediate rates is lower than a through rate, it is applicable.

JOINT VENTURE   Two or more firms invest into a single entity that is designed to provide an outcome of mutual benefit to each of them.

JONES ACT   Act of US legislation that requires ships of American flag to carry goods and persons between two points within the US.

JUMBO (BOOK)   A car record kept on sheets in binders large enough for posting the daily movements of fifty cars for thirty-one days (one month).

JUMPED THE PIN   The loss of the fifth wheel pin on the trailer that is used to couple the tractor to the trailer.

JUNCTION POINT   The connecting point where lines of two or more railroads meet, or where lines of the same company meet, including the connection of a main line and a branch line.

JURISDICTION   The extent or power of exercising judicial authority. Arises when a question of which country, state, or legal body has authority over a situation.

JURISPRUDENCE   The system of laws of a country.

JUSTIFICATION   The act of showing certain acts or deeds to be just or right.

JUST-IN-TIME   The practice of timing inbound inventory flows so that they arrive at the moment they are required resulting in minimized raw material inventories. Requires close links between the firm's forecasting production scheduling and its suppliers and linking carriers.

KKKK

KANBAN   A system of production flow control that uses cards to pull inventories through the plant. Goods are called for as they are needed. The result is minimized raw materials and work-in-process.

KDF CARTONS   Knocked down (flat) carton—unassembled. Permits higher density transportation and/or storage.

KEEL   The chief and lowest support of the whole frame of vessel, extending from stem to stern. Often seen as the "backbone" of the ship.

KEELAGE   The toll or charge that is placed on a vessel entering a port.

KEG   A small barrel. Kegs of different sizes have been used in various industries, whether they be beer, liquid forms of food, or hardware items (nails).

KENTLEDGE   Ballast along the keelson in the form of metal pegs.

KETCH   A two masted, fore and aft rigged vessel, strongly built.

KEY PERFORMANCE INDICATORS (KPI)   Those measures that are important to a firm or various departments or groups. In customer service to a certain customer, the KPI might be deliveries on-time and in-full.

KEY SUPPLIERS   Those suppliers that are deemed to be important to the firm and in which special attention is often applied.

K-FACTOR   An order point calculation in inventory control wherein some of the values apply to a group of items, and thus are calculated once and expressed thereafter as a value.

KICKBACK   Rebate usually given to person who is in position to purchase or order transportation service for his/her firm. Often the term is used negatively for a bribe. Ethics issue.

KICK DOWN   Shift down to lower gears on a truck transmission.

KICK THE DONUTS   Check the tires.

KIDNEY BUSTER   (slang) Hard riding truck.

KILOBYTES (KB)   A cluster thousand computer bytes.

KIRETSU   Japanese firms that are linked operationally and/or financially in order to compete against other sets of firms. It is a form of vertical integration.

KILOGRAM   The metric measure of weight equal to one one hundredth of a metric ton. Equivalent to 2.2046 pounds in the American measurement system.

KITTING   The act of combining components prior to manufacturing so as to smooth and simplify the firm's bill of material and production process. It typically involves having suppliers with lower labor costs subassemble goods prior to use by the firm.

KITTING AREA   An accumulation bin.

KNOCK DOWN (KD)   When articles are taken apart for the purpose of reducing the cubic space of the shipment, it is referred to as a knock down shipment. This is simply a process of disassembling.

KNOT   This represents a nautical mile of 6,082.66 feet. A measurement of speed in sea and air travel amounting to a nautical mile per hour. It may be used to measure the speed of the current.

KNOWN DAMAGE   Damage discovered at the time of delivery, or known before delivery.

KNOWN LOSS   Loss, or the absence of part of the shipment, discovered on delivery, or known before delivery.

KORT NOZZLE   A funnel shaped structure built around the propellers of tow boats to concentrate the water flow to and from the propellers.

KRONE   Stem term for Scandinavian country currencies (Sweden, Norway, and Denmark).

KUROSHIWO   The term applied to the warm northward stream of the Pacific Ocean. It moves northeast along Japan and the coast of China. It provides warm waters of beneficial effect. On the eastern side of the Pacific it is referred to as the Alaska current as it moves southward along the Western coast of North America.

LLLL

LABOR   Heavy working of a vessel at sea due to strong sea conditions.

LACHES   Neglect to do a thing at the proper time.

LADING   The contents of a vessel, car, truck, etc. is the freight lading.

LAKER   Vessels that navigate on the lakes, as contrasted to those that move on the high seas, are called lakers.

LAKE TYPE STEAMER   A steamer whose engines are located at the aft.

LAND BRIDGE   The movement of containers with a ship movement preceding and following a land haul. The land bridge movement is executed to shorten an origin-to-destination distance or time. Example is shipment from Japan to Europe that originally moves across the Pacific Ocean, then across the U.S. by rail, then finally by ship across the Atlantic Ocean for delivery.

LANDED COST   The total cost of producing, storing and transporting a product to the site of consumption or transfer to another port. Also, in a purchasing context: sum of all costs to the firm of acquiring and moving goods to where needed regardless of the department incurring each specific cost.

LANDED WEIGHT   The weight at the point of lading.

LANDFALL   The first sighting of land when coming from the open sea.

LAND GRANT   Land granted or given by the government to a transportation line.

LAND GRANT DEDUCTION   A deduction made from freight charges on government traffic in consideration of a land grant.

LAND-GRANT RATES   Reductions from the published tariffs for government movements on account of promotional land grants made to railroads many decades ago were called land-grant rates. It was estimated that total transportation costs reductions resulting from land-grant rates up to June 30, 1943 amounted to approximately $530 million. This was several times larger than the value of the land-grants at the time they were made.

LANDING CERTIFICATE   A document in which the foreign consignee takes an oath before an American consul or merchant, or two respectable foreign merchants, stating that merchandise described therein has actually been received.

LANDING GEAR   The device that supports the semi-trailer when it is not attached to the tractor.

L&R   Lakeandrail.

LASH   1) The process of binding tightly by rope or otherwise. 2) Acronym for

Lighter Aboard Ship, a system of loaded barges that can be carried on board ocean ships; avoids port handling of freight.

LASHING   A rope or wire that is used to secure two barges together.

LASHING EYES   Loops at the end of ropes which are used to secure.

LATENT DEFECTS   Faults that are not readily apparent through normal diligence. In accordance with the Hague Rules, the owner of a ship is not responsible for latent defects of a vessel which cause loss and damage.

LATITUDE   The angular distance measured from the equator to the North Pole or South Pole. The latitude is measured along the meridian that runs north south. The latitude lines run parallel to the equator. Distance is measured in latitude from the equator in degrees, which is zero degrees. The North and South Poles are each 90 degrees latitude.

LAWFUL RATE   An American transportation rate term for a situation of having a published rate, which is the legal rate, be deemed unreasonable and must be replaced with a reasonable rate, it is then unlawful. A lawful rate is reasonable, non-discriminatory, and it is not prejudicial or preferential in violation of the Interstate Commerce Act. Consequently, the legal rate may or may not be lawful and the lawful rate likewise may or may not be legal. However, any legal rate which is reasonable, non-discriminatory, nonprejudicial, non-preferential, etc. is both legal and lawful.

LAWFUL TRADE   A restriction against contraband aboard in a time-charter party.

LAY DAY   The allotted time for discharging a vessel (unloading), before demurrage charges begin.

LAYER   One complete row of boxes or product on a pallet or unitized stack.

LAYOUT   The design and planning of the storage areas and aisles of a warehouse.

LAYOVER   Eight hours or more rest before continuing the trip, or any off-duty period away from home.

LAY ON THE AIR   Apply the brakes.

LAZARETTO   (Italian) A place set apart in quarantine for fumigating goods.

L/C   Letter of credit.

L & D   Loss and damage. This term is usually applied when a loss or damage is discovered when the package is delivered. The term located loss or damage is used when the damage to goods, property, or persons occurs at a specific and identifiable time en route.

LEADMAN   Another name for a group leader. A working crew member who is responsible for the crew.

LEAD TIME   The period of time elapsing between when an order is placed and the order is received and is ready for use or consumption. In a fixed order interval system, this is often called replenishment time. Processing lead time is the time required to process an order. Delivery lead time is the time required for an order to be delivered.

LEADTIME INVENTORIES   A quantity of inventory that is sufficient between the time a replenishment order is made until it is delivered.

LEAD TRACK   A track that connects either end of a yard with a main track.

LEAKAGE   1) An allowance made for waste due to leaking of casks and barrels. 2) Liquid loss from a defective tank, valve, or vehicle.

LEAKER   A damaged container with contents coming out.

LEARNING CURVE   A common phenomenon that is found in most production activities. In basic form: the number of people-hours required to perform a task decreases with each repetitive successive unit of production.

LEASE, DIRECT   Can be almost any type of lease, but the lessor holds title to the asset.

LEASE, FINANCE (CAPITAL)   Lessee makes payments over the useful life of the asset and meets the requirements of Financial Accounting Standards Board Bulletin (U.S.) #13; similar to full payment lease.

LEASE, LEVERAGED   A group of investors provide a portion of the purchase price for the assets and the balance is borrowed from banks and/or institutional investors; the asset is then leased to a using party.

LEASE, MASTER   An agreement for the leasing of certain equipment with options for the lessee to lease additional equipment as necessary at a predetermined rate without a new contract.

LEASE, NET   Similar to a finance (capital) lease except that all other payments such as taxes, maintenance, insurance, and others are paid by the lessee.

LEASE, NON-FULL PAYMENT   A contract in which the lessor depends upon an unguaranteed portion of the residual value of the asset to recover costs plus a return on his investment.

LEASE, OPERATING   Lessor provides maintenance or some other service in addition to the use of the asset at a price that fills the requirements of the Financial Accounting Standards Board Bulletin (U.S.) #13; similar to non-full payment and a true lease.

LEASE/PURCHASE AGREEMENT   Similar to a conditional sale, but the lessee has the option to purchase the asset at a bargain price at the end of the lease period.

LEAST SQUARES METHOD　A statistical method of smoothing a curve to minimize the sum of squares deviations of the given points in a set of data.

LEG　A term applying to each origin-destination hop on an airplane trip; a New York-Chicago-Seattle run consists of two legs.

LEGAL RATES　The legal rate is the properly published rate filed with a regulatory commission. A carrier is required to charge in accordance with the published rate even if the published rate is in error and obviously incorrect. The carrier cannot change the published freight rate on its own volition. This is to be contrasted with the lawful rate, which is a reasonable rate in keeping with regulations.

LEGAL WEIGHT　The weight of the goods and interior packing but not the container. (used in foreign trade)

LENGTH BLOCK　A pallet pattern in which package lengths are loaded parallel to the pallet length side.

LESS THAN CARLOAD RATE (LCL)　Service formerly provided by railroads. Consisted of small shipments that the railroad moved in box cars.

LESS-THAN-CONTAINERLOAD　A shipment by container consisting of less than the weight or cubic capacity of the container.

LESS THAN TRUCKLOAD (LTL)　A quantity of freight weighing less than the amount required for the application of a truckload rate.

LESS THAN TRUCKLOAD RATE　Rate that is applied to a less than truckload shipment.

LETTER OF CREDIT (L/C)　The letter of credit may be revocable of irrevocable. If it is revocable, the bank reserves the right to withdraw from the operations. If it is irrevocable, the bank cannot withdraw its credit prior to the specified expiration date. Under the arrangements of the letter of credit, the bank guarantees that if the shipment is made and all the terms of the letter of credit filled, payment will be made soon. The importer normally makes the necessary arrangements with his bank to establish credit for a particular sum of money which would cover the arrangements of the letter of credit. The solvency of the buyer is of no concern under these circumstances to the seller since the bank stands behind the contract. The exporter normally has his own bank, called correspondent or confirming bank, which confirms the letter of credit arrangements. The purpose of the letter of credit is to provide a means for the bank to substitute its credit for that of the individual firm in order to make possible a foreign trade shipment. The buyer and exporter agree on the amount of the letter of credit. The buyer then applies to his bank for the letter of credit. The application lists the value of the merchandise to be shipped and describes the shipment in full detail. The exporter is named as the beneficiary of the credit and a time period is designated for the credit to be enforced.

LETTER OF CREDIT, BACK-TO-BACK　A secondary letter of credit issued to a beneficiary on the strength of a primary credit. In this instance, the beneficiary of the primary credit (the middleman) becomes the applicant of the secondary, but smaller credit. The issuing bank of the secondary credit does not have to rely on the creditworthiness of the applicant (the middleman) since it relies on the credit of the bank, who issued the primary credit. Secondary credits are usually issued for lesser amounts allowing the middleman a profit margin for handling the business transaction. This type of credit is usually issued for parties who have fully utilized credit lines, are not well established, or are unable to obtain a credit line from their banks. The issuance of secondary credits is always contingent upon the terms and conditions stipulated in the primary credit. Caution must be exercised prior to issuing back-to-back credits by very carefully determining their workability.

LETTER OF CREDIT, CLEAN   A letter of credit which requires the beneficiary to present only a draft or a receipt for specified funds before he receives payment.

LETTER OF CREDIT, CONFIRMED   A letter of credit issued by one bank to which another bank added its irrevocable confirmation to pay, thereby obligating itself in the same manner as the opening bank. Example: "We hereby undertake to pay drafts drawn in accordance with the terms and conditions of the letter of credit."

LETTER OF CREDIT, CUMULATIVE   A revolving letter of credit which permits any amount not utilized during any of the specified periods to be carried over and added to the amounts available in subsequent periods (See "Revolving").

LETTER OF CREDIT, DEFERRED PAYMENT   A letter of credit issued for the purchase and financing of merchandise, similar to acceptance type letter of credit, except that it requires presentation of sight drafts which are payable on installment basis usually for periods of one year or more.

LETTER OF CREDIT, IRREVOCABLE   An instrument, once established, which cannot be modified or canceled without the agreement of all parties concerned.

LETTER OF CREDIT, NON-CUMULATIVE   A revolving letter of credit which prohibits the amount not used during the specific period to be available in the subsequent periods (See "Revolving").

LETTER OF CREDIT, RESTRICTED   A condition within the L/C which restricts its negotiation to a named bank.

LETTER OF CREDIT, REVOCABLE   An instrument which can be modified or canceled at any moment without notice to and agreement of the beneficiary, but customarily includes a clause in the credit to the effect that any draft negotiated by the bank prior to the receipt of a notice of revocation or amendment will be honored by the issuing bank. Its negotiability is always restricted to the advising bank.

LETTER OF CREDIT, REVOLVING   An irrevocable letter of credit issued for a specific amount which renews itself for the same amount over a given period. Usually the unused portion of each period is non-cumulative and cannot be carried over to the next period. The contingent liability amount for such a credit is the amount of the credit multiplied by the number of periods the credit is to revolve. The amount in a revolving L/C is either cumulative or non-cumulative.

LETTER OF CREDIT, STRAIGHT   A letter of credit which contains a limited engagement clause addressed to the beneficiary stating that the issuing bank promises to pay upon presentation of the required documents at its counters or the counters of the named bank. In this instance, the issuing or the named bank verifies all documents and thus functions as the negotiating bank. The main difference between a negotiable and a straight credit is that a straight credit is payable only at the counters of the issuing or the named bank. A negotiable credit can be negotiated by any bank. This authority is given by the engagement clause which permits the credit to be negotiated by drawers, endorsers, or bona-fide holders.

LETTER OF CREDIT, TRANSFERABLE   A letter of credit that allows the beneficiary to transfer in whole or in part any amount of the credit to one or more third parties (second beneficiaries) provided that the aggregate of such transfers does not exceed the amount of the credit. Under this type of L/C partial shipments must be allowed when affecting partial transfers.

LETTER OF CREDIT, UNCONFIRMED   A letter of credit forwarded to the beneficiary by the advising bank "without engagement" on the part of the advising bank. In international transactions, the beneficiary must depend on the foreign bank for his payment. Thus, this type of L/C offers less protection to the seller than the confirmed type.

LETTER OF HYPOTHECATION   When a shipper authorizes a lien on certain goods in return for money advanced on them, he submits a letter of hypothecation.

LETTER OF INDEMNITY   When the consignor submits a guarantee to a consignee against any loss or damage arising out of a faulty or defective shipment of merchandise, he submits a letter of indemnity. This letter makes it unnecessary to add any statement to the bill of lading concerning the shortage or fault as noted on the ship's receipt.

LETTER OF INTENT   A communication from buyer to seller indicating an intention to purchase. Typically it is used to indicate to the seller that the firm will buy; it is used so that the seller can go ahead and order materials or start the job while the final purchase documents or contracts are being prepared. Letters of intent can have binding force unless carefully worded to the contrary.

LIABILITY, JOINT AND SEVERAL   An obligation undertaken by two or more carriers to carry out a contract or a claim or to assume an obligation.

LIABILITY, LIMITATIONS OF DAMAGES   Damages may be limited by a term in the warehouse receipt or storage agreement limiting the amount of liability in case of loss or damage, and setting forth a specific liability per article or item, or value per unit of weight beyond which warehouseman shall not be liable; provided, however, that such liability may on written request of the bailor at the time of signing such storage agreement or within a reasonable time after receipt of the warehouse receipt be increased on part or all of the goods thereunder, in which event increased rates may be charged based on such increased valuation, limitation of liability contained in the warehouseman's tariff, if any.

LIABILITY, WAREHOUSEMAN'S LEGAL   A warehouseman is liable for damages for loss or injury to the goods caused by his failure to exercise such care in regard to them as a reasonably careful man would exercise under like circumstances, but unless otherwise agreed he is not liable for damages which would not have been avoided by the exercise of such care.

LIEN   When a claim is made on goods to the satisfaction of a debt of duty, it carries the legal name of a lien.

LIE SHEET   The driver's log book.

LIFE CYCLE COSTING   Term for the sum of all costs of acquiring, using, and disposing of a capital asset. Includes the costs of purchasing, inbound freight, installation, energy, labor, maintenance, and disposal.

LIFELINE   Lines that are stretched fore and aft along the decks so that the crew members won't be washed overboard.

LIFO   1) Last-in-first-out method of inventory rotation. Goods cycled so that newest ones are shipped out first. 2) Method of inventory valuation that values the goods on the shelf in terms of the value of the most recent purchased lot prices.

LIFT TAIL GATE   A tail gate that is power operated and capable of lifting freight from street level.

LIGHT AIRCRAFT   A fixed wing aircraft having a maximum gross weight less than 12,500 pounds.

LIGHTER   1) This is an open or covered barge normally towed by a tugboat and used primarily in the harbor areas. This flat-boat is used for the transportation of freight between cars, vessels, and piers, and usually is towed by the tugboat. 2) Ship used to load or off-load cargo from a very large ship at sea that cannot enter ports due to size and depth limitations.

LIGHTERAGE   The duty or charge assessed for transferring, unloading, loading, etc. cargo by means of barges or lighters is called lighterage.

LIGHTERING   The hauling of freight on lighters or barges.

LIGHTERAGE LIMITS   The area within which, under certain rules, regulations, and charges, freight is regularly handled by means of lighters and barges.

LIGHT WEIGHT   This refers to the weight of an empty car.

LIMIT   An inventory management interpolation technique based on lot size. It looks at the lot sizes for groups of products to determine the effects of lot sizes on total inventory and set up costs.

LIMITED QUANTITY   Means the maximum amount of a hazardous material; as specified in the regulations, for which there are specific exceptions from the requirements of the regulations.

LINEAR PROGRAMMING   This is a method of mathematically allocating scarce sources between options to achieve a given objective when both the environmental constraints and the objective which limit the degree of achievement of the objective can be stated in terms of linear equations and equalities. Linear implies unchanging and definable relationships between the variables of the problem. The term programming only brings out the concept of an orderly process by which this type of problem can be solved in any of the following ways: (1) through the graphical method, (2) through the algebraic method; and (3) through the simplex method. The transportation linear programming problem employs only one form of the simplex method.

LINE DECK   Deck spaces of a barge between the bow and the forward cargo hold of the barge, and between the cargo hold covering and the stern.

LINE-FUNCTIONAL AREAS   These areas of the organizational table of an industrial firm which are involved in the actual creation of the utilities—the direct functions performed on the commodity as it moves through the vertical stream—are the line functional areas. Production, marketing, and logistics are the line functional areas of the industrial firm. Obviously, the line-functional areas of a service firm would be somewhat different. At one time it was thought that all economic activities performed in our society could be identified within the scope of the four utilities involving the creation of (1) time utility, (2) possession utility, (3) form utility, and (4) place utility. A more perceptive analysis of this subject matter reveals that most of the staff functional areas of the firm could hardly be identified with the creation of any of these four utilities. The provision of such staff services as credit, personnel hiring and terminating, etc. represent examples of staff areas of the industrial firm which do not create time, form, place, or possession utility. The line functions of the firm are directly involved in establishing the options, costing the options, and managing the execution of decisions throughout the vertical stream.

LINE HAUL   The movement of freight over the tracks of a transportation line from one town or city to another town or city (not a switching service).

LINE HAUL COSTS   Those fixed and variable costs of performing the intercity segment of the total transportation operation. It may be contrasted to the terminal costs, or it is sometimes contrasted to the local pickup and delivery costs.

LINE HAUL SWITCHING   The moving of cars within yard or switching limits of a station, preceding or following a line haul.

LINES   A transportation agency or carrier known as a rail line, water line, etc. Where a number of carriers are united by ownership, they are termed lines. Some forms of lines are: belt, branch, connecting family, independent, industrial, lateral, main number, short, tap and trunk.

LINE STEAMER   A vessel operating between certain points on time schedule.

LINK   In the post-production channel, there may be several nodes, or stop off storage and handling points. This would require several movements, rather than a single movement, to move through the channel from the manufacturing plant to the ultimate retailer. The transportation movement and the subsequent storage point represents a link. In the computation of the total logistics costs within a link, in order to eliminate duplication of costing, only the subsequent, or following, storage operation is added to the transport movement to involve the link. However, in the initial movement from the plant to the first node, it is necessary to compute both plant storage and initial mode storage with the transport cost to determine the total logistics costs in the first link. Beyond the first link, only the transport operation and the following node storage cost represent the link.

LIQUIDATE   To settle the accounts and distribute the assets of a business in bringing it to an end.

LIQUIDATION DAMAGES   Contract breach term. Liquidation damage is an amount stated in advance in a contract for the amount a vendor will be liable for in the event of late delivery or providing poor quality goods. An amount of damages that would be carried for in the event that the supplier would not perform. Example: $100 per day for each late delivery date. These damages are defined and stated in advance in a purchase order or contract.

LIST OF STORES   A document submitted to the customs authorities, containing a list of provisions and similar articles remaining on board a vessel at the end of a voyage.

LITIGATION   A judicial contest. The act or process of carrying on a lawsuit.

LIVE AXLE   A powered axle.

LIVE CHARTER RATE   Actual aircraft miles or hours of the charter passengers or cargo, which is proportional to that of the total charter rate charged by the carrier.

LIVESTOCK CONTRACT   A document taking the place of the bill of lading on shipments of livestock, due to unusual conditions surrounding their movement.

LIVESTOCK WAYBILL   A waybill used for shipments of livestock.

LLOYD'S   The internationally known association of marine underwriters.

LLOYD'S REGISTER   A yearly register issued by Lloyd's, containing the tonnage, age, build, character and condition of ships.

LOAD   The amount of scheduled work confronting the manufacturing facility, usually expressed in terms of hours of work.

LOAD CHART   A chart showing the weight of shipments loaded in a trailer and the position in the trailer of larger items.

LOAD FACTOR   The percentage of seats occupied by revenue passengers in an aircraft or for the entire airline over a period of time. Some freight carriers by air also measure the percent of total cubic footage of lift capacity on flights that are occupied by revenue freight and refer to this as load factor.

LOADING AND UNLOADING   In domestic shipping, a service usually performed by the shipper and consignee in carload lots and by the carrier in less-than-carload quantities. In marine shipping, a service performed by stevedores and called stevedoring (on vessel).

LOADING GATE   A passage in an airport finger where passengers are enplaned or deplaned.

LOADING PLATFORM   A flat surface to facilitate loading, usually erected alongside a warehouse at the approximate level of a car or truck floor, sometimes of the portable type.

LOADING SEALS   Seals applied to the doors of cars when cars are loaded, i.e., when the freight is checked from the freight house platform to the cars. They reveal break in.

LOADING SYSTEM   Some of the most common loading systems are: a) Unit loading (strap loading), b) Unitization (stacking strapping many packages); c) Bonded Blocking (loading like bricks); d) Cube loading (on pallets or unitized for grab trucks); e) Glued Loading (applying glue in strips on each side of the box to tie as many as 20 cartons together, usually on a pallet); f) Bulk Packing (loose and in bundles to permit one large fiberboard box as a substitute for smaller boxes).

LOAD LEVELING   A production scheduling term for the practice of assigning each job to manpower and machinery so as to smooth out flow to fully occupy each resource with a minimum of backlog and idle time.

LOAD LIMIT   The maximum allowable weight for a vehicle on a road, bridge, truck, or airport runway/apron.

LOCAL   A train which serves the principal function of stopping to deliver or pick up freight at each station between division points is called a local.

LOCAL CARTAGE   The service of display or delivery from a municipal terminal to particular commercial sites is called local cartage. It may be performed by a common or a contract carrier. It involves both pickup and delivery services in conjunction with line-haul operations.

LOCAL RATES   The local rate is applicable on a single carrier line. It's a movement between two points on a single carrier. It's to be contrasted with a joint movement which involves a movement between two points involving more than one carrier. Any additional switching service or pickup and delivery service performed by another carrier would have no effect on the structure of the rate.

LOCAL SERVICE CARRIERS   Domestic route air carriers operating between smaller traffic centers and principal centers or regional centers.

LOCAL STATION   A station located only on one transportation line.

LOCAL TARIFF   A tariff which lists the rates applicable between points on the same carrier's lines.

LOCAL TRAFFIC   All traffic that terminates or originates on the same railway line is referred to as local traffic. It does not involve any intermediate movement by connecting railway. Sometimes it is limited to a given classification territory.

LOCAL WAYBILL   A waybill covering the movement of freight over a single transportation line.

LOCATION   The exact spot in a warehouse where a particular product can be found.

LOCATION SYSTEM   Provides an efficient way to locate stock and increase handling and storage efficiency.

LOCATOR FILE   A record system that records where the product is stored. It is necessary where stock may be stored in varying, unpredictable locations.

LOCK   The water passage process which permits a vessel to move from one level of water to another between enclosed gates which lower and raise the water is referred to as a lock. This is necessary for all canals connecting water bodies of different levels.

LOCKING PADS   The mechanical device used to lock the container to the chassis of the ship hold or rail car.

LOCO   A term signifying that a quotation covers only the cost of goods as they stand, without packing cartage, or other charges which may accrue.

LOGAIR   Logistic air lift, which is a U.S. Air Force contract freight air lift service similar to that of the Navy's QUICKTRANS.

LOG BODY   A trailer or truck built to transport logs or other loads which may be boomed or chained in place.

LOG BOOK   This water transportation term refers to the official register kept by the master of a ship which spells out the daily record of events while at sea such as deaths, weather, births, accidents, or any other instance of significance.

LOGISTICS   The management of all inbound and outbound materials, parts, supplies, finished goods related information and cash flows. Logistics has evolved over the years to include more activities in firms. Originally it was confined to traffic and warehousing. Today it includes in many firms such activities as forecasting, order entry, inventory control, production scheduling, and product allocation among customers.

LOGISTIC TRAILER   A truck trailer capable of carrying double deck freight, thus creating a bigger payload.

LONG-AND-SHORT HAUL CLAUSES   A transportation regulatory requirement in many nations that prevents carriers from charging a higher rate for a short haul than the rate on the longer haul, when the short haul is contained within the long haul.

LONG DATED BILL   A bill of exchange with a long period to run before maturity.

LONGER   A row of barrels stowed fore-and-aft.

LONG HAUL   Distances of 1000 miles or more. (Air freight.)

LONG PRICE   Price after duties are paid.

LONG RANGE AIRCRAFT   Aircraft that will fly 1000 miles or more non-stop without refueling.

LONGSHOREMEN   The harbor employees who load and unload vessels.

LONG TON   A long or gross ton consisting of 2,240 pounds.

LOOP STATION   A through station in which the station track layout forms a loop or part of a circle, enabling trains to move in one direction only.

LOOSE   Not packed.

LORRY   In years gone by, the term lorry was applied to a low four-wheeled wagon without sides, of considerable length.

LOSS AND DAMAGE (L&D) CLAIMS—GENERAL   The terms of the Uniform Straight Domestic Bill of Lading reads that the carrier in possession of property shall be liable at common law for any loss or damage thereto. This makes the carrier practically an insurer against all losses except for Acts of God. A time limit of nine months for notification, and two years and one day for filing suit, is specified. The document entitled Standard Form for Presentation of Loss and Damage Claims is filled out.

LOSS AND DAMAGE CLAIMS PAPERS   The papers normally included in submitting a claim are: a) standard form of small L&D for presentation; b) proof of value (certified copy of invoice); c) statement of claim (itemized listing); d) transportation companies inspection report; e) paid freight bill or express receipt; f) original bill of lading; and g) copies of correspondence.

LOSS CLAIM (FREIGHT)   Expressive of injury to shipment of goods and generally referring to non-delivery.

LOSS, TOTAL   When there are no salvageable parts of the shipment remaining, and the destruction is complete, the term total loss is applied.

LOST SALE   A sale that could have been made but was not because of a stockout.

LOT   The units of goods for which a separate accounting is to be kept by the warehouseman.

LOT NUMBER   Identifying number or numbers used to keep a separate accounting for specific merchandise.

LOT SHIPMENT   If a shipment consists of only one piece, it is called a single lot shipment. If the shipment consists of more than one piece, it is given the term lot shipment.

LOT SIZE   The amount of a product ordered, shipped, or produced.

LOW BALL   Term for a price bid from a seller that is very low. The intent of the seller is to get the work then later make up for lost profits once the buyer is dependent upon the seller.

LOW BOY   A trailer built low to facilitate hauling equipment and other heavy machinery.

LUMPER   Term applied to independent contractor who assists owner–operator in loading or unloading of freight usually at food distribution centers, often coercive form of intimidation which adds to total cost of transportation. Need for this service often arises because of food facility refusing to perform truck loading or unloading and requesting a trucker to do so.

LUMBER BODY   A trailer body or platform truck with traverse rollers that was built to transport lumber.

LUMP FREIGHT   Payment in one sum to cover the hire of a vessel for a complete voyage or purpose.

MMMM

MAIN LINE   That part of a transportation system (railway or airline), exclusive of local operations such as pick-up and delivery services, switch tracks, branches, yards and terminals that are the long haul movements.

MAIN TRACK   All track of a rail carrier kept clear for the passage of trains is termed the main track for a line-haul railway. The term first main track is used.

MANDAMUS   The action of a court requiring a specific action to be taken is commonly referred to as a writ of mandamus.

MANDATORY   A proceeding or action containing a command or order.

MANIAC   Shop mechanic (slang).

MANIFEST   The document which lists the particulars of a shipment aboard a vessel or car is termed a manifest.

MANUFACTURER'S AGENT   An individual or firm who acts in the capacity of agent and is usually located at a port, in international movements. Often a sales person who sells for a manufacturer but is not employed by it. They are compensated by commission on the sales they make for the firm.

MANUFACTURERS   Articles which have been made or fabricated from raw form into finished form.

MARGINAL COSTS   The increase in total costs that result from the movement or production of one more unit.

MARINE INSURANCE   Insurance against loss or damage to property while in transit by water.

MARINE INSURANCE CERTIFICATE   A document certifying that a shipment is covered by insurance under an open cargo policy, issued by a merchant and duly countersigned for evidence. It is a negotiable document.

MARINE INSURANCE POLICY   The contract whereby the assurer (insurance company) agrees to pay the assured (one insured), for loss or damage incurred to ship or cargo to the extent of risk and to the amount of value expressly stipulated therein.

MARITIME   Business pertaining to commerce or navigation transacted upon the sea or in seaports in such matters as the court of admiralty have jurisdiction over, concurrently with the courts of common law.

MARITIME ADMINISTRATION (U.S)   Federal agency responsible for subsidy administration of the U.S. flag steamship industry that receives construction and operation differential subsidies; agency also studies and proposes efficient port design and practices.

MARITIME LAW   Legislation relating to ships, seamen and harbors.

MARITIME PERIL   Under the Marine Insurance Act of 1906, "Maritime perils mean the perils consequent on, or incidental to, the navigation of the sea that is to say, perils of the sea, fire, war, pirates, robbers, thieves captures, seizures, restraints and detainments of princes and people, jettisons, barratry, and any other perils, either of the like kind or which may be designated by policy." Only fortuitous accidents of the sea, not including actions of wind and waves, are included.

MARITIME POSITIONS   The location of sea related circumstances on the basis of longitude and latitude.

MARK   A letter, figure or device by which goods are distinguished.

MARKED CAPACITY   The stenciled or marked weight on a car denoting its carrying capacity.

MARKER   Rear train red light.

MARKET   A public place where provisions or other wares are sold.

MARKET COMPETITION   This is a term generally used in the making of rates. It is the competition of one market or set of sellers against others.

MARKET DOMINANCE   A concept that applies to situations in which a carrier or group of carriers experience a lack of competition that would otherwise place a ceiling on rates.

MARKET VALUE   As used in the adjustment of freight claims it denotes the value of a shipment at destination after freight charges (if uncollected) are deducted.

MARKING (FREIGHT)   Addressing packages for shipment and applying marks.

MARKING MACHINE   A machine that imprints or embosses a mark on a label, ticket, tape,

MARRIAGE RULE   A carrier has an option of stopping a car for completion of loading, or placing a separate car at a stopoff point to receive the transfer of a shipment. The marriage rule involves the process of placing a separate car at a stopoff point.

MART   A commercial center; same as market.

MARU   A name attached to all Japanese vessels which implies perfection or completeness. The original meaning was derived from sphere or circle.

MASTER CARTON   A single large carton that is used as a uniform shipping carton for many smaller packages of different products.

MASTER FILE   A file of major data on some aspect of business-like accounts receivable.

MASTER OF A SHIP   The commander or captain, who has chief charge of the government and navigation of a vessel, as well as the general command of crew and control of cargo.

MASTER PACK   A larger box made of fiberboard that is used to pack a number of smaller boxes or containers. A protection system to aid in handling and self packaging.

MASTER SCALE   Test cars are weighed and verified as to weight on a master scale.

MATERIALS AND SUPPLIES   Goods on hand required for repairs or replacements and for use in the general business of operations of carriers.

MATERIALS REQUIREMENTS PLANNING   An inventory and purchasing planning system that integrates product components, lead times and ultimate deadline to plan acquisition timings; called MRP.

MATE'S RECEIPT   A cargo receipt signed by the chief officer.

MATRIX   Arrangement of numbers in rectangular array for mathematical operations. It provides for solving rows of equations with certain column variables. Actually, any table of data is a matrix.

MATURITY   The time fixed for payment of a note, bill or draft.

MATURITY DATE   The data on which negotiable instruments become due for payment. Acceptances maturing on a non-business day are payable either before or after such date.

MAX.   Maximum.

MAXIMUM   The highest, or greatest; (sum, quantity, price, etc.)

MAXIMUM AND MINIMUM RATES   A maximum rate may be set by a regulatory authority to represent the highest rate a carrier may charge. The minimum rate represents the lowest rate that may be charged on any movement between given points for a given commodity. The maximum rate is to protect the public from excessive rates. The minimum rate is intended to restrain individual carriers from excessive competition.

MAXIMUM OBJECTIVES   The best possible terms that a buyer would seek to attain in a negotiation.

MEASUREMENT   The measurement of the tonnage according to well defined rules, in maritime transportation.

MEASUREMENT GOODS (CARGO)   That class of merchandise on which the freight assessment is based on measurement.

MEASUREMENT TON   Forty cubic feet or 2,240 pounds on the Atlantic, and forty-two cubic feet or 2,000 lbs. on the Pacific coast.

MEASURE OF DAMAGES   Rule or rules exercising the control in adjusting or apportioning the extent of damages to be compensated in actions at law for injury.

MEASURE MORE THAN IT WEIGHS   When the weight of a shipment is less than 56 pounds per cubic foot, the term "measures more than it weighs" is applied. It is not common for commodities to conform to these specifications. When this does occur, the assessment is made on the basis of the measurement rather than the weight.

MEMBER LINE   A carrier connected with an association or rate bureau.

MEMORANDUM BILL OF LADING   The third copy of the bill of lading is called the memorandum bill of lading.

MEMO WAYBILL   An internal railroad document usually used to route empty cars to a particular destination.

MERCANTILE AGENCY   A concern which procures and furnishes information on the financial standing and credit of business firms.

MERCANTILE LAW   Law pertaining to trade and commerce.

MERCANTILE PAPER   Notes or bills issued by merchants for goods consigned or bought.

MERCANTILE REGISTRY   An institution existing in most foreign countries for the purpose of insuring publicity of the essential facts as to the ownership or organization of business houses.

MERCATOR CHART   A charting methodology originated by Gerardus Mercator, 1512-1594. The earth charting was on the basis of the earth being a cylinder, being parallel and tangent to the equator. Distance per unit would increase as one moved toward the poles. Thus, an island at the poles would be larger than if near the equator.

MERCHANDISE   That which is bought or sold in trade other than real estate, bullion and negotiable paper.

MERCHANDISE BROKER   He who negotiates the sale of merchandise for another without having possession of the goods.

MERCHANDISE CAR   A rail car containing several less-than-carload shipments. Thus, containing several shipments from different consignors.

MERCHANDISE WAREHOUSE   A public warehouse for the storage and distribution of products, in great variety, that do not require refrigeration for their preservation. Some public merchandise warehouses provide air conditioned and humidity controlled facilities and may provide both refrigerated and merchandise warehousing services.

MERCHANT   One who buys and sells goods.

MERCHANTABLE   In salable condition; fit for market.

MERCHANTMAN   A commercial vessel.

MERCHANT MARINE   The commercial steamship fleet of a country.

MERCHANT MARINE ACT (U.S.)   An Act of Congress (1920), intended for the promotion, operation and maintenance of an American Merchant Marine and providing for a final adjustment of matters developing in connection with the construction and employment of ships built during World War I.

MERCHANT MIDDLEMEN   The merchant middlemen consist of the general classes: a) service wholesalers; and b) limited function wholesalers. The service wholesalers may be called regular wholesalers, jobbers, service wholesalers, and full function wholesalers. The term semi-jobber is applied to a wholesaler who serves the wholesale merchant and the retail merchant. Most service wholesalers service businesses within 100 miles of their establishment. Some operate regionally or nationally. Usually they sell to small retailers. They take title, assume ownership risk, and are independent. Among the services rendered are carrying stock, extending credit, making deliveries, and maintaining the sales force. Most wholesalers have a limited line of stock. That is, a grocery service wholesaler would service the grocery line for the retailers he services. The service wholesaler may be a) a general merchandise service wholesaler, or b) a specialty wholesaler. The limited function wholesalers do not provide the extensive services normally rendered by the service wholesalers. They are classified as follow: drop shippers; mail order wholesalers; cash-and-carry wholesalers; truck distributors; and converters.

METACENTER   Relates to ships. A point on a vertical line that marks the vertical line passing through the center of gravity of the displaced water of the vessel when it is listed or heeled.

METALLIC CURRENCY   Gold, silver and copper coins, forming the circulating medium of a country.

METER (METRE)   A meter is equivalent to 39.368 United States inches.

METRIC SYSTEM   The system which uses the meter as the unit of measurement of length is called the metric system. The liter and the gram are cubic and weight measurements, respectively, of this system. The other units of the metric system are decimal subdivisions of the liter and gram. Extensions of the metric system use milligram as 1/1000th of a gram, the centigram as 1/100th of a gram and the decigram as 1/10th of a gram. The decagram is 1/10th of a gram, the hectogram is 100 grams, and the kilogram is 1000 grams.

METRIC TON   A ton of 2204.6 pounds, or 1,000 kilograms.

MICRO-BRIDGE   Intermodal transportation from internal cities to/from seaports as part of a through movement transfer of container freight involving overseas ships.

MIDSHIPS   The center of the fore-and-aft line of the vessel. The middle of the fore and aft length. Also called amidships.

MILE   5,280 feet

MILEAGE   Length or distance in miles.

MILEAGE ALLOWANCE   An allowance made by carriers to owners of private freight cars and other equipment that is based on distance. The allowance is either applied as a reduction in the freight charges or an actual payment.

MILEAGE, CONSTRUCTIVE   An arbitrary mileage allowed a carrier in dividing joint rates based on a mileage prorate and not on the actual mileage.

MILEAGE GUIDE   A form of tariff that either states the distance between points, or prescribes how to compute the distance.

MILEAGE RATE   The division of the through charge to participating carriers on the basis of mileage.

MILEAGE TARIFF   When the rates of a tariff are based on mileage rather than involving a point to point rate, the tariff is normally referred to as a mileage tariff. Its value lies in the fact that it is possible to construct the total rate between any combination of points on the basis of the mileage tariff.

MILK CONTAINER CAR   A specially designed car, consisting of removable containers, each of which encases a glass-lined, heavily insulated tank, capable of carrying milk. Each container unit can be hoisted to and from motor trucks and platforms.

MILLING-IN-TRANSIT   Whenever a stopover is allowed under the tariff to permit a finishing process, or something comparable thereto, the term milling-in-transit is applied. While this term seems to imply only a milling process, it is more general.

MINI-BRIDGE   Ocean-rail container movement that replaces all water movement. Example: Europe to Charleston ocean movement with final rail move to New Orleans consignees in place of a complete Europe to New Orleans water haul.

MINI MAX   1) Inventory Systems. The upper and lower bounds, or high and low limits. Used as one method of inventory control. Orders for more are placed when lower limit is reached. Inbound flow stopped when maximum is reached. Also used for auditing and rejecting. Also known as min-max. 2) Quality Systems. The upper and lower bounds—or high and low limits. Used for auditing and rejecting out of spec items.

MINIMUM   The least, or lowest (sum, quantity, price, etc.).

MINIMUM BILL OF LADING   Many ocean bills of lading are known as minimum because they contain a clause which specifies the least charge that the carrier will make for the issuance of a lading. This charge may be a definite sum in currency, or it may be the current charge per ton or for any specified quantity of cargo.

MINIMUM CARLOAD WEIGHT   The minimum weight, as provided for in a tariff, classification, and exception thereto, shows the least amount of an article that will be accepted for shipment, in order that it may be classed and charged as a carload.

MINIMUM CHARGE   Applied to a commodity shipment, it establishes the minimum freight invoice charges, regardless of weight of the shipment, that will be assessed against the movement. It is expressed in terms of a total charge rather than a charge per hundredweight.

MINIMUM OBJECTIVE   The least that a buyer would like to attain in an upcoming negotiation with a seller. Example: current price is now $1.20; buyer would like $1.10, but would settle for $1.15 as a minimum objective.

MINIMUM RATE   As contrasted to the minimum charge, the minimum rate is the lowest rate per hundredweight that will be charged for a movement.

MINIMUM TRUCKLOAD WEIGHT   The weight at which a shipment is handled at a truckload rate.

MINIMUM WEIGHT   When a given rate is based on a minimum weight of shipment, this is referred to as the minimum weight for the rate.

MINNIE   Less than 100 lbs. in the shipment.

MIN. WT.   The minimum weight.

MISDELIVERY   A shipment that is delivered to the wrong consignee or the wrong location of correct consignee.

MISDEMEANOR   A crime less than a felony; a crime of a minor degree.

MISDESCRIPTION BY SHIPPER   Situation in which shipper's description of goods on bill of lading is not correct in relation to what is actually being shipped.

MISROUTE   When a carrier errs by violating the routing shipper's instruction, or sends a shipment via a route with a higher rate, this class of a mistake is termed a misroute.

MISROUTED FREIGHT   Freight that is sent to the correct destination, but by a route that results in a rate higher than that specified by the shipper's routing.

MISROUTING CLAIM   When an unreasonable utilization of high rated routes is used, the shipper has a right to file a claim for misrouting. Even though a legally published rate has been assessed, another lower rate may be applicable. The failure of the carrier to move by the route with the lowest rate often creates a condition which authorizes the shipper to file a claim for misrouting.

MISSHIPMENT   Shipping the wrong product, quantity, or to the wrong destination.

MISSIONARY RATES   When a rate is established at an unusually low level to aid in the development of a particular industry, it is called a missionary rate.

MIXED CARLOAD   Two or more different commodities in the same car.

MIXED CARLOAD RATE   The rate on a shipment of many less-than-carload shipments combined into a carload shipment.

MIXED LOAD   A load of different articles in a single shipment/consignment.

MIXED SHIPMENT   Two or more different articles in the same container or shipment.

MIXED TRAIN   A railroad train composed of both freight and passenger cars is a mixed train.

MIXED TRUCKLOAD RATES   Rated applicable on a single shipment composed of numerous small shipments, all moving from like origin to destination.

MIXING PRIVILEGES   The authorization to mix truckload freight in accordance with various combinations and alternatives. The rate applicable to each article is its truckload rate—as though its weight justified a truckload rate.

MODE   Mode is the vehicle system used for transportation. It is normally classified by the system for propulsion and the methodology of right of way. Carriers moving on highways are referred to as motor transportation mode or highway mode. Mode is a general term that covers all of the carrier classifications based on right of way, propulsion system, etc. Common use of the word mode means rail, motor, water, air, pipe, and sometimes intermodal.

MOLDED DEPTH   The measurement from top to keel of one, two and three deck vessels. Length from the top of the keel to the top of the upper deck beams at the side of the vessel.

MONEY ORDER   A non-negotiable order requesting one person to pay money to another.

MONOPOLY   1) The one seller available for a product or service. 2) Sole permission or appropriated power to deal in any species of goods or perform a service.

MONOPSONY   Term that applies to a market situation in which only one buyer is available.

MOORSOM'S RULE   A mathematical formula worked out for measurement of the cubical content of a vessel. It uses 11 cubic feet as a gross ton. Proposed and adopted in Britain in 1864. Adopted by U.S. in 1984.

MORE-THAN-ONE-CONSIGNMENT WAYBILL   A waybill used for more than one consignment of freight.

MOTIVE POWER   A term relating to the self-propelling equipment of a railroad.

MOTOR CARRIER   A transportation service company that transports in a motor vehicle over the highways.

MOTOR CARRIER ACT OF 1935.   U.S. Part II of the Interstate Commerce Act, which brought motor carriers under the regulatory jurisdiction of the I.C.C It involves regulation of common and contract carriers. It is incorporated into the Revised Interstate Commerce Act in 1978, motor carriers are referred to there as Subchapter II carriers. Most of this legislation was later phased out.

MOTOR FREIGHT ASSOCIATION   An association of motor carriers for any legitimate purpose, like issuing tariffs, lobbying, etc.

MOTOR TRANSPORT   A term used to signify transportation by auto truck.

MOTOR VEHICLE   Any vehicle, machine, tractor, trailer, or semi-trailer propelled or drawn by mechanical power and used upon the highways in the transportation of passengers or property.

MOUNTAIN-PACIFIC GROUP   The rail rate territory in the U.S. which is west of a line between North Dakota and Montana, between South Dakota and Montana, between Wyoming and South Dakota, until it comes to the main line of the Union Pacific, then extends west to Cheyenne, Wyoming, then south to Denver, and on through to Colorado Springs, Pueblo, Trinidad, and then follows the track of the AT&SF through Raton, Las Vegas, Albuquerque, and on to El Paso.

MRO   Term indicating maintenance, repair, and operating supplies. Those items and services that a firm purchases for its own consumption in the normal lines of activities. These are typically maintenance goods and services.

MULE   A small tractor used about the warehouse to move two-axle dollies. Also a yard tractor.

MULLEN TEST   Fiberboard and similar material is tested in strength by a device through what's called the mullen test.

MULTI-CITY-WAREHOUSE COMPANY   A firm operating warehouses in more than one city.

MULTI-MODAL INDIFFERENCE VOLUME   Analysis to determine the optimum carrier mode on the basis of transport rates alone. While this is incomplete logistics planning, under some circumstances it is helpful. Two competitive carriers will probably have different less than volume and volume rates, as well as different minimum volumes, to qualify for the volume rate. That volume at which the continuous per unit transport cost curves of the different modes cross is known as the multi-modal-indifference volume. At that volume it would be feasible to change carrier modes on the basis of transport rates alone.

MULTIPLE HAZARDS   A material meeting the definitions of more than one hazard class.

MULTIPLE CAR AND MULTIPLE TRAILER LOAD RATES   Lower than normal carload rates that apply when many of them are shipped as a single consignment.

MULTIPLE CLASSES   Rate classes which have a fixed multiple of a lower class. For example, three times the first class rate.

MULTIPLE LOADING   When two or more carload shipments are loaded on one car at the same origin for different destinations, or at different origins for the same destination, or a different origins for different destinations, any of these processes are referred to as multiple loading.

MULTI-SERVICE CARS   When hopper-type or gondola cars are adapted for carrying bulk commodities, and are equipped for discharge of content to the center of both sides of the track, the multiple use of cars is referred to as multi-service cars.

MULTIPLE SHIPMENT RATE   A transportation rate for freight whereby a lower rate applies on each shipment when many of them are tendered at the same time.

MULTIPLE UNITS   Railroad engines or powered passenger cars that operate simultaneously from one set of controls by one engineer.

MULTI-STOP BODY   A fully enclosed truck body with a quick and easy driver's compartment entry.

MULTI-STORY WAREHOUSE   A warehouse with more than one major floor level on which goods can be stored.

MULTI-TINE FORK   Attachment to a forklift truck that allows the movement of two pallets side-by-side, rather than the usual one pallet on the forks.

MUSHROOM LINE   A transportation company operating mushroom steamers.

MUSHROOM STEAMER   When a ship is put into effect on short notice, and has no specific operating policy but moves to and from ports seeking high revenue freight, it is called a mushroom steamer.

MUSTER   A collection of samples.

NNNN

NAFTA North American Free Trade Agreement, a customs and related economic alliance set by Canada, Mexico, and the United States.

NAMED LICENSED USER A practice in software sales and use whereby individuals in the customer firm are the only ones named to be permitted to access and use the software. Licensing agreements often contain this feature.

NANOSECOND One billionth of a second. A term used in data processing to a greater extent. Often used in reference to computer speeds.

NANO-SUPPLY CHAIN The smallest concept of a supply chain that begins with a manufacturing supply of raw material within the firm and further includes the optimization of production of that same firm. It typically ends at the finished goods end of the supply chain. This is a long standing concept of production and operations management.

NATIONAL AGREEMENT An agreement covering the needs of a commodity for a company at plants and facilities throughout the country.

NATIONAL AIR CARRIER ASSOCIATION A trade association made up of air carriers performing as supplemental carriers, and originally incorporated as the Military Air Carrier Association.

NATIONAL ASSOCIATION OF PURCHASING MANAGEMENT An American professional association in the purchasing and supply field. It has a certification program leading to the designation of Certified Purchasing Manager. Its headquarters is at 2055 E. Centennial Circle, Tempe, AZ 85285 U.S.A.

NATIONAL SUPPLIER A supplier that can and does supply a firm with goods and services at its sites throughout an entire country.

NATIONAL TRANSPORTATION POLICY A regulatory statement in legislation that provides direction and philosophy toward the regulation and development of a country's transportation industries.

NATURAL ADVANTAGE A benefit one locality possesses over another, due to its geographical location, its proximity to the seaboard and navigable rivers and general transportation facilities.

NATURAL DIFFERENCE A disparity between a shipper or dispute of a locality because of the presence or absence of natural advantages or disadvantages such as rivers and waterways, highways and mountains.

NATURAL SHRINKAGE The ordinary loss of weight of livestock, loss in weight because of evaporation of liquids and loss within tariff allowance on grain and seeds.

NAUTICAL   That which pertains to ships, sailors or navigation; maritime.

NAUTICAL ASTRONOMY   The use of astronomy to guide ships at sea by identifying points in the heavens and guiding on them.

NAVICERT   When it is desirable to exempt noncontraband shipments from seizure or search by patrols maintaining a blockade, a certificate called a navicert is issued.

NAVIGABLE   A term applying to waters that can be navigated by freight and passenger carrying vessels.

NAVIGATION   The science of conducting ships.

NEAPED   When the draft of the vessel exceeds the depth at high water neaps, the vessel cannot move until the high spring tides.

NECK-IN   A means of reforming a portion of a container to a smaller size than the rest of the container.

NEGLIGENCE   Any general process of failure to exercise the degree of care required by law results in a verdict of negligence.

NEGOTIABILITY   Credits are classified "negotiable" or "straight." Negotiability authorizes third parties to negotiate the beneficiary's drafts.

NEGOTIABLE INSTRUMENTS   An instrument such as a draft, promissory note, check or bill of exchange which is transferable from one person to another in good faith for a consideration. To be legal, the instrument must be in writing, signed by the drawer, must promise to pay a certain sum in money on demand or at a future date, and must be payable to order or to the bearer who must be named.

NEGOTIABLE PAPER   Bills, drafts, and notes, which may be transferred with all their rights by endorsement or assignment.

NEGOTIATING BANK   A bank named in the credit (or the credit freely negotiable) which examines the documents and certifies to the issuing bank that the terms are complied with. The bank may be authorized to purchase the draft and/or create an acceptance. In practice, the negotiating bank is usually the seller's bank and mails the documents to the issuing bank for payment or acceptance. When the discount charges are for the account of the seller, the seller has a choice of having drafts discounted by the negotiating bank.

NEGOTIATING POSITION   A loose term indicating the relative strength of the negotiator against the negotiator of the other firm. In a purchasing context, it can be a weak position if the supplier is in a seller's market position, or it can be the opposite.

NEGOTIATING STRATEGY/PLAN   The approach taken when about to undertake a negotiation with another party.

NEGOTIATIONS   Making a bargain or agreeing upon a mercantile transaction.

N.E.S.   Not elsewhere specified. A term used in an air freight tariff that means the rate specified applies to all commodities in the group not elsewhere appearing under their own name.

NESTED   The process of packing articles so that they rest partially or entirely within one another, thereby reducing the total cubic foot displacement, referred to as nesting or nested articles.

NESTED SOLID   Articles nested so that the bottom of one rests on the bottom of the one lower.

NET   The amount of revenue remaining after deductions, charges, expenses, losses, etc. Of course, this term also applies to a knotted rope or twine contrivance for the purpose of lowering or lifting cargo.

NET EARNINGS   Earnings remaining after the deduction of operating costs and necessary deductions pertaining to the carrying of passengers and property.

NET LEASE   Similar to a capital lease, but payments such as maintenance, insurance, taxes, and others are paid by the lessees.

NET OPERATING INCOME   The balance left after deducting all operating expenses from all income received from operation.

NET PRODUCT SALES   Gross revenue from sales less allowances and returns.

NET TON   2,000 pounds.

NET-TON-MILE   The movement of a ton of freight one mile.

NET TONNAGE   Represents the total cubic contents of those parts of a vessel closed in and devoted to the carrying of cargo and passengers, the weight measure being one gross ton for each 106 cubic feet of capacity. Net tonnage of vessel is ascertained by deducting from its gross tonnage, the cubic contents of certain spaces that are specified in the measurement laws and rules of the various maritime nations or in the measurement rules applicable at the Suez and Panama Canals. Net tonnage may be about 2/3 of gross tonnage, although not so with fast transatlantic liners, which have large coal bunkers, machinery and housing quarters.

NET WEIGHT   The weight of the contents of a shipment, without respect to the weight of the container or the car, is the net weight.

NEWSBOARD   In materials handling, it is a cheap board made from waste newspaper by means of a cylinder machine.

NO COMPETE CLAUSE   A contract term that does not allow someone to subsequently engage in work that would represent competition against the contracting firm.

NODE   All institutions which receive and hold goods moving in a channel are receiving and shipping points. The number of nodes in the channel has a significant effect on the length of haul, and therefore the volume of shipment, and the systems for logistics control.

N.O.I.   Not otherwise indexed.

NOIBIN   Not otherwise indexed by name. A common acronym found in tariffs that has the similar meaning as et cetera.

NOISE   Forecasting term. When breaking down historical data, statistical techniques can decompose the data, into a) base, b) trend, c) cyclical, and d) noise. The amount of information that can not be explained by either the base, trend, or cycle is considered noise.

NON-AGENCY STATION   A station at which a carrier has no agent.

NON-COMPETITIVE TRAFFIC   Where no competition exists between carriers in the movement of traffic, it is said to be non-competitive.

NONCONTIGUOUS COMMERCE   When the territory of a nation is not directly connected to the mainland, commerce between the mainland and the territory is referred to as noncontiguous commerce. Consequently, movements between continental United States to such areas as Puerto Rico, Alaska, etc. would be so regarded.

NON-DISCLOSURE AGREEMENT   A contract or contract term typically used by buyers and sellers that attempts to secure an agreement that the other party will neither use nor share with others the information gained in the relationship to the detriment of the firm requesting it. In a common way, a buying firm might ask a selling firm to sign such an agreement involving the knowledge and technology they learn about when dealing with it.

NON DUMPING CERTIFICATE   In order to prevent the whole market from being flooded by foreign exporters, many nations, notably Canada, require a value certificate. This certificate must stipulate the cost of the goods to the foreign buyer and the fair market value for home consumption.

NON-ECONOMIC REGULATION   As opposed to ECONOMIC REGULATIONS which deal with commercial entry/exit, services, and pricing, non-economic regulations are those that relate to pollution, employee management, safety, pensions, etc.

NONFLAMMABLE GAS   Any compressed gas other than a flammable compressed gas.

NON-POWERED AXLE   An axle used to support the load, but no driving power is used on the axle.

NON-PRIORITY MAIL   Mail bearing a surface carrier postage, that will go by air on a space available basis.

NONREV   A passenger transport term for a passenger that has been booked and boarded on a ticket that is zero in price. This is usually employees who are either deadheading or traveling as a company employee benefit.

NONSCHEDULED SERVICE   Flights for revenue not performed under schedule, and including all non-revenue flights incidental to such operations.

NONSTOP   Performance of a movement without stopping en route.

NON VALUE-ADDED ACTIVITY   Any activity, step, or process that is not seen as contributing to the value or competitiveness of a product or service.

NORMAL CRUISING SPEED   The standard cruising speed in statute miles per hour for an aircraft at flight altitude.

NORMAL DISTRIBUTION   A statistical concept indicating that events will occur in pattern centered around an average; the bulk of the pattern will be evenly spread near the average, and extreme occurrences will be few and outlying.

NORTH AMERICAN FREE TRADE AGREEMENT   See NAFTA

NORTH ATLANTIC TREATY ORGANIZATION   Military defense agreement among the United States, Belgium, Canada, Denmark, Germany, Greece, Iceland, Italy, Turkey, Portugal, Netherlands, Norway, Luxembourg, and the United Kingdom.

NOS   Not otherwise specified.

NOSE DIVE   Trailer tipped forward on its nose.

NO-SHOW   A person holding a flight reservation who fails to appear for a flight.

NO-SUSPEND ZONE   A former U.S. regulatory pricing regulation concept consisting of a band or zone within which rates could vary and not be subject to regulatory protest before the Interstate Commerce Commission.

NOTARY (NOTARY PUBLIC)   A public officer who attests or certifies to acknowledgement of bills, notes, protests and other papers.

NOTE   A written or printed paper acknowledging a debt and promising payment.

NOTE OF HAND   A written undertaking to pay money at a certain time.

NOTICE   The notification that an act has been performed—such as delivery of freight. It may involve an act to be performed.

NOTICE OF READINESS   The notice sent by the master of the vessel to the charter when the vessel is ready to load or unload.

NOZZLE, CAMELBACK   In materials handling, it is a unit with a control valve for regulating air intake.

NOZZLE, SUCTION   In materials handling, a device to lead materials into a suction line.

NUMBER BASE   Refers to the number of digit symbols used in performance of arithmetic manipulations and computations.

OOOO

OATH OF ENTRY In foreign trade, this term applies to a form which is required for the importation of goods into the country.

OEM Original equipment manufacturer; the firm in the supply chain that typically is the brand name of the equipment.

OBSOLESCENCE COST The decrease in value of inventory value resulting from the change in market value, or the introduction of more advanced substitutes, usually associated with time, is obsolescence cost. This cost results primarily in high-fashion goods, electronics, computers, and other industries of highly technical equipment with a high rate of innovation.

O/C Overcharge.

OCCUPIABLE STORAGE SPACE Warehouse net piling space. It includes the inside dimensions of the warehouse excluding interior walls, permanent aisles, elevator shafts, stairways, offices, receiving and shipping platforms or other areas where goods are not usually piled. It is measured in square footage. A key measurement used here is percent space occupied to the occupiable storage space.

OCEAN BILL OF LADING Under the Carriage of Goods by Sea Act of 1936, the conditions to be printed in the ocean bill of lading were specified. This bill of lading serves the same purpose as the domestic bill of lading in most countries. It is a contract for carriage, receipt of goods shipped, and it provides evidence of ownership. The ocean bill covers only an ocean movement. It is not, in and of itself, intended to cover a combination of land and water movements.

OCEANOGRAPHY The science of the oceans, tides, currents, temperatures, waves, flows, salinity and other ocean matters.

OCEAN SHIPPING REFORM ACT OF 1998 (U.S.) A regulatory change that among other things permitted confidential shipper/carrier contracts and eliminated tariff filings with the Federal Maritime Commission.

OFFER The first part of a contract creation. An offer is a form of power that a first party is giving to a second party to commit the first party to a requirement. In many ways a purchase order sent to a seller is a form of offer. If the seller acknowledges the terms of the purchase order, then an acceptance exists and a contract has been created.

OFFICIAL AIR CARGO TARIFF CIRCULARS A circular put out by the Air Tariff Publishers, Inc., specifying the requirement by state and federal governments for accepting and transporting special commodities. Used for the movement of livestock, human remains, gambling equipment, etc.

OFFICIAL AIRLINE GUIDE (OAG)   An airline timetable guide published for air services throughout the world.

OFFICIAL LOG BOOK   The log of events happening at sea on the vessel, includes deaths, births, marriages, accidents, fines, sickness, and other major actions involving the ship.

OFFICIAL RAILWAY GUIDE   A North American publication containing railroad information, distances between stations, names of officials and their addresses, and other major information.

OFF-LINE   Facilities and installations used by certificated air carriers for other than scheduled service.

OFF LOADING   To unload.

OFF-ROUTE POINTS   Points located off the regular route highways of line haul carriers and served either on irregular schedules on deliveries of LTL freight or on truckloads only, whenever freight is available. For scheduled ocean liner service, these would be ports not served by a carriers but ones they could arrange for delivery of cargo.

OFF-SEASON   Refers to periods of low traffic of which special fares, etc., are utilized.

OFFSET   Found in countertrade situations. Offset is any form of additional service or act that a seller from the U.S. must perform in order to gain the sale. Forms of offset include buying certain goods from the importing country, setting up a factory or research center within the borders of the country, helping local factories sell in the U.S. or other countries, and many others.

OFF SPEC MATERIAL   A purchasing term for goods received from a supplier that do not conform to the purchase specifications.

OILFIELD BODY   A heavily constructed truck body equipped with a bullnose.

OILFIELD HAULER   A motor carrier authorized to transport oil field equipment.

OLERON, LAWS OF   The code of the sea created by Richard Coeur de Lion from the Rhodian laws. All modern maritime law has emerged from these laws. They were very strict laws. For example, a master who cast away his vessel through ignorance could be beheaded without accountability.

ON CONSIGNMENT   Goods sent for sale at the best prices that the consignee can realize on behalf of the consignor. An example is when a supplier sends goods to a customer (per an order), the customer holds them and pays for them as they use or sell them. This saves capital costs for the customer, but it means a delay in receipt of payment for the seller. The benefit for the seller is the guarantee of eventual sale of the goods.

ONE TO MANY PURCHASING   A system of buying where the customer announces to many suppliers what price it is willing to pay for a specific good or service and then waits until one or more of the suppliers accepts the offer.

ONE TO ONE   Linkage by electronic means between one seller and one buyer firm.

ON-LINE   1) Transportation. Facilities and installations used in serving scheduled operations by the air carriers. 2) Electronic Systems. A general term for access to information via electronic means.

ON LINE CATALOG   A purchase catalog of goods and services that is in electronic form by way of the internet, extranet, or email as distinct from in paper form.

ON LINE COMMERCE   A general term for electronic linkages that a firm makes to other firms to consumers thereby allowing such activities as searching product/7service offerings, ordering, financial settlement, etc.

ON LINE ORDERING   Placing orders for goods or services via the Internet, extranet, or email rather than by phone, fax, or mail.

ON SHELF AVAILABILITY   A customer service measure of what percent of demanded sales in a given period could/can be satisfied with the goods on hand.

ON SITE SUPPLIER   A supplier that is physically on the purchaser's property performing such services as managing vendor stocking inventories, production activities, or managing the firm's overhead functions in an outsourcing type of relationship.

ON SOUNDING   Within the 100 fathom curve.

"ON THE BELL"   A railroad term for a train that has entered a block section of the road; arises from a bell that is rung automatically at a downline point from the train passing a specific spot.

ON THE BERTH   A term denoting that a ship is ready to load or discharge cargo.

ON TIME AND IN FULL   A customer service measure of shipments to customers, or from suppliers. Measures by the percentage of items in an order that were delivered on time. 100% means the order was complete as ordered.

OPEN ACCOUNT   Credit and billing arrangement whereby the seller bills the buyer periodically and payments are made over time. As distinct from cash on delivery or collect where payment is to be made upon delivery of the goods.

OPEN AND PREPAY STATIONS   An official list of freight stations in the United States with information as to whether goods may be consigned collect or whether charges must be prepaid.

OPEN CHARTER   A charter in which neither the destination or nature of the cargo is specified.

OPENINGS   The openings in the bottom deck of a double decked pallet that allow the finger wheels of a pallet truck to rest on the ground.

OPEN JAW TRIP   A round air trip that generally has different points for terminating the outbound trip and initiating the return trip.

OPEN POLICY   Insurance contracts which cover shipments throughout a specified period of time, or for all shipments of a certain value, but not committed to a single shipment, are referred to as open policy insurance contracts. The character of this contract specifies that the shipment insurance is automatic on each lot of merchandise, covering undefined risks and specifying that its terms should become definite by subsequent additions or endorsements to the contracts.

OPEN ORDER   A purchase order or contract that is outstanding with the goods yet to be delivered.

OPEN RATE   A rate for a commodity by a liner ocean carrier that is subject to negotiation on liner traffic for each and every voyage. It is a rate that is not subject to review and approval by a rate conference.

OPEN ROUTING   Situation in which a rate between two points applies over more than one route, any one of which can be used for shipping the goods or routing the passenger.

OPEN SKIES   An agreement between two nations that allows unrestricted or near unrestricted commercial flights between them by their flag carriers to and from any airport with customs and immigration facilities in the other countries. It is a form of modern deregulation. Japan and the United Kingdom are among the last hold outs of this form of deregulation in the world.

OPEN STATION   Any station at which an agent of a carrier is located and to which freight may be shipped collect.

OPEN TOP   Trailer with sides but without permanent top; frequently used when heavy equipment is transported, which is lowered into the trailer with a crane and covered with a fabric or plastic protection.

OPERATING AUTHORITY   Routes, points and other traffic that may be served by a carrier as granted by a regulatory agency.

OPERATING DIFFERENTIAL SUBSIDY   A traditional maritime subsidy by many nations that compensates its flag carriers for the difference in operating costs as against those other country carriers operating in the same markets with lower cost operations. It is designed to protect and preserve that flag nation's shipping capacity.

OPERATING EXPENSE   The cost of handling freight or passenger traffic.

OPERATING RATIO   Operating costs divided by total costs (or total revenue).

OPERATING REQUIREMENT   Any term in a contract with a supplier that requires it to adhere to certain practices that would normally be within their management discretion of them. Example: transportation is to be performed only by ships of a certain flag.

OPERATING REVENUE   Total money received by a carrier, from transportation and from operations incident thereto.

OPERATING STANDARDS   Specific features in a transportation contract that the shipper seeks to have the carrier follow. Examples are hiring qualified drivers, adhering to hazardous requirements, and maintaining safe equipment. The same is found in purchase of goods and service contracts.

OPPORTUNITY COST   An implicit or explicit cost that exists whenever one alternative is chosen over another; the foregone benefit from choosing other than the best alternative. If a firm has $1 million of inventory, but could invest in alternative money markets at, say 5-1/5%, then the holding of inventory incurs an opportunity cost to the extent of the short term money market returns of invested cash. In this case it would be $150 per day.

OPPORTUNITY SOURCING   The practice of searching for and analyzing suppliers with the intent of learning their offerings and capabilities without there being an immediate need for a specific product or service, as is the practice with traditional sourcing. The goal of opportunity sourcing is to discover potential suppliers with capabilities and technologies that the firm might be able to utilize in its own product innovation processes.

OPPOSED SWITCH   On a rail line a switch to another track or siding that can not be accesses by moving forward. An opposed switch requires a backward movement onto the track.

OPTICAL SCANNERS   Reading devices usually used in material handling to automatically record and/or affect sortation, stocking, picking, etc.

OPTIMIZING MODEL   A model or formula that results in an optimum (maximum or minimum) answer of the entire function.

OPTIMUM VALUE   Practice of purchasing the required quality items at the least total cost for the firm.

OPTION   The permission to choose, or privilege of taking or delivering something at a given day and price.

OPTION BID   A bidding approach whereby the supplier is to provide individual bid prices on different facets of the work involved. Prices are broken out for such things as the product (finished versus semi-finished), delivery included versus not included; warranty of 30 days, 180 days, and one year lot sizes of 100, 500, and 1000. Buyer can then select the mix of features that are best.

OPTIONAL CARGO   Cargo not yet sold when delivered at a port are termed optional cargo.

OR   Owner's risk.

ORAL ARGUMENT   In person presentation of evidence and other material before a court or regulatory body.

ORAL CONTRACT   A contract that was made orally and not reduced to writing.

ORDER   An instruction to purchase; directions to deliver goods or to pay money.

ORDER AND COMMISSION DEPARTMENT   (Express) One of the nontransportational divisions of the Express service embracing the purchase of supplies, payment of taxes, execution of legal papers, analyzing commercial conditions and locating new markets for shippers of fish, poultry, fruits and vegetables.

ORDER BILL OF LADING   A form of bill of lading that can be used to sell (by the shipper) or affect payment (by the buyer) for the goods en route in the care of the carrier.

ORDER CALL OFF   An order placed with a supplier where a long term or all-encompassing contract is in effect. This is in place of a traditional requisition and purchase order system. Order call offs are often performed by persons inside the firm who contact the supplier directly.

ORDER CYCLE   This includes the time and processes involved from the placement of the order to the receipt of the shipment. It includes the following processes: (1) communicating the order; (2) order processing; and (3) transporting the shipment. These are the functions performed in the lead time. It is similar to lead time.

ORDER FILL, MEASURE OF   A customer service and warehouse productivity measure that represents the total number of orders that were picked complete and/or shipped without stockouts or backorders in a given time period.

ORDER POINT SYSTEM OF INVENTORY CONTROL   An inventory control mechanism that causes a reorder when the level drops to a certain quantity of goods on hand.

ORDERING COSTS   All of the costs associated with the clerical work of preparing an order, transmitting the order, following up the order, and recording receipt of the order. It does not include machine set-up costs for manufacturing, since that is a part of purchase price. It does not include the costs of physically handling the inbound order, since that is accounted for in: (1) storage in-and-out costs, or labor costs; and (2) transportation shipping and receiving costs.

ORDER-NOTIFY (BILL OF LADING)   A document which is used for goods consigned or destined to the order of a person or company named on the lading.

ORDER PICKER   Mobile lift type equipment which allows the warehouseman to ride the pallet up and down to pick from various levels.

ORDER PICKING   The preparation of an order by the packer involving the packing according to the written order.

ORDER TO CASH CYCLE   The length of time required from when a firm receives an order from a customer all the way through to the date when it receives financial settlement from the customer. See also CASH TO CASH CYCLE.

ORDER TRANSPARENCY   A term that means that the progress of the order through the firm's purchasing department, supplier's order management system, their warehousing/manufacturing, etc. is completely visible or accessible easily by persons within the buying firm.

ORDER UP TO...   An inventory ordering policy used in periodic review systems whereby at certain points in time a check is made of an inventory level and an order is placed for a quantity that will bring that inventory level up to a predetermined quantity.

ORDINARY   A vessel in the harbor is known as in ordinary.

ORDINARY FREIGHT TRAIN   A train consisting of a locomotive, with or without a caboose or brake van, and including freight carrying cars.

ORDINARY LIVESTOCK   Defined as all cattle, swine, goats, sheep, horses and mules, except such as are chiefly valuable for breeding, racing, show purposes and other special uses.

ORGANIC PEROXIDE   An organic compound containing the bivalent—O—O structure and which may be considered a derivative of hydrogen peroxide where one or more of the hydrogen atoms have been replaced by organic radicals must be classed as an organic peroxide unless otherwise specified in the DOT regulations.

ORGANIZATION   The working structure of a company, corporation, association, etc., to handle efficiently various branches of work. Transportation organizations are divided into departments such as the executive, financial, operating, traffic, etc.

ORIGINAL   First in order; that from which anything is copied. In Commerce, the original bill of lading, original invoice, etc.

ORIGINAL BILL OF LADING   The one actually signed by the carrier and retained by the shipper; distinct from any of the copies or a facsimile copy.

ORIGINAL EQUIPMENT MANUFACTURER (OEM)   The prime firm or brand of a product. Though thousands of suppliers make parts for automobiles, the OEM would be the brand manufacturer of the car.

ORIGIN OF TRAFFIC   A point from which the traffic begins. The point or place which originates the traffic.

ORLOP DECK   The lowest deck in the vessel. The beams may or may not have the deck laid. It may not run the length of the vessel.

ORM-A   A material which has an anesthetic, irritating, noxious, toxic, or other similar property and which can cause extreme annoyance or discomfort to passengers and crew in the event of leakage during transportation.

ORM-B   A material (including a solid when wet with water) capable of causing significant damage to a transport vehicle or vessel from leakage during transportation.

ORM-C   A material which has other inherent characteristics not described as an ORM-A or ORM-B but which make it unsuitable for shipment, unless properly identified and prepared for transportation.

ORM-D   A material such as a consumer commodity which, though otherwise subject to the regulations of the DOT, presents a limited hazard during transportation due to its form, quantity and packaging.

OSCILLATION, PERIOD OF   The time of the roll, or oscillation, from port to starboard. If it includes the return roll to port, it is a double roll. The time required for a complete roll is the same regardless of the angle of the roll if there is no change in the trim. The swinging of the compass needle before coming the rest indicates a roll underway, and provides a means of timing the roll.

O.S.&D.   Over short and damaged.

OSHA   Occupational Safety and Health Act—a federal law in the U.S. governing safety features of the workplace.

OTIF   Acronym for "on time and in full," a customer service measure.

OTIFNE   Acronym for a customer service measure meaning "on time, in full, and no exceptions."

OUNCE   A weight of $1/16$ of a pound avoirdupois; $1/12$ of a pound, troy.

OUTBOARD   Away from the center fore-and-aft line of the vessel.

OUTLET   A supply chain term for any final firm in the cycle that sells to the ultimate user or customer.

OUT OF POCKET COST   Those carrier costs directly attributable to the movement of the traffic.

OUTPORT   A port or harbor located some distance from the chief port.

OUTPORT ARBITRARY   An extra charge in steamship tariffs for picking up or dropping off freight at a port that is not a regular stop along a liner's route.

OUTRAGE   The empty space in a container or drum to accommodate expansion, density change, etc., due to temperature change.

OUTRIGGERS   Equipment used to increase the width of the trailer.

OUTSIDE DIMENSIONS (O.D.)   The outside dimensions of a container or package. In drums it is measured by the diameter over the rolling hoops.

OUTSIDE STORAGE   Storing products outside of the building on the ground.

OUTSOURCE/OUTSOURCING   Turning a company operation or assets over to another firm for them to supply or manage. Distinct from ACCESS which is to seek something from an outside firm in a close relationship manner for which the firm is not capable of performing on its own and has a critical need for it.

OVERAGE   The extent that the freight exceeds that on the shipping document, or the quantity to have been believed shipped.

OVER- AND SHORT-LANDED REPORT   A report that shows missing packages, or short-landed shipments.

OVER-BOOKING   The act of selling more tickets than there are seats available. It is synonymous with over-selling.

OVERCHARGES   The extent of freight charges for transportation services in excess of those applicable thereto under the tariff or contract.

OVERCHARGE CLAIMS   When the shipper or consignee pays charges for a transportation service which exceed those applicable under the tariff, a condition of overcharge claim exists. A carrier may make an error and create an overcharge many of the following ways: (1) assessment of an incorrect rate; (2) errors in description on the bill of lading of the commodities being shipped; (3) errors in weight in which the weight designated on the bill of lading is incorrect, or an incorrect minimum weight is applied; (4) mistakes in tariff interpretation; and (5) clerical errors. Application for an overcharge claim must be filed in writing with the carrier within three years of time of delivery of the shipment. Normally, the claim is filed, the period is then extended six months from the time the claim would be disallowed. This permits the applicant to bring suit in the event application for an overcharge claim was disallowed by the carrier.

OVERDESIGNED   A term that signifies that a firm's specification for a particular good is more elegant than is necessary for the purpose for which the item is intended to perform in use. It is a target of standardization efforts.

OVERDUE   As applied to a draft or note, the specified time for payment of which has passed or matured.

OVER FLIGHTS   Aircraft flights over a country by planes of another country. This is typically done by way of prearranged agreements.

OVERFLOW WAREHOUSE   A warehouse that holds goods temporarily in peak demand or holding periods.

OVER FREIGHT   When freight is in the possession of a carrier without waybill or identifying marks it is normally referred to as over freight.

OVER INVOICING   A practice sometimes found when a seller is exporting goods to firm in a country with a closed or weak currency. The tactic is to show a higher price than normal for the goods being moved. The buyer then converts their local currency into U.S. dollars or other hard currency. Upon shipment and cash settlement, the seller receives the gross sum payment. He/she keeps the proper sales amount and deposits the excess in a bank account inside their hard currency country that belongs to the buyer. See also UNDER INVOICING.

OVERHANG   To extend or project beyond. It could refer to the overhand of products on pallets or rail cars beyond the width of normal clearance.

OVERHEAD GUARD   A protection overhead to protect the driver of a lift truck.

OVERHEAD PERCENTAGE   A percentage rate over and above the material and labor costs of producing a product that is charged to cover the overhead costs of the producer.

OVERHEAD RUNWAY SYSTEM   The overhead tracks which carry the lifting blocks and trolleys in warehouse operations. They operate in one plane, but may go straight or have curves.

OVERHEAD TRAFFIC   When traffic moves over a line which is a bridge in character, that is it is received by another carrier and delivered to a third carrier, it is called overhead traffic.

OVERHEAD WAYBILL   A document used to cover shipments by a carrier on whose line neither the point of origin nor the destination are located.

OVERLAND COMMON POINT (O.C.P)   A term stated on the bills of lading offering lower shipping rates to importers east of the U.S. Rockies provided merchandise from the Asia that comes in through West Coast ports. This traffic is in competition to the all-water Asia to mid-continent and U.S. East Cost Ports.

OVERLOAD   A vehicle that exceeds the regulation maximum in total weight or axle weight. Generally refers to motor transport vehicles.

OVER-SOLD   Selling more tickets than there are seats available. It results in a confirmed reservation without a seat.

OVERSPEC'D   Same as OVERDESIGNED.

OVER, SHORT, AND DAMAGE (OS&D)   When a freight agent submits a report showing discrepancies between the bill of lading and the freight on hand, this type of report is issued. Excessive freight is called over, absent freight is called short, and bad condition freight is referred to as damaged. In freight stations, a room is frequently set aside for unclaimed, shortweight, damaged items, etc. and is called OS&D room.

OVER-THE-ROAD (CARRIER)   A term denoting a motor carrier performing intercity service.

OVER WITHOUT BILL   Freight without its bill of lading or freight bill.

OWNER, OF A PROCESS   A general term for the person or department in a firm who oversees and is responsible for the performance of a process.

OWNER-OPERATOR   A driver who owns the vehicle he operates, and has leased it to a carrier.

OWNER'S RISK   Indicates that shipper relieves carrier from part of transportation risk.

OXIDIZER   A substance such as chlorate, permanganate, inorganic peroxide, or a nitrate, that yields oxygen readily to stimulate the combustion of organic matter.

PPPP

PACKAGE   A bundle, parcel or bale.

PACKAGE CAR   A freight car holding two or more less-than-carload shipments which are moved jointly from a point or origin to a principal break-bulk point.

PACKAGE FOOTPRINT   The shape and dimensions of the space occupied by a package on a packing line, shelf, or in a carton.

PACKAGE FREIGHT   Packages making up less-than-carload shipments which are billed on the basis of the number of pieces or packages and are subject to check and inspection.

PACKAGING ENGINEER   A professional trained in managing the packing operations of a firm.

PACKED   A term describing an article protected by, or with partitions wrappers, excelsior, straw, or other packaging and lining material, affording adequate protection against breakage or damage from handling or weather.

PACKING AND CRATING   A process as well as a common outsource service to prepare shipments for export.

PACKING LIST   The purpose of the packing list is to show the merchandise packed and all particulars. It is normally prepared by the shipper. It is not necessarily required by carriers. A copy is usually sent to the consignee to assist in verifying the shipment received.

PAS-CONTACT (PART OF SECURITY SYSTEM)   Plate completing electrical circuit affixed to a door or window. If door or window is opened the circuit is broken, resulting in a security alarm.

PADDY   Rice without the husks removed. A mixture of clean rice and paddy rice is called cargo rice.

PAJAMA WAGON   A tractor with sleeper facilities.

PALLET   The pallet is a device used for moving and storing freight. Commonly it is about four feet square and is so constructed to facilitate placement of a lift truck between the levels of a platform to move it on a freight car or into a warehouse.

PALLET, DOUBLE WING   A pallet that has the top platform extending out on opposite sides.

PALLET, EXCHANGE PROGRAM   An agreement between two firms that makes each responsible for the other's pallets. This is usually done on a one-for-one basis. Records are maintained on all pallet movements between the two parties.

This alleviates the requirement of having to off load products from one point to another and delivering empty pallets each time a product exchange takes place.

PALLET, FIRE   Safety platform that has emergency and fire fighting equipment stowed on it.

PALLET, FOUR-WAY   Permits forks to enter at any of its four sides.

PALLET, GMA   48″ × 40″ hardwood, four-way (4) entry pallet.

PALLET HOOK   A hook attached to a rope and used for lifting pallets.

PALLETIER RACK   Frame and pallet which stack on top of one another for higher stacking.

PALLETIZE   Placing specific size material on a specific size pallet in a prescribed arrangement.

PALLETIZER   A type of materials handling equipment that acts to palletize units in place o or in assistance with personnel performing same.

PALLET LOAD UTILIZATION   The percentage of total pallet square inches that are occupied by packages loaded upon it.

PALLET, ONE WAY   A pallet that can only be accessed by a forklift from its front or back.

PALLET PATTERN   The pattern of cases placed on each layer of a pallet or unit of merchandise.

PALLET, SAFETY WORK PLATFORM   48″ × 40″ pallet that has four sides 3′ high constructed on it. It is used in conjunction with a lift truck to safely raise personnel for maintenance or other duties.

PALLET, THROW AWAY   Designed to transport products one way and then disposed of Usually two-way entry constructed of soft wood.

PALLET, TWO-WAY   Permits forks to enter at only two of its four sides.

PANAMA CANAL ACT   An act of Congress (1912) prohibiting the ownership by railroads of water lines with which they compete.

PAN-AMERICAN UNION   An institution, with headquarters in Washington, D.C. very active in supplying information regarding South American countries. This institution is supported by the United States and the twenty Latin-American Republics.

PANCAKE   Brake diaphragm housing.

PANEL BODY   A delivery truck with a fully enclosed body commonly used for small package movements.

PANTOGRAPH   The apparatus atop electric locomotives and trains that reaches up to connect to the overhead wire electrical source.

PAPER, GUMMED   A dextrin coating on paper—or a coating of fish-animal glue. It is activated by moisture.

PAPER JACK   In ocean transportation, a master who secures command through influence and depends on his mate for professional assistance.

PAPER RATE   A published rate under which no traffic moves.

PAPER ROLL CLAMP   F/L attachment which permits grasping and rotating large paper rolls.

PAPER, VCI   Paper prepared with a volatile corrosion inhibitor.

PARADIGM   A way of thinking and acting.

PARALLEL TRADING   Also known as GRAY MARKET. Goods of a manufacturer that are purchased by someone from a low cost country and sold against that same manufacturer in a higher cost country.

PARATRANSIT   A term in the U.S. for transportation required by the Americans With Disabilities Act for forms of transport for persons with disabilities.

PARCEL POST   A part of the U.S. mail service providing for the carrying of merchandise and matter, up to and including certain dimensions and weights at zone rates.

PARCEL POST AIR FREIGHT   Air parcel post package shipment as air freight to the postmaster at the destination city for delivery within that postal zone or beyond. The destination postage is affixed by the shipper.

PARCEL RECEIPT   Receipt given by a steamship company for a parcel shipment.

PARCEL SHIPMENT   A small package restricted as to value, generally samples of goods or advertising matter.

PARETO'S LAW   A phenomenon found in many situations in which a relatively small number of products, sales or most activity comprise a large percentage of the total; see also eight-twenty rule. (ADD TO THIS)

PAR OF EXCHANGE   The actual value of a sum of money, as distinguished from theoretical value, of a similar sum in the currency of another country.

PARS   The name of one of the major airline reservation systems.

PARTIAL LOSS   Damage to property, but not such as to make it totally valueless or useless.

PARTIAL SHIPMENTS   Under letters of credit, one or more shipments are allowed by the phrase "partial shipments permitted." In bulk shipments (commodities, etc.), a tolerance of three percent is allowed.

PARTICIPATING CARRIER (TARIFF)   Each transportation line which is a participant in a tariff is referred to as a participating carrier. The tariff may be issued by the transportation line, or by a tariff publishing agent.

PARTICULAR AVERAGE   In marine insurance, particular average refers to partial loss on an individual shipment from one of the perils insured against, irrespective of the balance of the cargo, and so differs from general average. Such insurance can usually be obtained, but the loss must be in excess of a certain percentage of the insured value of the shipment, usually

PARTITION   A wall or panel used to separate sections or units. A means or separating commodities by slotted pieces for protection and packing.

PARTNER CARRIER   A carrier that is part of a marketing alliance. This might consist of shared codes for flights, joint marketing, combined frequent flier programs, etc.

PARTNERSHIP   1) Law. A legal entity whereby two or more persons combine and can act for each other. 2) Purchasing and Marketing. An original term that was used for alliances.

PART OWNER   In marine shipping, one of several owners of a ship.

PARTS BANK   An outsource service by a carrier or other third party logistics firm that holds spare parts for a brand manufacturer and distributes them when the brand firm customers order them. The concept was originally created by Federal Express in the United States for automobile parts.

PAR VALUE   The face or nominal value of a commercial paper.

PAR VALUE (EXCHANGE)   An exchange of currencies at the current rate without any additional fees, premiums, or discounts.

PAR WEIGHT   The steamship par between weight and measurement goods, determined by dividing a long ton (2,240 lbs.) by 40 cubic feet, and equal to 56 pounds.

PASS   An order providing for free transportation over specified lines or routes; known as annual or trip.

PASSENGER CAR   A car employed for the transportation of passengers; also known as a coach.

PASSENGER CARGO AIR CARRIER   A certificated air carrier holding right (certificate of public convenience and necessity) to transport scheduled passengers and ~freight over specified routes. It may be distinguished from an all-cargo or all-passenger carrier. They are commonly called all-purpose air carriers.

PASSENGER LIST   A list of the passengers of a vessel which is shown to custom house officials when entering port, either in the United States or abroad.

PASSENGER MILE   A term denoting the transportation of one passenger for a distance of one mile.

PASSENGER RATE   A carrier's charge or fare for transportation of a person from one point to another.

PASSENGER REVENUE   Revenue derived from passenger business of a railway company.

PASSENGER TARIFF   A schedule containing passenger rates (fares), excess baggage charges, routing, rules and privileges.

PASSENGER TRAFFIC   The handling of passengers which also includes baggage, express, mail and other traffic handled by passenger trains.

PASSING REPORT   The cars which are received or delivered in interchange between yards are identified on a passing report. This document is required by the traffic department to assure information on car movements which can be passed along to the shippers and consignees, or to the auditor's office. The passing report, obviously, becomes significant for bridge or overhead traffic.

PASSPORT   A document which certifies the nationality for a person or vessel. It assures safe conduct for the person identified.

PASS THROUGH   Any action or process that is streamlined to the point of not having to stop or be checked at a certain point.

PATENT CLAUSE   A standard boiler plate term in most purchase orders and contracts. This clause seeks to hold the buyers harmless from any possible patent infringement by the sellers.

PAVED RAIL PIT   Railroad track inside the building and area under and around tracks are paved, for ease of cleaning.

PAYBACK PERIOD, DISCOUNTED   The time period in which the initial investment cost of an asset is recouped from earnings inflows that are discounted with a present value factor to reflect the changing time value of money.

PAYBACK PERIOD, SIMPLE   The time period in which the initial investment cost of an asset is recouped in terms of earnings inflows in cash terms.

PAYEE   A party named in an instrument as the beneficiary (the recipient) of the funds. Under letters of credit the payee (the beneficiary) is either the drawer of the draft or a bank.

PAYEE   One to whose order a bill, draft, of note is to be paid.

PAYER   A party that is responsible for the payment as evidenced by the given instrument. Under L/C's, the payer is the party on whom the draft is drawn—usually the drawee bank.

PAY UPON CONSUMPTION   See PAY ON SCAN, a similar feature. In some hospital systems, the goods are paid for once they have been used by hospital personnel.

PAY ON SCAN   A transactional feature in many large retailers today whereby they pay the brand manufacturer for the goods once they have been scanned by a consumer at the retail store. This basically causes the goods to be in the retailer system on consignment.

PAYMENT   That which discharges a debt.

P. & D.   Pick-up and delivery of freight.

P.D. CAR   Permanent dunnage car—a boxcar equipped with dunnage.

P.O.   Purchase order.

PEAK TANK   A tank used to trim ship, located in the fore or aft sections of the ship.

PEANUT WAGON   A large trailer pulled by a small tractor.

PEDDLER CAR   When a shipment is discharged to various consignees, or is peddled to various consignees, the car containing the less-than-carload shipments is referred to as a peddler car. Each shipment takes the less-than-carload rate, subject to a car minimum charge. Peddler car deliveries are commonly made to branch houses of shippers.

PEDDLE RUN   A pickup and delivery operation over given routes involving frequent stops. It usually involves operations from one terminal, in one radial area.

PEGGED CURRENCY   A nation's currency that is held by it in a relative position against another currency. For many years the currencies of Hong Kong and Singapore were pegged to the U.S. dollar, and would float up and down in the world in line with the U.S. dollar. However, they would remain constant in relation to the U.S. dollar.

PEG LEG   A tandem tractor with only one power axle.

PENALTY   Legal punishment either on the person or goods, or by a fine imposed for misrepresentation, false billing, or non-compliance with

PENDENTE LITE   While suit is in progress.

PER   By; by means of; according to.

PER ANNUM   By the year.

PER-CAR RATES   The setting of a price or a rate per car on specific commodities is a per-car rate. This is commonly done with vegetables, fresh fruits, etc. Southeastern railroads use per-car rates as a means of competition against exempt motor carriers hauling into the east.

PERCENT   By the hundred; rates of interest, discount, commission, etc.

PERCENTAGE   An allowance figured by hundredth parts; also commission.

PERCENTAGE CLASSES   These are classes which have a stated percentage, relationship to an existing class, such as 27% of 1st, 85% of 5th, 90% of 6th, etc.

PERCENTAGE GROUPS   The related points considered as units in rate making; the same percentage applying to or from points within a group.

PERCENTAGE SYSTEM   The name given a method of rate making between Trunk Line and New England territories on the one hand and Central Freight Association territory on the other; these areas being divided into Eastbound and Westbound percentage groups, the same being determined in accordance with their relation to New York or Chicago. The commodity rates, New York and Chicago, are taken as a basis and rates between other points in the territories above named are made on a percentage of these rates.

PERCENTAGE TERRITORY   Area within which the percentage system applies.

PER CENTUM   By the hundred.

PER CONTRA   On the contrary.

PER DIEM (P.D.)   This implies for one day. It is a charge made by rail carriers against other rail carriers for the use of rail cars while on another line.

PER DIEM CHARGE   The amount paid by one carrier to another from each day it keeps a car belonging to the other and generally in the form of a certain sum per car per day.

PER DIEM RULES, CODE OF   The Association of American Railroads establishes per diem rules which govern the amount of the rate to be paid for the use of railroad rolling stock owned by another carrier. This is applicable to a common carrier railroad. The low per diem rates have been a matter of considerable contention over many years.

PERFECT ORDER   A quest in customer service whereby shipments to customers would be on time, in full, and without loss or damage.

PERFECT PURCHASE ORDER PERCENTAGE   A metric in customer service that measures the percent of orders received by customers according to their original purchase order.

PERFECT TRANSACTION   See PERFECT PURCHASE ORDER PERCENTAGE, PERFECT ORDER, OTIF, or OTIFNE.

PERFORMANCE BOND   A bond often required of vendors. The bond will provide payment to the buyer in the event that the supplier does not perform. Common in construction projects. Protection for buyer in event of vendor non-performance.

PERFORMANCE (CAR)   The performance of a car is the number of miles traveled by the car in a given period—loaded or empty. The performance also refers to the amount of freight carried, the average daily movement, the transportation receipts and any other information relative thereto.

PERFORMANCE REQUIREMENTS   A contract term between a buyer and seller that requires the goods or service to perform in a specified way. It might be as simple as light bulbs that are to last a minimum of 5,000 hours, or it might be a rate of speed of machinery. Some airlines seek performance of commercial aircraft in terms of fuel and costs of operations against the aircraft manufacturers.

PERFORMANCE SPECIFICATIONS   Specifications in the form of what the buyer wants the purchased product to do. Differs from other specifications which describe what the Item is to be made of and how it is to be manufactured. These specifications rely upon the seller to design and build the item so that it will perform according to the requested performance.

PERIOD COSTS   Costs that are incurred over a time span rather than from activity volume; examples are leases, interest, property taxes.

PERIODIC ORDER SYSTEM OF INVENTORIES   A system in which orders for good lots are placed in fixed time intervals; usually the lot size varies.

PERIODIC REVIEW   An inventory management process of checking the levels and consumption of goods according to a specified span of time, or points in time. For example, certain fast moving goods might be checked daily, slower ones weekly, and even slower ones monthly.

PERISHABLE FREIGHT   Commodities subject to rapid deterioration or decay; such as fresh fruits and vegetables, dairy products, and meats, which require special protective services in transit, such as refrigeration, heating, and ventilation.

PERMEABILITY   A characteristic of a film which permits liquids and gases to filter through.

PERMISSIVE OPERATING RIGHTS   Operating authority that may be utilized by a carrier and not required to serve.

PERMITS   Authority or permit granted by the I.C.C. To contract carriers by motor vehicle or water and freight forwarders to operate in interstate commerce.

PERMIT (WATER TRANS.)   A written authority to remove dutiable goods.

PERPETUAL INVENTORY RECORD   An inventory system that keeps constant track of all inflows, outflows and stock levels.

PERPETUAL INVENTORY SYSTEM   A stock control system that maintains a constant monitor of the level of goods.

PER SE   By and of itself.

PERSONAL PURCHASES   Making purchases for individuals who work for the form. Example would be adding one more car for an employee to a purchase of a fleet for the company. Personal purchases are discouraged in most firms.

PERT   Program evaluation review technique; a planning tool for projects, construction, etc. in which many tasks are to be performed in parallel with others while some must be completed in sequence; system determines the critical path that cannot incur any delay without causing a delay in the overall project completion time.

PERTURBATION   Procedure in data processing in which a variable at a time is changed to observe its effect on the overall system.

PESETA   The name of the national currency of Spain.

PESO   The name of many national currencies in Central and South America.

PETITIONS   Applications, protests or other statements presented to a regulatory body which calls for some action by that agency.

PETTY AVERAGE   Small charges, such as pilotage, port charges, etc., borne in part by both ship and cargo.

PH   A measure of acidity or alkalinity on a scale of 0 (acidic) to 14 (base) with 7 being neutral.

PHANTOM FREIGHT   The deficit weight placed on a freight bill for goods not actually in a shipment for purposes of qualifying the shipment for a higher weight break; lower rate that provides for lower total charges.

PHYSICAL CONNECTION   Indicative of a switching connection between two carriers, allowing from interchange of cars.

PHYSICAL DISTRIBUTION   Term that applies to the logistics activities that take place from end of the production line to the final user. Include such things as traffic, packaging, materials handling, warehousing, order entry, customer service, inventory control, and sometimes forecasting.

PHYSICAL INVENTORY   A physical count of designated items located within the warehouse.

PICKING ERROR   Removing wrong product or quantity from the warehouse inventory.

PICK PACK   A method of materials handling for outbound shipments. It is typically the picking of goods in quantities smaller than a carton.

PICK RACK   Storage rack used for assembly (order).

PICKUP   Those cars added to a train en route between dispatching and the receiving yards are generally referred to as pickup. Sometimes they are added at the dispatching yard to a train operating over several divisions on a continuous wheel report.

PICKUP ALLOWANCE   An allowance granted the consignor by the carrier for delivery of freight to the carrier terminal. It also means an allowance to the consignee for picking up freight at the terminal and taking to his business site when the rate called for carrier delivery.

PICKUP AND DELIVERY   A service involving the collection of freight from door of consignor and delivery to door of consignee.

PICK-UP SERVICE   The collecting of shipments by a transportation company from places of business, or residences, of the goods to be transported by said company. Formerly this service was principally performed by the express companies but is now extended to motor truck, airlines, and in some cases railroad and steamship companies.

PICK-UP TRUCK   A small truck with low sides and small carrying area behind the cab.

PIER   The projecting wharf, which may be either at an angle or perpendicular, which permits the side placement of ships for loading and unloading operations.

PIER HEADING   The United States engineers establish a fixed line beyond which a pier may not be extended.

PIG   A trailer transported on a rail flat car.

PIGGYBACK   The transportation of highway trailers or removable trailer bodies on rail cars specifically equipped for the service is called piggyback. It is essentially a joint carrier movement in which the motor carrier forms a pickup and delivery operation to a rail terminal, as well as a delivery operation at the terminating rail head.

PIGGYBACK, PLAN I   Through motor carrier service, shipper charged motor carrier rate, motor carrier performs pick up and delivery, line haul performed by railroad, motor carrier rate and liabilities apply for the shipper.

PIGGYBACK PLAN II   Through railroad service from door to door, railroad provides pick up and delivery, railroad rate and obligations apply.

PIGGYBACK, PLAN III   Ramp to ramp service with railroad performing line haul; shipper and consignee must arrange for pick up and delivery; railroad rate and liabilities apply for linehaul.

PIGGYBACK, PLAN IV   Railroad ramp to ramp service; shipper providing rail car and containers as well as arranging pick up; consignee arranges delivery; railroad rate for hauling equipment.

PIGGYBACK, PLAN V   Through railroad-motor carrier service in which offer joint service beyond their Dines; railroad provides rail car and the road or motor carrier provide containers as well as pick up and delivery; both responsible for obligations; each divides rate on division basis.

PIGGYBACK, PLAN V½ Innovation since deregulation of piggyback service in 1981; railroad provides through service of rail and motor links in railroad owned motor carriage service extending from its rail line territory.

PIGTAIL The cable used to transmit power to the trailer.

PIKE A turnpike.

PILFERAGE Felonious breaking into containers and taking and removing property of others.

PILOT In rail transportation this involves an employee who is assigned to a train when the engineer or conductor isn't acquainted with the rules. In water transportation the pilot is in charge of the vessel from the open seas through whatever channels may be involved to the proper dock.

PILOTAGE The charge for piloting a vessel, based on the draft or tonnage of

PINWHEEL PATTERN A type of package on pallet loading pattern that appears in a spiral-like form from the outside inward to the center.

PIPELINE A line of pipe used for transporting liquids, principally crude oil, or gas.

PIPELINE CARRIER A company owning and transporting liquids, principally crude oil, through pipes and treated as a common carrier.

P.I.V. VALVE Post indicator valve, indicates water pressure in that particular post (hydrant).

PLACARD (ING) The placement of signs on trucks and other transportation vehicles indicating the presence and nature of hazardous materials contained within them.

PLACE AN ORDER AGAINST A CONTRACT The practice of calling off goods against a supplier by a buying company that are covered in a blanket or systems agreement. These individual orders do not require full documentation as separate order transactions. They are contained with an overall existing contract.

PLACEMENT, ACTUAL When a rail car is placed in an accessible position for loading or unloading on a private or public delivery track or at a point designated by the shipper or consignee, it constitutes actual placement.

PLACEMENT, CONSTRUCTIVE When it is necessary to place a car as near as possible to the point of destination or the point promised by the carrier for the purpose of loading or unloading, or in circumstances in which the consignee's track or tracks are full, the approximation of optimum location involves constructive placement.

PLAINTIFF One who commences action in court to obtain redress for injury sustained.

PLATE B (RAIL CAR)   A rail car of standard length, width and height measurements that can travel over most lines in the nation.

PLATE C (RAIL CAR)   A rail car that is larger in length, width or height than the normal cars and must be carefully routed due to limitations on some rail lines; many of the larger, modern rail cars that have been built since the 1960s are Plate C cars.

PLATFORM BODY   A truck or trailer with no sides or top, but only the floor.

PLATFORM COSTS   The terminal freight handling costs.

PLATFORM HANDLING   The transfer of a load from one truck to another in the motor carrier business, regardless of whether or not the load touches the platform, is platform handling.

PLATFORM SLING   A platform used in place of a sling in water transportation, to which tackle is attached by bridles to the corners.

PLEADINGS   The written or oral position in a legal case, or in a hearing before the regulatory authority.

PLIMSOLL MARK   The depth to which a vessel may safely load is identified by a horizontal line painted on the outside of the ship. In British merchant vessel this is normally referred to as the plimsoll mark. This mark must remain above the surface of the water.

PLUG DOOR   A special tight sealing type of door often found on box, insulated and refrigerator rail cars.

PLY   To beat to windward. Steamers also ply between ports to load and unload. Also a layer or fold.

PLYWOOD   A laminated wood veneer, glued together.

POINT   A word used synonymously with city, town or place and usually indicating some important traffic characteristic.

POINT OF ORIGIN   The station at which a shipment is received by a transportation line from the shipper.

POINT OF SALE   The location of a sale between a seller and a buyer. It is generally used for the site of the final sale in a supply chain to a consumer.

POINT OF USE   The site where an item is consumed or used. This is a particularly important point in field service operations.

POINTS   The tapered ends of rails in a railroad switch that separate from or join other rails in order to change train course.

POISON A   Extremely dangerous poisons, poisonous gases or liquids of such nature that a very small amount of the gas, or vapor of the liquid, mixed with air is dangerous to life.

POISON B   Less dangerous poisons, substances, liquids, or other solids (including pastes and semi-pastes), other than Class A or irritating materials, which are known to be so toxic to man as to afford a hazard to health during transportation; or which, in the absence of adequate data on human toxicity, are presumed to be toxic to man.

POLE TRAILER   A form of truck trailer consisting of the axle unit and a rigid pole that attaches to the truck pulling it.

POLICY   The written contract of insurance.

POLICY MANUAL   A document used in purchasing and traffic departments that spells out the processes, authorities, and organization of the department.

POOL   An assembly of equipment to be drawn on by those creating the pool.

POOL DISTRIBUTION   Technique of combining small orders to get truckload (TL) or carload (CL) rates.

POOLED PURCHASING   Common in government purchasing; the needs of various cities, counties, or states are pooled together into one purchase for advantage of volume buying.

POOLING   The practice of two or more transport firms combining operations so as to take capacity out of the market and share the total revenue that is possible along the route thereby minimizing their collective operating costs.

POOLING AGREEMENT   The process of agreeing on the divisions of revenues, or the divisions of tonnage business, between several carriers in accordance with a contract or agreement.

POOLING (CAR)   When individual carrier equipment is managed through a central agency which serves several railroads for the joint benefit of the carriers and the shippers, a pooling action is involved.

POOLING EQUIPMENT   The joint or common use of the station facilities,

POLYETHYLENE   A synthetic material attained by polymerization of ethylene under great pressure.

POLYSTYRENE FOAM   A plastic foam used for packing and protection. It is composed of open or closed cells.

POOP (DECK)   A light deck, raised above the main or upper deck and extending a short distance forward from the stern.

POROSITY   A condition of being permeable or of loose texture that permits the passage of liquids or gases.

PORT   1) Geographic Location. A harbor for ships. 2) Ship Structures. The left side of the ship.

PORTAL   Gateways to the internet that act to simplify the search process for users. Portals are provided by groups having an interest in a specific area. For example, a forestry research group at a university might provide a single web site that acts as a portal for efficiently finding any other related forestry web sites.

PORT CHARGES   The general assessment for pilotage, lighterage, towage, wharf services, etc. compose port charges.

PORT DIFFERENTIALS   When a rate is added to the port-to-port rate for the continuous movement from a port to the interior, a port differential is applied. Interestingly enough, along the North Atlantic ports, New York uses it as a basing point for rates and the differential is the added charge from New York to whatever North Atlantic interior point is involved. Baltimore has also been used as a basing point for such rates.

PORTER MODEL   A popular value chain concept for an individual firm as espoused by Michael Porter.

PORT EQUALIZATION   In order to assure a shipper the lowers possible charge from an interior point to a given port, it is common to have the steamship line absorb the differential between the cost of shipping freight from the interior point to the steamship's port for all excess charges beyond the movement to a rival port which might be shorter.

PORTERAGE   The charge made by dock companies for the numerous services rendered by the porters.

PORT, FREE   When a port is provided for the landing and holding of shipments for re-export without the imposition of the usual custom procedures and charges, this is termed a free port.

PORT MARK   In international water movements, the final destination is the port mark. It need not necessarily be the port of entry if the port of entry is not the final destination.

PORT OF CALL   A port in which vessels may load or discharge their cargo is a port of call. When it is necessary to provide extra transportation service to points beyond the port of call the process is normally referred to as beyond port of call.

PORT OF DEPARTURE   The port from which a ship clears or sails and known as Port of Exit.

PORT OF DISTRESS   Any port to which a vessel may turn in the event of trouble.

PORT OF ENTRY   The port at which a custom house provides services for the importation of goods into a country.

PORT OF ORIGIN AIR CARGO CLEARANCE PROCEDURE   A procedure designed to expedite international transportation of goods. It permits the performance of customs formalities at nongateway cities, rather than holding up the customs operations until the shipment is at the gateway city.

PORT-TO-PORT   From one port to another port.

PORT WARDEN   An of official whose activities embrace the valuation, measurement, etc., of cargo or ship.

PORT WARDEN'S FEE   A charge made at a port for a survey of cargo, hull, valuation, measurement, etc., of goods or ship.

POSSOM BELLY   A livestock trailer with a drop frame that permits hauling small livestock and chickens under heavy livestock.

POSTAGE STAMP RATE   A rate which is uniform throughout a large territory is referred to as Postage Stamp Rate because of its semblance to postage charges.

POST AUDIT   A study conducted of a new warehouse, fleet, etc. to ascertain how well it is performing in relation to the proposal and financial analyses used to originally justify It.

POST ENTRY   A statement of goods made after they have been unloaded and the particulars ascertained.

POSTING (TARIFFS)   The filing of tariffs and other schedules for public use in compliance with the law at local and general offices of the carrier and to which the carrier is a party.

POSTPONEMENT   The practice of delaying the final stages of manufacturing until the last point in the line or upon ordering by the customer. By maintaining the product in a generic form as far as possible on its journey through distribution and performing final finishing near the customer, the seller generally increases response service to customers and minimizes overall total inventory costs in the system.

POTATO CAR   An especially designed car for the transportation of potatoes.

POTENTIAL COMPETITION   A competition existing in possibility and not in reality. For example: A river or other waterway paralleling a railroad and upon which no boats or steamships operate is considered potential competition.

POTS   Warning flares that indicate an obstruction, breakdown, or other hazard.

POUCH CHECK   When a check is made by the American Association of Railroads through its Car Service Division at certain points to determine the transit of freight in selected cars at the station at a given rate for the purpose of trying to locate delayed freight, it is referred to as a pouch check.

POULTRY CAR   Car usually triple or quadruple decked, and constructed specially for the transportation of poultry.

POUND   The name of the currency of the United Kingdom.

POWER BRAKE   Applying the brake with an open throttle.

POWER OF ATTORNEY   Authority to do or forbear derived by one person from another. Also, authority granted by a transportation line to an agent to act on its behalf within the defined permission or authority granted in the power of attorney document.

PRACTICE   That which has become customary through frequent action; the exercise of any profession.

PRATIQUE   The temporary quarantine of a vessel is raised by granting the master of the vessel a pratique certificate. When granted pratique, the vessel is unrestricted. It is granted by the health officer.

PRE-AWARD SURVEY   An analysis of bidders to determine their capabilities and capacities to perform the work as outlined in the bid.

PREBLOCKING   Practice of having a prior railroad arrange rail cars in a certain sequence so that the current carrier does not have to reclassify or resequence the cars.

PREBUILD INVENTORIES   The practice of increasing inventories in the supply chain in advance of promotions or product launch so as to meet expected market demand.

PRECEDENT   A former court or regulatory agency decision that acts as the basis of subsequent decisions involving similar circumstances.

PRECLEARANCE   A process in some nations import customs and immigration systems whereby passengers and freight are cleared at the outbound country terminal facilities so that they may pass through the inbound terminals with a minimum of delay.

PRECOOLING   A process employed in the shipment of citrus fruits and other perishable commodities. The fruit is packed and placed in a cold room and the heat gradually extracted. The boxes of fruit are packed in a solid mass in cars that have been thoroughly cooled. The bunkers are completely filled with large cakes of ice, and the car is hauled through to destination without unsealing or opening bunkers.

PREDATORY FARES/RATES   Freight rates and passenger fares by established carriers that are very low so as to cause a new entrant in the market to drop out of it. These fares and rates are below full costs of the seller but are seen as short term losses to maintain long term market presence by the dominant carrier.

PREFERRED CUSTOMER   Any customer that is designated in favorable status by a seller firm. This is typically based upon high volume purchases or the potential of the customer to become an important one in the near future.

PREFERRED SUPPLIER   Any supplier that is designated in favorable status by a buying firm. This is often done after careful quality certification and capability analyses have been conducted by the buying firm.

PREJUDICE   Failure to give one shipper the same treatment as another shipper, under similar circumstances and conditions.

PREMIUM   A sum beyond par value.

PREPAID   Payment in advance of freight and/or other charges prior to delivery of shipment at destination, usually by shipper at point of origin.

PREPAY   Pay before, or in advance.

PREPAY STATION   When a station is identified for the purpose of requiring pre-payment, it is referred to as the prepay station. Normally this is a non agency station.

PRESENTING A DRAFT FOR COLLECTION   Means that the bank accepts the documents from a shipper and effects collection through their branch or corre-spondent at foreign destination and credits the shipper's account upon receipt of advice that the draft has been paid by the consignee.

PRICE INDEXING   The tracking of commodity or service prices over time and creating a numerical and often graphical chart of them. This is often done in order to measure the prices paid by the firm against the index which is an average of most transactions in the market.

PRICE LIST   A list of articles with prices attached.

PRICE, LONG   The price of goods after all duties have been paid.

PRICE ON DELIVERY   A price term found in the buying and selling of some minerals. The price that is determined is the one that is in effect on the day of delivery of the shipment.

PRICE PROTECTION CLAUSE   1) A contractual term between a buyer and seller that states that the price will not rise to the buyer during the term of the contract. 2) A purchase contract term required by some retailers of their suppliers stating that if the prices of the products in the general consumer market were to drop during the course of them holding the goods available for sale, then the manu-facturer is to compensate the retailer for the lost margin opportunity.

PRICE TARGETING   A negotiating and buying objective of setting the maximum price that a buyer seeks to settle upon in a purchase.

PRICE TRANSPARENCY   Prices that are widely known across a region or coun-tries. The advent of the Euro has caused price transparency of the same products in the markets across various nations of Europe. Transparency allows clear analysis of choices.

PRICE UNIFORMITY   Prices that are held constant by a seller across many mar-kets.

PRICE VARIATION/VARIANCE A purchasing term for the difference between prices paid and the prices that were projected in the budgets for that period. Any difference between them is a variance.

PRICE VOLATILITY Prices that fluctuate widely in a short period of time, often so fast that they can not be related to easily noted supply and demand causes.

PRICE, WALK AWAY The price that a buyer sets in his/her mind at the beginning of a negotiation that is the maximum they will be willing to pay. Any price that is settled upon that is higher than it would result in no sale taking place—they will "walk away" from it.

PRICING CUBE A pricing concept whereby the seller offers the lowest possible price for a) full truck/lorry loads, b) set periods of time, and c) in single commodities. Any deviation from any of these will be charged at different prices. The cube concept means that prices will be higher for a) differing quantities, b) multiple commodities, and c) over different changing points in time.

PRIMA FACIE At first view or on the face of it.

PRIMAGE An allowance of 5 to 10 percent added to ocean freight rates in the early days of shipping to be given to ship's officers and crew for the safe handling, stowage, and delivery of cargo consigned to their ship; now usually included in the tariff and quotation.

PRIMAGE AND AVERAGE ACCUSTOMED A prorate levy assessed by the steamship companies on consignors to cover the cost of wharf age, pilot age, and other port charges.

PRIMARY PACKAGE The package in which a product is placed for its display on the retail shelf. This is a bottle, box, tube, can, etc.

PRIME ENTRY A statement of goods based on details given in the bill of lading.

PRINCIPAL BILL The first of a set comprising a foreign bill of exchange to be presented and therefore the one which is accepted and paid.

PRINTER-SLOTTER A machine that prints, slots, creases and trims solid and corrugated box materials.

PRIORITY That which is first in rank, time or place; first claim.

PRIORITY MAIL Mail bearing air mail service rates for transportation by air on a priority basis.

PRIOR TRANSPORTATION A term found in some regulatory areas for a situation in which the leg of movement under examination had been preceded by movement by another mode.

PRIVATE AIR CARRIAGE Also called proprietary air transportation and business flying. It involves the use of company owned planes, or leased planes, to carry passengers, property, or freight for business purposes. It is not usually used to refer to personal private transportation.

PRIVATE AIRCRAFT   Any aircraft that is not commercial or military.

PRIVATE CAR LINE   A private concern owning its own rolling equipment, or leasing cars to or from railroads and operating them as private cars.

PRIVATE CARRIER   A carrier that provides for movement of goods for the manufacturing or merchandising firm for which it is owned.

PRIVATE LABEL   The practice of a retailer to have goods produced and labeled in their own brand. These are placed side by side on the shelves to compete against the goods of branded manufacturers.

PRIVATE LINE CAR   A freight car not owned or leased by a railway company.

PRIVATE SIDING   The rail track which serves a particular industrial plant is referred to as a private siding. The track may be owned or rented by the plant.

PRIVATE WAREHOUSE   A warehouse operated by the owner of the goods stored there. A small stockroom at a manufacturing plant is a private warehouse, as is the huge order picking facility of the catalog mail order house.

PRIVATIZATION   The selling off of enterprises, agencies, and activities by a government to the private sector. In the 1980s and 1990s many governments of the world sold off their national oil firm, airlines, railroads, banks, highways, ports, shipping firms, etc.

PROBLEMIZATION   See ISSUE ASSESSMENT.

PROCEDURE   The rules and principles established for the conduct of cases before a regulatory commission or court.

PROCESS   A set of activities, resources, and flows designed to produce a desired outcome or output.

PROCESS FOCUS   A special attention made to identifying, improving, and managing critical processes in a firm or organization.

PROCESS IMPROVEMENT   See PROCESS FOCUS.

PROCESS MANAGEMENT   See PROCESS FOCUS

PROCESS ROADMAP   The act of capturing all the steps in a chain of activities and analyzing them for levels of sophistication. Some firms perform a basic process of a current operation and then apply a next tier of target enhancements, then a next, etc.

PROCESS VERSUS FUNCTIONS   An activity view of a firm or organization rather than a traditional departmental one. For example, a functional organization might be viewed in terms of departments for Marketing, Selling, Innovation, Manufacturing, Distribution, Production, Materials, and Purchasing. A process oriented firm would, on the other hand, be viewed horizontally in terms of Plan, Source, Make, and Deliver processes in the overall quest for competitiveness.

PROCESS FLOW CHARTING   Capturing all the steps and activities in an overall process.

PROCURATION   A general letter or power of attorney.

PROCUREMENT   Overall activity of inbound logistics including purchasing, value analysis, cost analysis, inventory control, etc.

PROCUREMENT CARD   A credit card used by firms for small and odd item purchases. This greatly reduces the need for petty cash and requisition/purchase orders for these items.

PROCUREMENT PLAN   The overall plan of how a purchasing group will obtain the needed goods and services for its organization over a period of time. It typically contains strategies for specific commodities and services, key suppliers to approach and use, and it often contains system enhancements that are to be made during the period.

PRODUCE   Farm products of all kinds.

PRODUCER'S MARKUP   The difference between price charged by a producer and the costs of production and distribution.

PRODUCT AVAILABILITY   Measure of the number of products available for use or shipping in relation to the total possible number manufactured or marketed by the firm at any point in time.

PRODUCT CODE   Identification number or letter.

PRODUCT IDENTIFICATION   Any number or marking clearly showing the type or lot numbers on freight bills, etc.

PRODUCT LIABILITY   The liability that a seller has relating to the item it is selling in the market. This liability is generally for safety related factors.

PRODUCTION COSTS   The actual costs of producing a thing. This does not include profit or capital investment.

PRODUCTION LOGISTICS   Generally, the planning, movement, and flow of goods into, through, and out of a manufacturing facility.

PRODUCTIVITY   A work effectiveness measure that is, in general terms, the sum of outputs divided by the sum of inputs.

PRODUCT LIFE CYCLE   A cycle that products experience throughout their life that consists of a conception stage growth, maturity and decline, each part of the cycle calls for different materials management and distribution strategies; product life cycle can be as short as a few months as with fad items or as long as several decades.

PRODUCT MANAGEMENT PROBLEM   The determination of the product mix resulting from the production activities of the industrial firm would represent its product management problems. The introduction of a new line for production requires the comparison of the total effect on one option product with another. This would necessitate anticipating the changes in production, marketing, and logistics costs with revenue for each product option.

PRODUCT POSTPONEMENT   See POSTPONEMENT

PRODUCT PROLIFERATION   A common phenomenon in most firms, indicates that over the years the number of products or stockkeeping units a firm produces or distributes has greatly increased.

PRODUCT RECALL   The seeking out and arranging for product that has been sold or distributed by the firm to be brought back to it; usually for defective goods or health problem items.

PROFIT CENTER   An accounting approach to internal operations in which all or most related revenues and expenses are assigned to specific functions, product lines or managers. A profit center approach for a private warehouse or private fleet would require the managers of those operations to charge for services in such a way so as to cover expenses and make a profit.

PRO FORMA   For the sake of form.

PRO FORMA INVOICE   An invoice that is prepared and sent to a buyer in advance of producing a lot of goods. Often done for buyers in foreign countries who use the pro forma invoice in the exchange the local currency into the currency required for payment.

PROGRAM   A set of instructions to perform a computer operation. It performs a phase of a job or algorithm usually.

PROGRESSION OF CLASSES   A series of classes increasing in relation to a basic class. For example: The first class being a basic class, all classes higher bear a relation to it.

PROGRESS PAYMENTS   Intermittent payments made to a supplier according to progress in producing goods, services, construction, or project work that require a long time to complete.

PROHIBITED ARTICLES   Goods which the carriers will generally not handle at all, or is so, only in accordance with separate and special set of rules and regulations.

PROMOTION OPTIONS   Since the close of World War II, there has been a growing recognition of the need for determining public demand, and influencing that demand. Promotional activities are involved in each of these two classes of activities. The optional promotional plans of a firm may be regarded as involving different plans for promotion. Each plan would involve its own projected change in market demand, its own combination of media required, the uniquely different time of positive effect for each media, the allocated cost involved in the given plan for expenditure in each media, etc. Consequently, when two promotional plans are compared, the change in anticipated demand resulting from the promotion activity must be measured against the changes in total cost—production, logistics, and marketing costs. It cannot be measured against promotional costs alone.

PRO NUMBER   The number placed on its freight bill by a carrier. The prefix pro is derived from the word progressive, i.e., consecutive.

PROOF OF DELIVERY (POD)   A document or other certification that goods have been delivered to their intended destination and party.

PROPORTIONAL RATES   The proportional rate may be used only in constructing through rates on shipments which begin or terminate at points beyond the points from or to which the proportional rate applies. Sometimes they provide a means of establishing a competitive through rate where one of the carriers refuses to be a party to a competitive joint rate. The I.C.C. defined proportional rate as one which applies to a part of a through transportation which is entirely within the jurisdiction of the Act to Regulate Commerce." The proportional rate is used to equalize rates via one gateway to rates that are available via another gateway. Sometimes they induce the movement of through traffic from origin to a destination when the traffic is similar to the intermediate local traffic between the points covered by the proportional rates. Export and import rates are examples of proportional rates. If export rates through Boston were made similar to export rates through New York, it would be an example.

PROPORTIONAL TARIFF   A tariff containing only proportional rates.

PROPOSAL   An act on the part of a shipper to change the rates, rules or regulations in the tariff. Action taken with the publishing agency or rate.

PROPOSAL   The document with summarized technical information used to justify the acquisition of a capital asset.

PROPRIETARY AIR TRANSPORTATION   See Private Air Transportation. The use of company owned or controlled aircraft for business flights.

PRO RATA   In proportion.

PRO-PATA CHARTER   A charter for an aircraft on a flat fee basis in which the passengers share the flat charter rate, on an equal basis. This form of charter is more common than the entity charter.

PRORATE   A proportional distribution; according to a certain rate.

PRORATE, COMBINATION MILEAGE AND RATE   In interline traffic, an average of the percentages determined between given points, by use of mileage prorates and rate prorates.

PRORATE, MILEAGE   A division of revenue on interline shipments based on the ratio of each carrier's miles to the total miles.

PRORATE, RATE   On interline shipments, a division of revenue on the basis of the percentage of each carrier's local rate to or from the interchange point to the total combination rate from origin to destination.

PRORATING POINT   A traffic point upon which a rate is prorated.

PRO-RATING TERRITORY   Indicative of a territory to which shipments by several carriers in a joint shipment would divide the transportation rate on a prearranged percentage basis. In other words, the through rates constructed to such territory will be prorated, or divided, on an established basis of divisions between the carriers handling the traffic.

PROTECTIVE SERVICES   Such services as refrigeration, icing, salting, and heating rendered en route, for which the tariff authority makes specific charges and allowances.

PROTECTIVE TARIFF   Duties imposed on imports to encourage local manufacturing

PROTEST   1) A document filed by a party in an attempt to prevent a rate from going into effect or an application being approved. 2) A legal means of proving presentation and default of a negotiable instrument, as well as providing notice to interested parties that the instrument was not paid.

PROTEST (CAPTAIN'S)   A document prepared by the master of a ship on arrival at port concerning accidents or damage to ship or cargo during a certain voyage, generally for the purpose of relieving the ship owner of liability. In instances of jettison, the ship's master must note his protest before the consul of the country from which his vessel sails within 24 hours of his arrival at the first port he reaches, reporting the circumstances of protest is a process whereby a more complete statement giving all details is drawn up after the expiration of the 24-hour period.

PROTESTING A BILL   Attestation by a notary public, for the purpose of taking legal action, that a bill of exchange has been presented and refused acceptance or payment.

PROXIMO   In the next month.

P-SYSTEM   The system for managing inventory which involves ordering on a specific date each order, for the quantity required until the next fixed reorder date— plus the amount of the lead time stock. Thus, it involves a fixed review period, but a variable order quantity.

PUBLICATION   Making public in the manner required by the Act, of tariffs, circulars, billing, instructions, guide books, territorial directories, classifications, exception sheets, etc., which in any way effect the handling of traffic.

PUBLIC PURCHASING   General term that applies to purchasing by city, county, state, and federal bodies.

PUBLIC SERVICE COMMISSION   A name given to a State body having control of or regulating public utilities.

PUBLIC UTILITY   That which is made use of by the general public, and the operation and conduct of which is vital to everyone.

PUBLIC WAREHOUSE   A warehouse operated by a warehouseman engaged in the business of storing goods for hire. The word public refers to the fact that the warehouse provides a service to the public, and does not indicate public ownership.

PUBLISHING AGENT   A person authorized by transportation lines to publish tariffs of rates, rules and regulations for their account.

PU&D   Pickup and delivery. This operation involves the door-to-door pickup of freight from the consignor and the delivery operation to the consignee.

PULL DISTRIBUTION   Situation in which demand at the retail or final level acts to stimulate inventory and transportation flows at preceding points in warehousing, etc., back to the factory and purchasing.

PULL THE PIN   The process of releasing the fifth wheel lock.

PUL-PAC   Another name for a Push/Pull attachment for a lift truck.

PULPBOARD   A form of paperboard without sizing, with crude formation and low finish. It is composed of ground wood pulp mixed with sulphite or sulphate pulp to add strength.

PUNCH (CAR IDENTIFICATION)   A small device on the outside of a freight car containing a punching die representing the car number. Cards are inserted into the punch by means of a paddle which transfers car number to the card by marginal punching.

PUNCHED TAPE   In data processing, it is a paper tape perforated to represent data.

PUNT   The national currency of Ireland.

PUP   A short semi-trailer used jointly with a dolly and another semi-trailer to create a twin trailer.

PURCHASE AGENTS (INTERNET)   An electronic mechanism that a potential buyer sets into motion to search out prices that are offered by various sellers through their sites.

PURCHASE ORDER   The basic document in purchasing systems for acquiring goods from vendors.

PURCHASE ORDER COST   The computed total cost incurred by a buying firm for initiating, processing, and settling a purchase order transaction. This is used in analysis regarding PROCUREMENT CARDS, SYSTEMS CONTRACTS, BLANKET AGREEMENTS, and other alternative forms of purchase mechanisms.

PURCHASE ORDER DRAFT   A purchasing technique that utilizes a separate document in the placement of each order.

PURCHASE QUANTITY DISCOUNT   If a reduction in purchase price per unit is made for buying in larger quantities, it represents a purchase quantity discount. Thus, a standard pace per unit may be charged but reduced to a lower per unit price based on a minimum volume of purchase. The existence of purchase quantity discounts creates the need for computing the indifference volume just as it is computed in transportation logistics costing. At some volume less than the specified minimum volume for a purchase discount, the total cost of the purchase would be exactly the same when computed at the regular price times the indifference volume or at the minimum volume times the discount price.

PURCHASE PAYMENT DISCOUNTS   Whenever a reduction in purchase price is made as a result of payment within a specific period of time, the extent of the reduction in purchase price for early payment is called a payment discount. If a purchase agreement should specify "2 percent—10 days—30 days net," it offers an opportunity to reduce the price 2% by payment within 10 days. This is a 2% discount on the required invoice price to be paid.

PURCHASING BUSINESS PLAN   See PURCHASE PLAN.

PURCHASING COUNCIL   A body composed of purchasing people from various decentralized divisions of a single firm. The purpose of this body is to collectively negotiate and acquire goods using the clout of the entire body.

PURCHASING SHARE   The percent of total purchases of a firm or organization that is sourced and handled by the purchasing department.

PURE MATERIAL   One that experiences little or no weight or cubic loss from extraction or other raw form through to being a finished product, has implications for optimal plant location.

PUSH DISTRIBUTION   A distribution strategy that consists of stocking distribution centers, retail and sometimes use points in anticipation of an increase in future demand.

PUSHER-AXLE   A non-powered axle on a trailer.

PUT AWAY   The overall process of receiving goods, inspecting them, entering them into the inventory system, and placing them into their intended storage site within the facility.

PUT AWAY TIME   The total time required from receipt of inbound goods in a warehouse until they come to rest at their intended storage site in the facility.

PUT ON THE AIR   Apply brakes.

PUT ON THE IRON   Put on chains.

PYROFORIC LIQUID   Any liquid that ignites spontaneously in dry or moist air at or below 130F.

QQQQ

QUADRANT TECHNIQUE   A purchasing field method of classifying goods and services according to their value/profit potential and risk. Generally, the four quadrants are named criticals, distinctives/bottlenecks, generics, and leverage/commodity items.

QUALIFIED SUPPLIER   A particular supplier that has been evaluated to be fit for supplying the firm with goods it needs from it. It generally consists of a quality audit as well as an assessment of technical capabilities and financial stability.

QUALIFYING A SUPPLIER   The process of examining a supplier with the possible result of it becoming a QUALIFIED SUPPLIER.

QUALITY   The grade established by a standard. Purchasing field term for the attributes or characteristics of a product or service being specified and/or acquired.

QUANTITY   Anything that can be increased, diminished, divided or measured as to bulk, weight or number.

QUALITY GAP   The difference between the attributes of a current product or service against an ideal or goal of quality attributes.

QUANTITY DISCOUNT   In purchasing, this is a reduction in the purchase price contingent on a large quantity purchased in a certain lot or over time for a particular commodity.

QUALITY FUNCTION DEPLOYMENT   Systems analysis into a physical item or process to determine each component or step in terms of its contribution to the final performance or outcome. The purpose is to remove anything that does not add value or contribute to the desired performance of it.

QUARANTINE   A control process placed on an operation to protect against a health hazard. A ship may be quarantined so that it cannot leave or arrive in a protected point. The Q flag is hoisted during the quarantine period.

QUARTER   The fourth part; 28 pounds, avoirdupois; 8 bushels.

QUARTER DECK   That part of a ship which is abaft the mainmast.

QUASI   Almost. As if that which resembles.

QUAY   A term for a wharf, usually of solid as distinguished from open-pile construction, accommodating vessels on only one side, and parallel with the shore line.

QUAY DUES (QUAYAGE)   A charge for berthing at a quay.

QUAY-PIER   A structure either extending from the mainland or lying between two docks or basins of sufficient size to permit all the necessary elements of terminal facilities to be arranged parallel with the ship and serving ships or both sides.

QUEUE   The lining up of vehicles, passengers, freight, or messages or otherwise for processing.

QUICK-CHANGE (QC)   This term is applied to the procedure for transforming a passenger aircraft into a cargo carrying plane, and vice versa. It has passenger seats and galleys set up on pallets for quick removal and conversion from passenger to cargo aircraft.

QUICK DISCONNECT (QDC)   A system or device for expediting the change of the lift truck, computer equipment, telecommunications equipment, etc.

QUICK RATIO   The sum of cash, accounts receivable and marketable securities divided by the amount of current liabilities.

QUONDAM   Former.

QUOTA   A system of controlling imports by specifying the limitation on the amount that can enter the country during a certain period of time.

QUOTATION   Current prices of commodities, etc.; also, the act of quoting or that which is quoted. A price offer received from a seller from requesting the price of its goods or services.

QUOTE   The current price (or rate) of something; the price offered to a buyer for certain goods or services.

Q-SYSTEM   This management inventory system involves the optimization of the order quantity, and the standardization of the order quantity. It involves a variable review time, and a fixed order quantity.

RRRR

R&L   Rail and lake.

R&O   Rail and ocean.

R&T   Rail and truck.

RL&R   Rail, lake and rail.

RACK CAR   A freight car equipped with racks at both ends and used for the movement of pulpwood. It is a term used for rail flatcars with racks for handling automobiles. The 85 foot flatcar may have two or three levels of cars.

RACKING   Hooks, racks, stilts and stripping placed in a refrigerator car on which meats and other perishable commodities are arranged for proper transportation.

RACK JOBBER   A middle person in a distribution chain who distributes manufacturer's goods that includes placing them into position at the customers' sites for final sale and use. Distinct from straight delivery to an inbound loading dock, this person often inventories the goods, rotates the stock, replenishes it, and is responsible for its care.

RACK, PIT   Storage rack located in the warehouse where a small supply of each item is stored specifically for efficient picking.

RACK, SHIPPING   Rack designed to transport a specific product.

RADIOACTIVE MATERIAL   Any material, or combination of materials, that spontaneously emits ionizing radiation, and having a specific activity greater than 0.002 micro curies per gram.

RADIO FREQUENCY IDENTIFICATION (RFID)   A system of short distance radio signaling that is generally used for sending instructions within a warehouse to forklift operators for picking and putaway processes.

RADIUS   Besides its standard meaning in geometry, in materials handling it means the horizontal distance between the centerline of a hook and the perpendicular going through the center of the rotation of the hook.

RAGS   Bad tires.

RAG TOP   An open top trailer with a tarpaulin cover.

RAIL AND WATER TERMINAL   A terminal where freight is transferred between railway cars and boats.

RAIL BUMPER   Metal device affixed to the rail track, designed to stop a rail car.

RAIL DOCK   The platform which runs along the railroad track.

RAIL DOOR Large overhead door where rail enters building for entering and exiting of railcars.

RAIL FLEET SIZING The analytical process undertaken by a shipper or receiver firm to determine the optimal size and configuration of rail cars needed for their leasing/ownership and use.

RAIL-LAKE RAIL (RL&R) The carrier modes participate in that order in a movement.

RAIL PIT Area where inside rail track is located.

RAILROAD BOND A bond issued by a railroad for the purpose of financing improvements, extensions, etc., and generally secured by mortgages on tracks, rolling stock and other property.

RAILROAD RETIREMENT ACT An act of Congress, passed on August 29, 1935, and amended in 1937, establishing a retirement system for employees, subject to the Interstate Commerce Act.

RAILROAD STORAGE CHARGES In addition to the demurrage rules, hazardous shipments are also subject to charges for storage on railroad tracks. These charges vary from $8 to $20 per day, depending on the rate territory and the materials. Storage charges are assessed as penalties, since railroads are not in the warehousing business. The charges are specified in the demurrage and storage tariff of the contract terms and conditions of the carrier's bill of lading.

RAILROAD UNEMPLOYMENT INSURANCE ACT An act of Congress (June 25, 1938) establishing an unemployment-insurance system for employees of certain firms engaged in interstate commerce.

RAILROAD WAYBILL This is normally called the historical record of the shipment. It is prepared for each carload and less-than-carload shipment from the shipping order. The shipping order is the carrier's copy of the bill of lading. The railroad waybill moves with the shipment from point of origin to destination regardless of the number of carriers over which the shipment is transported. The waybill consists of a list of added information such as the weights, the carton numbers if transferred en route, special services performed, etc. The original waybill will eventually be forwarded to the auditor's office. The Interstate Commerce Commission requires that the original waybill be retained for three years before destruction.

RAILS In materials handling, it means the fixed or removable horizontal members of the post pallets.

RAIL TRAFFIC That which pertains to the movement of goods and persons on rails.

RAILWAY FINANCE ACCOUNTING The keeping or examining of the revenues accruing from and expenses chargeable in the operation of the railways.

RAILWAY LABOR ACT   An act of Congress (May 20, 1926) providing for the disposition of disputes between carrier and employees. An amendment (June 21, 1934) created the National Railroad Adjustment Board and the National Mediation Board.

RAILWAY LINE CLEARANCE   The weight and size limitations for movements.

RAILWAYS   Synonymous with railroads and signifies the collective rail transportation lines of a country.

RAMP   An inclined roadway or passage used to facilitate a loading or unloading operation. It is used, for example, to load semi-trailers on flatcars.

RAND   The name of the currency of the Republic of South Africa.

RANDOM ACCESS   A computer term indicating that data is stored on a high speed rotating disk in random arrangement thereby speeding its access by a user.

RANDOM NOISE   In data processing, it represents a procedure for simulating unpredictable events.

RANGE   A term used with reference to a provision in Cork (Ireland) for orders Charter Party, by which the loading port is not specified when the charter is signed but limited to ports within a certain range of coastline.

RATE   The price of a carrier for providing transportation and related services.

RATE, ALL-COMMODITY   A rate, usually based on a carload, applied to an assortment of merchandise or shipments which move at one time in one vehicle from one consignor to one consignee.

RATE, ALTERNATIVE   A rate employed when the tariff provides for the use of more than one rate on particular kinds of traffic.

RATE, ANY QUANTITY   A rate applied regardless of quantity shipped.

RATE BASIS   The economic factors which are involved in the making of a transportation rate.

RATE, BERTH   In maritime traffic, the rate charged on general cargo by regularly operating water lines as distinguished from the rates charged on full cargoes and chartered vessels.

RATE, BLANKET   A special rate covering several different articles in a single shipment.

RATE-BREAK POINT   When two independent movements are added to provide a lower rate than the through rate, the point at which they connect is called the rate-breaking point. For example, if the rate from New York to Chicago was added to the rate from Chicago to Peoria, and this provided a lower combination than the through rate from New York to Peoria, the rate would be said to have Chicago as the rate-breaking point—or the rate is said to be made "over" Chicago.

RATE BUREAU   An organization of carriers legalized under the Reed Bulwinkle Bill for the purpose of establishing agreement on rates. The bureau also publishes the tariffs for the participating carriers.

RATE CARD (SYSTEM)   A card file system of keeping rates, showing article, commodity or class rates, I.C.C. authority, routing, marks, and classification governing.

RATE, CARGO   A rate applying to a consignment which takes up all the freight carrying space in a vessel.

RATE, CHARTER   A rate which applies when a charterer leases or hires a vessel for a trip, usually based on the weight of the cargo. The ship owners usually pay all charges agreed upon. Since this form of charter eliminates the element of risk from calculation of shipper, it is the form used most commonly. When a ship is hired for a period of time rather than by the trip, the rate is based on the net tonnage of register of the vessel, calculated monthly. The owners of the ship usually supply food and maintenance of crew and keep the ship in repair; the charterer furnishes fuel, passport and terminal charges.

RATE CHECK   A freight bill audit for the purpose of discovering errors and overcharges.

RATE, CLASS   A rate applied to an article not assigned a special or commodity rate and not covered by an exception. Class rates apply to the numbered or lettered groups or classes of articles that are contained in the territorial rating column in the classification schedule.

RATE, COMBINATION   A through rate from point of origin to destination, made up of two or more rates added together.

RATE, COMPELLED   A rate between points adjacent to rivers, lakes, and so forth.

RATE CONSTRUCTION   The science, method or factors employed in the making of rates.

RATE, CORPORATE VOLUME   Discount rate that is based upon the amount of freight that the entire firm tenders to a carrier. As distinct from the volume that a particular site might tender to the carrier.

RATE, DECLARED (VALUATION)   A transportation charge based upon the declared value of an article or articles. (See VALUATION, DECLARED.)

RATE, DISTANCE   A rate constructed on a mileage basis, usually local or joint, and applicable to a specified distance only. As the length of the haul increases, the per-ton-mile factor decreases.

RATE, EQUALIZING   The rate that results from a voluntary adjustment of rates on a basis that equalizes natural disadvantages of shippers and localities as regards transportation facilities and costs.

RATE FACTORS   The component rates which make up a through rate.

RATE MAKING   Calculations used to determine charges for handling and clerical—plus any additional expenses.

RATE-MAKING LINES   The transportation companies in a geographic area that control the rates established.

RATE, PAPER   A published rate that is never assessed because another published rate or rates would instead apply to a particular shipment.

RATE, POSTAGE-STAMP   When a rate is uniform throughout a large territory it is termed a postage-stamp because of its similarity to fixed postage charges.

RATE QUOTATION   A rate provided by a carrier.

RATE, RELEASED   A rate that applies when responsibility for the full value of the freight is not assumed by the carrier.

RATE, RETURNED-SHIPMENT   A rate applied to mineral-water carriers; packages, drums, or cylinders used for transporting acids, ammonia, and gas; and to bags and sacks which are returned to the original shipper after their contents have been emptied.

RATE SCALE   A table of rates graduated according to distance or zones.

RATE STRUCTURE   Is that foundation upon which a series of related rates are based.

RATE TERRITORY   The geographic division of the country to establish the jurisdiction for rate making purposes, establishing rate bureaus, or forming associations.

RATE, THROUGH   A rate applicable from point of origin to destination.

RATE, VOLUME (VR)   In motor-carrier tariffs, a term used to denote rates at quantities heavier than LTL lots (6,000 pounds) and lighter than TL lots (10,000 pounds).

RATE WAR   The name given the action when carriers cut rates in an effort to secure tonnage; at the present time not so frequent among rail carriers as water lines.

RATING   1) A class to which an article is assigned; 2) Computation of proper charges for shipment.

RATING, VOLUME   The rating established for high-density freight.

RATIONALIZE   1) Efficiency. The act of analyzing a system in order to make it more efficient. 2) Organizational. To downsize.

REACH TRUCK   A form of fork truck with forward mounted load wheels that permit the fork carriage to extend forward for picking up or dropping a pallet or unit block of goods.

REAL TIME   An electronic system term for the capability of immediate access to data. This is distinct from BATCH which is done in consolidated mode only at certain points in time.

REAR END DEVICE   A light and signal device placed on the rear freight car of a train to warn approaching trains of its presence. This is in place of the lights that were on brake vans and cabooses.

REASONABLE CARE AND DILIGENCE   See LIABILITY, WAREHOUSE-MAN'S LEGAL.

REASONABLE DISPATCH   A transit time concept in claims.

REASONABLENESS (I.C.C.)   A requirement under law (common) and by statute that a rate shall not be higher than is necessary to reimburse the carrier for the actual cost of transporting the traffic and allow a fair return.

REBATE   That part of the transportation charge, returned by a carrier to a shipper, and now unlawful.

REBILLING   Issuing a new waybill at the junction point to which the connecting line has billed the cargo.

RECEIPT   A written acknowledgment of payment.

RECEIVE   Inbound movement of goods.

RECEIVER   Document listing the goods received on a particular shipment—quantity and description.

RECEIVER (OF FREIGHT)   One to whom a shipment is consigned; the consignee.

RECEIVER'S CERTIFICATE   When a receiver acts for a carrier by acknowledging an indebtedness under court authority to provide funds for equipment, supplies, fuel, and other requirements for the carrier's operation, a receiver's certificate is the term applied to the written acknowledgment.

RECEIVER WITH INTERNAL CYCLONE   A vertical cylinder used in materials handling that enables the material to fall into the hopper by air being forced into the base of the cylinder.

RECEIVING   The process of entering goods, data, or people into a system.

RECEIVING PAYMENT (FOREIGN)   The manner of receiving payment for goods sold in foreign countries can be divided into three principal methods: 1) Cash in advance, 2) Open Credit, and 3) Payment against Draft, a) documents deliverable on acceptance of draft (D.A.), and b) documents deliverable on payment of draft (D.P.).

RECEIVING TALLY   An independent listing of goods on a shipment which is prepared by receiving personnel at the warehouse.

RECHARGE BILL   When two rail carriers serve the same point and agree to absorb one another's local switching charges, a reciprocal switching agreement is in effect. Under these circumstances an industry that is located on the railroad and wishes to route its shipment via another railroad may do so without paying extra charges for the switching performed by the rail carrier on whose line the industry is located.

RECIPROCAL TREATY   A commercial treaty between two nations, providing mutual advantages.

RECIPROCITY   In purchasing or traffic settings, a selection process whereby one firm buys from another because the second also purchases or uses the first firm.

RECIPROCITY, CARRIER-SHIPPER   A purchasing and carrier selection practice that consists of a carrier purchasing products needed in the company in effective exchange for the manufacturer selecting the carrier for shipments.

RECLAMATION   In shipping, a claim made against the seller of goods which prove deficient or defective.

RECONSIGN   To change the name of consignee and/or the destination while shipment is still in transit.

RECONSIGNMENT (R/C)   The process of changing the consignee while a shipment is en route through a change in the bill of lading is called reconsignment. Reconsignment can only take place before the shipment is delivered to its original destination. A charge is made for reconsignment. The charge varies with the tariff provisions and depends upon the extent of change in destination. Reconsignment can take place only at the request of the owner of the goods. It is not available on LCL shipment. It is not practiced to any significant extent by motor carriers, airplanes, freight forwarders, or water carriers. Normally diversion will not change the name of the consignee while reconsignment will change it. This practice is indispensable to the lumber, perishable goods, and comparable industries. It permits reconsignment to the most advantageous market. Reconsignment is a change in the name of the consignee while en route, as contrasted to diversion, which does not change the consignee, but is also made while the shipment is en route.

RECONSIGNING CHARGE   Charge for re-billing a shipment en route to other than original destination.

RECOOP   Inspection of damaged goods, repacking, returning good stock to storage and disposing of the bad stock.

RECOOPERING   Cooperage repair on wooden containers. It is often used to refer to the repair of all containers and packages used in shipping.

RECOUPER AREA   Area set aside in warehouse for recartoning, etc., of damaged products.

RECURRING MANAGEMENT PROBLEMS   Each business operation is confronted with a series of management problems of a general class that occur over and over again. While recurring management problems may be of a major or minor nature, it is possible to classify major management problems facing the industrial firm into a relatively few significant classes of problems. One classification of recurring management problems may be on the basis of whether they occur before or after the operations of the firm. Those occurring before the operations of the firm, for example, would be illustrated by location management problems and product determination management problems. It is necessary to determine what will be produced and where it will be produced before operations begin. Operational management problems can be divided into pre-production, in-production, and post-production recurring management problems. An example of a pre-production management problem would be planning the pre-production logistics channel. An example of a production management problem would be determining the optimum equipment for production. A post-production management problem might involve optimizing the post production channel. In this classification basis, recurring management problems may be rather limited in number.

RECYCLE(ING)   The act of disposing of waste or left over items in a manner that allows the materials to be used again in a manner that avoids landfill or other undesirable disposition.

REDETERMINATION   A process used in purchasing of large projects or construction. An initial determination is made as to the labor, material, and time requirements for the new work. At a certain point in the work's progress, a final estimation is made as to the exact labor, time, or materials requirements. A final negotiated rate is then determined.

RED LABEL   A label required on shipments of articles of an inflammable character.

REDUCED RATE   A rate that has been reduced since some specified time.

REDUNDANT EFFORT   Any activity that is duplicated where the second one provides little or no value (unlike double checking in a critical quality system).

REEFER   This is a broad term covering refrigeration equipment in general. It may be more specific such as a reefer car, referring to a rail car with refrigeration equipment.

REENGINEER(ING)   A process of system improvement that generally starts with determining the AS-IS set of activities. It then analyzes them for possible reduction or elimination of redundancies. The resulting SHOULD BE chart then becomes the template for system improvement.

REEXPORT   Term signifying the act of importing of goods only to later export them. The original importing might have been for storage, some manufacturing, or packaging.

REFERENCE INQUIRY   A form used by manufacturers when asking for references regarding the experiences of other manufacturers with foreign firms.

REFINING IN TRANSIT   The stopping of shipments of sugar, oil, etc., at a point located between the points of origin and destination to be refined.

REFRIGERATED WAREHOUSE   A public warehouse providing temperature control at 0 degrees F for the freezer space, 60 degrees F for the cooler space, and 25 to 60 degrees F in the atmospheric controlled space—where the humidity is held to 50–70 percent.

REFRIGERATION   The process of keeping freight in a low temperature state. Usually performed by ice, liquid nitrogen or by mechanical refrigeration.

REFRIGERATION CHARGES   The charge made for icing a refrigerator car, in some cases on per 100 pounds basis, and in other instances, per car.

REFRIGERATOR CAR   A specially constructed car, insulated and equipped with ice bunkers or baskets, or a cooling system, and usually adapted for the installation of heating units, used primarily for the movement of commodities that need protection from heat or cold.

REFUND   The term refund applies in circumstances of an overcharge collected by a carrier for charges billed or paid.

REFUSE BODY   A truck body built for the movement of refuse—garbage.

REFUSED FREIGHT   Freight which the consignee or owner refuses to accept; freight which, for any reason, cannot be accommodated on the flight of intended departure.

REGENERATE   A form of recycling, generally of chemicals, so that they may be used again in the same way as they were originally.

REGIONAL   A geographic concept that is larger than local in scope. Regional can mean several states or provinces in a country, or it can be parts of continents made up of several countries.

REGIONAL CARRIER   Local service carriers that provide air transport services between smaller cities, or between principal cities and smaller cities.

REGIONAL DISTRIBUTION CENTER   A warehouse or distribution facility that serves a wide geographic area.

REGIONAL PURCHASE AGREEMENTS   A purchase contract for goods or services that spans the lines of businesses or divisions of a firm throughout an entire region.

REGIONAL SOURCING   Sourcing of products in purchasing for use in regional operations (many sites of the firm).

REGISTER   A specific storage location in the computer; or a document submitted by the custom officers which permit a vessel to pursue foreign trade. It specifies the major characteristics of the vessel.

REGISTER (OF SHIPS)   A list, kept by the collector of customs, containing the names, ownership, and other facts relative to vessels registered in the merchant marine of a country. Three terms are used in the United States to designate the admittance of a self-propelled or sailing vessel to American nationality and privileges: Registered refers to vessels in a foreign trade. Enrolled refers to vessels in coastal and Great Lakes trade. Licensed refers to vessels of weights under 20 tons. All are referred to as Documented.

REGISTERED TRADEMARKS   A trademark is known as registered when certain requirements have been set and proper filing made in Washington, D.C.

REGULAR COMMON CARRIER   A carrier authorized to serve the public in general, by set rates, over set routes, between given points, hauling general commodities.

REGULAR ROUTE CARRIER   A carrier with an operating right that defines specific points on specific routes.

REGULAR ROUTE COMMON CARRIER   A carrier offering a service to the public in general over a given route, on schedule, between specific points.

REGULAR TRAIN   A train represented on the timetable and may consist of sections.

REGULATION   The supervision by federal and state regulatory commissions of the affairs of the various transportation agencies.

REHEARING   Second hearing. Is the opening of a complaint, case or discussion already concluded.

REINSURANCE   The transfer of part of the contract of insurance from one insurer to another.

RE-INTERMEDIATION   Placing back into a system some segments that were originally eliminated.

RELABELING   A common foreign trade zone activity of applying different labels and markings on products so they may be sold and used in different markets.

RELATED POINTS OF DESTINATION   A group of points the rates to which are made the same as or with relation to rates to other points in the group.

RELATED POINTS (ORIGIN)   A number of points the rates from which are made the same as or with relation to rates from other points in the same group.

RELATIONSHIP MANAGEMENT   A marketing field practice of developing loyalties with customer based upon linkages between persons in the selling firm with many people in the buying firm.

RELAY   In motor carriage it involves a line-haul movement that involves a change of driver and vehicle.

RELEASED RATE   A rate based on a limitation of the carrier's liability for loss and damage, and therefore less than a rate applying without such limitation.

RELEASED VALUATION   The value of a shipment set by the shipper which establishes the maximum liability of the carrier.

RELEASED VALUE RATES   When a shipper declares in writing the value of a product being shipped, a choice of rates is made available. Under a higher rate, unlimited liability is placed on the carrier for the full value of the shipment. Under lower rates, the shipper is given a reduced rate but agrees that a claim in the event of loss and damage would not exceed a given dollar amount of the declared value. Authorization by the I.C.C. must be obtained before the carrier can publish rates based on released value. This is specified in 10730 of the Act. It is usually necessary for a carrier to prove to the I.C.C. that movement of this commodity has been highly susceptible to loss and damage and that variations in commodity values make claim settlements difficult.

RELIEF CLAIM   A claim filed by the freight agent with the auditor of a carrier asking that a particular uncollectible item be taken out of his account.

RELIEF TRACK   An extended siding long enough to allow an inferior train to continue running.

REMITTANCE   The transfer of funds from one party to another.

REMOTE CONTROL   A means of operating a crane from a point outside of the cab.

REMOTE ENTRY   The ability to enter data or access to an electronic system from locales away from the central data source.

RENEWAL (OF NOTE)   Extension of time or giving a new note for an old one.

RENEWAL STORAGE   This is the rebilling on a monthly basis for products stored in the warehouse.

RENEWING A BILL   Accepting a new bill of exchange in place of one which has become overdue.

RENTAL CONTRACT   A short-term contract for the use of assets, including maintenance and insurance.

REORDER POINT QUANTITY   In inventory management, this term is synonymous with the lead time inventory. It is the average quantity required to service production of sales for the time required to order, process and transport the new order.

REPACKAGING/REPACKING   A common retail industry and foreign trade zone activity of removing goods from their original packages and placing them into other ones for special market purposes. This is often done in order to conform to the marketing or customs requirements of other countries to which they will be exported.

REPAIRING   A foreign trade zone activity of fixing damaged goods.

REPARATION   This is a compensation presented to a shipper to atone for excess payments by the shipper. Reparations are awarded for discrimination, unreasonableness under RICA Chapter 107, departures for the long and short haul rule, etc. Proceedings may be formal or informal. A refund ordered by the I.C.C. as an award for damages under circumstances when a charge which has been paid as judged to be unlawful is called a reparation payment. Payment in excess of legally applicable charges results in overcharge claims, but if the legally applicable charge is in fact unlawful, a reparations claim rather than an overcharge claim should be filed.

REPARATION CLAIMS   A reparation claim is a request for damages by a shipper against a carrier through an action of law or an action before the Interstate Commerce Commission. Reparation payments may be due when the Commission finds that legally published charges were unlawful on past shipments and must be made between overcharge claims and reparation claims. If a payment exceeds the legally applicable charge, an overcharge exists. However, if the charges paid are the legally applicable charge, but are found to be unlawful, reparation payments should result.

REPARATION (ORDER)   Redress in the form of adjustment or reimbursement on account of an assessed charge proved to the Interstate Commerce Commission to be unjust or unreasonable.

REPLENISH(MENT)   The act by a supplier to replace the inventory level of goods used by its customer. Replenishment is a seller's activity that includes keeping track of inventories and delivering them to the customer as they are used or according to plan by the customer.

REPLENISH UPON CONSUMPTION   A form of REPLENISHMENT that is based upon actual use by a customer.

REPLEVIN   The action to regain possession of goods which have been wrongfully taken from a party complaining.

REPORT   An official statement of facts; description, an account of a meeting or a report of the regulatory commission, expressive of its findings.

REPOSITORY   In shipping, a warehouse or storehouse.

REPRISAL   The seizure of ships or property to indemnify for unlawful seizure or detention.

REQUEST FOR BID (RFB)   A document sent by a buyer to potential sellers requesting that they provide the buyer with bid prices and certain terms for work that is needed.

REQUEST FOR PROPOSAL   A document sent by a buyer to potential sellers requesting proposals from them for work that is needed by the buyer firm.

REQUEST FOR QUOTE (RFQ)   See REQUEST FOR BID.

REQUIREMENTS EXPLOSION   A step used in determining all the required components and items needed to manufacture a given amount of finished product. Entails using the bill of materials listing of required items and the total number of finished items that will be produced. Thus, the bill of materials is "exploded" to provide the number of each sub-unit item that will be needed.

REQUISITION   Document that is sent from user department to purchasing. It contains what items are requested by the user department. Purchasing uses the requisition as the basis of a purchasing contract or purchase order.

RESALE   Goods that are purchased and sold by the firm in their original form.

RESELLER   A general term for a wholesale or retailer.

RESERVE BUOYANCY   The buoyancy created by all enclosed and water-tight or detention.

RESERVED FREIGHT SPACE   An agreement between some airlines and shippers permitting them to reserve freight space for certain flights.

RESERVED MATERIAL   Products that are still in a distribution center but are earmarked for outbound shipment to a particular customer.

RESERVE INVENTORY   Inventory that is being held for future use. (See RESERVED MATERIAL.)

RESHIPMENT   The carrier has a responsibility of placing the car on a private siding under an original bill of lading. Any subsequent movement would involve a new contract or reshipment. However, in diversion and reconsignment, the through rate is from the origin through the point of diversion and on to the final destination. Under these circumstances, the diversion or reconsignment charge is not an additional charge.

RESHIPPING RATE   Almost synonymous with the proportional rate and usually applicable to commodities that are stopped in transit for some treatment or manufacturing process, and eventually forwarded to a final destination.

RESOURCING   The act of reducing the number of suppliers the firm will buy from in the future. It consists of evaluating all the current ones and selecting the best for future purchases.

RESPONDENTIA BOND   A bond placed on a vessel by the master for emergency repair operations. Usually performed in a location distant from the owner and involving a lien on the vessel.

RESTORATION   In shipping, the placing in effect again of a rate or service after once having been removed, canceled or suspended.

RESTRAINT OF PRINCES, RULERS OF PEOPLE   Under the Hague Rules, the common water carrier is relieved of any liability that results from restraints imposed by rulers of a people.

RESTRAINT OF TRADE   Contracts in restraint of trade are those held to interfere unjustly with competition and therefore illegal. A number of laws have been enacted to prevent illegal restraint of trade, foremost among them the Sherman Antitrust Law.

RESTRICTED ARTICLES   Articles which are handled only under certain conditions.

RESTRICTIVE ENDORSEMENT   An endorsement on a bill of exchange which restricts the rights of further transfer of its ownership or which stipulates conditions for dealing with it.

RETAIL CONCENTRATION   A general supply chain and marketing/selling term indicating that the number of final sellers in the chain are being reduced through consolidation or from some of them dropping out of the market.

RETAIL MARKUP   Difference between sales price that a retailer receives for an item and the original purchase and inbound freight cost.

RETARDER YARD   A large freight yard where certain tracks are constructed over a hump so that cars can be pushed by a locomotive on to the hump and the released to roll down the incline by gravity. As the cars move downhill, a tower man, by remote control means (a series of mechanical devices known as car retarders and switches) can divert each car to appropriate track so that they can be readily made into a freight train in the proper order to best facilitate their delivery to destination. See hump yard.

RETIRE A BILL   To pay a bill at maturity or under discount.

RETROACTIVE   When a tariff, or a rule in a tariff, is applied to a date prior to the date of the publication of the tariff or rule, It is normally termed retroactive.

RETROFIT   A process of modifying an aircraft after reduction, or even after some service, to install changes put on later models. For example, many 707-120 turbojet aircraft were retrofitted with turbofan engines, as well as changes in wing leading edges and leading-edge flaps. They were identified as 707-120B turbofans. Retrofitting is again an issue with noise regulations being enforced at some major airports in the world.

RETURNABLE BOXES   Common in Europe, these are containers that were used in outbound distribution and are then brought back to the manufacturer for further use by it.

RETURN CHANNEL   A channel that is designed to return goods to the firm from either recall or recycling needs.

RETURNED SHIPMENT RATE   A rate applicable to mineral water carriers, packages, drums, or cylinders used in the transportation of acids, ammonia and gas, also bags and sacks which are returned to the original shipper after being emptied of their contents.

RETURN ON ASSETS   A profitability measure of asset investment in a firm; basically, net profit divided by assets; often referred to as ROA.

RETURN ON CAPITAL EMPLOYED   A measure of the profit of a firm divided by the total value of all debt, equities, and retained earnings in the firm.

RETURN ON EQUITY   A profitability measure of funds invested in the firm by debtors and investors divided into profits for a year.

REUSE   A general term indicating that something that was originally sold can be used by someone else after use by the original buyer.

REVENUE DILUTION   A diminishing of revenue received by a seller. It can be from a lowering of price due to competition or it can be from splitting of revenue with resellers.

REVENUE TON-MILE   Two thousand pound movement of revenue freight for a distance of one mile.

REVENUE WAYBILL   A waybill showing the amount of charges due on a shipment.

REVENUE YIELD   A carrier management term for the revenue generated by each rail car, trailer or airplane seat in a given period.

REVERSE DISTRIBUTION   Product recall.

REVERSE FLOWS   Distribution channel movement of goods in the backward direction from customers and retailers back to the manufacturer or on to the original supplier.

REVERSE LOGISTICS   A term that is used for REVERSE FLOWS or in situations when product is being recalled by the manufacturer and needs to be brought back from customers and consumers.

REVIEW PERIOD   The time in which a contract may be examined for possible amendments or rejection.

REVISED INTERSTATE COMMERCE ACT (RICA)   The Interstate Commerce Act was recodified in 1978 into the Revised Interstate Commerce Act.

REVISION   The corrections made on freight bills following an audit.

REWAREHOUSING   1) Moving product to other locations in a warehouse in order to have another storage configuration. 2) Combining part lost of the same product within a warehouse so as to free up storage slots.

REWORK   Steps that a buying firm has to take in order to fix purchased goods to a condition that they should have been in according to the original specifications sent to the supplier.

RFB   Request for bid.

RFQ   Request for quote.

RHUMB LINE   Refers to a straight course followed by a vessel. It may not be a straight line of sight course, but a straight line on a Mercator chart which cuts each meridian at the same angle. On a sphere, it is a straight line.

RIDER (INSURANCE)   Insurance coverage on goods that extends from when they are in the factory or warehouse to when they are delivered from a transportation shipment.

RIDE SHARING   A commuter practice similar to car pooling.

RIDE SHOT GUN   The assistant driver, riding on the right of the cab, not driving.

RIG   Any combination of truck and trailers or semitrailers.

RIGHTING LEVER   The distance between those vertical lines which would pass through the center of gravity and the center of buoyancy. It is said that when the vertical line of the center of buoyancy meets the central line of the ship above the center of gravity, the lever is a righting one. If it is below, it is an upsetting one.

RIGHTING MOVEMENT   An action to right a listing vessel.

RIGHT OF EMINENT DOMAIN   The right of the sovereign power to appropriate property for public use.

RINGGIT   The national currency of Malaysia.

RISER   Water pipe that supplies water to a section of the sprinkler system.

RISK   The probability of loss.

RISK EVALUATION   The examination of a process or situation to identify the possible risks and the nature of them.

RISK, PROCUREMENT AND SUPPLY   The chance that the supply of an item might a) not be available, or b) not available in the quality and quantities needed by the firm.

RIYAL   The national currency of the Kingdom of Saudi Arabia.

ROAD-BED   The foundation on which the track of a railroad is placed.

ROAD HOG   One who takes more than his share of the road.

ROADMAP   See PROCESS ROADMAP and PROCESS FLOW CHARTING.

ROADRAILER   Innovation in late 1970s piggyback trailer that has wheels for movement on rails and highway; transfer from one to the other takes place in minutes; does not require separate rail car.

ROADSTEAD   A tract of water, not necessarily enclosed in any way, but usually near the shore line, where ships at anchor may ride with protection from the heavy seas afforded by the headland.

ROBINSON-PATMAN ACT   An act that prohibits product sales in discriminatory ways (pricing, availability, etc.).

ROCK IT   The process of freeing a vehicle from mud or snow by forward and reverse action.

ROLL   The undulation of the sea that oscillates the vessel from one side to the other.

ROLL AND REST   The process of stopping to rest at regular intervals by a long-haul driver.

ROLL CAGE   A unitizing medium, often used in retail distribution. A metal cage used in picking operations for store deliveries. Typically, it contains many boxes and cartons of many SKU's. It can be rolled onto trucks and onto store aisles.

ROLLER TRAILER   A trailer with rollers on the floor. Product will slide easily on the rollers to aid in loading or unloading.

ROLLING STOCK   The freight and passenger cars owned by a rail carrier, not including motive power equipment; also buses, trucks and trailers.

ROLLTOP   A trailer with a sliding roof to facilitate crane loading.

ROOT CAUSE ANALYSIS   The examination of an issue or complex system to determine the possible causes of failure or problem development.

ROOT MODULES   In data processing, it is a technique for solving very complex problems that cannot be algebraically resolved.

ROSE BOX   A strainer located at the base of the suction pipe of a bilge pump.

ROTARY SEAL AIR LOCK OR FEEDER   A multiple blade rotor in a casing that delivers materials into hoppers continuously without permitting the passage of gas.

ROTARY VAN FEEDER OR STAR VALVE   Three or more rotary vans in a housing that permits materials to be discharged from a hopper at a controlled rate. It is not suitable for use as a gas seal.

ROTATING FORKS   Forklift attachments.

ROTATING HEAD   A clamp attachment or fork on a lifting carriage of the fork truck that permits the rotation of the load.

ROUGH MATERIAL RATES AND RATIO   Shipments of rough lumber or unfinished article of forest products, shipped into a mill point at a local rate, with the privilege of reshipment of finished products from mill point via the inbound carrier, provided the outbound weight is a specified percentage of the inbound weight of the rough material, on the basis of the local rate on the finished product from the mill point. The inbound charges are then reduced to basis of the rough material rate, which averages approximately 50% of the local rate assessed.

ROUNDHOUSE   A building, usually semicircular, at a terminal, terminus, or division point into which locomotives are sent at the end of a run for cleaning and overhauling.

ROUND TRIP   A journey that starts and ends at the same point. In origin and destination statistics. It involves going and returning by the same route and the same class of service.

ROUTE (RTE)   The combination of carriers transporting a shipment, and the points through which they travel.

ROUTE CLASSIFICATION OF CARRIERS   Transportation carriers are classified by the character of the routes they service in the following manner: 1) regular routes scheduled service; 2) regular route non-schedule service; 3) irregular route radial service; 4) irregular route non-radial service; and 5) local cartage service.

ROUTINE   A set of computer instruction devised to perform an algorithm.

ROUTING   The process of determining how a shipment will move between an origin and destination is referred to as routing. This requires the destination of the carrier, the route of the carrier, and directly or indirectly, the time en route. The party holding title to the goods en route should retain the right to route to protect his interests. Specific right routing is published either in a rate tariff or a routing tariff that might be referred by the rate tariff. Commodity rates are more restrictive on the routing options than are class rates. If the shipper shows a rate lower than the rate applicable on the route specified, it is the legal obligation of the railroad agent to so inform the shipper and ask for instructions as to routing. According to Section 10763 of the Interstate Commerce Act, the shipper may prescribe the rail route. Routing by motor carrier is different since RICA does not confer on the shipper the right to route shipment when two or more motor carriers are required. However, most reliable motor carriers respect the wishes of the shipper. When the initial motor carriers select a joint motor carrier, they must protect the shipper by selecting one with the lowest through charges.

ROUTING CODE   A financial coding system used for the wiring of funds. Each bank has a special routing code that channels funds to them.

RTX   Real time trading exchange—buying off the web.

RUBLE   The national currency of Russia.

RUDDER   A contrivance hung vertically on the after side of the stern post that serves as hinges for lateral motion of the vessel. The stock of the rudder head. The orders to the quartermaster are given in terms of the rudder rather than the helm by international agreement.

RUDDER CHAINS   Chains used to control the rudder in the case of accident. They are secured to the horn of the rubber and lead to each quarter.

RULE 40   A rule in the Consolidated Freight Classification that specifies container construction requirements.

RULE 41   A rule in the Consolidated Freight Classification that establishes policy on bursting strength, dimensions, and the requirements for solid and corrugated fiberboard cartons and fiber drums.

RULE MAKING PROCEEDING   A process in which a regulatory agency develops and implements administrative regulations.

RULES OF PRACTICE   Rules governing the procedure to follow by parties to proceedings before regulatory commission. Parties to proceedings are complainants, defendants, interveners, protestants, respondents, applicants and petitioners, according to the nature of the proceeding and their relation thereto.

RUNNING DAYS   Every day, including Sundays and holidays.

RUNNING DOWN OR COLLISION CLAUSE   An agreement whereby if a vessel is to blame for a collision with another vessel, the underwriters pay for three-fourths of the damage to the other vessel, up to three-fourths of the value of the insured vessel. Provided for under the Institute Time Clauses.

RUNNING TRACK   A track reserved for traffic movement through a yard.

RUN-THROUGH TRAIN   A train that operates over two or more railroads without change of engines and caboose.

RUNWAY DROP SECTION   Facilities for raising or lowering the runway track so they can line up with other levels.

R&W   Rail and water.

SSSS

SL&C   This refers to the shipper's load and count.

SL&T   This refers to the shipper's load and tally.

SABRE   One of the world's major airline reservation systems.

SADDLE TANK   The fuel storage area that is located on the tractor.

SAFE BERTH SAFE PORT   A berth is safe for a vessel if it can be reached. To be safe while at berth, the vessel should not touch the bottom at low tide.

SAFETY ANGLE   That stage in the roll of a vessel beyond which the righting power of the vessel is in danger.

SAFETY APPLIANCE ACT   An act of Congress (1893) requiring the railroads to provide safety devices, such as air brakes, couplers, hand guard rails, and so forth, for their equipment.

SAFETY STOCK   The average amount of stock on hand when the new order is received. This will vary with the no-stock-out safety assurance level established. The safety stock would be rated for a 90 percent assurance safety stock requirement than for an 80 percent. The safety stock level depends on the deviations in 1) delivery time for the carrier, 2) order fulfillment time required for the vendor, and 3) sales or production requirements which are serviced by the storage operation. Safety stock costs, which are the costs of retaining stock to meet deviations of an unpredictable nature, may be added to the other direct and hidden logistics costs in computing an optimum economic logistics quantity (ELQ) in logistics channel planning. Safety stock would be classed as a constant cost, since it does not vary per cwt. with changes in the volume of shipment.

SAGGED   When a vessel has settled structurally amidships, it is said to have sagged.

SAID TO WEIGH   According to the Hague Rules, the water carrier should issue bills of lading which show the weight or the quantity of the shipment as provided by the shipper. The carrier need not show a quantity or weight which he believes to be incorrect.

SAILING   Within the meaning of a charter party, a stipulation that the vessel has her cargo on board and is ready to proceed at once on the voyage.

SAILING DAY   The specified time that water carriers will receive cargo for a certain vessel and destination.

SAILING TRIM   A vessel loaded to the proper draft fore and aft.

SAINT ELMO'S FIRE   When the air is supercharged with electricity, a luminous brush-like appearance is seen on the ends of the yardarms, stays, or mastheads, on the vessel. The electrical discharge represents the relieving of the difference in the electrical potential between the atmosphere and the earth.

SALE/LEASEBACK CONTRACT   A company sells some or all of its assets to a firm and leases some or all of them back under a direct lease; usually done by a company needing cash.

SALE AND LEASEBACK   A common terminal financing method in the motor carrier industry in which the firm constructs the facility, sells it to recapture the initial cash outlays, then leases it for a long-term period.

SALES BASED ORDERING   A purchasing practice of ordering replenishment items from suppliers according to the sales experienced by the firm.

SALINITY   The amount of salt in the sea water. Usually it ranges from 33 to 37 parts salt in 1,000 parts water. A salinometer is a hydrometer that measures the salinity of boiler water. The normal content of seawater in parts per 1,000 is as follows: Sodium Chloride 27.213, Magnesium Chloride 3.807; Magnesium Sulphate 1.658; Calcium Sulphate 1.280; Potassium Sulphate 0.863; Calcium Carbonate Residue 0.123; and Magnesium Bromide 0.076.

SALTING (IN TRANSIT)   A service correlative with the services of refrigeration and ventilation, and imperative for the preservation and protection of certain commodities.

SALTY   A Great Lakes area term for an ocean ship.

SALVAGE   An award allowed those who voluntarily rescue ships, passengers, or freight.

SALVOR   One who voluntarily engages in rescue at sea.

SAME AS   A term meaning that the classified ratings for such articles are identical.

SAME STORE SALES   A measure of economic activity, either up, down, or flat, based upon a retail firm's sales by stores that were also measured in a previous time period. This avoids contamination of data from an increased or decreased number of store outlets in the firm.

SAMPLE   A small portion of merchandise taken as a specimen of quality.

SAMPLING   1) Purchasing. The practice of requesting a sample of product from a supplier for testing and determining its fit for use by the firm in the future. This avoids the need for specifically describing the specifications of the item when buying it. 2) Foreign Trade Zones. Making goods available for sampling by potential customers in this customs-free zone.

SANITATION   The formulation and application of measures designed to maintain healthy surroundings.

SANITATION LINE   A margin of space, typically 18″ or 36″ wide, painted around the inside of warehouse walls so that any signs of rodents can be easily seen and to mark the area so that no merchandise will be stored there. Traps are usually placed in this area.

SANS RECOURS   Without recourse.

SATELLITE TERMINAL   The use of a separate ticketing and loading facility by one or more airlines at a large airport complex. Sometimes it is called a satellite terminal.

SCALES OF RATES   Numerous rates adjusted with relation to each other.

SCALE TICKET   Axle weights of a vehicle on a form.

SCAN-BASED TRADING   See PAY ON SCAN.

SCANNER   An electronic device used to read bar and other codes on products. They are used either at fixed locations, like cash registers, or they are portable hand-held units. They are used to record sales, items passing certain points, counting, and progress in a distribution channel.

SCANTLINGS   The dimensions of the various parts of the ship's structure. It involves frames, stringers, plating, girders, etc. Rules concerning these dimensions are printed by the American Bureau of Shipping.

SCEND OF THE SEA   The lifting of a vessel to the leeward as a result of the waves.

SCHNABEL CAR   Specially designed rail cars for moving very heavy and large ladings.

SCHEDULE   1) Designated time consumed or which is supposed to be required (and usually presented in tabular form) for a movement between two points. 2) The term also applies to a tariff or other publication containing a list of prices for services rendered or other kinds of specific information. 3) In a time-table, the schedule is that part prescribing the class, direction, number and movement of a regular train.

SCHEDULE, COMPARATIVE-RATE   A table of rates that shows the difference, if any, in charges via two or more routes or via two or more of the several forms of carriage, such as rail, water, express, and parcel post.

SCHEDULES, AIR TAXI   A third level air carrier that offers passenger service from outlying suburbs and minor airport to the large municipal airports. These are also called nonscheduled carriers, though some nonscheduled carriers also carry cargo. Supplemental air carriers were granted restricted operating certificates under a 1961 amendment to the Federal Aviation Act.

SCHEDULED SERVICE   A transportation service over the carrier's certificated routes on scheduled flights.

SCOOPCAR   A car, constructed for use in railway service, having a scoop which is pushed along on top of the track, for removing snow, rock, or earth slides.

SCOPE OF WORK   The method of describing specifications in a service contract.

SCORE   To cut or indent a piece of flat material to facilitate bending, creasing, tearing, or folding.

SCORING MACHINE   A machine to make a cut or indentation to facilitate folding, creasing, etc.

SCOW   A light draft vessel shaped like a box used in local transportation of bulk shipments—like coal, sand, gravel, etc.

SCRAP FACTOR   An extra amount of product (percentage) that is used to increase the requirements of raw materials in order to be able to produce a net amount of finished product.

SCRATCHED   Non-available items that are taken off a customer order with the intent that they be reordered at a later date.

SCREW   1) Air. A slang term for propellers on an aircraft. 2) Ships. The oft-used term for the ship's propeller.

SCRIPT   A term applied to bridge and tunnel toll tickets.

SCRIPT SHEET   A document carried by the truck driver showing the details of the shipment on the truck. It is a manifest.

SCUPPERS   The vessel drains running from the waterways of the weather deck and spar.

SCUTTLEBUTT STORY   A rumor.

SEADOCK   Liquid petroleum loading or unloading facility at sea which very large ships can serve; product is then shipped via pipeline to and from dock on land.

SEA KINDLY   A general condition of good trim of a vessel that results in comfortable movement.

SEAL   A device used for locking a freight car or motor vehicle door. An unbroken seal serves as evidence that the door fastening has not been tampered with since the time of applying the seal.

SEALED BID   A bid, and bidding method, whereby it is not opened and read until all bids are received and evaluated in the open. This avoids the chance of a favored bidder being told of early bids and given a chance to finalize their's prior to the deadline date.

SEAL LOG   Document used to record seal numbers.

SEAL RECORD   A record of the number, condition and marks of identification of seals made at various times and places in connection with movement of cars between points of origin and destinations.

SEALS, CONTINUOUS   Car seals successively applied, without a check of the freight being made at the time they are applied. This means that when cars are stopped in transit to unload part of the freight, the seal is removed; when part of the contents have been unloaded, a new seal is applied with no check of the remaining contents of the cars.

SEALS, LOADING   Seals applied to a freight-car or motor-vehicle door when the freight is checked from the freight-house platform to the car or in transit.

SEALS WITH EXCEPTIONS   Seals that do not agree (either showing a different number or signs of having been tampered with), with record previously taken or reported by someone else.

SEARCH ENGINE   An Internet site that is useful for searching needed web sites. Common brands are Yahoo and Excite.

SEA ROOM   In water transportation, offshore a good, safe distance from shoals.

SEAT PITCH   The distance between the rows of seats in a passenger aircraft.

SEASONAL RATE   A rate instituted for specified articles or commodities and effective only certain periods of the year.

SEASONAL TARIFF   A tariff containing seasonal rates.

SEAWAY   Sea motion when clear of the shoal water.

SEAWORTHY   A vessel properly constructed to go into service. It is properly designed, equipped, manned and constructed.

SECONDARY PACKAGING   The packing into which several primary packed goods are placed. These are generally the cartons in which 6, 12, or 24 units of a product are sold to retailers.

SECOND TIER SUPPLIER   A firm's supplier's supplier.

SECOND, THIRD, AND OTHER MAIN TRACKS   Main tracks laid parallel to the first main track.

SECOND VIA   Copy of a bill of exchange forwarded by different ship, route or mail, from the first or principal bill.

SECOND WORLD   A term that was traditionally used for the communist nations of the world that were not active in the economic activity of the rest of the world.

SECTIONAL TARIFF   A unique tariff which presents several different rates between the same pairs of points by putting them in different sections of the tariff. The provisions for different application of the sections are in the tariff.

SECTION-22 RATES   A long-standing term for reduced railroad rates for shipments made by federal, state, and local government agencies in the United States.

SECURE FOR SEA   The process of preparing for sea movement by lashing all movable objects, placing grips on the boats, tying down the furniture, etc.

SECURITY PASSWORD   A personal code that is used to restrict entry into electronic systems and security areas and is known only to the person using it.

SEGMENTATION, CUSTOMER   Any method a seller uses to categorize customers according to selected characteristics.

SEGMENTATION, SUPPLIER   Any method a buyer uses to categorize suppliers according to selected characteristics.

SELF UNLOADER   A ship capable of unloading its own cargo rather than rely upon dockside assistance; usually found on coal, grain and other bulk ships.

SECURITY AREA   Part of a warehouse protected by fence, electric eye, etc.

SEEL   The action of the vessel to roll in a seaway.

SELECTION CRITERIA   Those characteristics and attributes used to select certain items and reject others. This is a practice of evaluating suppliers, carriers, and even customers.

SELF BILLING   1) A purchasing practice of allowing the supplier to submit an invoice to its customer based upon what it sent or replenished to them. This is now a common practice with in-house supplier activities. 2) Similarly, it is the practice of a buying firm creating the invoice it will pay after the seller delivers the goods to them.

SELF INSURANCE   The process of providing for the assumption of risk under some self-organized provisional insurance fund, rather than taking outside insurance coverage.

SELLER'S MARKET   Market condition whereby selling firms have power to set prices, terms, and conditions to greater degree than buyers.

SELL IN   The time to get a new product on the shelf to where a brand firm can then start advertising it.

SEMI   A semitrailer, although it usually means both the trailer and tractor.

SEMI CONTAINERSHIP   Vertical cells to accommodate containers on a cargo ship.

SEMITRAILER   A freight-carrying vehicle without its own motor power, attached to a tractor by means of a fifth wheel; sometimes called a box.

SEPARATION CLOTHS   Fabric used to ward off moisture in certain cargo, such as sugar. Sheets of the cloth are spread over and under the cargo.

SERIES (OR SERIAL) NUMBER   A number used principally by tariff publishing agents and transportation companies to identify a tariff or other publication. For example, if the first issue of a tariff is designated Series Number/00, the first reissue would be called / 00A.

SERVICE CENTER   A warehouse or wholesaler that performs value-added functions to the product. A common example is metals service centers that perform shaping, cutting, and other services for customers.

SERVICE FEE   A system of pricing by suppliers whereby they charge for a service they perform upon raw materials and charge for these activities separately rather than bundling them into a single price for the goods. This is also an unbundling practice.

SET   The direction of the current. It also refers to the direction the vessel moves as a result of the tide, wind, etc. The drift is the extent of influence of the current on the vessel. Drift is often confused with set.

SET IT DOWN   Slang. To stop quickly.

SET-OFF   A claim which one party has against another who has a claim against him; a counter claim.

SETTLEMENT   The closure of a transaction with the final cash payment and deposit/clearance by the seller.

SET-UP (SU)   When articles are shipped ready for use, as contrasted to being knocked down, it is referred to as a set-up shipment. It is a completely assembled shipment.

SET-UP COSTS   The variable costs involved in a machine set-up operation to produce for an order, or to change the rate of production to meet an order. It is manufacturer's cost, which should be included in purchase (sales) price. It is an added production adjustment cost.

SHAFT ALLEY   The extended alley in which the shaft operates.

SHAG   A small city trailer.

SHAPING A COURSE   In water transportation, the process of calculating a course by taking it from the chart with parallel rulers, making allowance for deviation and presenting the course to the quartermaster for steering.

SHARED DISTRIBUTION   Distribution functions that are shared by two or more firms, even sometimes competitors, that serve to reduce the overall total cost of warehousing and transportation to each of them. This is being prompted by many firms in Europe in markets where there is low vehicle utilization and many small just-in-time direct store deliveries. Some supermarkets are forcing competitors to make combined single deliveries in one truck/lorry.

SHARED INFORMATION   The transmission to or allowing access by another firm in the supply chain. Typically, firms at the end of chains are starting to share forecasts so that their suppliers can more efficiently service them.

SHARED RISK   An arrangement between two firms, one usually being a supplier, in which one provides investments. When profits are earned from the venture, then the profits are shared on some predetermined formula basis. On the other hand, if the project does not result in profits, both have incurred losses on their investments. This is starting to be common in oil field projects where major suppliers are investing into oil rigs along with the brand oil firm on a shared risk basis.

SHARED USER TRANSPORT   See SHARED DISTRIBUTION.

SHARED USER WAREHOUSING   See SHARED DISTRIBUTION.

SHARP PRACTICE   Any action by a buyer that takes unfair advantage of a seller.

SHEDS   A common British term for warehouses.

SHELF REPLENISHMENT SEQUENCE   The order in which goods come from a retail store warehouse or backroom and will be place on the actual retail store shelf. Many distribution operations are picking goods and arranging them in cages and on trolleys in the order in which they can be most efficiently stocked on store shelves. This is in recognition that as much as 50% of the total cost of a retail good supply chain takes place between the store dock and store shelf.

SHELF TAKE-OFF   Demand for consumer goods as they are sold by the retailer to the buying consumer. This is the farthest point in a distribution channel at which to measure demand other than actual use by the consumer at their consuming site.

SHEEP HERDER   A slang phrase meaning a truck driver of questionable ability.

SHEER   The upward curve of the deck. The term also applies to a change in the course of the ship due to shoaling or from another vessel in close proximity which displaces the water. A very sharp action of this form is called a rank sheer.

SHEER STRAKE   The upper line of plates and/or planking.

SHELF LIFE   The length of time a product can remain in storage or available for sale before it is necessary or desirable to remove it for quality reasons.

SHELL PLATING   The outside skin of a steel or iron vessel.

SHERMAN ANTITRUST ACT   Legislation that prohibits practices that will cause or tend to cause monopolistic situations.

SHIFTING BEAM   This refers to a portable support for the hatch covers.

SHIFTING BOARDS   Temporary partitions placed in the hold of a ship to prevent bulk cargo from shifting.

SHIP   In proper terminology, this term should apply only to a vessel that is square rigged on all masts from three up. However, it is used to apply to all vessels. When sea water comes aboard, it is said to be shipped. Also anything put in place is said to be shipped.

SHIP AGENT   Person or firm who is hired to attend to details necessary when a ship is in port. Typically hired by shipowner or charterer; includes such things as attending to port fees, renting of pier, etc.

SHIPBOARD, ON   On a vessel, or within it.

SHIP BROKER   An individual who makes contracts for the employment of vessels; or one who negotiates the purchase and sale of ships.

SHIP CHANDLER   A person who deals in cordage, sail cloth, and other supplies for ships.

SHIP CHARTER   The rental of a charter ship.

SHIP DEMURRAGE   A charge for delay to a steamer beyond a stipulated period.

SHIP FIXTURE   The term for the agreement that results in a ship charter.

SHIPMENT   A single consignment of one or more pieces from one consignor at one time, at one origin address, receipted for in one lot, and moving on airbill (or waybill) to one consignee at one destination address.

SHIPOWNER   The person or company under which a vessel is officially registered is the owner.

SHIPPED   Goods which have undergone transportation.

SHIPPER   Many meanings. 1) Person who will pay freight bill. 2) Person who has right to route goods. 3) Person who technically owns goods while en route as defined by the FOB terms on the bill of lading. 4) Slang for the bill of lading.

SHIPPER'S ASSOCIATION   A non-profit cooperative that serves to consolidate shipments for member firms.

SHIPPER'S CERTIFICATE   A form filled out by the shipper and presented to the outbound carrier at the transit point, along with instructions and the inbound carrier's freight bill, requesting reshipping privilege and transit rate on a commodity previously brought into the transit point.

SHIPPER'S EXPORT DECLARATION   The declaration of the merchandise and its value for purposes of shipment to a foreign country, or to non-contiguous territories of the United States involves making out of the Shipper's Export Declaration. This is filed with the United States Collector of Customs, and a copy is left with the port or border point of exit. This is required on all shipments, whether they are foreign or domestic, except for some shipments which only move in transit through the United States from one country to another.

SHIPPER'S INTEREST INSURANCE   Amount for which the shipment is insured, as declared in appropriate box on the Air Waybill. In no event can such value exceed actual value of the property at destination plus 10%.

SHIPPER'S LETTER OF INSTRUCTIONS   A document in which a shipper provides details as to how a shipment is to be undertaken and is sometimes used as the basis for creating the details of a letter of credit.

SHIPPER'S LOAD AND COUNT (SL&C) OR SHIPPER'S LOAD AND TALLY (SL&T)   A notation made on a bill of lading that the loading and counting was performed by the shipper without the carrier's supervision or verification, is referred to as the shipper's load and count.

SHIPPER'S ORDERS   The official document which authorizes that a shipment traveling under an order bill of lading is released for pickup.

SHIPPER'S ROUTING   The directions concerning the carrier or carriers that will perform the transportation operation.

SHIPPING   A collective term for a number of ships or vessels, also the act of loading, unloading and transporting goods.

SHIPPING ACT   An act of Congress (1916) which created the United States Shipping Board for the purpose of developing water transportation, operating the merchant ships owned by the government, and regulating the water carriers engaged in commerce under the United States flag.

SHIPPING ACT OF 1984   U.S. Legislation that deregulated some aspects of ocean liner shipping. Major item was the allowance of volume contracts between shippers and ocean carriers.

SHIPPING ARTICLES   The contract which is entered into by the officers and crew of the ship. The contract specifies the voyage, wages, etc. The articles are a contract between the master and crew.

SHIPPING CLERK   One having charge of the packing and forwarding of goods.

SHIPPING COMMISSIONER   An officer, appointed to a port of entry by the circuit court having jurisdiction over it, whose duties are to supervise seamen's contracts and enforce laws made for their protection and relief.

SHIPPING DAY   A term used by carriers to specify the time they will accept freight for certain points.

SHIPPING ERROR   Shipment of wrong product, quantity, or to wrong destination.

SHIPPING INSTRUCTIONS   In general usage, the instructions given the transportation company by the shipper relative to the movement of his goods. Freight forwarders sometimes provide shippers with a shipping instruction form, which is filled out and accompanies bill of lading. It contains instructions as to the name of consignee, class of steamer, kind of insurance, and any special information as may be required for the proper and expeditious handling of the shipment.

SHIPPING LAWS   The laws of shipping related to vessels, their construction, ownership, inspection, registration, nationality, tonnage—in fact covering everything that has to do with the rights and duties of those engaged in shipping, as well as the contracts and general movements of merchandise.

SHIPPING ORDER (SO)   Usually the triplicate copy of the bill of lading containing instructions from the shipper to the carrier for forwarding of goods.

SHIPPING POUND   The gross weight of a package of silk, including the spool, bobbin, warp beam or cone on which it is wound.

SHIPPING PERMIT   When the exporter of goods arranges for space, steamship company issues a shipping permit to either the shipper or its agent. This document provides instructions to the receiving clerk at the pier concerning the quantity and character of the shipment. It is a common practice for the dock receipt to be attached with the shipping permit for signatures by the receiving clerk when the goods are delivered to the dock. When several shipments are made by truck, it is a common practice to provide a memorandum receipt to the truck men. When the shipment is complete and all deliveries have been made, the memorandum receipts are exchanged for a dock receipt.

SHIPPING RELEASE   1) Direct communication from a user to a selling firm for items that are being drawn against a blanket or national contract. 2) A communication from a firm's order entry operation to a distribution center.

SHIPPING SUBSIDIES   Financial aid to shipping by public grant. The terms bounty and subvention may be employed in the same sense.

SHIP'S (SHIPPING) ARTICLES   The official agreement between master and crew, specifying such matters as the voyage, name and position of each crew member, wages, time of service, and provisions agreed upon.

SHIP'S BILL   The copy of the vessel's bill of lading retained by the ship's master.

SHIP'S BUSINESS   The standard paperwork of the ship. This includes records, surveys and all documents.

SHIP'S DOCUMENT   Papers issued by a water carrier in its dealings with government authorities and in the operation of its vessels. Among these are the shipping permit, shipper's export declaration, consular invoice, certificate or origin, non-dumping certificate, exporters' invoice, and ocean bill of lading.

SHIP'S HUSBAND   The owner of a vessel, or an agent who acts for him in obtaining cargo and attending to whatever is essential to the due prosecution of the voyage.

SHIP'S MANIFEST   A statement listing all the consignments on board a vessel, together with the quantity, marks, and destination of each. A copy of the manifest must be filed with the collector of the port before a vessel clears or enters. This copy, together with individual manifests filed by shippers, becomes the basis of the government's official foreign-trade statistics and, in the case of imports, serves as a check upon import duties. One or more copies are carried with the vessel to serve as means of cargo identification in case of search or detention. A ship's manifest is also used as a basis for freight accounting in the same way that a railroad waybill underlies railroad-freight accounts.

SHIP'S MASTER   The commander of a merchant vessel. He has complete control of navigation and over all on board and represents the owners on a voyage and in foreign ports. He has authority to board the ship by contracts for necessary supplies and repairs and may even pledge the cargo, if necessary.

SHIP'S OPTION   The choice of a vessel to accept freight by weight or measurement tons.

SHIP'S PAPERS   Documents which a merchant ship is required to carry consisting of 1) register; 2) log book; 3) charter party, if ship is under charter; 4) muster roll; 5) ship's articles; 6) bill of health; 7) bills of lading, or duplicate receipts of cargo from master to shipper; 8) manifest, or general statement of cargo; 9) invoices, or statements of costs of goods; 10) clearance, or permission from port authorities to sail; 11) certificate of inspection; 12) passenger list, if passengers are carried; 13) bill of sale if ship has been sold by citizens of one country to those of another, together with consular certificate; 14) officers' licenses; and 15) license to carry on a port trade. Sometimes the ship's register is replaced or accompanied by a passport, issued by the sovereign authority, and/or a certificate of enrollment, if the ship is employed in the United States coastal trade.

SHIPSIDE   Alongside a vessel.

SHIP'S TACKLE   All blocks, rigging, and other working gear utilized on a ship to load or unload cargo.

SHIP-TO-ORDER   Outbound transportation from a factory that is in response to actual customer orders, rather than producing and moving the goods to stock for movement later in time.

SHIP-TO-STOCK   Outbound transportation from a factory to a warehouse from which shipments will be made later in response to actual customer orders. This system insulates the factory, somewhat, from short-term fluctuations in customer demand.

SHOO-FLY   A temporary track constructed around a tunnel, bridge, or washout for purpose of detouring traffic during course of performing repairs and renewals to tracks, bridges and tunnels. This reduces delays to freight and passenger trains while the railroad is being repaired.

SHORE   To support. To set blocking under an overloaded deck to shore it up. Also refers to a coastline or land near a body of water.

SHORTAGE   A deficiency in the quantity of goods shipped; also, that part of a shipment that remains undelivered.

SHORT CAUSE ACTION   An action to provide prompt trail for cases in chancery, which includes admiralty, providing documentary evidence is provided. There is no appeal on the decision. This is an action by England and others to save time.

SHORTENED PROCEDURE   A procedure inaugurated by the Interstate Commerce Commission with a view toward simplifying, shortening and making less expensive complaints filed with it. Briefly, this procedure upon consent of all parties to formal complaints, permits the presentation of evidence and argument by sworn statements of fact and dispenses with oral hearings. The case is assigned to an examiner for preparation of a proposed report to be served upon the parties and thereafter the procedure is the same as proceedings in which oral hearing is had.

SHORT EXCHANGE   Payable on sight, demand, or within ten days.

SHORT FORM BILL OF LADING   A deviation from the regular straight bill of lading which only refers to the contract terms but fails to include them.

SHORT-HAULING   A term applied when a railroad accepts a shipment of goods to be hauled for a short distance over its own line and then transfers it to another, to be hauled to a point which the initial carrier also services. According to Section 10726 of the Interstate Commerce Act, "no common carrier may be compelled to short-haul itself," a carrier may refuse such a shipment if, by accepting the short haul, it would lose business which it otherwise might have hauled to its ultimate destination by a noncircuitous route and without causing an extra freight rate to be charged the shipper.

SHORT LINE   That carrier or combination of carriers having shortest mileage between two points.

SHORT LISTED SUPPLIERS   Those suppliers that have made a cut and are still included in a buyer's rationalization process.

SHORT NOTICE   The process of filing a tariff in less than the required thirty days under approval of the Interstate Commerce Commission.

SHORT OF DESTINATION   Before reaching final destination.

SHORT TON   2,000 pounds.

SHOTGUN CHANNEL   The shotgun channel is the single warehouse channel, or single node channel. Under the shotgun channel system, goods flow from the manufacturing plant directly to a wholesaler or warehouse which services the retail facilities. With the exception of direct shipments from the manufacturing plant to the retailer, this represents the most simplified form of a port-production channel. (See SINGLE WAREHOUSE CHANNELS.)

SHOULD BE   A general reengineering term for what an optimum process would consist of after analysis of WHAT IS. In a reengineering effort, any step, activity, or process that does not add value is removed. The resulting chart or schematic is often called a Should Be process.

SHOULD BE COST   The costs that a supplier would be incurring for work being performed for a buyer firm that is based upon benchmarking the lowest and best in class costs for such work.

SHOW-CAUSE ORDER   A directive to respondents issued by a regulatory authority, such as the Civil Aeronautics Board, requiring the respondent to show cause why the Board should not implement its findings.

SHOVELING   Slang reference to hasty loading or unloading of freight.

SHREVEPORT CASE   A case decided by the United States Supreme Court in which it held that the Interstate Commerce Commission had the power to decide that intrastate rates might not be used for any undue or unreasonable or unjust discrimination against interstate traffic moving under like conditions.

SHRINKAGE   Reduction in bulk of measurement. Natural shrinkage is the ordinary loss of weight of livestock, or reduction in weight because of evaporation of liquids, and reduction in bulk within the tariff allowance on grain and seeds.

SHRINK WRAPPING   A packaging process that releases the strains in a plastic film resin the temperature of the film. The package is wrapped while the film is still hot. As it cools, it shrinks and more closely fits the content of the package.

SHROUD   A waterproofing process by means of covering the top and sides, while permitting air to circulate from the bottom.

SHUNTING (CARS)   Switching, moving, or turning a car from the mainline to a side track.

SICK HORSE   Slang—a tractor in poor mechanical condition.

SIDE TRACK (SIDING)   A short track running parallel with another track, usually the main line, and connecting with it at both ends. An assigned siding is a side or team track owned-by a carrier and assigned to one or more industrial concerns for the purpose of loading or unloading.

SIDE-TRACK AGREEMENT   When a rail carrier and a shipper or receiver complete a contract covering the mutual responsibilities for the use and operation of a rail siding, it is referred to as a side-track agreement.

SIDING   A track auxiliary to the main track for meeting or passing trains, or a track for industrial purposes.

SIGHT   The time when a bill is presented to the drawee.

SIGHT DRAFT   One payable at sight, i.e., when presented.

SIGHT ENTRY   A procedure that must be put through to release goods from Customs, occasioned by the use of incorrect invoice form, and particularly applicable to traffic into Canada.

SIGNATURE SERVICE   A system for safeguarding a shipment by having each person who passes on a shipment to the next carrier receive a signature of transfer.

SIGNED UNDER PROTEST   The master of a vessel may sign bills of lading under protest if the charters object to the insertion of a certain clause in the bill. This forbids his signature being placed in evidence.

SIGNING AUTHORITY   The highest amount that a buyer may approve on a purchase order or contract before having to have the purchase checked by a person of higher authority.

SILICA GELL   A drying agent, or a desiccant, commonly placed inside containers to prevent moisture drainage. It is a colloidal silica possessing fine properties and is highly absorbent.

SILK SCREEN PROCESS   A process for decorating containers by using a silkscreen stencil rather than metal plates. It is applicable to any shaped container.

SILO   The generic term for a department structure in an organization where there is a low amount of coordination and sharing of information across them.

SILO OPTIMIZING   In a traditional organization, based upon former scientific management and organization principles, this would be the continuing focus upon making each and every department operate as efficiently as possible. This is in contrast to a complete systems view whereby some functions and processes would incur higher costs in exchange for greater reductions by others.

SILOUTTE JUDGMENT   A 1998 European Union ruling that prohibited stores from performing GRAY MARKET purchases in countries from which the same branded goods might be available at lower prices.

SIMPSON'S RULES   Rules used to find the areas of figures such as a parabola bounded by a curve on one side and a straight line on the other side.

SIMULATION   One of the most powerful planning tools available to management is simulation. It consists of representing an operational procedure on the basis of its cost. The simulation of an operation is a model run-through of the operation as represented by cost and revenue figures. Simulation could take an infinite number of forms. It may be better understood in football. Preparation for a game frequently takes the form of one practice team simulating the plays of the coming opponent to help prepare the defense for the specific plays.

SINE DIE   Without a day appointed.

SINGLE-CITY WAREHOUSE   A firm operating a warehouse in one city.

SINGLE CONSIGNMENT WAYBILL   A waybill involving only one shipment.

SINGLE PLANE SERVICE   A transport service from origin to destination without need for changing planes, even though several stops may be required.

SINGLE-STORY WAREHOUSE   A warehouse with one major floor level on which goods can be stored.

SINGLE SOURCE   Generally, the act of using only one source for a product even though others are available.

SINGLE TRACK   A main track upon which trains are operated in both directions.

SINGLE WAREHOUSE CHANNELS   In the single warehouse channel, the manufacturer would transport directly to a single warehouse in the post-production channel and each warehouse would service only the retail requirements within the area. The single warehouse channel is often referred to as the shotgun channel and involves a direct shot of the goods from the plant to the wholesaler who then services the retail need without the involvement of a more complex echelon system.

SINKING FUND   A fund set apart from revenue to pay a government or corporation debt.

SISTER SHIP CLAUSE   A clause that specifies that if an insured vessel collides with another, or receives salvage services by another which belongs wholly or in part to the same owner, or are under the same management, the injured will have the same rights under the policy as they would have were the vessel entirely the property of parties with no interest in the vessel involved.

SIX BANGER   Slang. A six cylinder engine.

SIXTEENTH SECTION ORDER   An old term for an order issued by the Interstate Commerce Commission in pursuance of Section 16 of the Interstate Commerce Act; now Chapter 11, RICA.

SIXTH-FREEDOM TRAFFIC   Air service that originates in one foreign country. stops in the home country of the airline, and then terminates in a third country. The stop in the home country may or may not involve a stopover for the passengers or a change of planes. The so-called freedoms involve rights of an airline relative to flying over, stopping off, picking up and dropping off traffic in other countries.

SKID   Set of legs or planks used alone or in combination with wheels and platform to elevate and to transport articles. Also a slang for pallet.

SKILL   A person's ability to perform a certain task. In the late 1990s many firms investigated and developed essential skills in all areas of their firms. In the supply chain some example skill areas that are being identified are establishing and setting strategies, negotiating, identifying customer service offerings, etc.

SKINNIE AXLE   Slang for a single axle trailer.

SKINS   Tires.

SLEEPER   A tractor having sleeping compartments.

SLEEPING MONEY   Money that is invested in assets that are not working to produce revenue or profit at the moment. An example would be idle capital goods and excess inventory. (See WORKING MONEY.)

SLIDING FIFTH WHEEL   A fifth wheel that can be moved forward or backward on the tractor to obtain the desired distribution of weight between the trailer axles and the tractor.

SLIDING SCALE DISCOUNT   A price or rate that is reduced as a customer purchases or a shipper ships more during a given period.

SLIDING TANDEM   A two axle arrangement that can be moved forward and backward on the trailer body to provide the optimum weight distribution.

SLING   A net of rope or chain in which goods are hoisted from ship to dock and vice versa.

SLIP   A water space between two piers or wharves, or the slot in a dock in which a vessel ties up.

SLIP OF THE WHEEL   The percentage of distance lost through the mobility of water for a vessel. To get the slip, determine the distance run by the engines (or the pitch) times the minutes run, and divide by 6080 feet.

SLIP SHEET   Piece of cardboard used to handle unitized loads with a push/pull attachment.

SLITER   A machine used to cut roll stock according to desired directions.

SLOT AVAILABILITY   An aviation term indicating that a landing and gate position is available for purchase or lease by an airline into a certain airport.

SLOTTING ALLOWANCE   A charge that is made by retail stores to brand manufacturers for the ability to sell their goods in the store. This is a charge to be paid up front before any goods are placed on the store shelf for sale to consumers. While many observers see this as a second revenue stream for stores in addition to the margins earned on the goods sold, others have stated that this is little more than an extorted form of corporate bribe. Either way, it is a form of cost for branded manufacturers to overcome in their efforts to reach the consumer.

SMALL SHIPMENTS   A relative term for shipments that are often mentioned in a negative sense as being close to marginal or unprofitable for carriers due to small weight and low freight charges.

SMART CARD   A credit or debit card that contains information useful to the user or issuer.

SMART TAGS   A tag placed on products that contains data concerning them. These are typically scannable tags.

SMOKE HIM   Slang phrase for passing another vehicle.

SMOKER   A term applied to a tractor emitting too much gas fumes.

SMOKESTACK   The vertical exhaust tube on the side of the tractor cab.

SMOKE VENTS   Vents in the roof of a building allowing smoke to leave the building during a fire.

SMOOTHING   A procedure for evening out data that inevitably is variable. The use of averaging and multiple exponents helps accomplish this.

SMUGGLER   One who avoids the payment of duties by secretly bringing (importing) goods into a country; also a name given a vessel engaged in smuggling.

SMUGGLING   Bringing goods into a country without paying duties.

SNAIL MAIL   A slang term for the postal service as opposed to e-mail.

SNOW PLOW   A work equipment unit moved by, but not attached to, locomotive to clear away snow from the right of way.

SNUB NOSE   A cab over tractor.

SOCIAL COSTS   A cost of an economic activity that also incurs costs for others in a society and economy but are not captured in the accounting by either the buyer, seller, provider, or user. An example would be pollution caused by transport vehicles.

SOFT CURRENCY   A currency that is not readily acceptable to persons and firms in other countries. A currency that is difficult to exchange or one that does not hold value in relation to other currencies.

SOFTWARE   The programs and routines used in computer processing. It may include compilers, sub-routines, general purpose utility programs, etc.

SOLA   In case that only one copy of a bill of exchange is in circulation.

SOLE SOURCE   There being one and only one source available.

SOLICITUDE   Given to avoid a fine by promising to produce shipping documents that have missed carrying steamer, within thirty days.

SOLUTIONS BUSINESS   A firm that presents itself to the market as one that identifies problems and opportunities for its customers and sells its products and services in ways that provide solutions to the customers' needs.

SORT   1) Logistics. The act of selecting and arranging goods in a particular order for further use or movement. 2) Electronic. The taking of random data sampling and arraying them in a desired order. This is a common feature of data base programs.

SORTING TRACKS (YARD)   A system of yard tracks where cars are classified in greater detail after having passed through classification tracks.

SOUNDINGS   A vessel is said to be on or off soundings depending on whether the bottom can be reached by deep-sea lead. The 100 fathom curve is the dividing line depth.

SOURCING   1) Purchasing. The act of seeking out potential suppliers for a product or service that the firm requires. 2) European Supply Chains. The process of efficiently identifying which factories should provide goods to which country marketing group in a multinational company.

SOURCING OPTION   Any alternative method or source of acquiring a needed product or service.

SPC   See STATISTICAL PROCESS CONTROL.

SPACE   In marine shipping, space is generally considered as a unit for occupation of goods.

SPACER   Short noticed metal bar used to connect storage rack uprights together in a parallel line.

SPACE WEIGHT RATE   A rate that applies to weight or cubic measure, usually whichever is greater, to determine total freight charges, common in the ocean steamship industry.

SPAR AND BOOM GEAR   This is a cargo handling set up. A boom is placed over the hatch and another over the side. The hatch tackle hoists the cargo, while the boom tackle carries the sling across the deck.

SPEC   Specification.

SPECIAL AGENT   One authorized to act only on a specific matter or on one occasion.

SPECIAL CARGO   Cargo with high value per unit weight or measurement. Precious metals and specie are examples. An extra charge is made for handling.

SPECIAL COMMODITIES DIVISION   A division of a motor carrier that carries freight requiring specialized equipment such as for steel hauling, heavy loads, bulk liquids, etc.; usually handled with owner-operators on trip leases.

SPECIAL DAMAGES   A carrier obligation term for damages in which goods have lost their value due to delay.

SPECIAL RATES   The air special rates are special freight rates for transportation between specific cities. It involves movements by container, deferred air freight, import rates and surface air rates.

SPECIAL REPARATION DOCKET   That part of the record of the Interstate Commerce Commission whereby application of the carriers for permission to refund unlawfully collected transportation charges are passed upon.

SPECIAL SERVICE TALLY   Document prepared for any extra charges over and beyond standard charges.

SPECIAL SERVICE TARIFF   A tariff containing switching, storage, demurrage, etc. charges, rules and regulations.

SPECIAL TRACKS   In a typical yard there will be several tracks devoted to special purposes, varying with local conditions. Some of these are: caboose, scale, coaling, ash pit, bad order, repair, icing, feed, stock, transfer, sand, and depressed.

SPECIFIC COMMODITY RATE   As contrasted with a general commodity rate, this is set upon individual commodities.

SPECIFICATIONS   The methods used to communicate from a buying firm to a selling the exact attributes needed in the product or service being acquired. Can be brand name, commercial descriptions, blueprints, method of manufacturing, and others.

SPECIFICATION (PACKAGING)   A summary of a packaging component, in great detail.

SPECIFICATION COMPLEXITY, REDUCING   The actions taken by a firm to reduce the number of different specifications used for primarily the same basic functions. In a fastener example, it would be the process of reducing the number of nuts, bolts, and screws used in manufacturing items from many of them to a smaller number of them.

SPECIFICATION, INDUSTRY STANDARD   A specification of an item that was created as a norm in a particular industry. For example, in the food processing industry, the Number 46 can is one of a certain size, shape, and configuration that is used by many branded firms.

SPECIFICATION, REFORMULATION   Actions taken to change the exact specifications of a product or service.

SPECIFICATION, RESTRICTED   Any product or service specification that is so unique that it is available from only one supplier. This is often an artificially created single-supplier situation that buying firms attempt to avoid today.

SPECIFICATION, SIGN OFF   Gaining approval within the firm from the person or group that had originally created a specification in order to change it to another, typically, more standard one.

SPECIFICATION, STANDARDIZING   Acts to simplify the specifications of products and services used by the firm. This is typically done by adopting those that are SPECIFICATION, INDUSTRY STANDARD.

SPECIFICATION, TIGHT   See SPECIFICATION, RESTRICTED.

SPECULATION   Purchasing raw materials in excess of known requirements with the intent of reselling them at a profit in their current form at a later point in time. The difference between speculation and hedging is that hedging involves the intent to use the product.

SPEDITEURS   Forwarding agents.

SPEED TO MARKET   The length of time it takes a firm from the time it decides to launch a new product or service until it is made available in the market. (See also, TIME TO MARKET.)

SPIDER DIAGRAM   A schematic consisting of concentric circles and divided into sectors that represent certain product or service attributes. Firms then compare their current product offerings (from low to high on the concentric circles) for each attribute against a competitor or customer demands. It is valuable for competitive analysis and gap studies in skills and competencies.

SPLIT DELIVERY   In addition to stopping-in-transit specified carriers sometimes offer a split-delivery service on carload freight. The rules are published in the agency tariffs. Delivery may be made to one or more parties. Multiple deliveries at more than one siding requires a switching service. Additional charges are made for added switching services and the unloading of cars.

SPLIT LOAD   A loaded trailer that is moved to two or more destination terminals. The multiple terminals may be close.

SPLIT MONTH BILLING   Merchandise received before the 15th is assessed one month storage charge. Merchandise received after the 15th is assessed a two month storage charge.

SPLIT MONTH STORAGE   A full month's charge for goods received from the 1st of the month through the 15th. One-half month's charges assessed to all goods received from the 16th through the last day of the month. A full month's charges assessed to all goods on hand on the first day of the next month.

SPLIT PICKUP OR DELIVERY   Multiple pickup and/or deliveries, involving one or more places of business.

SPLIT SHIPMENT   Situation in which an entire shipment is separated for movement; done either by initial shipper or carrier.

SPLIT SHIFTING   The process of shifting the main and auxiliary transmission gears simultaneously.

SPOILAGE   One form of deterioration cost. A sub-set of deterioration. The reduction in consumption value resulting from inadequate facilities or opportunity for preservation.

SPONTANEOUSLY COMBUSTIBLE MATERIAL (SOLID)   A solid substance (including sludges and pastes) which may undergo spontaneous heating or self-ignition under conditions normally incident to transportation or which may upon contact with the atmosphere undergo an increase in temperature and ignite.

SPOON DRIFT (SPINDRIFT)   The sea mist blown from the waves.

SPOT   A vessel at her loading port and ready to load or unload.

SPOT PRICE   The price of goods that are coming on to the market at the current time and must be sold. Prices of goods that are now available on the market due to harvesting. Prices of goods that are now available for delivery after long periods of speculation under futures contracts.

SPOTTER   A terminal yard driver who parks vehicles brought in by regular drivers. The term is also applied to a supervisor who checks on line haul driver.

SPOT THE BODY   Slang for parking a trailer.

SPOTTING   The process of placing freight cars or trucks at a particular dock for loading is referred to as spotting the cars.

SPOTTING CARS   Switching to a specified location.

SPREAD   The gap between maximum allowable load and actual load carried.

SPREADER   A device used to spread lifting cables, so it lifts straight up from the container corners.

SPREAD SHEET   Computer software that allows for easy computations involving numerical data.

SPREAD TANDEM   A two axle arrangement on a trailer with the axles spread more than usual.

SPRINKLER   Fire protection water outlets that automatically spray water if the temperature rises above a certain degree.

SPUR-TRACK   A track which extends a short distance from a regular railroad track is a spur track. It may serve one or more industries.

SQUARE FOOT STORAGE   Contractual agreement for a specific amount of square footage. Charge is determined by multiplying square foot rate by number of square feet contracted for.

SQUEALER   A slang phrase for a tachograph.

SQUEEZE   Slang for carton clamp.

STABILITY   The degree of force which holds a vessel upright, or returns it to up-right if keeled over. Weights on the lower hold will increase the stability.

STACK   The exhaust pipe on a diesel.

STACKER   An individual who loads the freight on the truck, or unloads it.

STACKER CRANE   Crane installed within a rack enabling the stack to be as high as 100 feet.

STACKING   Placing of merchandise on top of other merchandise.

STACKING HEIGHT   The distance as measured from the floor to a point 24″ or more below the lowest overhead obstruction. Stacking height is usually controlled to coming into contact with overhead obstructions and to maintain clearances required by local fire regulations and ordinances.

STACKS   Refers to product which is stacked up in the warehouse. Storage area.

STAFF FUNCTIONS   Those functions in the industrial firm which service the line functional areas by providing them legal services, credit services, finance availability, personnel services (hiring and terminating), etc., are termed staff areas. The staff areas do not provide a time, place, form, or possession utility service in the firm.

STAGING   The practice of picking goods in a warehouse and bringing them to rest at the dock so that further checking and load planning can take place. This is distinct from DIRECT LOAD.

STAGING AREA   A temporary storage area in a warehouse or terminal where goods are accumulated for final loading at one time.

STAKE BODY   A trailer platform body with removable stakes, which are usually joined by chains, panels or slats.

STAKING   Stakes used on open cars to prevent the lading, such as poles, lumber and structural iron from shifting and rolling off cars.

STALE DATED BILLS OF LADING   Shipping documents which are present to the negotiating bank after 21 days from the day of issuance. The L/C may substitute a shorter or a longer period for presentation.

STANCHIONS   The pillars used to support the deck. Stanchions are also used on deck to support awnings.

STAND   The spot at which an aircraft can be brought to rest so that freight and passengers may be loaded and unloaded.

STANDARD BILL OF LADING   A form of lading used to some extent in the Southeast, the conditions of which differ with those of the uniform bill of lading.

STANDARD CLASSES   Those which are established as a fixed rule and are complete in themselves.

STANDARD DENSITY   The compression of a flat bale of cotton to standard density of approximately $22\frac{1}{2}$ pounds per cubic foot.

STANDARD FORMS   Forms adopted for general use with a view to uniformity.

STANDARD GAUGE   The distance between the rails of practically all North American railroads is 4 feet $8\frac{1}{2}$ inches. This is standard gauge distance between the rails.

STANDARD INTERNATIONAL TRADE CLASSIFICATION   A numerical identification of commodities moving by air. Adopted by the U.S. scheduled air carriers and developed by the United Nations.

STANDARD METROPOLITAN STATISTICAL AREA (SMSA)   A designated zone for major population centers in the U.S.; useful in population, marketing and other analyses.

STANDARD RATE   A rate established via direct routes from one point to another in relation to which the rates via other routes between the same points are made.

STANDARD ROUTE   The carrier or carriers having the direct route between two points.

STANDARD SETTLEMENT INSTRUCTION (SSI)   The methods used to settle wire and cash transfers from one bank to another.

STANDARD TRAFFIC FORMS   Forms that have become standard through continued use or which have been prescribed for use by the Interstate Commerce Commission.

STANDARDIZATION PROGRAM   An effort, usually within a purchasing department, to find commonality among parts, components, and raw materials so that fewer of them can be used in the firm's many products. Benefits of purchasing volume buying and inventory control often accrue.

STANDBY FARE   A low fare in the airline industry that is only available to passengers if no other revenue paying passenger shows up to board the flight.

STANDING APPOINTMENT   A prearranged date and time at a warehouse or factory for pick up of goods. These can be extended to the same time each week, month, etc., of the same configuration of goods in the order.

STANDING ORDER   An agreement whereby a customer agrees to purchase a certain quantity of specified goods at certain intervals, and vendor agrees to ship at those times.

STAPLE   Principal commodity of a country or district; a commodity in everyday use.

STAPLING MACHINE, STRAP   A machine that staples over-trap on cases requiring strong binding.

STARBOARD   The right side of the vessel, looking forward. At one time a steering board was used on the right side of the vessel.

STATED REFRIGERATION CHARGE   A freight refrigeration charge for service en route used for a cwt., package, track or other method of quoting the charge.

STATEMENT OF BILLING   Brief of a waybill without names of consignors and consignees.

STATEMENT OF CHARGES   An itemized list often submitted separate from the commercial invoice (the price or bill of goods), and embracing inland and ocean freights, cartage to steamer, insurance premiums, consular fees, and cooperage charges.

STATE TOLL   A charge made by a State for the use of its highways or other roadways (tunnels, bridges, etc.).

STATION   A place designated on the timetable by name, at which a train may stop for traffic, or to enter or to leave the main track, or from which fixed signals are operated.

STATION COSTS   Costs of rating, billing and routing a rail shipment.

STATION INDEX   A list of points to, from and between which rates apply, and appearing in a tariff or other traffic schedule.

STATION ORDER CAR   A car loaded by shipper with several less-than-carload shipments in destination order, for different points along the same route. This car is placed into a train without its contents being rehandled at the carrier's terminal at point of shipment.

STATION PIER   A pier having no rail connections; where freight is received and delivered by car-floats.

STATISTICAL PROCESS CONTROL (SPC)   An approach to quality enforcement. Statistical process of measuring output of production line or other activity. Output guides producer as well as being sent to buying firm. Accept/reject decisions are made from the data as are rules to adjust the machinery or system.

STATUS QUO   The existing conditions or state of things.

STATUTE OF LIMITATION   A statute law limiting the time in which claims or suits may be instituted.

STATUTORY NOTICE   The length of time required by law for carriers to give notice of changes in tariffs, rates, rules, and regulations—usually thirty days, unless otherwise permitted by authority from the Interstate Commerce Commission.

STAVE   The breaking of the boat planking. Also a term for an external puncture in a ship's hull.

STEAM RAILWAY   A carrier whose principal motive power is steam.

STEAMSHIP   A vessel whose principal motive power is steam and not sails. There are three classes of steamships: 1) Freight carrying vessels (liners and tramps); 2) Combination vessels (freight and passenger); and 3) Passenger carrying vessels.

STEAMSHIP AGENT   A firm that represents the owner of a vessel in ports for purposes of handling port clearances, arranging dock space, stevedores, etc.

STEAMSHIP FREIGHT CONTRACT   Sometimes the shippers in a steamship line contract for space and rates relative to future sailings.

STEAMSHIP GUARANTEE   An indemnity issued to the carrier by a bank, which protects the carrier against any possible losses or damages arising from release of the merchandise to the receiving party. This instrument is usually issued when the bill of lading is lost or not available.

STEERING AXLE   An axle which has the directional control of the vehicle attached. There may be more than one steering axle on a single unit.

STEM   The leg of a transportation vehicle trip to reach the first pick up or delivery site in an area.

STEM WINDER   A slang phrase for a vehicle with a crank starter.

STENCIL   Applies to any paper, board, metal, etc., that makes lettering by passing ink over a sheet with letters perforated.

STENCILING   Required on all orders under 5000 lbs. It provides positive identification of each shipment and can often prevent claims.

STENCIL WEIGHTS   Weights stenciled on a car or container showing the capacity, light weight of car or container, and the maximum weight to be loaded in car or container.

STERILE AREA   1) Airlines. That area within the security zone. 2) Manufacturing. Any area that is maintained in very clean conditions with a minimum of contamination. Examples are food processing and especially "clean rooms" for manufacturing micro chips and other technologies.

STERN THRUSTER   A propulsion device that is placed sideways on the rear of a ship that assists in its docking and undocking. This provides sideways movement.

STET   Let it stand.

STEVEDORE   A person having charge of the loading and unloading of the boats.

STICKY PRICES   The name for prices that tend to rise with small upward opportunities arising in the market but are slow to come down when these same conditions recede.

STIFF   The quality of a vessel to be stable, or to return to an upright position.

STITCHER   A procedure for stapling box bottoms, tops, joints, etc., in solid fibers or corrugated containers.

STOCK CAR   A car designed for the transportation of livestock.

STOCK KEEPING UNIT (SKU)   The unit of distinct product and package size in a supply chain system. A specific brand of breakfast cereal in a 12 ounce box and the same product in an 18 ounce box are two stock keeping units. Each has a separate UNIFORM PRODUCT CODE.

STOCKLESS DISTRIBUTION   A term for distribution that does not involve stopping the goods in warehouses. This is often the term used for CROSS DOCK distribution.

STOCK LOCATOR SYSTEM   A system whereby all spots within the warehouse are lettered or numbered.

STOCK MIXING   When a marketing firm buys from different manufacturers and keeps a full line of products at the warehouse for shipments to customers.

STOCK OUT   The condition of running out of the materials, parts, supplies or finished products required for production or sale. A deficiency of stock in storage.

STOCK OUT COST   When the supply of an article or commodity runs out, losses are sustained. If the immediate effect of a loss is to shut down manufacturing or processing operations, the extent of the loss may be the combination of profits lost as well as production costs incurred during the period of shutdown that could not be forestalled. If the stock out eliminates the availability of goods for sale in the post-production channel, the stock out cost may be measured by the combination of lost profits from potential sales, and marketing costs that could not be forestalled, and that will result in marketing facilities operating at less than full capacity.

STOCK REPORT   A record of items on hand by type and number, based on the paperwork recording of receipts and shipments during a given period.

STOCK ROTATION   First in, first out.

STOCK SPOTTING   A distribution method whereby goods are moved to forward storage points for fast, short replenishment order cycle times to customers; primary rationale for stock spotting is for customer service needs.

STOL   Short takeoff and landing aircraft. Aircraft capable of landing and taking off on reduced length runways.

STOP IN TRANSIT   The process of stopping en route to partially load, unload or perform another service.

STOP-OFF OPERATIONS   The process of stop-off is a privilege granted to a shipper for the purpose of completing a loading or for partial unloading. A shipper must designate the intended stop-off operation on the bill of lading by designating the points at which the car should be stopped, the name and address of the party who will load or unload at the stop-off point, and the purpose of the stop-off operation. An example would be, "stop this car at Spokane, Washington to complete loading by the Johnson Produce Company." Freight may be prepaid or otherwise at the stop-off point. If freight is prepaid, a special form is used or a memorandum bill of lading is applied. When goods are stopped for partial unloading, the carrier must obtain a receipt for the unloaded portion of the car. The point at which the car is stopped must be directly intermediate and on the authorized route.

STOP-OVER   Many carriers allow a stop-over privilege on carload freight shipments at stations between points of origin and final destination, for the purpose of finishing loading or partly unloading, or taking advantage of transit or other privileges permitted in accordance with tariff rules and regulations.

STOPPAGE IN TRANSIT   This term is very different from stopping in transit. Stoppage refers to the right of a shipper of goods moving on a straight bill of lading to withhold final delivery and return the shipment to its origin because of the unwillingness or incapacity of the consignee to pay for them.

STORAGE   A charge for storage for freight in carrier's warehouse in excess of free time authorized by tariffs.

STORAGE AISLE   An aisle used to gain access to a storage bay, pallet slot, pallet rack or bin.

STORAGE BAY   That portion of the occupiable storage space that faces either a handling or storage aisle where merchandise can be stored.

STORAGE CHARGE   Fee for holding goods at rest.

STORAGE COSTS   The sum total of all costs associated with storage. It includes a) inventory costs, b) warehouse costs, c) administrative storage costs, d) deterioration costs, e) insurance costs, f) in-and-out (labor) costs, and g) taxes. It does not include ordering costs, since these are a part of purchasing costs.

STORAGE EFFICIENCY   The degree to which the minimum space can be used for a customer account.

STORAGE-IN-TRANSIT   This term is applied to a tariff privilege which permits freight to be stopped en route for storage without a change in the rate. However, it may involve an added switching charge.

STORAGE REVENUE   Money received for the storage of a customer's product.

STORAGE TRACK   A track on which cars are placed when not in service, or when held awaiting disposition.

STORE ASSORTMENT   The makeup of a package or carton of many individual products that are then shipped to a small store. This also includes special multi-product packages that are combined to be sold in one overall package to consumers.

STORE-DOOR DELIVERY   The movement of goods to the consignee's place of business, customarily applied to movement by truck.

STORE FRIENDLY PICK   The picking of various products in a retail distribution center and loading them onto pallets or into cages according to an efficient unloading flow pattern in the retail store.

STOREKEEPER   An officer in charge of a bonded warehouse.

STORES   1) Purchasing. Those operations in a firm that hold and make available to users required maintenance, repair, and operating supplies. 2) Ocean Shipping. Provision and supplies aboard a vessel. List of stores is a document listing stores aboard a vessel at a given time.

STORM TRACK   In the northern hemisphere, the cyclone moves in a right curve, while in the southern hemisphere it moves in a left curve. The line of the storm motion is called the storm track. A vessel in the storm track will not experience wind, but the barometer will fall. If in the northern hemisphere, the vessel would put the wind on the starboard quarter and run a right circle.

STOVE   A case or cask broken in from the outside.

STOW   To place the vessel gear in its proper place.

STOWAGE   The careful arrangement of freight in a ship's hold.

STOWAGE, BROKEN   The space in a ship lost between units of cargo.

STOWAGE FACTOR   The relation between measurement freight (40 cubic feet of space to the long ton) and the weight of cargo. Stowage factors vary from 9 cubic feet for pig lead to 1000 cubic feet for wicker baskets.

STRADDLE CARRIER   A truck lifting device to pickup containers within its own framework.

STRAIGHT JOB   A truck with the chassis and body permanently attached.

STRAIGHT RE-BUY   The purchase of goods from a supplier via purchase order, without bidding or negotiations, that are the same products as a previous order.

STRAIGHT SHIPMENTS   Goods consigned directly to a named consignee.

STRAIGHT TRUCK   A vehicle with the cargo body and tractor mounted on the same chassis.

STRAPPING TOOL   A device used to pull strapping tightly on a case or to draw it closely so that seals or other fastening may be applied.

STRATEGIC ALLIANCE—HORIZONTAL   A linkage with another firm for the purpose of extending one's marketing reach and geographic scope. In the airline industry, two or more carriers will often develop a marketing alliance that is referred to as "strategic" in order to extend both their route structures.

STRATEGIC ALLIANCE—VERTICAL   A relational linkage with another firm for the purpose of accessing advantages and competencies that the original firm does not have the capital, skill, or geographic reach to attain on its own. An example might be an alliance with a supplier in order to gain access to its technologies that they do not sell to or through any other firm.

STRESS   The force required to change to shape of an object. It may involve twist, thrust, pull or otherwise.

STRETCH WRAP   A process and means of applying a sheet of plastic to a small load of packages in such a way that they are secured together in a convenient unitized manner.

STUB STATION   A station in which the tracks are connected at one end only.

STUFFING   Loading a container(s).

SUB-BLOCK   One of the units contained in a main (express) block and including certain points for rate-making purposes.

SUBCONTRACTING   The act of having another firm produce part of a product.

SUBLEASED CARS   Private line rail cars that are then released to another party, usually for short periods.

SUBPOENA   An order to require an individual to present testimony.

SUBROGATE   To put in the place of another.

SUBROGATION   Putting one thing in place of another; substituting one creditor for another.

SUBSIDY   A compensation by a government agency in situations in which inadequate or no service has or will be rendered by commercial carriers.

SUBSTITUTE   Any product or service that can be used in place of another. This is a common issue when a firm seeks to slim down the number of stock keeping units in its system by combining them or using ones with similar attributes.

SUCKER BRAKES   Vacuum brakes.

SUE   Abandoned high and dry.

SUE AND LABOR CLAUSE   The action taken to recover the costs of action taken to avert or minimize loss from a casualty is taken under the sue and labor clause by the master against the underwriters.

SUFFERANCE WHARF   A wharf licensed and attended by customs authorities.

SUNDRIES   Unclassified articles.

SUNSET LAW   Law that requires an agency or law to be analyzed and rejustified or else its existence will be automatically terminated.

SUPERCARGO   An agent who accompanies cargo to the foreign market to care for and sell it to the best advantage, and to buy a return cargo and accompany it home.

SUPER CENTER   A master wholesale or service center that replenishes individual field warehouses. Many such centers are used to receive and breakdown consolidated import consignments; they then distribute the goods to the field warehouses.

SUPERIOR TRAIN   A train given preference by train order.

SUPER TANKER   An ocean tanker ship in the range generally from 75,000 to 100,000 deadweight tons. See VLCC and ULCC.

SUPPLEMENT (TARIFF)   A publication containing additions to and/or changes in a tariff.

SUPPLEMENTAL AIR CARRIERS   A class of air carrier performing passenger and cargo charter services which are supplemental to the scheduled service of the certificated route air carriers. They hold restricted certificates of public convenience and necessity from the Civil Aeronautics Board.

SUPPLEMENTAL ORDER   An order made by a court of a regulating body altering or adding to an order which was previously issued by them.

SUPPLIER   The current term for a company that supplies the firm with its purchased goods and/or services. An older, and less used, term is vendor.

SUPPLIER ACTIVITY PROFILE   A report or data base listing of the amount and type of purchases a firm makes with an individual supplier. This might also include subsequent quality and delivery experience data.

SUPPLIER COST MODEL   The act of researching the costs and cost structure of a supplier and benchmarking what their best-in-class costs should be. This is used to construct component costs for negotiations.

SUPPLIER DEVELOPMENT   Any act that helps a supplier enhance their operations and performance for the buying firm.

SUPPLIER INTEGRATION   Any activity that involves close linkages with a supplier. These can include sharing forecasts, combining transportation activities, conducting mutual research, etc.

SUPPLIER LIST   Those suppliers that a buying firm has as available for selection for individual purchases. This list is generally developed after quality inspection and visits to suppliers.

SUPPLIER MANAGEMENT   Any activity that has the effect of exerting control over suppliers for the purpose of shaping their behavior in favorable ways for the buying company.

SUPPLIER RATIONALIZATION   The conscious act by a purchasing group of a firm to reduce the number of suppliers they use for a particular good or service.

SUPPLIER SATISFACTION INDEX   A measured listing of how well a supplier performs for a buying company. Such indexes are computed based upon quality of the product, reliability of deliveries, willingness to do business with the customer, etc.

SUPPLIER TURNOVER   A measure of the degree to which a firm's suppliers are dropped from the purchase list and others are selected to replace them.

SUPPLIER'S SUPPLIER   The second tier supplier that is used by the supplier a firm acquires goods and services from in their market.

SUPPLY BASE   1) Broad. All the firms that could be considered for purchase of goods and services by a firm's purchasing department. 2) Narrow. The suppliers on a firm's approved supplier list.

SUPPLY BASE REDUCTION   See SUPPLIER RATIONALIZATION.

SUPPLY BOATS   Boats that bring provisions from shore to off-shore oil platforms.

SUPPLY CHAIN   1) Goods Firms. The design and execution processes used by a firm to acquire, convert, and move goods to markets. 2) Service Firms. The design and execution processes used by a firm to configure and mobilize its offerings to the market. Supply chains can be built in many forms and serve many purposes. Some of these are to seek cost synergies, compete against another set of firms in the market, tap innovation in the supply and customer markets, etc.

SUPPLY CHAIN COLLABORATION   A conscious cooperation and integration among firms in a supply chain. This is typically conducted for purposes of increased efficiencies or extended competitiveness.

SUPPLY CHAIN, EXTENDED   A view by a firm that its supply chain includes suppliers, sometimes supplier's suppliers, customers, and even ultimate consumers.

SUPPLY CHAIN KNOWLEDGE   Data that is accessed across a supply chain by a firm or the firms integrated in the chain and is combined to form competitive advantage. This can be in the form of knowledge about ultimate consumers, technologies, or logistics advantages.

SUPPLY CHAIN MANAGEMENT   The overall planning and execution of supply chain activities.

SUPPLY CHAIN, MICRO   A supply chain that extends from a firm's purchasing through to the end of its production line.

SUPPLY CHAIN, NANO   A supply chain view that includes only raw material inventories, production planning, and production management.

SUPPLY CHAIN OPTIMIZATION   Actions designed to view the costs of a supply chain and its performance as an end goal rather than lowest individual cost of each of its components.

SUPPLY CHAIN ROADMAP   See ROADMAP.

SUPPLY CHAIN TEAM   A group of people, typically comprising different supply chain components, who are assembled for the purpose of discovering and implementing efficiency improvements.

SUPPLY CHAIN TRANSACTIONS   A loose term for the four activities of Plan, Source, Make, and Deliver.

SUPPLY LEADERSHIP   The act of shaping supplier and supply market behavior and investments for the benefit of the buying firm.

SUPPLY MANAGEMENT   1) Most expansive view, it involves all activities required by the firm to acquire goods and services and in some cases use and sell them. 2) Narrow view: management of maintenance and repair items in the firm.

SUPPLY MARKET MANAGEMENT   See SUPPLY LEADERSHIP.

SUPPLY RELATIONSHIP   The name for the specific form of relationship a firm has with a supplier of a product and/or service. These range from arm's length to full integration.

SUPRA   A legal term used to signify that a case or ruling has been previously decided upon or adjudicated by either a court or regulatory body.

SUPRA PROTEST   A form of acceptance by a second party to save the credit of the drawer of a bill of exchange which has been protested.

SURCHARGE   A charge above the usual or customary charge.

SURCHARGE, FREIGHT   An increase in the freight charge resulting from the rate advances allowed in the Fifteen Percentage, 1931, Ex Parte 103.

SURPLUS GOODS   Materials that have accumulated within the firm that are in excess of requirements.

SURTAX   An additional or extra tax.

SURVEY   1) Transportation. An examination requested by the master to the port authorities and his consul, when entering port with such damage as bulwarks or masts down, the vessel leaking, etc. The vessel is checked for proper stowage. The master may extend a protest to the survey. 2) Exporting. A general term for the service of an outside inspection firm that will attest to the quality and attributes of goods that are ready for export. Many letters of credit require that goods be inspected by a survey firm prior to export from the producing country.

SURVEYOR   In shipping, one who officially examines and reports on applications for marine insurance. '

SUSPENSE ACCOUNT   An account to record an incomplete transaction awaiting additional information or audit for its adjustment, such as interline.

SUSPENSION   The withdrawal of a privilege or opportunity for a short period.

Applied to rates, it implies the I.C.C. is holding up a proposed rate from going into effect until a hearing or study is completed.

SUTTLE WEIGHT   Weight after tare is deducted.

SWAMPER   An assistant who rides with the driver.

SWAPS   Practice of exchanging commodities between two firms rather than have two buying-selling arrangements. Gasoline firms often practice this so as to reduce transportation expenses.

SWIFT   Society for Worldwide Inter-Bank Financial Telecommunications, a funds wire transfer consortium of banks and other financial institutions.

SWINDLE SHEET   A slang phrase referring to the I.C.C. Log.

SWITCH   A connection between two lines of track to permit cars or trains to pass from one track to another. Also, to move cars from one place to another within switching limits.

SWITCH CREW   The people that move a rail car from one place to another within switching limits.

SWITCH ENGINE   An engine used in the service of switching cars.

SWITCHING   Movement of cars within terminal areas for loading, unloading, train make-up or breakup. Switching within the plant is intraplant, switching between plants is interplant; switching between points within the terminal area is interterminal.

SWITCHING AND TERMINAL COMPANY   A company performing switching service only, furnishing terminal trackage, bridges or other facilities only, operating ferries exclusively, or performing any combination of these functions, and which may incidentally conduct a regular freight or passenger service.

SWITCHING CHARGE   An added switching charge for performing a switching service that is not within the switching limits.

SWITCHING LIMIT   Switching limit is the area at a station within which Lionel carload freight is picked up or is switched for loading or unloading without added charge above the line-haul freight rate. It may be the same area as yard or less but rarely greater than the yard limit. Tariffs filed with regulatory bodies define such switching limits at important stations. At intermediate stations it is all tracks within the station layout or yard limit.

SWITCHING LIMITS   Boundaries within which switching rules and charges apply.

SWITCHING RECIPROCAL   A mutual interchange of carload freight, inbound and outbound, which is switched to or from a siding of another carrier under a regular switching charge. The carrier receiving the line-haul usually absorbs the charge.

SWITCHING SERVICE   A railway service performed under yard rules and regulations. It may involve the classification of cars according to commodity and destination; the assembling of cars for train movement; changing the position of cars for purposes of loading, unloading, and weighing; the placing of locomotives and cars for repair and storage; and the moving of equipment in connection with the carrier's work service not constituting a road movement.

SWITCHING TARIFF   A schedule containing charges for (switch) movement of cars.

SWITCH ORDER   An order to move a car from one place to another within switching limits.

SYNCHRONISM   That situation in which the action of the waves and the oscillation of the vessel are in tune. If the ship and waves reach their greatest angle of inclination simultaneously, an excessive roll follows. To correct this, the speed and/or direction of the vessel is changed.

SYNCHRONIZED PRODUCTION   Manufacturing operations that are linked with customer demand and enables fast replenishment, typically PRODUCE-TO-ORDER rather than PRODUCE-TO-STOCK type of production.

SYNDICATE "A"   A U.S. Salvage Association which performs the survey of marine property.

SYNDICATE "B"   An association of insurance companies which insures the Shipping Board's equity in a vessel under sail.

SYNDICATE "C"   An association of insurance companies that specializes in hulls and machinery for American flags and foreign owned vessels.

SYNERGY   The ability to gain economies from combining or coordinating separate functions across a firm.

SYNERGY CHAIN   A supply chain that is created for the purpose of taking costs out of a complex firm's overall supply chain processes. This consists of coordinated warehousing, transportation, and sometimes a common order management system.

SYSTEM (RAILWAY)   The entire trackage equipment and facilities of a line of railroad, inclusive of main tracks, side tracks, branch lines, yards and terminals.

SYSTEMS CONTRACT   A contract typically covering maintenance, repair, and operating supplies for a particular plant from a vendor.

SYSTEMS ANALYST   The supervisor who approves the instructions, concepts, etc., in the program.

SYSTEMS PROGRAMMER   The person preparing the instructions to meet the objectives of a computer program. He also makes up the flow-charts.

TTTT

T&R   Truck and rail.

TAB   The identification card attached to an article or container shipped.

TABLE, BALL TRANSFER   In materials handling, this is a table with freely mounted balls used to facilitate transfer from one conveyor to another.

TACHOGRAPH   An instrument used to record miles driven, speed, number of stops, etc. It is placed in the cab of the truck.

TACK   Short for tachograph. Also short for tachometer.

TACK-ON ORDER   An order placed with a supplier by one customer for the same type of goods that are already being produced by a supplier for another customer. This avoids the need for the supplier to change over the production line and incur related costs of doing so.

TACTICAL DIAMETER   The deviation from the course a vessel experiences in traveling through 180 degrees.

TAGGING   An activity in the supply chain of retail goods where they are tagged with identification and other labels for their final sales.

TAIL, OF THE INVENTORY   See INVENTORY TAIL.

TAILBOARD ARTIST   Meaning one who regards himself a perfect driver.

TAILGATE   The removable or opening rear wall of the truck body which permits rear end unloading—or permits spill-unloading by raising if it is a dump truck. The tailgate term was originally applied to wagon boxes.

TAILGATING   Following too closely in trucking.

TAKE OR PAY AGREEMENTS   A pricing agreement made between a buyer and a seller that requires the buyer to pay for a defined quantity over a period of time, regardless of the quantity they actually need. These are usually discount price agreements. Risk of total consumption or use is upon the buyer firm.

TALE QUALE   Such as. A term used generally in grain trade to denote that cargo is presumed to correspond with sample and that the buyer takes all risk of subsequent loss or deterioration.

TALLY   A tally sheet is made up when goods are received and a record of their condition on arrival is tabulated.

TALLY FORM   A record of such items as amount, description, marks, etc., of goods being loaded or unloaded.

TALLY NUMBER   Sequential number listing; one given to each tally.

TANDEM   A semitrailer or tractor with two rear axles.

TANDEM AXLE   A two axle arrangement on the rear of the truck, either or both of which may be powered.

TANGIBLE ASSETS   Assets in physical form such as inventories, plants, equipment, and even financial instruments.

TANK BODY   A tank truck used to carry liquids.

TANK CAR   A car consisting of a tank, or more than one tank, mounted on car frame or directly on cradles over truck bolsters, used for the transportation of liquids and gases.

TANK CAR GAUGE BOOK   A publication showing capacities, names of owners, series numbers, etc., of tank cars in the country.

TANKER   A liquid hauling truck. A tractor with a tank body.

TANK SHIP   A vessel used for transporting bulk liquids. It is divided into compartments for facilitating multiple liquids, safety, etc.

TANKTAINER   A container with a built-in tank for transporting liquids.

TANK TRAILER   A fully enclosed trailer designed for the transportation of liquid commodities in bulk.

TANK TRUCK CARRIER   A motor carrier that hauls liquid and/or dry bulk products in tank trailers, containers, or vans.

TAPE DRIVE   In data processing, the equipment which passes the magnetic tape past the recording heads.

TAPE, GUMMED CLOTH   A packaging tape which may take many forms. Typically they are cloth and paper gummed for packaging. Some are fiber-filled and clay-filled in design.

TAPE, GUMMED SEALING   A wide tape used for packaging consisting of kraft paper in many weight forms. The most common weight compositions are 35, 60 and 90 pounds.

TAPE, GUMMED SISAL   A form of packaging tape composed of sisal fibers or great strength combined with asphaltic or non-asphaltic laminants between sheets of kraft paper.

TAPE, KRAFT   A packaging tape made from brown kraft paper gummed with many forms of animal or vegetable glues. They require moistening for use.

TAPE, PRESSURE SENSITIVE   A type of packaging tape that does not require moistening when used. Like others, it is covered with adhesive and can be applied with pressure in any temperature or degree of moisture.

TAPE, SEALING   A packaging tape made from cloth, paper, etc., and an adhesive which is applied with pressure. It is used for containers and packaging.

TAPE, SHIPPING SACK   A heavy-duty packaging tape made of creped-kraft, coated with gummed substance. It IS applied over the paper ends on multiwalled shipping sacks, usually after the closures are sewn.

TAP LINE   A short line railroad, sometimes called a feeder line, usually owned or controlled by the plants served by it.

TARE   The amount to deduct from the gross weight of the shipment because of the packaging weight.

TARE WEIGHT   The weight of an empty container or an empty car, without any references to the weight of contents, is called the tare weight.

TARGET BREAK-EVEN   A form of break-even analysis whereby the buyer fixes a maximum price for the seller then computes the quantity needed for he/she to purchase while covering all costs and margin of the seller.

TARGET COSTING   A purchasing field analysis of what component costs should be for the supplier against which buyers will negotiate. This is based upon benchmarking what reasonable and best practice costs should be. See also SHOULD BE COSTS. Target costs are typically determined for materials, packaging, labor, labor productivity, equipment costs, and freight.

TARGET PRICE   A price goal in a negotiation. Also, the price that is constructed after target cost negotiations and determination of a reasonable margin to be allowed the supplier.

TARIFF   Rate books which provide the dollar charge on a given class of transportation movement are called tariffs. Separate tariffs are provided for motor shipments as compared to rail shipments, and for commodity, class, T.O.F.C., in-transit charges, and many other different classes of charges. A tariff is a rate book and should not be confused with the term applicable to international trade which refers to a tax on exports.

TARIFF, AGENCY   A tariff published by an agent on behalf of two or more carriers.

TARIFF, ALTERNATIVE   A schedule divided into two or more sections, each of which provides for the application of rates in some other section when the use of such rates will produce lower charges.

TARIFF AUTHORITY   The tariff or other schedule referred to in support of statement and containing rate or regulation applicable to specific traffic. It is usually sufficient to create the number under which it is filed with the Interstate Commerce Commission or state regulating body.

TARIFF CIRCULAR   A publication of a regulatory commission that presents the regulations related to carriers and how they are to publish their tariffs.

TARIFF, CLASS   A schedule that contains rates from one point to another for the several groups or classes to which articles are assigned in a classification or an exception sheet.

TARIFF, CLASS AND COMMODITY   A schedule that contains both class and commodity rates and provisions for their alternative application.

TARIFF, COMBINATION   A tariff containing class and commodity rates.

TARIFF, COMMON   A tariff published by an agent for the account of two or more transportation lines as issuing carriers.

TARIFF, CONVENTIONAL   A tariff which contains and represents all the concessions provided for by the commercial treaties concluded by the particular country.

TARIFF FILE   Copies of tariffs, classifications, supplements, reissues and other schedules, maintained for the purpose of ascertaining, quoting and checking rates and determining the rules and regulations governing traffic.

TARIFF INDEX   A list, kept by a carrier, of the tariffs it issues or is a party to, together with points from, to and between which the rates contained therein apply.

TARP   The tarpaulin used to cover the top of the trailer.

TATTLE-TALE   The term applied to the tachograph.

TAXI   The movement of the aircraft about a landing area on its own thrust. Occurs before take-off and after landing.

TEAM TRACK   The team track is not for the sole use of a particular industry, but is provided for the general use of the public for loading and unloading freight cars.

TEAR STRENGTH   The measurement of resistance to tear under commonly accepted measurement tests.

TECHNICAL BUYING   A European term for the purchase of capital goods and maintenance/engineering items as opposed to the purchase of raw materials that will be used in the finished goods of the firm.

TECHNICAL PURCHASING   See TECHNICAL BUYING.

TECHNICAL REVIEW   Examination of a process, proposed product, or capital project in terms of its technical feasibility.

TECHNICAL STOP   A stop on an airline route for the purpose of crew change and/or fuel; not for passenger enplaning or deplaning.

TECHNOLOGY SHARING   Turning key technology knowledge over to a supplier for their use in making goods for the buying firm that created or possesses the technology.

TELECOMMUTING   A practice of workers staying at home and conducting their work via phone, fax, and computer thereby avoiding commuting and the resulting congestion that physical commuting would incur.

TELEMARKETING   Soliciting customers by calling them by phone. Also termed tele-selling.

TELEPHONE BIDDING   Quick bidding through calling suppliers by phone or fax and requesting their bid prices in this manner.

TELEPROCESSING   In electronic systems, it involves attaching peripherals online to a CPU by telephone to perform on-line processing devices.

TELETYPE (TELETYPEWRITER)   An electric typewriter using the telegraph lines to take in messages and provide information continuously or intermittently between two long-distance terminals that carry on continuous information transfers. The teletype can handle about 10–15 characters per second.

TELETYPEWRITER   TWX, high speed typewriter which picks up and sends information through the phone line from one point to another.

TELPHERAGE   The carriage of goods by telpher.

TELPHER SYSTEM   An overhead track used for moving a beam-type trolley. It permits hoisting bulk material or containers. It can be operated automatically and remotely if needed.

TEL QUEL   The rate charged for a bill of exchange which is of such currency as not to be subject to the long rate on three months' bill or upwards, nor subject to the short rate which applies to bills up to ten days, but which falls somewhere between those limits.

TEMPERATURE CHIMNEYS   A means of determining the temperature of cargo in the hold in water bulk cargo movements by providing pipes into the cargo which permit the lowering of thermometers. The problem is to avoid spontaneous combustion.

TEMPORARIES   Workers who are not permanently employed by the firm.

TENDER, ISSUE THE   See REQUEST FOR BID and REQUEST FOR PROPOSAL.

TENOR   Time and date for payment of a draft, stated in one of the following forms: At sight (A/S)—A draft so drawn that it is payable upon presentation to the paying bank. (No. of days) days sight (D/S)—The draft is payable a fixed number of days after acceptance. (No. of days) days date (D/D)—The draft is payable on a certain date; e.g., 30 days from date of invoice or issuance of other shipping documents.) days sight/documents against payment (D/S D/P)—The term is used in the collections process. The draft must be presented for acceptance to the drawee (usually the buyer). Documents can be released only against payment in full plus charges, if need be. These terms are used mainly in Hong Kong.

TENDER   The presentation for transportation by the shipper, or delivery by the carrier, of a shipment.

TERMINAL   Facilities provided by a railway at a terminus or at an intermediate point on its line for the handling of passengers or freight, and for the breaking up, making up, forwarding and servicing trains, and interchanging with other carriers.

TERMINAL CARRIER   The carrier making the delivery in a joint carrier movement.

TERMINAL CHARGE   The charge for such facilities as docks, wharves, piers, switching tracks, belt-line railroads, hoists, warehouses and elevators for the loading, unloading, interchange, and storage of freight.

TERMINAL OPERATIONS   As applied to a switching and terminal company, the use of the facilities furnished at such locations as a freight or passenger union station, bridge ferry, and other terminal joint facilities, usually measured by the number of cars handled for tenant companies.

TERMINAL SWITCHING   The moving of cars originating at destined to points.

TERMINAL TRACKAGE   Track facilities at terminal stations provided for the joint use of two or more carriers.

TERMINI (POINTS)   Synonymous with terminals and specifically referring in the case of the Western Termini to certain points originally the western terminals of eastern railways and now important in rate construction.

TERRITORIAL   A qualifying term and expressive of that which is applicable to a designated section or territory.

TERRITORIAL DIRECTORY   A publication embracing description of traffic territories, rate points, crossings, termini, etc., and issued to avoid duplication of matter so extensive that it would not be practicable to incorporate it in each tariff applicable.

TERRITORY   In transportation, a designation of a part or section of the country.

TERTIARY PACKAGING   The outer packaging used for units of product. It is a unitizing medium in which individually packaged products and multi-units of them are contained. This might consist of an overall carton that contains 24 secondary packages of product each containing 6 units of product.

TEST, DROP   A system of testing resistance to damage of containers through controlled drop testing.

TEST, DRUM   The process of testing shipping containers by revolving them inside a hexagon drum.

TEST, ELMENDORF TEAR   A tear testing system by controlled weight application to various layers of paper or board.

TEST, FLAT CRUSH   A crush measurement system by applying incrementally increasing forces to corrugations in a sheet of fiberboard, etc.

TEST, FOLDING ENDURANCE   A system of testing the endurance of packaging paper or film to the folding stress. A schopper machine performs a frequent folding operation.

TEST, HYDROSTATIC PRESSURE   A test to establish the capacity of metal drums to meet specifications to authorize their use in the movement of dangerous commodities.

TEST, INCLINE IMPACT (COBUR TEST)   The purpose of this test is to establish the ability of packaging to resist impact that might occur in freight car movements. The test consists of rolling a dolly down inclined rails so it will impact against a solid wall.

TESTING   A common foreign trade zone activity, though not limited to them, of examining goods and attesting to their quality, attributes, and condition.

TEST, LEAKAGE   A system for testing metal containers for leakage. Underwater seams are tested, and sometimes heavy oil or soapsuds are used for testing.

TEST SHIPMENT   A shipment made in a package or form of shipping not specified in the tariff for purposes of evaluating the new package or shipping method.

TEST, TENSILE   A package testing process that captures an ability to resist external and/or internal rupture.

THEFT   Feloniously taking and removing property with intent to deprive the rightful owner; the taking of the entire container or article.

THEORY   An exposition of the abstract principles of a science considered apart from practice.

THE TRADE   A general term for large retail firms in the supply chain.

THICKENER   A materials handling facility for arranging the solid to liquid concentration by systems of gravity, suction or precipitation.

THIRD LEVEL CARRIER   Air carriers that provide passenger and/or freight service between outlying small cities, or from these cities to trunk line cities.

THIRD PARTY FIRM   Any person or organization that provides services in a logistical or production process other than the seller or buyer. Examples are public warehousemen, carriers, rate auditing firms, outside manufacturing firms, etc.

THIRD PARTY LOGISTICS   Outsourced logistics activities for such things as traffic management, warehousing, inventory control, order management, field service, etc.

THIRD RAIL   A rail either along side a rail track or between the running rails that carries electricity for the locomotive or train source of power.

THIRD STRUCTURE TAX   The first two levels of tax on motor vehicles consist of registration and fuel taxes. Any other tax on transportation service or the vehicle used in transportation would be a third structure tax.

THIRD WORLD   Those economically underdeveloped nations of the world.

THREE (OR MORE) TRACKS   Three (or more) main tracks, upon any one of which the current of traffic may move in either specified direction.

THROUGH BILL OF LADING   A bill of lading drawn up to cover goods from point of origin to final destination when interchange or transfer from one carrier to another is necessary to complete the journey.

THROUGH FARE   A single fare for a transportation movement from the point of origin of the passenger to the destination. It is usually lower than the sum of individual fares that might be involved. It could take the form of a joint fare, or the combination of several separate fares.

THROUGH FLIGHT   Any flight that does not require the transfer to another plane (or other modal vehicle). It could be very circuitous and involve many stops. It could also involve an equipment interchange movement in which several different carriers are involved, that interchange jointly used common equipment.

THROUGH FREIGHT   As distinguished from local, this class of service is maintained between important junctions and terminals, usually between the large producing and consuming centers of the country. This traffic is largely carload but includes merchandise or package cars.

THROUGH PACKAGE CAR   A through package or merchandise car is one loaded with less than carload shipments to break bulk at a given point, in some cases containing package freight for one station only and in other cases shipments for many stations beyond.

THROUGH RATES   A charge applied to an interline shipment. The sum total of all rates that apply via a through route. A through route is the combination of connecting carriers by which they offer through transportation service from one point on the line of one carrier to the destination on the line of another carrier In Southern Pacific Terminal vs. I.C.C., 219 U.S.98 1911, the four essential characteristics of a through rate were established to be: 1) a through bill of lading, 2) uninterrupted movement, 3) continuous possession by the carrier, and 4) unbroken bulk. In a more recent case in 1956 (Denver vs. Union Pacific Railroad Co.), the Supreme Court stated that a through route exists only when the carriers hold themselves out as offering through transportation.

THROUGH TICKET(ING)   A passenger ticket that is sold by the originating carrier that applies over a connecting carrier's segment of the total movement.

THROUGH TRAIN   A train which does not stop at all stations on its route.

THROWING MACHINE, BULK MATERIAL, VANE TYPE   A rotating drum that throws bulk material through the use of moving paddles or vanes.

TICKET BY MAIL   A new means of ticketing passengers. These are tickets that are sold when the passenger contacts the carrier directly and purchases them without use of travel agents or other intermediaries.

TICKET SCALPER   A person who buys and sells the unused parts of railway tickets or airline tickets.

TIE   One complete layer of material on a pallet or unit.

TIE (RAILROAD)   The wood or concrete cross-member that rests on the surface onto which rails rest.

TIED UP   A common expression for a roadway that is blocked.

TIER   A layer of packages placed on a pallet.

TIERS AND BELTS (MERCHANDISE TRAFFIC REPORTS)   A numeration of the Equi-Graphic Rate Blocks, starting with the northwest corner of the United States.

TILT-BED TRAILER   An arrangement of a truck trailer on one or more axles, so centered that it may be tilted to facilitate loading or unloading.

TILT CAB   A type of cab that will tilt to permit access to the engine.

TIME BUCKET   The time period used in a materials requirements planning system.

TIME CHARTER   The time charter party in water transportation is a contract for leasing which spells out the terms of the leasing arrangement between the shipowners and the lessee. It would state, for example, the time of the lease in years or voyages.

TIME COMPRESSION   The act of taking less time to perform an entire set of activities than was traditionally done.

TIME FREIGHT   A term used to signify that payments for the hire of a vessel are being made periodically instead of in one lump sum.

TIME LINE   A demarked graphical continuum showing subactivities in an overall process.

TIME RATE   The price per hour assessed by service providers for the work they perform.

TIME-SHARING   A sharing of computer facilities by many different users. It involves a special teleprocessing operation.

TIMETABLE   Authority for the movement of regular trains subject to railway train rules, with a schedule that prescribes train classification, direction, identification, and movement. Timetable schedules usually are in effect for 12 hours after their time at each station, and a train behind schedule for more than the prescribed time limit can proceed only as authorized by train order. Timetable authority may be superseded by rules providing for block signals and interlocking signals.

TIME TO MARKET   A general term for the total length of time it takes a producer to develop and launch a new product.

TIPPER SEAL   A device for emptying materials from a hopper by reciprocation without reducing the vacuum.

T.O.F.C.   This refers to trailer-on-flatcar. It is also called piggyback. Shipments going T.O.F.C. receive special rates in special tariffs provided for that class of shipment.

TOLERANCE   A weight allowance is frequently made to reconcile weight variations of certain commodities due to circumstances that may frequently arise. The deviation allowance in the weight is called the tolerance.

TOLERANCES   The allowed deviations from the specifications that a buyer will permit of a seller.

TOLL   1) Transportation. The charge made for the use of a bridge or roadway. 2) A traditional term for outsource manufacturing.

TOLL PACKAGERS   Outside firms who receive a manufacturer's goods, package them, and return them to the original firm for further manufacturing and distribution.

TOMMING DOWN   This is the counterpart (opposite meaning) of shoring up. One would brace under a deck to hold cargo down.

TON   A measurement of weight, commonly equivalent to 2000 lbs. avoirdupois (short, or net, ton); 2240 lbs. (long ton); or 2240.6 lbs. (metric ton). The short ton is generally used in domestic transaction, and the long ton in the export trade of the United States. However, since the practices of ocean carriers are not uniform, the long ton is not always used. Countries which have adopted the metric system of weights and measures use a ton on 2204.6 lbs., particularly in weighting exported cargoes.

TONGS, SCISSOR   A forklift attachment that grips the load when the fork is lifted through scissor action.

TON-MILE   The movement of one ton of freight a distance of one mile. Ton miles are computed by multiplying the weight in tons of each shipment transported by the distance hauled.

TON-MILE COST EARNINGS   A unit employed in comparing freight earnings or expenses, i.e., the cost of, or the amount earned from, transporting a ton of freight one mile.

TON-MILE TAX   A system for assigning highway costs to motor vehicle operators. It is a criterion for allocating highway costs, and should not be confused with the taxing system for collecting the predetermined user's share.

TONNAGE   In ocean commerce, the weight a ship carries expressed in tons, or the carrying capacity of a vessel, less specifically, the number of tons of freight handled. Cargo tonnage refers to the quantity of cargo shipped, and vessel tonnage to the tonnage of the ship in which goods are transported.

TONNAGE (CAPACITY), DEADWEIGHT   The number of tons of cargo which a deducting displacement light and displacement loaded tonnage. Deadweight capacity, expressed in long tons or metric tons, usually serves as the basis for charter rates when vessels are operated on time charters.

TONNAGE, GROSS   The total measured cubic capacity of a vessel expressed in tons of 100 cubic feet, found by dividing the cubic measurement of its capacity by 100.

TONNAGE, NET   The total cubic contents of those parts of a vessel closed in and devoted to the carrying of cargo and passengers, the weight measure being one gross ton for each 100 cubic feet of capacity. Net tonnage of a vessel is found by deducting from its gross tonnage the cubic contents of certain spaces that are specified in the measurement laws and rules of the various maritime nations or in the measurement rules applicable at the Suez and Panama Canals. Net tonnage may be about $2/3$ of gross tonnage, although in the fast transatlantic liners, which have large coal bunkers, machinery, and housing quarters, it is likely to be lower.

TONNAGE TAX   A tax assessed on all vessels coming into the United States ports from foreign countries whether owned by Americans or not. Charge is so much per ton at each entry and not to exceed a certain sum per ton in one year.

TON, REGISTER   100 cubic feet, a unit used for measuring the entire internal capacity of ships or for register of tonnage.

TOOLING DOWN THE HIGHWAY   Slang for driving a vehicle at the legal or normal speed.

TO PAY AVERAGE   A marine insurance term having the same meaning and used alternatively to WITH PARTICULAR AVERAGE.

TOP FREIGHT   Freight that can only be loaded on top inside a trailer or container. Generally, freight that is light and/or fragile and cannot withstand weight from other goods stored on top.

TOP-HAMPER   The sum of all gear and spars over the ship's deck.

TOP OFF   A transportation term for taking on additional freight or passengers just prior to the initiation of a voyage or trip in order to maximize the revenue of the entire trip.

TOTAL ACQUISITION COST   The computed total life cost of planning for, acquiring a capital good or piece of equipment, operating it over a long period of time, and eventually disposing of it.

TOTAL AVERAGE INVENTORY   The sum of average order quantity (one-half of order quantity), plus safety stock. Likewise equal to one-half of ELQ, plus safety stock. The safety stock is the amount on hand after the arrival of the order. Total average inventory is the average normal use stock, plus the average lead stock, plus safety stock.

TOTAL CASH CYCLE   See CASH TO CASH CYCLE.

TOTAL COST OF DISTRIBUTION   The sum of the purchasing, transportation and storage costs in the movement of finished products through the post production channel. Distribution is only the post-production channel. All direct and indirect (hidden) logistics costs are included in the total distribution costs. This could mean over fifty different logistics costs.

TOTAL COST OF OWNERSHIP   See TOTAL ACQUISITION COST.

TOTAL COST RELATIONSHIP   The relationship established by a buying firm with a seller whereby close attention to total supply chain costs between the two of them is the major focus of the relationship. This is often attempted when the two firms are in a closely aligned joint supply chain arrangement and are competing against another set of firms that are also in a close supply chain relationship and they are all competing for the same customers.

TOTAL EXPORT CONCEPT   An analytical and managerial concept and viewpoint proposed by the British National Economic Development Office in the 1960s in order to aid exporting firms in their overall processes of selling out of the country.

TOTAL LIFE CYCLE COST   See TOTAL ACQUISITION COST.

TOTAL LOSS   Nothing salvageable; completely destroyed.

TOTAL VALUE RELATIONSHIP   The relationship established by a buying firm with a seller whereby close attention to mutual product/service innovation by the two of them is the major focus of the relationship. This is often attempted when the two firms are competing against another set of firms that are also in a close supply chain relationship and they are all competing for the same customers.

TOTE   A basket-like device used in materials handling operations for picking and moving many small units of goods over short distances. In some industries totes are moved inside transport containers for efficient handling from one facility to inside a destination one.

TOW   The pulling of another vessel by a hawser. The term tow also means the process of a tug pulling barges or other floating material. A tow is also the short ends of manila fiber used in making rope. Usually, tow means the vessel towed.

TOWAGE   The fee charged for moving or towing a vessel from one point to another.

TOWLINE   Materials handling medium that consists of carts that move via cable line in floor; does not require manual movement on main system.

TRACE   To follow the movement of a shipment.

TRACER   The process of requesting the carrier to give a record of a location of a shipment is a request for a tracer. It would normally ask for the name of the party who signed for the shipment, as well as a record of the arrival and the delivery time. It is not to be confused with expediting.

TRACING   The process of following the shipment in order to determine the nature of its movement primarily for the point of determining where it was lost and how it can be recovered is called tracing. While expediting must take place prior to a shipment, tracing takes place after a shipment. While some shippers seem to make a request for tracing for most of their shipments, normally this request should only be made to locate a shipment that has been lost. Among the facilities used in a tracing operation are: 1) passing reports; 2) telegrams; 3) telephone; 4) post cards; 5) records of delivery, from connecting lines. When a tracing act is performed, particularly for motor carriers, the request for a tracing act should include the way-bill number, date, tractor number, trailer number, carded data, manifest number, consignee, and destination.

TRACING FREIGHT   An endeavor to locate a shipment.

TRACK   In motor transportation, this is the precision of the rear axle wheel to follow the preceding axle wheel—particularly when making a turn. Also ties, rails, and fastenings, with all parts in their proper relative positions.

TRACKAGE   A charge made by a carrier to another carrier operating over its rails. The carrier using the track acquires trackage rights.

TRACKAGE RIGHTS   All tracks operated and maintained by others but over which the respondent has the right to operate some or all of its trains. On a road of this class, the respondent has no proprietary rights but only the rights of licensee.

TRACK, BODY   Each of the parallel tracks of a railroad yard upon which cars are sorted, switched, or stored.

TRACK CAPACITY   The number of cars a length of track will hold.

TRACK, HOLD   A track in a storage yard where cars are held pending delivery.

TRACK, HOUSE   A track running alongside or entering a freight house, used by cars that receive or deliver freight at the house.

TRACK, INDUSTRIAL   A track that serves one or more industries.

TRACK, LADDER   A track connecting the body tracks of a yard in a regular sequence.

TRACK, LEAD   A track extended to connect either end of a yard with the main track.

TRACK, PASSING   A track auxiliary to the main track for the meeting of passing trains, limited to the distance between two adjacent telegraph stations.

TRACK, SPUR   A track of indefinite length extending out from a regular railroad track.

TRACK STORAGE   A charge made for exceeding the loading time in rail movements. The car is held on the carrier's line too long for loading or unloading. This charge is not to be confused with demurrage, and is made in addition to demurrage.

TRACK, STUB   A track connecting with another at one end only and usually protected by a bumper at the stub end.

TRACK, TEAM   A side track for general use of the public in loading and unloading freight directly from cars to highway vehicles and vice versa.

TRACTOR   A vehicle designed and used primarily for drawing other vehicles and not so constructed that no part is to carry a load other than a part of the weight of the vehicle and load so drawn.

TRACTOR, AGRICULTURAL   In materials handling operations, this four wheeled vehicle is used for pulling loads. Its large rear wheels permit it to operate over very rough ground.

TRADE   1) Commerce. 2) See THE TRADE.

TRADE ACCEPTANCE   A time draft or bill of exchange drawn by the seller of merchandise on the buyer for the purchase price of the goods and having on its face the signed acceptance of the buyer with the date and place of payment.

TRADE ACCEPTANCE   See ACCEPTANCES.

TRADE DISCOUNT   An allowance made to dealers in the same line.

TRADELOAD   The practice of selling and shipping large quantities of goods to a retailer at the end of a quarter or year so that the manufacturer can post these to sales and accounts receivables on their accounting statements for that period. This practice creates a tremendous distortion in the efficient planning and management of the supply chain.

TRADE MARGIN   The difference between what a retailer pays a manufacturer for goods and the price it receives from the consumer. This is a measure of gross margin.

TRADEMARK   Figures, letters, or devices, used on goods and labels which the owner has the sole right to use.

TRADE-OFF   The application of offsetting advantages or costs in planning costs which integrate cost planning. It may involve trading off transportation costs for storage costs, or trading off faster service for greater transport costs.

TRADER   A merchant; a broker

TRADE RESTRICTIONS   Any limitations to the free flow of goods from manufacturers to the final retail sector of firms. These can be limitations on quantity, allocation to certain markets, and minimum sales price requirements.

TRADE ROUTES   Lanes of the sea customarily followed by merchant ships.

TRADING BLOCK   Any group of nations that create agreements among themselves to reduce or eliminate import tariffs and importing restrictions, regulations, and processes.

TRAFFIC   Persons and property carried by transportation lines.

TRAFFIC AGREEMENT   A working arrangement between carriers relative to the interchange of cars, divisions of revenues and rates, and such items as enter in when traffic is to be handled between the lines.

TRAFFIC EXPERT   One who is skilled through practice or experience in traffic matters, one who acts for shippers and receivers in an advisory capacity or takes entire charge of their traffic matters.

TRAFFIC MANAGEMENT   In the industrial firm, traffic management involves all functional operations related to the buying and management of transportation services, and/or the management of private transportation services. Consequently, traffic management is responsible for the selection of carriers (if there is no logistics manager), the preparation of shipments or the carrier, loading and unloading on the shipping platforms, tracing, expediting, rate analysis and applications, tariff controls, reconsignment, diversion, preparing and filing bills of lading, and all other operations related to preparing, documenting, loading, unloading, handling and approving shipments into and out of the industrial firm. By way of contrast, the traffic department of a motor carrier is responsible for rate determination, whereas the traffic department of a rail carrier firm was traditionally involved in sales functions.

TRAFFIC MANAGER (INDUSTRIAL)   An official having complete supervision of the shipping and receiving departments and general transportation activities of an industrial concern.

TRAFFIC POOLING   An illegal procedure of sharing the revenue between carrier providing a common service on a pre-arranged basis. This eliminates competition by eliminating the possibility of more revenue by seeking out traffic. In fact it encourages directing traffic to the competing line, who would be required to share the revenue after providing the service.

TRAFFIC SIGNAL PRIORITY   An urban traffic flow method that causes traffic lights to turn green with upcoming buses, trolleys, or emergency vehicles.

TRAILER   A vehicle designed without motive power, to be drawn by another vehicle and so constructed that no part of its weight rests upon the towing vehicle.

TRAILER, ARTICULATED   A trailer with a coupling to the tractor by an articulating tractor attachment. The trailer has its own front wheels to permit jockeying around when it is not attached to the tractor.

TRAILER, DROP FRAME (SINGLE)   A trailer which facilitates loading or unloading by dropping the platform behind the front wheels.

TRAILER-FLATCAR OPERATION   A railroad operation commonly called piggyback in which highway semi-trailers of a Motor Carrier (or those owned by a rail line) are loaded at shippers, loading docks or place of business and driven by Motor Carrier to railroad loading point where they are loaded on specially equipped flatcars and hauled to unloading points in fast merchandise trains operating on passenger train schedules. At unloading point, semi-trailers are removed from flatcars and driven by Motor Carrier to consignee's place of business.

TRAILER INTERCHANGE   In motor transportation, this activity involves the interchange of the shipment between carriers on a joint movement, and it usually involves the transfer of the shipment to the vehicles of the joint carrier.

TRAILER INTERLINE   This operation is the transfer of trailers between carriers on a joint movement. This involves large volume interline shipments, since it is a trailer volume interline transfer.

TRAILER POLE   This trailer system is used for transporting long loads. It consists of a single steel attachment between two carriages. The trailer is adjustable in length.

TRAILER SHIP   A vessel that transports motor trailers, and has ramps for direct drive-on loading and unloading of the trailers.

TRAILER SUPPORT   A trailer support device at the front end of the trailer which is retractable.

TRAIN   An engine, or more than one engine, coupled with or without cars displaying markers.

TRAIN-MILE   The movement of a train one mile.

TRAIN OF SUPERIOR RIGHT   A train given preference by train order.

TRAIN ORDER   An order issued by or through a proper railway official to govern the movements of a train.

TRAIN SWITCHING   Switching service performed by train locomotives at terminals and way stations.

TRAM   A term for a passenger trolley.

TRAMP LINE   A transportation line operating tramp steamers.

TRAMP (VESSEL)   A ship not connected with any particular service which carries any cargo to any port and does not operate under a given schedule. Tramp vessels are sometimes chartered by regular carriers and operated as line ships.

TRANSACTION   An agreed upon event between two parties that involves a trade of goods and financial commitment. A loose term for any document related activity within a firm or supply chain.

TRANSACTION COST   The cost of conducting a transaction.

TRANSACTIONS—SUPPLY CHAIN   These are plan, source, make, and deliver, the basic transactions a manufacturing firm must manage efficiently in its supply chain.

TRANSCO   For-profit controllers of electricity traffic in a deregulated environment.

TRANSFER ORDER SERVICE   Orders from customers that are accepted by one firm and then turned over to a wholesaler or manufacturer for completion.

TRANSFER PRICE   Term applied to a charge one part of a firm assesses another for services rendered or products transferred to it; common in private trucking and private warehousing.

TRANSFERS   A term used to describe points where shipments are rehandled before reaching final destination. Transferring consists of the movement of a shipment or shipments from one car to another or from one depot to another or in the case of a terminal or junction transfer, from one railroad to another.

TRANSFER SLIP   A protected landing place for car floats with adjustable apron or bridge connecting the tracks on the land with those on the car float.

TRANSFER UNIT   A piece of equipment that facilitates the transfer of a container from a motor chassis to a rail car without heavy lift equipment.

TRANSSHIPMENT   Shipment of merchandise to the point of destination in another country on more than one vessel or vehicle. The liability may pass from one carrier to the next, or it may be covered by "through bills of lading" issued by the first carrier.

TRANSIT AIR CARGO   This is a procedure initiated by the Customs Bureau to expedite international air freight movements. It permits the constant flow of freight traffic between airlines and flights without previously required paperwork.

TRANSIT BALANCE   The freight rate applicable under transit rules on shipments moving from transit point to destination. It is the difference between the through rate from origin to destination and the flat rate from origin to transit point.

TRANSIT CHARGES   The charges for services given while a shipment is in transit.

TRANSIT DUTIES   Taxes imposed on goods passing through a country.

TRANSITING OR TRANSITED   Passing or having passed through; applicable particularly to traffic through a canal or waterway.

TRANSIT POINT   An intermediate point at which freight is held for finishing processes or other treatment.

TRANSIT PRIVILEGE   A privilege specified in a tariff permitting a consignment to be stopped for processing, reloading or other charges, the freight to be reshipped with the application of the through rate from origin to destination. An extra charge may or may not be assessed for the privilege.

TRANSIT RATE   A rate restricted in its application to traffic which has been or will be milled, stored or otherwise specially treated in transit.

TRANSIT TIME   Travel time to get from shipping point to destination point.

TRANSLOADING   On shipments to be stopped in transit to partially unload, a carrier, on request of shipper or at carrier's convenience with consent of shipper, transfers at any point on its line authorized by tariff, the portion of shipment to be partially unloaded or the portion for final destination and forwards each from transfer point in separate cars.

TRANSPORTATION   That activity of commercial life embracing the movement of goods and persons from one point to another.

TRANSPORTATION ACT, 1920 (U.S.)   Approved February 28, 1920, 41 Stat. L. 456, provided for the termination of federal control over railroads, enacted provisions relating to the settlement of disputes between carriers and their employees, and other important amendments to the Interstate Commerce Act at that time.

TRANSPORTATION ACT, 1940 (U.S.)   Approved September 18, 1940, 54 Stat. L. 899, provided for declaration of a national transportation policy, regulation of water carriers in interstate and foreign commerce, establishment of a board of investigation and research to investigate the various modes of transportation.

TRANSPORTATION AND EXPORTATION ENTRY   In international trade, this is a form which specifies the goods entering the country (U.S., for example) and will be subsequently exported through a domestic port. All warehouses and carriers used must be bonded.

TRANSPORTATION FACILITIES   A term which embraces the services rendered by carriers in moving property or persons from one point to another; the cars, vehicles, airplanes or ships used in the act of carriage; and such things as terminals and depots, that form a part of the carrier's plant and are devoted to the act of transport.

TRANSPORTATION OF EXPLOSIVES ACT (U.S.)   An act (March 4, 1909) that regulated the transportation of explosives and other dangerous articles in interstate commerce and provides penalties for any violation of the regulations. Today, these are subject to the U.S. Department of Transportation Hazardous Materials Regulations.

TRANSPORTATION RATE   The rate charged for a line-haul.

TRANSPORTATION WAREHOUSING   This represents a warehousing cost saved. It should be termed a transportation warehousing cost saving. Traffic routing under circumstances of reconsignment and diversion offer opportunities for maximizing the time in transit and thereby receiving a free warehousing service. The savings equal the warehousing costs saved by free storage aboard the carrier instead of storing in a private or public warehouse. This is not a savings if the market could have been predetermined and the shipment routed more directly. Under these circumstances, it would represent an added inventory-in-transit cost, rather than a reduced warehousing cost.

TRANSPORT INTERNATIONAL DES ROUTIERS (T.I.R.)   An agreement between European countries which authorizes sealed container units to cross boundaries by motor transport without going through inspection, and without paying duties. The inspection and duties are handled at the final destination country.

TRANSPORT OR CONVEYING LINE   Pipes used in materials handling for carrying entrained solids.

TRANSSHIP   A term denoting the transfer of freight shipments between boat lines and railroads; the rehandling of goods en route.

TRANSSHIPPING   Where there is no steamship line operating between the United States and a foreign port, it is necessary to ship to some point where cargo can be transferred to another carrier for transportation to final destination. The act of transferring is called transshipping, and the point where the transfer occurs, the place of transshipment.

TRAP CAR   This term is used interchangeably with the term FERRY CAR. It refers to a car loaded by a single shipper at his industrial site containing shipments to various destinations. Another meaning applied to these terms is a car that is loaded by the transportation carrier which contains numerous less-than–carload shipments for various origins.

TRAVELER   A commercial agent; a salesman.

TRAVELING   This is a term used to describe the motion applied to move the crane.

TRAVELING REQUISITION   A requisition that travels from frequent user to the purchasing department and returns. It is used for high volume recurring purchases. The return step acts as an advise that the goods have been ordered and from whom.

TRAVEL WELL   A term that indicates that chemicals, wines, and other products can endure the rigors of transport and are received at the destination in a condition that is or near their intended condition. There has been no deterioration in condition to the goods resulting from the transport movement.

TREATY   A compact or agreement entered into between the governments or sovereigns of two or more states.

TREK   To travel by wagon, truck or other conveyance, with accouterments (in search of a new settlement).

TRESPASSER   As used in connection with accident reports, one who goes on the right of way without right, including pedestrians and occupants of vehicles passing closed gates or similar barriers or attempting to pass over or under trains or cars at highway grade crossings.

TRET   Allowance for waste of 4 lbs. in 104 lbs., after tare has been deducted.

TRI-AXLE   A three axle trailer or tractor.

TRICK   A railroad tour of duty, can range from one day to two or more depending upon the schedules.

TRI-LEVEL CAR   A three level freight car used for transporting automobiles.

TRIM   The nature of a vessel's float. The trim could be an even keel, or it could be trimmed by the head of stern. The term trim is often omitted by saying a vessel is by the head.

TRIMMING CHARGE   A charge assessed at so much per ton for distributing coal or grain in a ship so that the load will not shift at sea and in order that the weight will be evenly distributed throughout the hold.

TRIP DELAY   The loss of driver time after he is available for a trip but is forced to wait for loading, paperwork, trip assignment, repairs, etc.

TRIP LEASE   This term refers to equipment leasing. It may be between two carriers, or between a private carrier and a common carrier.

TRIPLICATE   To make three copies; the third copy.

TROLLEY   1) Passenger Transportation. An urban electric vehicle capable of carrying high volumes of passengers, generally at grade and in streets. 2) Materials Handling. A wheeled cart used for distributing or collecting small quantities of goods.

TROLLEY BRAKE   A means of operating a trailer brake, independent of the tractor brake, by means of a hand valve.

TROLLEY, LOAD (OVERHEAD RUNWAY TYPE)   A trolley moving system operating two or more wheels on overhead tracks by a self-powered or manually operated action.

TRUCK, DRIVERLESS   An automatically controlled vehicle that can pull trailers or carry loads. The direction comes from control wires in the floor or road surface. It can be applied to any set of directions in this way. These trucks may be operated by remote radio.

TRUCK JOCKEY   Slang for a truck driver.

TRUCKLOAD   A shipment transported by motor carrier that meets the minimum weight required for the application of a truckload (TL) rate.

TRUCKMAN   One who transports goods by means of trucks, drays, carts or wagons.

TRUCK MASTER   A truck driver.

TRUCK MAIL   This is not the movement of public mail, but the carriers' business mail between terminals or stations in its own vehicles.

TRUCK MILE EARNINGS   The earnings per truck mile. Attained by dividing gross revenue by the miles traveled.

TRUCK RUN OFF   A prepared path at the side of a downhill road that is designed for out-of-control trucks to safely turn to and come to rest without causing accidents.

TRUCK, SKID   An elevating vehicle that may be inserted under the skid that permits raising and then moving the skid.

TRUCK, STACKING   A truck with extended legs that may straddle or go under the load. Elevation of the load is performed with hydraulic pump. The forms on the truck may be alternated with a platform.

TRUCK TRACTOR   The trailer pulling vehicle. Used to pull trailers and semi trailers.

TRUE LEASE   One in which the lessor has the benefits and risks of ownership; the lessee acquires the use of the asset for a stated period of time without building any equity in the asset.

TRUNK LINE   A carrier operating over a large territory. A term now used interchangeably with Main Line.

TRUST BASED PARTNERSHIP   A relationship between a buyer and seller in which each trusts the other not to exploit the other in changing market conditions nor to share joint confidential information with outsiders.

TRUST RECEIPT   A document given banks by exporters and importers in exchange for a bill of lading.

TUBE   The term for the London, England subway system.

TUG AND SMALL TRACTOR   A small powered unit that tows trailers. The driver may ride or walk. It is battery operated. A bumper permits pushing some loads.

TUGBOAT   A small boat used to tow or move other boats, lighters, barges, etc.

TUMBLE OR FALLING HOME   The extent the sides of the vessel turn in from the perpendicular.

TUNDISH   A container used for collection of liquids from several sources. It is conical in shape.

TURBOFAN   The type of airplane engine in which the thrust of the turbojet engine has been increase by applying a low-pressure fan. The turbofan engine may have a separate fan driving the turbine, or it can have a low pressure compressor on the front which permits part of the airflow to bypass the engine.

TURBOJET   An engine that has an air compressor to facilitate combustion with the gas combustion serving to rotate the turbine as well as create the thrusting power.

TURBOPROP   A jet engine, not a piston engine, that drives a propeller. The propeller shaft operates the propeller and the compressor for the jet combustion.

TURBULENT FLOW   A flow with different direction and magnitude at all points.

TURN   A general term used about the vessel. The seaman turns in for the night. The tide turns, etc.

TURN AROUND   The combined movement from and to a given terminal. This commonly used term in motor transportation refers to the action of the driver returning to his point or origin after a delivery. Usually it involves the same vehicle, but it may not.

TURNAROUND (VESSEL)   The time it takes between the arrival of the vessel and its departure.

TURNING CIRCLE (OF A STEAMER)   The circle followed by the vessel when steaming under a hard-over helm.

TURN KEY   The practice of having an outsider perform an activity that is normally or traditionally performed by the firm. Turn key is also a noun denoting the firm performing such services.

TURNOUT   Another term for a railroad switch.

TURNOVER   The term for revenue in European and other nation accounting systems.

TURNOVER ASSETS   Total sales of a firm divided by the sum total of assets.

TURNOVER, INVENTORY   The total flow of inventory handled in a given period divided by the average amount held on hand.

TURNOVER, OF A PRODUCT LINE   To eliminate items in a firm's product offering and replace them with new items.

TURNTABLES, RUNWAY (MANUAL OR POWERED)   A device which may be rotated to allow the trolley that carries the lifting blocks to be diverted to other tracks which are usually at right angles to the main track. All tracks are on the same level or plane.

TURNTABLE STEERING   The front axle of the vehicle pivots around a king pin for a turntable type of rapid direction change.

TWEEN   Means between decks.

TWIN SCREW   The power applied to two rear axles in a truck—with the same power source for each axle.

TWO-MAN OPERATION   The joint driver operation of two alternating drivers on the same rig on long haul movements. This facilitates a through movement without stopping for rest under single driver operations. Since the vehicle tie-up costs during the stop and rest period exceed the extra driver costs during the total tap time, the operation is sometimes economically feasible.

TWO STEP BIDDING   The practice of conducting initial bids to ascertain suppliers' ideas for a proposed form of work. The buyer then collects the best ideas in the proposals and re-bids to the suppliers by seeking the best prices from them in this second round of bidding.

TWO-WAY OR Y JUNCTION   Equipment that permits conveyor load to be diverted to one or two branches.

UUUU

UBIQUITOUS MATERIALS Materials that are universally available are ubiquitous. For practical purposes, materials that are somewhat generally available are normally termed ubiquitous. Thus, one might consider water for soft drink production and clay for brick production to be ubiquitous materials. The significance of ubiquitous materials is that they encourage decentralization of production.

U.C.C. Uniform Commercial Code, the American legal basis for contract law between buyers and sellers and warehousemen.

ULLAGE The amount a cask or container lacks of being full.

ULTIMO Last (month).

ULTRA LARGE CRUDE CARRIER In ocean shipping, these are tankers over 300,000 deadweight tons.

UMBRELLA RATES When regulatory policy requires that the minimum rate for one carrier mode is held higher than it would prefer in order to permit another carrier, usually with a higher variable cost, to compete, it is called an umbrella rate. It is the process of making rates sufficiently high to protect the high cost agency. This is a pricing policy frequently adopted in cartelized industries. This is most unreasonable when it provides protection for a high cost carrier. In the Ingot Molds Case of 1965, the U.S. Supreme Court permitted the Commission to use out-of-pocket cost, fully distributed cost, or some other measurement of cost in setting the minimum level for a rate.

UNBALANCED TRAFFIC A greater movement of freight or passenger traffic in one direction than in the other.

UNBUNDLED The reverse of BUNDLING. This is the practice of offering customers individual features of products or services in a pick-and-choose format rather than one full bundled product.

UNCLAIMED FREIGHT Freight that cannot be delivered as a result of improper address, though it has been called for by the receiver or owner.

UNCLAIMED GOODS Goods in government storehouses not called for within three years of time of storing, or on which duties have not been paid.

UNCONCEALED LOSS OR DAMAGE CLAIMS Claims resulting from loss and damage which are apparent on delivery. The consignee specifies in writing on the carrier's delivery receipt the nature of the loss and damage. This should be signed by the consignee representative and delivery time noted. The local freight agent is notified immediately.

UNDERCHARGES Charges for transportation services, which are less than those applicable thereto under the tariffs lawfully on file with the Commission.

UNDERHANG   The space on a pallet between the outer edge of the packages and the pallet edges; indicates less than 100% pallet area utilization.

UNDER INVOICING   Situation whereby a foreign seller asks a domestic buyer to agree to understating the charges on the official documents. A real price is negotiated, but a lower official price is used for exporting, moving, and importing. The intent is to pay the full price, but something less than the full price goes through official channels to the exporter. The remaining amount is to go direct from the importer to the exporter's bank account in the U.S. This is a scheme used where foreign countries do not allow exporters to keep the hard currency they generate upon exporting. The governments convert the hard currency into local currency and remit the local currency to the account of the exporter. With under invoicing the exporter has a horde of hard currency cash outside the country. (See also OVER INVOICING.)

UNDERWAY   In water transportation this implies that the anchor has been weighed and the vessel is underway. Even if the vessel has been stopped, it is underway if disconnected with the dock. The terms under weigh and underway are synonymous, but underway is now preferred among seamen. The term weigh generally means the raising of the anchor.

UNDERWRITER   An insurance firm. In water transportation, it insures the cargo and vessel. It is common practice in water insurance for several underwriters to cover a portion of the total coverage.

UNDUE OR UNJUST DISCRIMINATION   A discrimination which is unwarranted by the facts in a particular case. Under the Interstate Commerce Act it is unlawful for any common carrier subject to the Act to make or give any undue or unreasonable preference or advantage to any particular person, company, firm, corporation or locality, or to subject them to any undue or unreasonable prejudice of disadvantage. Thus, if a carrier establishes different rates on identical services, it would be unjust, and upon complaint the carrier would be ordered to remove the unjust discrimination.

UNIFORM COMMERCIAL CODE (U.C.C.)   The body of American state laws that cover basic contracts, warehouse-goods owner relationships. Of particular application are Titles 2 and 7 which pertain to sales of goods between businesses as well as liabilities of warehousemen (storage of product).

UNIFORM CUSTOMS AND PRACTICES FOR DOCUMENTARY CREDITS (U.C.P.)   The U.C.P. is a set of rules for letters of credit drawn up by the Commission on Banking Technique and Practices of the International Chamber of Commerce in consultation with the banking association of many countries. It was revised and became effective in October 1975 and is published under I.C.C. Publication No. 290. All major trading countries adhere to the U.C.P.

UNIFORM DEMURRAGE RULES   Schedules providing rules and charges for demurrage which are in general used throughout the United States, having the approval, but not prescribed by, the Interstate Commerce Commission.

UNIFORM EXPRESS RECEIPT   A receipt furnished the shipper for goods entrusted to the Express Company for transportation.

UNIFORM LIVESTOCK CONTRACT   The bill of lading used to cover the transportation of livestock or wild animals.

UNIFORM PRODUCT CODE   A North American bar code and classification system for consumer products that enables them to be scanned by cash registers. This is also a coding system for keeping track of goods through the supply chains.

UNIFORM THROUGH EXPORT BILL OF LADING   This unique bill of lading is only used for land and water transportation movements. It is divided into three parts. The first part covers the rail movement to the port. The next part covers the ocean transportation. The third part covers the transportation from the foreign port to the ultimate destination. At the present time the through export bill of lading is used only on rail carload or LCL shipments originating at Denver and points east for export through west coast ports. It is issued in both the straight and order forms. The rail carrier issuing the through bill signs the contracts for all carriers.

UNIT COST   The total cost of producing a product or service divided by the number of units in the run or lot.

UNITED PARCEL SERVICE   Referred to as U.P.S., a commercial privately owned firm engaged in shipping packages. Not to be confused with the United States Postal Service.

UNITED STATES RAILROAD ADMINISTRATION   A body created by Act of Congress and charged with the operation of Federal controlled lines during the period January 1, 1918 to March 1, 1920.

UNITED STATES SHIPPING BOARD   A body created by Act of Congress and charged with the administration and operation of such merchant marine activities as are under the control and jurisdiction of the federal government.

UNITIZATION   The consolidation of a number of individual items onto one shipping unit for easier handling. It is also the securing or loading of one or more large items or cargo into a single structure, or carton.

UNITIZE   To consolidate by banding, binding, etc., several packages into a single unit for shipment.

UNIT LOAD   The process of combining a number of packages, by binding, banding, etc., so the unit package can be moved as a singe unit.

UNIT LOAD DEVICES   Any materials handling and storage device or system that combines goods into quantities so that they can be handled or stored in combined single unit quantities. Thus, the placement of 48 packages of a product onto one pallet and stretch wrapping it enables the system to efficiently handle them all as one unit.

UNIT OF ISSUE   The quantity of normal sale or distribution. Example: 48 boxes to a case.

UNIT OF TRAFFIC   The average number of passengers or tons of freight transported.

UNIT PRICE   The price for each unit of saleable good.

UNIT RATE   Buying products or services in unit terms so as to relate consumption or use to the amount paid. An example would be converting a copier contract from one that is for lease of the machine, cost of toner, cost of paper, and labor rate of the employee to one where the using firm paid for all of these costs in a cost-per-printed page. In the airline and railroad industries, these firms pay for leased engines on the basis of "power by the hour."

UNIT RECORD EQUIPMENT   The standard punched card data processing machinery operated by controlled panel, rather than by stored program computers.

UNIT TRAIN   Movement of a particular commodity in trainload lots on an arranged schedule.

UNIVERSE   In statistical computations, this is the total population from which a sample has been taken.

UNLATCH   In motor transportation, this term is applied to the releasing of the lock on the fifth wheel of the trailer to permit dropping the trailer.

UNLAWFUL   Opposed to law.

UNLOCATED LOSS OR DAMAGE   Injury to goods, person or property occurring at some time or place not exactly known.

UNPRICED ORDER   An order that has been placed with a vendor without knowing what the price will be for the lot.

UNROUTED   A shipment tendered to a carrier without specific shipper routing instructions.

UNSEAWORTHY   Unfit for a sea voyage in equipment or condition.

UNSOUND   In bad condition.

UPCHARGE   1) Logistics. The practice by many third party logistics firms of charging the client a single fee for all the handling, storage, and services rather than individual invoices for each of these cost components. This makes the client's own sales and logistics costing processes more streamlined. 2) Purchasing. A practice used when a firm asks a distributor to no longer charge a margin on product they are purchasing from it. Rather, the system is based upon the distributors own prices paid to their suppliers plus, say, 5% up charge to the buying company. In this way the buying company has visibility into the original price by the supplier's supplier.

UPDATE   In data processing, the act of bringing a file of data up-to-date by adding current data and correcting old data is termed update.

UPLOAD   To move data from one computer to another. The receiving computer experiences a download.

UPRIGHT   Vertical metal frame supporting the bars or shelves of a rack facing.

UPSETTING MOMENT   This may be computed by multiplying the tonnage by the upsetting lever (in feet), presented in foot-tons.

UPSTREAM   In the oil industry, this is all the activities starting with exploration, drilling and production. Distinct from refining and marketing, which are downstream activities.

USAGE   The number of units consumed during a given period of a particular commodity.

USAGE OF TRADE   Custom, or the frequent repetition of the same act in business.

USAGE RATE   See Usage.

USANCE   The time allowed by established usage or custom for the payment of a bill of exchange, differing according to the countries.

U.S. CONSULAR INVOICE   A statement on merchandise required before a ship may leave any foreign port bound for the United States. It must be sworn to in triplicate or quadruplicate at the American consulate located nearest the point where the goods are assembled for shipment.

U.S. CUSTOMS BONDED WAREHOUSE   The federal government retains goods until import duties are paid in a customs bonded warehouse. The importer pays the expense of warehousing, but the U.S. government retains control of the goods. The warehouseman must provide a bond that the goods will not be released until the duties are paid. The custom bond provides no protection to the depositor of the goods.

USEFUL LIFE   The length of time in which an asset lasts, as different from depreciable life.

USEFUL LOAD   The dead weight tonnage of the vessel.

USER   Purchasing field term for the person requesting a purchasing of something by the purchasing department. Often the person named on an internal requisition.

U.S. FLAG CARRIER   In air transportation, the holder of a certificate of public convenience and necessity to transport freight and/or personnel between the U.S. and/or its territories to one or more foreign countries. This operating authority requires both Civil Aeronautics Board and Presidential approval.

U.S. GOVERNMENT BILL OF LADING   The United States Government is the world's largest shipper. A special bill of lading is made out for government ship-ments. It is a draft on the Treasury of the United States. These bills specify the people who are accountable under the government bill of lading contract. It is important that a traffic manager recognize that the government consignee has no latitude in accepting or refusing shipments.

U.S. INTERNAL REVENUE BONDED WAREHOUSE   Goods which must be held until internal revenue has been paid are placed in a U.S. Internal Revenue bonded warehouse. This must be on goods produced in the U.S. and it offers no protection to the depositor of the goods.

USURY   Interest beyond the lawful rate.

U-WAGON   A wheeled vehicle that is U shaped and used to station around a con-tainer, lift it, and permit towing to a preferred location.

VVVV

VACATION NOTICE OR ORDER   An order setting aside a ruling of a regulatory commission, agency, or court.

VACUUM PACKAGING   The process of packaging goods in a vacuum, or when all air has been removed prior to sealing. It may be performed on flexible or rigid containers. Desired effects can be smaller cubic space occupied, removal of air to reduce growth of contaminants, or to preserve items for long periods of time.

VALID   Binding; good in law.

VALUATION, ACTUAL   The value as specified on the bill of lading by the shipper. Pertinent when transportation rate reflects the value of the commodity as well as a basis for claim in the event of loss or damage.

VALUATION, AGREED   The value of an article or shipment agreed upon by shipper and carrier in order to establish a specific liability in case of loss or damage.

VALUATION, DECLARED   The valuation placed on an article or shipment when it is delivered to the carrier for transport.

VALUATION, RELEASED   A condition which limits the carrier's liability for damage for freight while in transit. Usually this form of freight arrangement provides for a lower charged rate in exchange for the carrier being liable for less than full value for the goods. In international air shipments, most rates are released to a valuation of $US20.00 per kilo of weight.

VALUE   1) Economics. A concept in economics that roughly means the benefit of consumption that a buyer obtains for the measure of the price paid for it. 2) Business-to-Business. Whenever a firm can exact a price premium over and above its costs, that amount is seen as value as perceived by the customer. 3) Purchasing. Functionality of a product or service to the actual user. Similar concept in the field of quality.

VALUE ADD   To perform a task or activity that increases the value of a product or service.

VALUE ADDED ACTIVITY   Any step, activity or process that increases the desirability and salability of a product or service as seen by a customer or ultimate user.

VALUE ADDED NETWORK (VAN)   In electronic data interchange systems, a VAN translates the codings used by the buyer into ones used by the sellers, and vice versa. Thus, both firms can be linked without having to eliminate the investment in neither one's coding and cataloging systems.

VALUE ANALYSIS   Purchasing processes directed at improving the design of a product that is produced by the firm. Involves questioning all parts, components, materials, designs, with eye toward reducing costs, improving performance, using substitute products in greater supply, etc. It is generally a multi-functional team process aimed at enhancing the competitiveness of the product or service.

VALUE CHAIN   A rough term for supply chain. Many people make the distinction when examining a chain for only those activities that actually add value (or do not) to the products as they move from raw material through to use by the ultimate consumer. Example: a step that has inventory that is sitting is seen as non-value added and subject to analysis for change.

VALUED POLICY   A marine insurance policy covering risks to a fixed amount of valuation.

VALUE ENGINEERING   Similar to value analysis, only this is performed upon development of the product prior to production and product launch.

VALUE, EXTRAORDINARY   A degree of value which entirely prohibits the movement by freight of goods so priced, rated or classed, or permits it only under certain specified conditions.

VALUE OF SERVICE   In transportation pricing, it is the practice of charging on the basis of what the traffic will bear," as opposed to pricing according to cost-of-service for a specific commodity. Long used in rail and motor carrier transportation, it is the practice of pricing commodity rates so that the mix of the volume of movements and prices charged would provide the carrier with the maximum over-all total revenue or contribution to profit. In the United States, the Hoch-Smith Resolution of 1926 by the U.S. Congress directed the then Interstate Commerce Commission to set rates on agricultural commodities at levels that would move the traffic and not be so high as to prevent their movement.

VALUE RECEIVED   A phrase used in bills or notes to express an indefinite consideration.

VALUE TO WEIGHT RATIO   A long used concept in transportation value-of-service pricing whereby the higher the value of the product being shipped, the more that it can withstand higher freight rates and still be able to be marketed by its producer.

VALVE   A device that serves to control the flow of liquids. In pneumatic or hydraulic operations valves may take the form of sluice, shovel or flat, nonreturn, ball and disc, plug, gate, and diaphragm.

VALVE, AIR RELIEF   A valve that serves to facilitate air escape in the line. It is installed at the highest point in the line.

VALVE, BUTTERFLY   A special type valve which has a disc rotating in an axial bearing.

VALVE, COUNTERWEIGHTED FLAP   A valve designed to control the outflow of the material in the line, and prevent entry of air or gas.

VALVE, CYCLONE TAIL   In materials handling, this valve is installed in the tail leg of a cyclone to allow the solids to leave the cyclone, but prevent the entraining fluid to escape. It also prevents the entry of air.

VALVE, MOTORIZED HOPPER, FOR CONTINUOUS OPERATION   A combination of upper and lower valves which provide continuous alternating performance. This gives continuous discharge of the line without permitting reverse flow of the fluid.

VALVE, MULTI-WAY   A valve that can serve many lines. It has a rotating chamber with an inlet and outlet which can be rotated to service many radially spaced conveying lines.

VALVE, PRESSURE RELIEF   A valve with an automatic release for fluids when pressure builds up.

VALVE, SLIDE OR SHUTTER   A shutter type valve that has a plate that slides across the pipeline or hopper to control the flow.

VALVE, SONIC   This is a type of nozzle with an adjustable needle to allow air to flow at high sonic velocity and thus provide constant quantity of air for back pressure.

VALVE, TWO-WAY   A device that is able to divert a single stream of material to two alternating flows.

VALVE, VACUUM RELIEF   A type of valve which permits fluid to enter the pipeline under vacuum conditions.

VAN   A large covered motor vehicle, used principally for moving pianos and household effects. A rail car that is basically an enclosed box on wheels that is used for movement of goods.

VAN BODY   A motor vehicle body that is fully enclosed, and commonly used in the transportation of general freight.

VAN CONTAINER   A container commonly used to transport freight.

VANNING   The process of loading a container.

VAPOR   Gas or condensation that is given off of something.

VARIABLE COSTING   A method of inventory valuation that applies only the variable costs of an activity or function. Variable production costs would include labor, materials, utility costs, etc. The system is helpful for internal management.

VARIABILIZED FIXED EXPENSES   Whenever an outside firm takes over an overhead function for a client firm and charges them back on the unit of service or activity, they have variabilized fixed expenses for the client. This reduces the financial break-even point for the client company.

VARIANCE   The deviation between planned and actual.

VARIETY CONTROL   Another term for STANDARDIZATION endeavors.

VARNISH FINISH   A protective fluid used to coat a surface for both protection and appearance. Common on ship deck and railing surfaces.

VEGETABLE CAR   A car equipped with facilities for safe and proper handling of vegetables.

VEHICLE   Any carriage or other contrivance capable of being used as a means of transportation on land.

VELOCITY, CRITICAL AIR   The critical air velocity which is required to facilitate fluidization.

VELOCITY, CRITICAL SETTLEMENT   The level of velocity, which if lowered, will permit the largest particles to settle out.

VELOCITY, OPTIMUM   That velocity which requires the lowest power requirement without the process of settlement taking place.

VELOCITY, PARTICLE   The velocity of a particle at any specified time.

VENDEE   One to whom something is sold, a buyer.

VENDOR   A seller. The company supplying the product. The term is used less as time goes on. A more popular term is supplier.

VENDOR FILL RATE   A purchasing term for evaluating a supplier in terms of the percent of all orders that were received from them complete.

VENDOR LEAD TIME   The time extending from the supplier receiving an order from a buyer until the goods are received at the warehouse or plant. This is also called the lead time, or the purchasing cycle.

VENDOR MANAGED INVENTORIES   The practice of suppliers managing their goods on the property of the buying company.

VENDOR PERFORMANCE INDEX   A rating of experience factors when dealing with vendors; based upon quality, on-time performance, etc.

VENDOR RATING SYSTEM   Any means used to evaluate the quality of a vendor. See DOMINANT CHARACTERISTIC, WEIGHTED POINT, and COST-RATIO.

VENDOR RATIONALIZATION   The process of reducing the number of vendors or suppliers used for specific products or services. Done for reasons of increasing buying power, improving service, tapping supplier innovation, administrative simplification, and other reasons.

VENDOR STOCKLESS SYSTEM   System of acquiring goods from a vendor whereby the vendor agrees to hold the goods near the buyer firm. Purpose is to have inventory available through short lead time without having to directly invest in the goods.

VENTILATE   To admit air, or exhaust smoke and gasses in a fire.

VENTILATED CAR   A car equipped with openings at top, sides and/or ends to admit air.

VENTILATION   The regulation of the circulation of air.

VENUE   The place where an action in the law arises.

VERBAL ORDER   A purchasing order placed orally with a supplier. Often followed up by written order.

VERTICAL INTEGRATION   The purchasing or acquisition by a firm of its supplier firms as well as those enterprises in the chain in the direction of the customer. Example: a manufacturer of machine would be seen as vertically integrating if it purchased a metal producer or a wholesaler or retailer.

VERY LARGE CRUDE CARRIER   An ocean tanker in the range of 150,000 to 299,999 deadweight tons.

VESSEL, FOREIGN   A term sometimes applies to a vessel not registered or licensed, in reference to the privileges derived from the revenue system. In a number of instances the term designates a vessel navigating under the flag and with the papers of another government.

VESSEL, PUBLIC   A vessel belonging to a nation or government.

VESSEL'S MANIFEST   Statement of a vessel's cargo (revenue, consignee, marks, etc.)

VESSEL TON   100 cubic feet.

VIA   By way of.

VIABLE SUPPLIER   A supplier that is financially sound, and/or is one selected by a company as one that is capable and willing to provide quality products and services to it.

VIRTUAL   An Internet industry term for the visibility and availability of something without it being in actual form as such.

VIRTUAL CENTRALIZATION   A term for the coordination of separate functions within lines of businesses in a firm in such a way that they present a single point of contact with suppliers and customers. They are not actually centralized, but they behave to the outside world as though they do.

VIRTUAL ORGANIZATION   An organization that is made up of persons and systems that belong to other ones but has an identity as an entirely new one.

VISIBLE CAPACITY   That which is known or is apparent as to the carrying capacity of a car, its type and the nature of the commodity to be loaded and shipped, considered.

VISUAL REVIEW SYSTEM   An inventory control system that involves determining the reorder time by walking around and taking note of the stock levels. This is usually used for low value items and items seldom required.

VOICE GRADE   This term applies to a voice telephone line used in electronic data transmission that has a capacity of as much as 500 characters per second.

VOLUME DISCOUNT   A price discount that is predicated upon large quantity purchases either at once or over a period of time.

VOLUME RATE   A rate applicable in connection with a specified volume (weight) of freight.

VOLUMETRIC BASIS   Measurement of the volume of something.

VOLUME SHIPMENT   A shipment that qualifies for the volume rate, or the minimum weight or quantity required for a rate reduction.

VOLUME TO WEIGHT RATIO   A measure of product density. A cubic foot of feathers would be very light whereby a cubic foot of mercury would be very heavy.

VOLUNTARILY SEPARATE   An airline term used when a passenger offers to travel on a flight earlier than planned without their luggage being on the same flight with them.

VOUCHER   1) A receipt, document, or other proof to the accuracy of something. 2) A document sent from purchasing to accounting, along with other documents, with the instruction to pay a supplier.

VOYAGE   In water transportation, the outward and homeward trips are termed a voyage, though the movements between port are termed voyages in insurance underwriting.

VOYAGE CHARTER   A contract for hiring a vessel for specific voyage. The terms of the contract are specified in the charter.

VOYAGE POLICY   An insurance policy based on a voyage, rather than on travel for specific time period. Normally, a time policy will cover the vessel for maximum of one year, subject to extension.

VULNERABILITY ANALYSIS   Investigation into how and where an organization, process, or activity would incur risk of operation.

WWWW

WAIT TIME   The time expended while a job awaits processing.

WAIVER   The forfeiting of a right.

WAIVER CLAUSE   The waiver clause normally used states: "And it is expressly declared and agreed that no acts of the insurer or assured in recovering, saving or preserving the property insured, shall be considered as a waiver or acceptance of abandonment."

WAKE   The track which follows the vessel as it moves through the water. The term is also used to refer to the efficiency of the propeller while operating in forward moving water of the wake current. The wake of the hatch is directly behind the hatch opening. A wake of air, or a vortex, often trail a jet through the air.

WALL TO WALL INVENTORY   A condition when materials, parts or supplies are involved in processing from one end of the plant to the other without involvement in formal stock.

WAR CLAUSE   An extra insurance surcharge upon ocean ships and cargo for when they operate in areas of the world deemed to have risk from war. This is reflected in extra tariff and contract charges that are levied upon the cargo.

WAREHOUSE   A place for the reception and storage of goods.

WAREHOUSE, BONDED   A place used for the storage and custody of import merchandise which is subject to duty until the duties are paid or the goods are reshipped without entry. The owners of such warehouses must be approved by a government body and must give guarantees or bonds for the strict observance of revenue laws.

WAREHOUSE CONTRACT   A contract that applies between a client owner of goods and a warehouse operator for handling, storage and services to be performed.

WAREHOUSE COST   The warehouse cost may be incurred under private or public warehouse storage, the warehouse rate determines the warehouse cost if the public warehouse is used. The average warehouse cost represents the computed cost of rendering a private warehouse service involving the same operations as those provided by the public warehouse under the warehouse rate. The warehouse cost under private facilities for multiple commodity storage circumstances is an average approximation.

WAREHOUSE DELIVERY ORDER   A document authorizing the release of merchandise from a warehouse.

WAREHOUSE EDUCATION RESEARCH COUNCIL   Professional organization in the warehousing field. Central office located in Oak Brook, IL., USA.

WAREHOUSE ENTRY   The document or form which identifies goods imported when placed in a bonded warehouse. The duty is not imposed on the products while in the warehouse, but will be collected when they are withdrawn for consumption.

WAREHOUSE LABOR COST   This is commonly referred to as the in-and-out costs. It is a flat charge assessed per hundredweight and cannot be influenced by the volume of shipment. Each hundredweight of a shipment must be moved in and out, so the average warehouse labor cost cannot be influenced by the volume of shipment. In most public warehouse tariffs, a separate charge is made for labor costs. Surprising to most people, the labor cost is usually about twice the warehouse rate. However, the average warehouse cost, which is the warehouse rate times the time in storage cost may become larger per hundredweight than the labor cost per hundredweight if the volume of shipment is so large as to require an extended period of time in storage.

WAREHOUSEMAN   A person who receives and ships goods and merchandise to be stored in his warehouse for hire.

WAREHOUSE, PRIVATE   A warehouse that is owned and operated by the firm that owns the products contained within it.

WAREHOUSE, PUBLIC   A place of storage used by the general public. In addition to the service of storage, many public warehouses perform the functions of a distributing agent or forwarder.

WAREHOUSE (RAILROAD)   With the changing of the liability of the carrier from that of common carrier to that of warehouseman, resulting in a decrease in degree of liability, the railroads have provided extensive storage facilities in the shape of warehouses. Two general kinds of storage are available: 1) storage in transit as a necessary part of the service of carriage, manufacturing or milling; and, 2) Enforced Storage, resulting from inability of the carriers to make deliver.

WAREHOUSE RATE   The charge for the storage of goods by a public warehouse is the warehouse rate. It is also called the storage rate. The warehouse rate does not change per hundredweight as the volume of shipment changes. It is a fixed cost. Under most circumstances, there is not a reduction in warehouse rate for varying volumes of shipment. The warehouse rate does not include labor costs associated with the in-and-out services on the goods. Warehouse cost is the product of the warehouse rate times the volume in storage.

WAREHOUSE RECEIPT   A receipt, usually negotiable, given for goods, known as a lot, placed in a warehouse for storage.

WAREHOUSING   The storing of goods.

WARES   Goods, merchandise and commodities, bought, sold and shipped.

WARRANT (WAREHOUSE)   A receipt issued by a public or bonded warehouse.

WARRANTY   See express warranty, implied warranty of fitness, implied warranty of merchantability.

WAR RISK INSURANCE   Insurance coverage for losses resulting from war activity.

WAR TAX   A tax on the total freight charges, including demurrage, etc., assessed on all classes of freight for domestic consumption. (War measure.)

WASHOUT   An erosion of the permanent roadbed by storm or flood to such extent as would cause delay of trains, or endanger traffic.

WASH PLATE OR BULKHEAD PLATE   This is a baffle plate.

WASH PORT   An opening in the bulkhead of the ship for the freeing of water. It is usually a barred opening.

WASTAGE   Loss in handling; shrinkage or decay.

WATCH (SHIPBOARD)   On ship board for equal apportionment of labor and discipline, the crew is mustered in two divisions, the Starboard (right facing bow) and Port (left). The day commences at noon and is divided into seven watches as follows: Afternoon watch (noon to 4 pm); First Dog watch (4 pm to 6 pm); Second Dog watch (6 pm to 8 pm), First Watch (8 pm to midnight); Middle watch (Midnight to 4 am), Morning watch (4 am to 8 am); Forenoon watch (8 am to Noon).

WATER BALLAST   Water carried in the low flat tanks or double bottom of the vessel for the purpose of trimming the ship. It may be released by pumps or flooded by sea cocks.

WATERBED PRICING   Pricing of products and services by a firm or market that is fluid to the extent that if they are driven down in one area the firm raises them for others.

WATERBORNE   Floating.

WATER CARRIER ACT OF 1940 (U.S.)   An act of Congress delegating to the Interstate Commerce Commission regulatory powers applicable to common and contract water carriers operating in domestic trade.

WATER COMPELLED RATE   Rate charged by railroads that are depressed in a specific market in response to coastwise or barge competition.

WATERLOGGED   A situation in which the vessel is floating only as a result of the buoyancy of its cargo. The vessel has lost its buoyancy.

WATER REACTIVE MATERIAL (SOLID)   Means any solid substance (including sludges and pastes) which, by interaction with water, is likely to become spontaneously flammable or to give off flammable or toxic gases in dangerous quantities.

WATERTIGHT COMPARTMENTS   Compartments made water free by the application of watertight bulkheads and doors.

WATER TRAFFIC   This applies to the movement or handling of goods and persons by vessel.

WAVE PERIOD   The time required for two successive waves to crest.

WAY   Refers to the ship's action through the water.

WAYBILL   The official document which is used to identify the shipper and the consignee, present the routing, describe the goods, present the applicable rate, show the weight of the shipment, and make other useful information notations.

WAYBILL DESTINATION   The destination of the shipment.

WEATHER   The weather side is the windward side.

WEATHERBOUND   Held up by weather.

WEATHER DECK   A deck out in the weather—without overhead protection.

WEATHER INTERFERENCE   That level of weather activity which retards the loading, unloading or other logistics activity.

WEATHER WORKING DAY   Day which permits work operations so far as weather conditions are concerned.

WEB, EDI   An Internet based ordering and customer linkage.

WEIGHING AND INSPECTION BUREAUS   A railway organization to secure for its members uniform practices in complying with tariff regulations and requirements of government authorities relating to weight, classification, and condition of shipments.

WEIGHT   That which it weights. In shipping, weight is qualified as gross (the weight of the goods and the container); net (the weight of the goods themselves without any container); and legal (similar to net and determined in such manner as the law of a particular country may direct).

WEIGHT, AGREED   A specific weight agreed upon by shipper and carrier for commodities transported in a particular container or package or in a certain manner.

WEIGHT AGREEMENT   A form of agreement between shippers and carriers when shippers desire to use estimated weights not already incorporated in classifications and other traffic schedules.

WEIGHT CAPACITY   The carrying capacity of a car designated in weight is referred to as the weight capacity.

WEIGHT CARGO   A cargo on which the transportation charge is assessed on the basis of weight.

WEIGHT CERTIFICATE   A certificate, sometimes signed by a public weigher, certifying as to the weight of a shipment.

WEIGHTED AVERAGE   The statistical process of running an average of man forms of date, with each class of data given a percentage value which jointly equals 100 percent.

WEIGHTED AVERAGE COST OF CAPITAL   A measure of a firm in terms of its weighted average cost of short- and long-term debt, preferred stock, common stock, and retained earnings. It is a measure against which capital project returns and profits are evaluated.

WEIGHTED POINT VENDOR RATING SYSTEM   A method to evaluate vendors that uses percentage weights to various attributes (price, service, quality, etc.). A weighted average is used for all the characteristics and a total quality rating is determined.

WEIGHT, ESTIMATED   The weights provided in classification and tariff schedules for goods shipped in certain packages, in a certain manner, or under certain conditions. The general practice of the carriers, however, is to base charges on the gross or combined weights of the articles and containers.

WEIGHT, GROSS   In shipping, the total weight of the goods plus the weight of the container and packing materials.

WEIGHT, LANDED   The weight of a shipment as the point of landing.

WEIGHT, LEGAL   Usually the same as net weight.

WEIGHT LOSING MATERIAL   A commodity that tends to loose weight in the production process.

WEIGHT, NET   The weight of the goods alone, not including the weight of the container.

WEIGHT NOTE   A document issued by dock companies giving details of marks, weights, date of entry, etc., of imported goods.

WEIGHT OR MEASUREMENT, SHIP'S OPTION   A term denoting a charge assessed on the basis of weight if the weight of the shipment exceeds its cubic measurement, or on a measurement basis if the cubic measurement exceeds the weight of the shipment.

WEIGHT OUT   Term in freight carriage when vehicle reaches weight limit though some empty space still exists in it.

WEIGHT, PAR   The steamship par between weight and measurement goods: 56 pounds, found by dividing a long ton (2,240 lbs.) by 40 cubic feet.

WEIGHTS AND WEIGHING   Under law, a shipper has a right to have the correct weight of his shipments ascertained so that the charges computed may be correct.

WEIGHT SHEETS   The listing with weights of the articles in a shipment. Presented to the weighing bureaus.

WEIGHT, TARE   The weight of the container alone.

WELCH FORMULA   A formula used to reduce the inventory carried for a number of products. It seeks to reduce ordering costs without increasing inventory, or reduce inventory without increasing set-up costs.

WELL CAR   A flatcar with a depression or opening in the center to allow the load to extend below the normal floor level in order to come within overhead clearance limits.

WESTBOUND OR WESTWARD   The direction of train movements in which the distance by rail from San Francisco is decreasing. A few exceptions have been established on branch lines where this rule would result in confusion because of so-called westbound trains actually operating in eastbound compass direction.

WESTERN HEMISPHERE TRADE CORPORATION   A United States corporate enterprise that performs business anywhere in the Western Hemisphere—North and South America, Central America, or the West Indies—and operates under tax advantages.

WEST TEXAS SWEET   An American benchmark for oil produced in the United States that is quoted daily in commodity markets.

WET GOODS   Liquids for shipment in bottles or cask.

WET LEASE   Airline charter that includes the crew.

WET STRENGTH   Wet tensile strength is the measure of resistance of paper when saturated with water. Wet bursting strength applies to containers filled with water.

WHARF   A place for berthing vessels in order to facilitate the loading and discharging of passengers and freight; usually a platform of wood, stone, or other material parallel to a stream or other body of water, alongside of which a vessel may wharf for loading or discharging.

WHARFAGE   The charge against a vessel for use of a wharf for the purpose of loading, discharging, or docking.

WHARFINGER   One who owns and/or operates a wharf.

WHARFINGER'S RECEIPT   A document acknowledging receipt of goods for shipment by a wharfinger.

WHAT-IF ANALYSIS   Usually computerized analysis that is directed toward trying various alternatives for the feasibility of their outcomes. Common in distribution analysis.

WHAT-IF SCENARIOS   An analytical technique of considering and evaluating all the likely outcomes of a situation in the future. It is an effective and fairly encompassing planning technique.

WHEELBARROW   A one-wheeled device for the hand pushing of materials, etc. The elevation of the hand shaft end of the box permits concentrating most weight on the wheel, while the single wheel optimizes maneuverability.

WHEEL REPORT   A document, made from waybills, which lists the cars in a train as it leaves a yard and on which the conductor posts setoffs and pickups. On trains reaching a yard, the document is known as the inbound (train) consists; on departing trains, as the outbound (train) consists. A copy of the wheel report is sent to the car accountant's office, to be posted to the car record.

WHITE TAIL   A commercial aircraft that currently has no operating owner and is available for lease or sale.

WIDE BODY   Large jets such as B-747, 777, L-1011 and DC-10. It is generally an aircraft with two aisles when it is in a passenger configuration.

WIDE-SPREAD   Motor truck axles which exceed eight feet apart. (On the trailer.)

WILLIE   Railroad slang term for a waybill.

WINCH RIG   A straight truck which carries a hoist for pulling or lifting.

WINGS   The outer bridge of a vessel. That part of the deck near the sides of the vessel.

WINTER LOAD LINE   A load line on a vessel that is lower to provide for rougher weather conditions.

W-I-P   Work-in-process.

WITHOUT ENGAGEMENT   A phrase incorporated in a quotation and used to avoid having to accept an order at the price quoted. A safeguard against prices fluctuating in the interval between the giving of the quotation and the order being placed.

WITHOUT RECOURSE   A phrase preceding the signature of a drawer or endorser of a negotiable instrument and signifying that the instrument is passed onto subsequent holders without any liability to the endorser in the event of non-payment or non-delivery. Many negotiable instruments are signed "with recourse," meaning that in the event of nonperformance, the holder has the right to make a claim on the last endorser.

WITHOUT RECOURSE CLAUSE, BILL OF LADING (SECTION 7)   Common carrier bill of lading part; when signed by shipper, carrier cannot seek freight bill payment from shipper if consignee fails to pay charges.

WITH PARTICULAR AVERAGE (W.P.A.)   Under this insurance arrangement, partial loss or damage to merchandise is covered. It is used in application to loss by seawater. Payment will be forthcoming with little damage. It is often extended to include losses from pilferage, leakage, breakage, theft, nondelivery, etc.

WITNESS   A person produced to testify as to the correctness of a statement, fact or action.

WOOD CHIP CARS   A converted box car with roof removed used in hauling fuel (sawmill refuse, etc., i.e., wood trimmings, and sawdust used for fuel).

WOODCHUCK   A slang term applied to a driver with little seniority.

WORD   In data processing, a word is a combination of bytes to facilitate computational requirements. The availability of third generation systems has eliminated the difference between word machines and byte machines.

WORK   The action of the vessel or the cargo which results from the movement.

WORK CENTER   In production and inventory, the term refers to a section of the plant where a specialized form of work is underway.

WORKING CAPITAL   The short-term assets and liabilities of a firm combined into a single measure. It can either be a) cash, accounts receivables, and inventories less current liabilities, or b) accounts receivables and inventories less current liabilities.

WORKING CAPITAL COSTS   The computed cost of working capital based against an opportunity cost of capital.

WORKERS COMPREHENSIVE   An insurance that covers employee accidents and other risks.

WORKING MONEY   A slang term for cash that is invested in assets that are earning the firm a profit at the moment. Machinery would represent monies that are earning money at the current time. On the other hand, assets that are idle would represent sleeping money.

WORK-IN-PROCESS   Goods that are between various stages of production. As distinct from raw materials or raw components and finished goods.

WORK SAMPLING   The application of random samples to establish frequency of performance.

WORK STATIONS   The place of operation for a worker.

WORLDSCALE   A worldwide benchmark measure of charter ship prices particularly in the oil business. It fluctuates with supply and demand.

WORLD TRADE ORGANIZATION   A worldwide set of countries that seek to reduce tariffs and other trade barriers among nations of the world.

WORST ANALYSIS   A means of concentrating effort on the most unstable phase of a system. The use of partial differentials is one way of converging on an unstable system. Applies to data processing.

W&R   Water and rail.

WRAPAROUND   A wooden cage placed on top of pallet, adding extra support to the product on the pallet, enabling higher stacking.

WRECKAGE   Merchandise (saved) from a wreck.

WRECKER   A special vehicle for towing and pulling disabled vehicles.

WRECK MASTER   A person legally appointed to take charge of goods, etc., thrown ashore after a shipwreck.

WRONG MAINING   The operation of a train in the opposite direction track on a multitrack railroad line. Special operating rules apply in this situation, because signals are generally not governing that train.

XXXX

X-DOCKING   Another term for CROSS DOCKING.

YYYY

YACHT   A quick sailing vessel, used for pleasure.

YARD   A system of tracks within defined limits, whether or not part of a terminal, designed for switching services over which movements not authorized by time-table or by train order may be made, subject to prescribed signals, rules, and regulations.

YARDAGE   The charge made in addition to the transportation and other charges for shipping livestock to a stockyard located in various sections of the country. This charge, usually assessed on the basis of so much per head, varies in amount according to the nature of the livestock.

YARD CART   A form of trailer used to transport containers in a yard storage area.

YARD, CLASSIFICATION   An area in a railroad yard where freight trains are made up according to destinations.

YARD CONTROL   The dispatching and control of trains or trucks in a yard area.

YARD ENGINE   An engine assigned to yard service and used for work within yard limits only.

YARD (FREIGHT)   A unit of track systems within a certain area used for sorting cars, loading and unloading freight, and making up trains, over which movements not authorized by time-table or by train order may be made, subject to prescribed signals and regulations. These units are further qualified according to the service each performs as: Receiving Yard (where trains or cars are received); Storage Yard (where cars are held pending disposition); Classification Yard (where cars are segregated according to their kind, contents and destination); Hump Yard (where trains are broken up, a car being pushed over the summit and after uncoupling run down from the hump by gravity. This is an artificially constructed elevation overtopping a wide expanse of freight yards networked with tracks and switches); Make-up Yard (where trains are made up); Gravity Yard (where the classification of cars is accomplished by gravity); Poling Yard (where movement of cars is done by use of poles by an engine on an adjacent paralleled track).

YARD HOSTLER   A truck tractor of sorts that is used to move trailers around and within a terminal.

YARDING-IN-TRANSIT   The process of stopping in-transit to store, load, un-load, sort, and otherwise handle forest products.

YARD JOCKEY   See YARD HOSTLER.

YARD MASTER   The one person who is in charge of the yard.

YARD SWITCHING　Switching service performed by yard locomotives in yards where regular switching service is maintained, including terminal switching and transfer service in connection with the transportation of revenue freight and incidentally of company freight. (See TRAIN SWITCHING.)

YAWL　A light, two-masted boat.

YEN　The name for the currency of Japan.

YIELD　The total revenue derived by a transportation vehicle, plane seat, etc., in a given period.

YIELD EROSION　A term for the decline in profitability of sales. In the airline industry, a long term period of increased competition would be said to result in yield erosion in terms of the revenue obtained for each seat sold on airplanes.

YIELD POINT　That point in stress which identifies the beginning of deformation.

YIELD PRICING　An airline and hotel industry practice of fine-tuning prices based upon near real-time demand. In heavy demand periods, high prices are charged; in low periods, discount prices are offered.

YORK-ANTWERP RULES OF 1890　Rules adopted in Antwerp in 1890 which established the standard basis for adjusting general average. The code states the rules for adjusting claims.

YUAN　The name of the currency for South Korea and China.

ZZZZ

ZERO DEFECTS   An objective in purchasing and production in which 100% quality is sought.

ZERO SUPPRESS   In data processing, this is a utility module used to remove non-significant zeros to the left of a number before the printing process takes place.

ZERO-ZERO WEATHER   Weather where flying visibility is not effective, in any direction.

ZINCS   Plates made of zinc placed between steel and bronze to prevent an electrolytic process.

ZONE OF RATE FREEDOM   A zone within which a carrier may raise or lower its rates without them being subject to lawful charges from shippers, consignees, or other carriers. A concept used in transportation rate regulation.

ZONE PICKING   Process of picking goods whereby persons are assigned to specific areas of a warehouse. Picking by each person is confined to each area. Orders are often picked by many persons in the different zones and accumulated (staged) at or near the outbound docks for shipment.

ZONES (EXPRESS)   Districts of the United States (blocks and subblocks) used in rate-making in connection with express traffic and rates.

ZONES (PARCEL POST)   The eight divisions of the United States and its possessions made for the purpose of establishing parcel-post rates.

ZONE STORAGE   Merchandise stored in the warehouse in large areas and given area location.

ZONES (TIME)   Wide areas used for uniform time making purposes. Examples in the U.S. are called Eastern, Central, Mountain and Pacific zones; in Europe, U.K., and Central European.

TRANSPORTATIONS RATES—ALL CARRIER MODES

ACCESSORIAL CHARGES   Supplementary services and privileges associated with transportation are accessed an added charge. Examples of such services are loading, unloading, pickup, transit privileges, stopoffs for loading and unloading, inspection, grading, switching, etc. They are not included in the freight charge, and usually take the form of a flat charge not based on a unit of weight.

ACTUAL VALUE RATES   Rates that have carrier liability up to the full value of the goods in case of loss or damage. This requires a grouping of commodities in accordance with value and relating the rate with the value. In the event of loss or damage, the value of the shipment may be recovered, rather than a released or agreed value. This system is the counterpart of released value rates.

AGGREGATE TENDER RATE   A reduced rate on separate shipments that are included within a single motor carrier pick up move; the economies of the single consolidated pick up, and often part of the line haul, are passed onto the shipper in this lower rate.

AGREED CHARGES   A form of rail contract rate in which a reduced rate is applied in exchange for the shipper routing a certain percent of total movements over a certain carrier.

AIR FREIGHT RATES   Air freight carriers have their own special tariffs.

ANNUAL VOLUME RATE   A rate that is tied to a minimum annual tonnage volume by a shipper; a form of contract rate.

ANY QUANTITY RATES   Any quantity (AQ) class ratings apply to those articles for which no minimum or volume is required. They are a substitute for TLT or LCL rates, and a substitute for volume rates. They apply for any volume of shipment. Any quantity rates are also applicable to commodities that usually do not move in carload lots, and may take commodity rate form.

ALTERNATIVE RATES   Whenever the tariff rules permit either a class or commodity rate to be substituted for a higher rate in another section of the same tariff, or another tariff, when it is lower, it becomes an alternative rate. The rules sometimes permit circumventing the standard rules for rate priorities.

ARBITRARY RATES   An arbitrary rate is added to a base point rate to provide regional zone. Commonly, the arbitrary is given to the short line carrier. This permits setting rates to a few base points, rather than setting specific rates to each terminal in a region. The movement, of course, need not go through the base point.

ASSEMBLY AND DISTRIBUTION RATES   These are rates on multiple shipments which are moving under a consolidated bill of lading. Motor carriers provide A & D rates at about 10 percent lower level than ordinary separate small shipments to account for the lower cost of handling the consolidated movement. They are used on shipments that originate or terminate at points beyond the terminal areas of freight forwarders or consolidators. An industrial shipper that regularly performs a consolidated operation, or uses a consolidator, would reap savings from such rates.

BARGE-RAIL RATES   A joint barge-rail movement may have a single joint through rate, or a combination of several rates, computed on various segments of the haul. Congressional legislation requires that barge-rail rates will be lower than all-rail rates between the same points.

BASING RATES (or BASING POINT RATES)   Rates which are constructed by assuming the rate to a base point, or adding a differential or arbitrary to a base point are known as basing rates. A basing rate is used in combination with other rates to form a through rate.

BLANKET RATES   The establishment of a large blanket area from or to which equal rates apply. The blanket area may be the origin, destination, or both origin and destination. The transportation rate would be the same per hundredweight from any point in the blanket area to or from a given point or area. Some regard a blanket rate as being synonymous with a group rate, but is usually considered to cover a greater geographic area than a group rate. A blanket area may cover all points east of the Mississippi River, while a grouped area may cover only the New England states. Blanket and grouped rates encourage dispersion.

BREAKDOWN RATES   The provision for incrementally reduced rates for incrementally greater volumes of shipment is a process of breaking down rates. While rail carriers have various types of rates which permit lower rates under varying packaging, container, volume, etc., circumstances motor carriers are more inclined to have graduated breakdown rates base exclusively on volume of shipment.

BUSINESS FARE   A rate for a class of airline service that is between coach and first class.

CAR-FERRY RATES   A transportation movement which combines a rail movement with a water transportation of the rail car on a ferry is assigned a car-ferry rate. They may be the same as an all-rail rate.

CARGO RATES   Shipments large enough to employ cargo capacity in water transportation are granted cargo rates. Cargo volume IS usually considerably larger than that needed to acquire volume rates for other carrier modes.

CARLOAD RATES   In railroad movements, shipments which qualify for a specified minimum volume are entitled to a carload rate. There is no necessary relationship between a minimum carload volume and the amount required to utilize the capacity of a rail car. These rates are appreciably lower than less-than-carload rates.

CLASS RATES   Rates applied to groups of commodities between specific point, rather than on specific commodities. The class rate structure assures equal class rates on a given class of commodities for any given distance anywhere in the United States. This does not mean that the same cost per ton-mile would prevail for different lengths of haul, since terminal costs make up varying proportions of the rate for varying lengths of haul.

COLLECTION RATES   Rates for inbound movement of many shipments that are consolidated at an intermediate point for long haul; it is the reverse of distribution rates.

COMBINATION RATES   Rates determined by adding rates on each segment of a through route make up a combination rate. Often they tend to be greater than a single through rate.

COMMODITY RATES   Rates on specific commodities between specific points are commodity rates. They are usually lower than class rates, and put into effect to reflect a lower cost of transportation per hundredweight as a result of the volume of the traffic, reduced handling costs, or otherwise. The commodity rate is a special commodity tariff for the carrier mode.

COMPARATIVE RATES   An application for a lower rate in a hearing is justified by documenting that rates for comparable movements by others or the same carrier exists. Comparative rates are rates used to illustrate a more favorable rate under comparable circumstances.

CONTRACT RATE   A rate that is based upon a negotiation and applied between a carrier and a particular shipper or receiver.

CORPORATE VOLUME RATE   A lower than normal rate charged to shippers that provides increasing discounts with increasing tonnage shipped from each firm over a particular carrier throughout specified time periods.

DIFFERENTIAL RATES   Differential pricing is reduced pricing, or at least differences in pricing, based on circumstances which provide an excuse for the reduction. Differential rates in transportation result from a type of movement which seems to offer inferior service at a reduced price. Thus, a more circuitous route, or a joint modal (rail-barge) route, might encourage traffic by giving reduced rates which are not really justified by reduced costs of service.

DEMAND SENSITIVE RATE   A rate designed to smooth out the peaks and valleys of seasonal product transportation demands; generally higher in peak season, sometimes lower in low season.

DENSITY RATE   A transportation rate that is generally lower per hundredweight for products that are dense (heavy per cubic foot) and vice versa.

DISTANCE RATES   Rates which reflect the principle of varying rates with distance, though not in proportion to distance, are termed distance rates. These rates usually reflect a constant amount for a terminal charge, and an added amount to reflect the distance of the haul. The term block rates is often applied to distance rates.

DISTRIBUTION RATES   A lower rate provided for the consolidation of many small volume shipments all destined for a single commercial area. The distribution rate covers the distribution process in the terminal area, which is added to the low volume line haul rate. The combination of a consolidated line haul rate, plus the distribution rate for the delivery at the destination on each LTL part of the consolidated shipment make up the total combination rate.

ESCORT RATES   Rates for a person accompanying a special shipment, e.g., high, wide and heavy.

EXCESS-OF-CAPACITY RATES   Motor carriers, seeking to compete with railroads, publish rates on minimum weights which exceed the legal capacity of a single vehicle.

EXCURSION FARE   A low fare that is applied for certain elastic submarkets, such as the occasional traveler on vacation who is price sensitive.

EXPORT RATES   Rates on domestic portion of an international export shipment are granted lower rates than comparable movements not destined for export. Export and import rates take precedence over other rates—be they class or commodity, import or export rates.

FREIGHT FORWARDER RATES   Freight forwarders publish their own tariffs. Today their rates are predominantly governed by motor classifications. Years ago, when rail carriers presented most of the line haul service, the freight forwarder rates were primarily based on the railroad classification. Freight forwarder tariffs are both class and commodity, and provide for both less-than-volume and volume shipments. The freight forwarder pays the line haul carrier TL and CL rates on the line haul service, but the forwarder is forced to provide an assembly and distribution service, which forces the actual cost of the service considerably higher than that of the volume rate. The tariffs must reflect this.

GROUP RATES   The granting of identical rates for all points in a grouped area, whether a grouped origin or destination (or both), represents a grouped rate. Grouped rates encourage the dispersion of industry.

GUARANTEED RATE   1) a contract carriage rate; 2) an annual volume rate.

IMPORT RATES (see export rates)   The reduction in the domestic portion of an international movement below the rates on domestic traffic between the same points provide a low domestic combination rate which is referred to as an import or export rate. They take precedence over other rates between the same point— be they either class or commodity import rates.

INCENTIVE RATES   Reductions in truckload rates for shipment volumes that exceed the minimum truckload volume by a given amount, or percent. The amount of the reduction in the rate is usually established as a percent of the truckload rate. Thus, a shipment volume that exceeds 28,000 lbs. by at least fifty percent, would be granted a reduction in the truckload rate by 10 percent. Motor carriers commonly employ incentive rates, as they do breakdown rates, but the latter are incremental rate reduction.

INTERLINE RATES   These rates must involve more than one carrier in the transportation service. They may take the form of a joint rate, or a combination rate (two separate rates).

INTERMEDIATE RATES   An intermediate rate is a rate to or from an intermediate point in a movement. According to the aggregate- of the intermediate rate, if the combination of intermediate rates, whether class or commodity, is lower than the through rate, the lower rate prevails. However, if another tariff contains a specific commodity rate on the through movement, which should take priority over a commodity rate on an intermediate movement, the commodity rate under the intermediate rule will not be applicable.

INTERSTATE RATES   Any rate on a movement passing through more than one state. Even if the origin and destination is in one state, if the haul passes through more than one state, it is an interstate haul, with an interstate rate.

INTRASTATE RATES   Rates on movements which originate and terminate in the same state, and do not pass through another state, are intrastate rates.

JOINT RATES   Joint rates involve a single through rate—not a combination of separate rates (which are called combination rates). A joint rate is a single rate published for the several carriers involved. Joint rates involve more than one carrier, agreeing on a single through rate.

LAND GRANT RATES   Rates on U.S. government movements which were lower than the published rates as a condition of the land grants to the railroads were collectively called land grant rates. They were repealed, October 1, 1946. It has been estimated that the total savings to the government under the land grant rates, inclusive of voluntary reductions of rates by competing carriers amounted to 580 million dollars by the end of June, 1943.

LAWFUL RATES   A lawful rate is one that conforms with the low, or the approval of the I.C.C. or other regulatory authority. A lawful rate may not be the rate published in the tariff, and thus, may not also be the legal rate.

LEGAL RATE   The legal rate is the published rate in the tariff. The carrier is legally bound to collect on the legal rate, whether it conforms to the lawful rate or not.

LESS-THAN-CARLOAD RATES   The term carload rates applies to both commodity and class rates. It is commonly said that a truckload minimum weight is based on the weight that can be safely loaded in a trailer of 1,500 cubic feet and conform to the legal limits on the vehicle. The railroad carload classification minimum weight is based on the weight that can safely be loaded on a 40-foot car. This is somewhat academic, however since minimum carload and truckload weights may be considerably less than this. The less-than-carload rate is the rate applicable to shipments which do not qualify for the minimum weight specified for the carload rate.

LESS-THAN-TRUCKLOAD RATE (See less-than-carload rate above)   The less shipment is not sufficiently large to equal the minimum volume specified for a truckload rate—or the shipper is not willing to pay for the minimum volume specified for a truckload rate. If the actual shipment volume times the less-than-truckload rate exceeds the minimum volume times the I truckload rate, the lesser charge of the two systems applies on the shipment.

LOCAL RATES   The rate on a transportation movement performed on one carrier line, regardless of the length of the haul, is a local rate. If it is not a local rate, it must be a joint rate or a combination rate. It may involve a combination of two rates as a single combination rate, or it may be two joint rates on the movement—but It must involve only one carrier to be a local rate. One rate, by one carrier, on one movement is a local rate.

MAXIMUM RATES   In order to protect the public from exorbitant rates, the regulatory authority frequently will establish a maximum rate that may be charged. This ceiling rate is commonly set to cover the costs of operation, committed capital costs, and provide a fair return on investment. A minimum rate is a price floor placed on rates to prevent destructive competition. Between the minimum and maximum rate is the zone of reasonableness.

MEASUREMENT RATES   A measurement rate is usually quoted on a cubic basis or a gross ton basis. One may find measurement rates on ocean movements and bulk shipments by rail. Other forms of measurement rates might take the form of a rate per cord of wood—based on a specific number of cubic feet per cord. In ocean transportation, the rate may be based on a rate per gross ton of 2240 pounds, or per measurement of 40 cubic feet, whichever produces the highest charge.

MILEAGE RATES   Mileage rates are also called distance rates. (See distance rates.) Mileage rates vary directly, but not proportionately, with an increase in the length of haul. They tend to have a fixed terminal cost and an added cost per mile of movement. However, mileage blocks provide an equal rate for all distances within the block. Distance or mileage rates may be class or commodity, fiat or proportional, local or joint, and may be import, domestic or export rates. According to Tariff Circular No. 20, the mileage class rate may be used only when no specific through rate or commodity rate prevails. Mileage commodity rates may only be used when there is no specific commodity rate.

MINIMUM RATES   A floor placed on rates, below which they cannot go, is a minimum rate. It is common to establish that the minimum rate cannot go below the variable costs of performing the transportation service.

MISSIONARY RATE   Missionary rates are a form of a promotional rate that is often called a proportional rate. Missionary and proportional are used synonymously, though the term proportional rate is more common. A proportional rate is a lower rate of a segment of a through movement than the rate that terminates at the intermediate point. Many countries have long had subsidized transportation to outlying colonies and affiliated countries in order to encourage growth of these distant locales.

MOTOR CARRIER CLASS (COMMODITY) RATES   Motor carriers have their own uniform freight classification, which is a modification of the docket 28300 scale of class rates. The National Motor Freight Classification deviates from the 28300 scale for classifications less than about Class 40 or 45. Motor carriers also issue their own competitive commodity rate tariffs which present commodity rates on specific products between specific points.

MULTIPLE CAR RATE   The I.C.C. now permits multiple car rates, which are a lower level of rates for shipment volumes that require more than one car. These rates must at least cover out-of-pocket costs, and must be made available as a result of proven competition. In years gone by, the I.C.C. discouraged these rates because: (1) they were thought to be discriminatory against single car shippers, and (2) it was believed there was little difference in the cost of service between single car and multiple car shipments.

MULTIPLE SHIPMENT RATE   A rate for freight whereby a lower rate applies on each shipment when many are tendered at the same time.

MULTIPLE-TRAILER LOAD RATES   Rates which are lower for shipments re-quiring more than one trailer load are multiple trailer load rates. The justification for these lower rates is the same as the presented in multiple car rates discussed above. (See multiple car rates.)

PAPER RATES   A rate which is published but has never been used is termed a paper rate.

PER CAR RATE   A fixed charge per car on specific commodities, between specific points is a per car rate. Sometimes it is referred to as a sealed carload rate. The flat charge is assessed regardless of the volume of the shipment in the car.

PREDATORY RATES   Low prices charged by transportation companies that are designed to drive a competitor from the market.

PREJUDICIAL RATES   When a rate exists which is deemed to be in violation of Section 10741 on matters of preference and prejudice, it is generally referred to as a prejudicial rate. The term is used as an adjective.

PROPORTIONAL RATES (see missionary rates above)   A lower than normal rate on a segment of a through movement to encourage traffic, or capture competitive traffic, is a proportional rate. Normally, it will allow a rate below the published rate commonly prevailing (though it too is published) that reduces the rate to a geographic intermediate point, for traffic destined to points beyond. This type of rate may be used in international movements, providing a lower rate to the gateway port. The proportional rate may be a percentage of the standard rate, or a flat rate which is lower between given points.

REASONABLE RATES   This is a regulatory phrase which deals with the character of a particular rate to be just and reasonable in accordance. While the adequacy of a rate to cover costs is often used to appraise its reasonableness, more often than not, reasonableness is measured by comparing a rate.

RELEASED VALUE RATES   Released value rates are based on an agreed value of the commodity shipped. While this provides a lower rate, it also provides a lower liability to the carrier. The of agreed value to actual value is applied to the dollar loss to establish the carrier liability.

SATURDAY NIGHT FARE   A low airline fare designed for the vacationer or other casual passenger. It is designed to not appeal to the business passenger who generally pays higher midweek fares.

SECTION 22 RATES (US)   Reduced rates are granted federal, state and local governments under Section 22 of the original Interstate Commerce Act.

SHORT NOTICE RATES   The regulatory statute provides that provides for a few number of days' notice must be provided before filed rates become effective.

SPACE WEIGHT RATE   A rate that applies to weight or cubic measure, usually whichever is greater, to determine total freight charges, common in the ocean industry.

THROUGH RATES   A through rate is the total rate applicable on a haul. It may be a single joint through rate, it may be a single local rate, it may involve combination rates or any other charge on a continuous carriage by one or several carriers. When more than one carrier is involved, a through rate has been agreed to by carriers for continuous service.

TRUCKLOAD RATES   In motor movements, a shipment volume which qualifies for a minimum volume required for a truckload rate is granted this lower rate. If the truckload rate times its minimum weight requirement is lower than the actual rate times the LTL rate, the lower rate and payment is the legal and lawful rate. There is no needed relationship between the amount required to fill a truck and the minimum truckload weight. (See LESS THAN TRUCKLOAD rates for further amplification.)

VOLUME RATES   Rates based on a minimum volume of shipment (weight) are called volume rates. It is a motor rate, and it includes the loading and unloading by the carrier—in contrast to the railroad carload rate in which the carrier does not load and unload. The term volume rate is also used for lower motor carrier LTL rates based on minimum volumes.

WATER COMPELLED RATE   Rate charged by railroads that are depressed in a specific market in response to coastwise or barge competition.

STANDARD ABBREVIATIONS

24-7-365	24 hours a day, seven days a week, 365 days of the year
3PL	Third party logistics
4PL	Fourth party logistics
5PL	Fifth party logistics
a	At to. At the rate of.
A	Acceptance or accepted in commercial language.
A.D.A.	Americans with Disabilities Act
A.G.	Aktien-Gesellschaft, German stock company
A.G.V.	Automatic guided vehicle
A.P.	Aktiebolager, Swedish stock company
A.S.	Aktieselskabet, Danish stock company
A.T.C.	Air Transport Command, air traffic control
A.W.O.	American Waterways Operators.
A/C, or acct cur.	Account current.
A/cs. Rec	Accounts receivable.
A/O	Account of.
A/P, A/cs. Pay.	Accounts payable.
A/R	All rail (insurance), All risks (identical with W.P.A.).
A/S	After sight.
A/V	Ad valorem.
A/W	Actual weight, all water.
A1	Top rate. First class condition. The highest rating given by Lloyds of London
AAA	American Automobile Association.
AAFA	Assistant Auditor Freight Accounts.
aar.	Against all risks.
AAR	Association of American Railroads.
AB	Able bodied seamen.
ABS	American Bureau of Shipping.
abn.	Airborne.
abst, abstr.	Abstract.
Ac, acc or acct	Account, accountant.
AC.C.	Air Coordinating Committee.
ACI	Air Cargo, Inc.
act wt	Actual weight.
Act, actg.	Acting.
ACW	American Chain of Warehouses
ad inf., or ad fin. (ad infinitum)	To the end without limit.

ad int (ad interim)	Meanwhile or in the meantime.
ad val. (ad valorem)	According to the value.
ad.	After date.
AD	In the year of our Lord. Anno Domini.
ad., adv., advt	Advertisement.
add	Addition
Adm.	Admiralty, administration, administrator.
Adm. Ct or Adm Co.	Admiralty Court.
admr.	Administrator.
adv.	Advance.
adv. chgs(-es).	Advance charges.
advps., or avoir.	Avoirdupois.
AF.CA	Assistant Freight Claim Agent.
AF.O.C.	Auditor Freight Overcharge Claims.
AF.R.	Auditor Freight Receipts.
AF.T.	Auditor Freight Traffic.
AF.T.B.	Atlanta Freight Traffic Bureau.
AF.T.M.	Assistant Freight Traffic Manager.
AFA	Auditor of Freight Claims.
AFAA	Airline Flight Attendants Association.
affd.	Affirmed.
AFFT.	Affidavit.
Ag (argentum)	Silver (metal).
agcy.	Agency.
AGFA	Assistant General Freight Agent.
agr., agrl.	Agriculture, agricultural.
agt	Agent.
ah.	Aft hatch.
ak	All right, or correct.
alc	Alcohol.
ALJ	Administrative Law Judge
ALPA	Airline Pilots Association.
alt	Altitude, alternate.
ALTA	Association of Local Transport Airlines.
altr.	Alternate, alternative.
a.m.	Ante meridiem (before noon).
AM.2	Air Mail Route No. 2.
AM.F.	Air mail field.
AMA	Automobile Manufacturers Association.
amdt	Amendment.
amt	Amount.
amt per veh.	Amount per vehicle.
AN.	Arrival notice.
an. (anno)	In the year.

anal.	Analysis.
Ann. Cas.	Annotated cases.
Ann. Rep.	Annual Report.
annot	Annotated.
annum	Year.
ans.	Answer.
ANSI	American National Standards Institute
ANSI-X12	ANSI EDI standards
ante	Before
AO.C.	Auditor of Overcharge Claims.
APA	Administrative Procedure Act.
APC	automatic passenger counter
APEC	Asia Pacific Economic Cooperation
APICS	American Production and Inventory Control Society
App. Div.	Appellate Division.
app., appln., appn.	Application.
approx.	Approximate.
appx.	Appendix.
APS	advanced planning and scheduling solutions
AQ.	Any quantity.
AR.	Auditor of receipts, auditor of revenue, Allegheny Region.
ar., arr.	Arrives, arrival.
arb., arbry.	Arbitrary.
ARINC	Aeronautical Radio, Inc.
Arr. N.	Arrival Notice.
arrd.	Arrived.
art	Article.
as	Same as.
AS.LR.	American Short Line Railroads.
ASN	advanced shipping notice
assn., assoc.	Association.
asst	Assistant.
asstd.	Associated, assorted.
ASTL	American Society of Traffic and Logistics
ATA	Auditor of Traffic Accounts.
at wt	Atomic weight.
AT. (marine insurance)	American terms.
AT.CA	Air Traffic Conference of America.
AT.M.	Assistant Traffic Manager.
AT.S.	Army Transport Service.
ATA	American Trucking Associations, Inc.; American Transit Association

ATAA	Air Transport Association of America.
Atl.	Atlantic.
att or att,v.	Attorney.
Au (Latin, aurum)	Gold.
aud	Auditor.
Aud Disb.	Auditor Disbursements.
Aud Pass. Accts.	Auditor Passenger Accounts.
Aud Rev.	Auditor of Revenue.
Aud Sta Accts.	Auditor Station Accounts.
Aud. Frt Accts.	Auditor Freight Accounts.
Aud. Frt Rec	Auditor Freight Receipts.
auth	Authority, authorization.
av.	Average, avenue.
Ave.	Avenue.
avg	Average.
AVI	Automatic vehicle identification.
AVL	Automatic vehicle locator system.
AWA	American Warehousemen's Association.
B	British, breadth.
B B.	Break bulk, bill book.
b	Bag, bale.
B of C	Bureau of Customs.
B&IB	Billing and instruction book.
B. Pay.	Bills payable.
B.C.C.T.	British Columbia Coast Terminals.
b.d.i.	Both dates inclusive.
B.F. or B. Fir.	Firkin of butter.
B.O.	Buyer's option, bad order, branch office, back order.
B.O.R.	Bureau of Operation Rights (I.C.C.).
B.P.	Between perpendiculars.
B.S.	Balance sheet, bill of sale.
B.W.I.	British West Indies.
B/A	Billed at.
B/D	Bar-Draft.
B/E	Bill of Exchange.
B/F	Brought forward.
B/M	Benchmark(ing).
B/P, B P.	Bill of Parcels, bills payable.
B/R, B.R., B.	Rec Bill of rights, bills receivable.
B/S	Bill of Sale.
B2B	Business-to-business (commerce).
B2C	Business-to-consumer.
Bal.	Balance.

Barb.	Barbados.
bbl., bbls.	Barrel, barrels.
BBs.	Below bridges.
bd	Board.
bd. ft	Board foot (feet).
bdl., bdle, bdis.	Bundle, bundles.
bds.	Boards.
bet	Between.
bg., bgs.	Bag, bags.
Bk, Bank	Book; banks.
Bkt, bskt	Basket.
BL, B/L	Bill of Lading.
bl., bis.	Bale, bales.
bldg.	Building.
blk	Block.
blt	Built.
BM.	Board measurement.
BPR	Business process redesign.
bque.	Barque.
Br.	Branch, British.
br., brs.	Branch, branches.
Braz	Brazil.
Brit	Britain.
Bskt	Basket.
bt	Berth terms.
bt	Boat.
bu.	Bushel, bureau.
bx., bxs.	Box, boxes.
c	Coupon, carton.
C Degree	Centigrade.
C of C.	Chamber of Commerce.
C of S.	Commissioner of Ships.
C to S	Carting to shipside.
C&C	Coal and coke.
C&D	Collection and delivery.
C&E	Clothing and equipage.
C&F	Cost and freight.
C&L	Canal and lake.
C&R	Canal and rail, canal and river.
C&SMFA	Central & Southern Motor Freight Association.
C. (Cerdum)	A hundred, currency.
C.B.	Cash book, Customs Bureau.
C.B.D.	Cash before delivery.
C.B.E.	Cab-beside-engine.

c.c	Contra credit, current cost, cubic centimeter.
C.C.	Chief clerk, connecting carrier.
C.C.B.	Canadian Custom Bonded.
C.CA	Circuit Court of Appeals.
C.E.	Consumption Entry.
C.F., C&F	Cost and freight.
c.f.	Cubic feet.
C.F.A.	Central Freight Association, Canadian Freight Association.
C.F.C.	Consolidated Freight Classification.
C.F.I.	Cost, Freight & Insurance.
C.F.R.	Code of Federal Regulations.
C.F.T.B.	Central Freight Tariff Bureau.
C.G.	Consul General.
C.H.	Custom house, clearing house.
C.I.	Cost insurance.
C.I.F.&C.	Cost, insurance, freight and commission.
C.I.F., C.I.&F.	Cost, insurance and freight.
C.I.F.&E	Cost, insurance, freight and exchange.
C.I.F.C.&I.	Cost, insurance, freight, collection and interest.
C.I.F.I.&E.	Cost, insurance, freight, interest and exchange.
C.I.T.	Cleaning(-ed) in transit.
C.L	Carload, connecting line.
C.L & R	Canal, lake and rail.
C.L.F.	Connecting line freight.
cm	Centimeter.
C.M.	Common meter, certified member.
C.O.D.	Cash (or collect) on delivery.
C.O.F.C.	Container on flatcar.
C.O.S.	Cash on shipment.
C.P.A	Certified (Chartered) Public Accountant, Combination Publication
C.P.C.&N.	Certificate of Public Convenience and Necessity.
C.P.G.	Cotton piece goods.
C.P.M.	Certified Purchasing Manager.
C.R.C.	Canadian Railway Commission.
cs	Cases.
C.S.	Car Service, civil service, cold storage.
c/s	Cotton seed.
C.S.D.	Car Service Department.
C.S.M.F.B.	Central States Motor Freight Bureau.
C.S.S.	Car Service Station.
C.T.B.	Chief of Tariff Bureau, Consulting Traffic Bureau.

C.T.C.	Central (or Centralized) Traffic Control.
C.T.L.	Certified in Transportation and Logistics (term in AST&L certification).
C.T.M.	Coal Traffic Manager, Certified (or Consulting) Traffic Manager.
C.U.F.	Cushion underframe.
c.v.	Chief value.
C.W.O.	Cash with order.
C.W.R.	Central Western Region.
C.Z	Canal Zone.
C/A	Capital Account, current account.
C/N	Correction.
CA	Commercial agent, car accountant, claim agent, Central America.
CAAdm.	Civil Aeronautics Administration (Authority).
CAB.	Civil Aeronautics Board.
CAD	computer aided dispatch, Cash against document.
CAF	Currency adjustment factor.
CAF.	(French) Coute (cost), assurance (insurance), fret (freight).
Cal., Calif.	California.
CAM	Commercial air movement.
Can.FA	Canadian Freight Association.
cancig.	Canceling.
cap.	Capital, capitol.
Capy.	Capacity.
car acct	Car accountant.
car ser. agt	Car service agent.
cash., cashr.	Cashier.
CASL	Committee of American Steamship Lines
cat.	Catalogue.
Cbm	Cubic meter.
CDS	Construction differential subsidy.
cent (centrum)	Hundred, century.
Cent(s)	centime(s).
cert, certif.	Certificate, certified.
cf. (confer)	Compare.
CFR	cost and freight
Ch. Acet Off.	Chief Accounting Officer.
Ch. Clk	Chief clerk.
Ch., Chin.	China.
ch., ehap.	Chapter.
Cham. Comm.	Chamber of Commerce.

char.	Charter.
chg., ehgs.	Charge, charges.
Chi., Chgo.	Chicago.
Chin.	Chinese.
chm, chman.	Chairman.
CIA	Cash in advance.
Cie.	(French, compagnie) Company.
CIF	Cost, insurance and freight.
CIP	Carriage and insurance paid to.
CIPS	Chartered Institute of Purchasing and Supply.
cir. (circa, circum)	About.
cir., circl.	Circular.
cit	Citation, citizen.
CITL	Certified in Transportation and Logistics.
ck, cks.	Cask(s), check(s).
cl.	Claim.
cl. ht	Ceiling height.
class7 elasstn.	Classification.
cld.	Cleared.
clk	Clerk.
CLM.	Couneil of Logisties Management
CM, AST&L	Certified Member, American Society of Transportation and
CMI	Co-managed inventories.
Co.	Company, county.
col.	Column.
coll.	Collect.
com'g.	Commencing.
com'l, cml.	Commercial.
Com. Merch.	Commission Merchant.
com. pts.	Common points.
com., comm.	Commission, committee, commerce.
comb.	Combination.
commod.	Commodity.
commr(s).	Commissioner, commissioners.
Comptr.	Comptroller.
con't, cont'd.	Continued.
con. (contra)	Against, in opposition.
conf.	Conference.
Cong.	Congress.
Cong. Rec.	Congressional Record.
const	Consignment.
cont	Controller.
cor.	Corrected.

Cor. L	Corrosive liquid.
corp.	Corporation.
coun.	Counsel.
cp d	Chaners pay dues.
cp.	Compare.
CPFR	Collaborative, planning, forecasting, and replenishment.
CPT	Carriage paid to.
CR.	Carrier's risk, class (or commodity) rate.
cr.	Creditor, credit, creek.
cross., crossg.	Crossing.
CSR	Customer service response.
Ct	Court, count.
ct, cts. (centum)	Cents, cent.
ct, cty.	County.
ctg., ctge.	Cartage, containing.
ctl.o.	Constructive total loss only.
cu.	Cubic, (cuprum) copper.
cu. ft	Cubic foot (feet).
cur.	Current (this month), currency.
cwt	hundredweight (U.S.—100 pounds, U.K.—112 pounds).
cy., cyls.	Cylinder, cylinders.
d	Day, a penny, or pence.
D.	(Roman notation) Five hundred, depth.
D.B.	Day book.
D.B.&B.	Deals, battens and boards.
D.C.	Direct Current.
D.D.	Double deck, demand draft.
D.D. of T.	Director, Division of Traffic.
d.do.	Dispatch discharging only.
D.E.I.	Dutch East Indies.
D.F.A.	Division Freight Agent.
D.F.B.	Damage free bracing.
d.l.o.	Dispatch loading only.
D.LO.	Dead Letter Office.
D.M.	District (or Division) Manager.
D.N.A.	Delta Nu Alpha.
D.O.P.	"dropping the outbound pilot" (term in ship charter).
D.O.T.	Department of Transportation.
d.p.	Direct port.
D.P.	Documents for payment.
D.R.	Dock receipt, differential rate.
D.S., Div. Supt	Division Superintendent

D.S.T.	Daylight Saving Time.
D.T.	Director of Traffic (or Transportation).
D.T.A.	District Traffic Agent.
d.w.	Dead weight.
D/A	Days after acceptance.
d/a clause.	Vessel must discharge afloat.
D/B/A	Doing business as.
D/D	Days after date, demand draft.
D/S	Days after sight.
D/W	Dock warrant.
D1 or 2T1	Double First Class.
DA	Documents for acceptance.
da (ditto)	The same.
DAF	Delivered at frontier.
dbk	Drawback.
dbl.	Double.
DDP	Delivered duty paid.
DDU	Delivered duty unpaid.
deduct	Deduction(s).
def.	Definition, defendant, deferred.
deft	Defendant.
deg.	Degree.
Del.	Delaware.
delv'd.	Delivered.
dely., delvy.	Delivery.
demm.	Demurrage.
dep.	Depot.
dept or dpt	Department.
DES	Delivered ex ship.
desp.	Despatch.
destn.	Destination.
dft	Draft.
di., dia, diam.	Diameter.
dif	Differential, different.
dig.	Digest.
dir.	Director, direction.
Dir. of P.S.	Director of Public Service.
dis., disc. or disct	Discount.
disp.	Dispatch, dispatcher.
dist.	District, distance.
distr.	Distributor, distribution.
distrb.	Distributes.
div.	Division, diversion.
dk	Dock.

dkt	Docket.
dm.	Decimeter.
Dm.	Dekameter.
DOB	dealer own brand
Doc.	Document, docket.
DOE	Department of Energy.
dol., dols.	Dollar, dollars.
dom.	Domestic
doz, dz	Dozen.
dpt	Depth, department, deponent.
Dr.	Debtor, debit.
dr.	Dram.
DRP	Distribution requirements planning.
DSD	Direct store delivery.
dun.	Dunnage.
dup.	Duplicate.
dw	A pennyweight (Latin denarius and English weight).
dwt	Deadweight tons.
dz	Dozen.
E&OE	Errors and omissions excepted.
E&OE	Errors and omissions excepted.
E.B.&B.B.	Eastbound Basing, Billing Book.
E.D.S.T.	Eastern Daylight Saving Time.
E.F.I.B.	Eastern Freight Inspection Bureau.
e.g. (Latin, exempli gratia)	For example.
E.H.	Eggs in hatching (parcel post).
E.M.F.	Electromotive force.
E.O.N.	Except as otherwise excepted.
E.R.	East River (N.Y.C.), Eastern Region.
E.S.T.	Eastern Standard Time.
E.T.O.	Express Transportation Order.
e/c.	Emergency charges.
e/i	Certificate of insurance.
e/o	(In) care of
ea	Each.
EAN	European Article Number
EB.	East bound.
EC	European Community
ECMCA	Eastern Central Motor Carriers Association.
ECR	efficient customer/consumer response
ECU	European Currency Unit
ed.	Editor, edition.
ED.	End door(s).

EDLP	Every day low pricing.
edtd.	Edited.
EE.	Errors excepted.
EFT	Electronic funds transfer.
Eft	Electronic funds transfer.
EL	Eastern Lines.
el.	Elevated, elevator.
elec.	Electric.
elev.	Elevation, elevator.
emb.	Embargo.
eml.	Commercial.
EMV	(Europay/MasterCard/Visa)
EN.	Exceptions noted.
eng., engr.	Engineer.
EPA	Environmental Protection Administration.
EPI	Early purchasing involvement.
EPOS	Electronic point of sale.
eq.	Equal, equivalent.
equip.	Equipment.
ERP	Enterprise resource planning.
ESI	Early supplier involvement.
est	Estimated, established.
est. wt	Estimated weight.
et al. (Latin, et alia)	And others.
et seq. (Latin, et sequentia)	And the following.
ETA	Estimated time of arrival, emergency temporary authority.
etc. (Latin, et cetera)	And so forth, and other things.
Eth.	Ethiopia.
EU	European Union
Eur.	Europe.
EW.	End width of boxcar, eave to eave.
ex (Latin)	From.
ex.	Example, exception, exchange, extra, express.
Ex. B.L	Exchange Bill of Lading.
Exc.	Exception, except.
excep., except	Exception.
excg.	Exchange.
excidg.	Excluding.
excpt.	Exception.
exd	Examined.
exp.	Express, export, expense.
EXW	Ex works.
exw.	Extreme width.

F	Fragile (parcel post).
F Degree	Fahrenheit.
F&W Chg.	Feeding and watering charge.
f.a.s.	Free alongside (ship)
F.B.	Freight bill.
F.C. Adj.	Freight claim adjuster.
F.C. Aud.	Freight claim auditor.
F.C.A.	Freight claim agent (or Association).
F.C.B.	Freight Container Bureau (A.A.R.).
F.C.C.	Federal Communications Commission.
F.D.	Finance docket, freight department.
F.F.	Freight forwarder, folded flat.
F.F.L.	Fast Freight Line.
F.FA	Foreign freight agent.
F.G.A.	Foreign general agent.
F.I.	Falkland Islands.
f.i.a	Free in and out.
f.i.a	Full interest admitted.
F.I.R.	Floating-in-rate.
f.i.w.	Free in wagon.
F.M.	Fine measurement.
F.M.C.	Federal Maritime Commission.
F.O.B.	Free on board.
F.O.R.	Free on rail.
f.o.w.	First open water.
F.O. Adj.	Freight overcharge adjuster.
F.PA	Free of particular average.
F.PA (AC.)	Free of particular average (American conditions).
F.PA. (E.C.)	Free of particular average (English conditions).
F.R	Federal Register.
f.r. and cc.	Free of riot and civil commotion.
F.S.	Fourth Section (Interstate Commerce Act).
F.S.A.	Fourth Section application.
F.S.O.	Fourth Section order.
f.t	Full terms, disuatch money payable on all time saved on the chartered time
F.T.B.	Freight Tariff (or Traffic) Bureau.
F.T.C.	Freight Traffic (or Tariff) Committee, Federal Trade Commission.
F.T.D.	Freight traffic department.
F.T.M.	Freight traffic manager.
F.T.Z.	Federal Trade Zone.
F/A	Free astray.
FA	Freight agent, freight auditor, freight association.

FAA	Federal Aviation Act (Agency), free of all average.
Fah., Fahr.	Fahrenheit.
FAK	Freight all kinds.
FAM	Foreign Air Mail Route No. 2.
FAQ.	Fair, average quality.
FAS	Free alongside ship.
fath, fth.	Fathom.
FCA	Free carrier.
Fe.	(Latin, ferrum) Iron.
Fed Aud.	Federal Auditor.
Fed.	Federal Reporter, U.S. District Courts.
Fertz	Fertilizer.
ffa	Free from average.
FFI	Freight Forwarders Institute.
fin.	Financial.
fir.	Firkin.
flt	Float.
fltg	Floatage.
fl.	Florin.
fl. ld.	Floor load (in pounds per square foot).
fm.	From.
FMCG	Fast moving consumer goods.
fms.	Fathoms.
FOB	Free on board.
for	loading and discharging the cargo.
for.	Foreign.
FPA	Free of particular average.
fr.	Franc, from.
frt	Freight.
ft	Foot, feet, fort.
Ft Assn.	Freight association.
fur.	Furlong.
fut	Future.
fwd.	Forward.
fwdg.	Forwarding.
fwdr.	Forwarder.
FX	Freight Tariff Concurrence, FX I, FX2, etc.
G CA	General claim agent.
G.	Grain, gage, gauge.
G.	Guineas, gulf.
G. Aud.	General auditor.
G. Supt, Gen. Supt	General superintendent.
G.B.	Guidebook, Great Britain.
G.B. & I.	Great Britain and Ireland.

G.B.L.	Government Bill of Lading.
G.B.S.	Government Bureau of Standards.
G.C.	General circular.
g.c.m.	Greatest common measure.
G.C.T.	Greenwich Civil Time.
G.F.D.	General freight department.
G.F.F.C.	Gulf Foreign Freight Committee.
G.F.O.	General freight office.
G.F.T.C.—E.R.	General Freight Traffic Committee—Eastern Railroads.
G.FA	General freight agent.
G.I.C.	Gulf Intercoastal Conference.
G.L	General letter.
G.LSA	General Livestock Agent.
G.M.	General Manager, general merchandise.
G.M. or G. Mdse.	General merchandise.
G.m.b.H.	Gesellschaft mit beschraenkter Haftung—lim. liab company
G.O.	General order, General office.
G.O.C.	General operating committee.
G.P.D.	General passenger department.
G.P.O.	General Post Office.
G.S.	General specials, General superintendent.
G.S.A.	General Services Administration.
G.S.F.C.	General superintendent of freight claims.
G.S.O.	Car Service Order.
G.T.	Gross ton.
G.T.&T.M.	General traffic, transportation manager.
G.T.D.	General traffic department.
G.T.I.	General transportation importance.
g.tc.	Good till canceled.
GA	General agent, general average (marine insurance).
GAE	General Air Express.
gal. cap.	Gallon capacity.
gal., gals.	Gallon(s).
GAO	General Accounting Officer (Office).
GATT	General Agreement on Trade and Tariffs
gds.	Goods.
Gen. Aud.	General auditor.
gen., gen'l	General.
Ger.	Germany.
gi.	Gill (Measure).
gm.	Gram.
gov., govt	Government.

GPS	global positioning system
gr.	Grain, gross, group.
gr.	Great gross.
Gr.	Greece.
gr. prod.	Grain products.
gr. wt	Gross weight.
gt (Latin, gutta)	A drop-like marking, great.
gtd.	Guaranteed.
H	Hydrogen.
h.	Harbor, high, height.
h.a. (Latin, hoc anno)	This year.
H.D.	High density (Cotton).
H.G	Hauling class (or code).
H.H.G.	Household goods.
H.I.	Hawaiian Islands.
H.M.	His (or Her) Majesty.
H.M.S.	His (or Her) Majesty's Ship.
h.p.	Horsepower.
H.R	House of Representatives.
H.W.	High water.
H.W.M.	High water mark.
haz	Hazard.
hbr.	Harbor.
heat	Heater charger.
hf.	Half.
hg.	Hectogram.
hg. chts.	Half chests.
hgt	Height.
hhd., hhds.	Hogshead, hogsheads.
hl.	Hectoliter, metric system.
Hon.	Honorable.
HOV	High occupancy vehicle.
hr., hrs.	Hour(s).
HST	High speed train.
ht	Height.
HTML	Hypertext markup language.
hund.	Hundred.
hypoth.	Hypothesis or hypothetical.
I&S	Iron and Steel; Investigation and Suspension.
I&S (articles)	Iron and steel (articles).
I&S (docket)	Investigation and suspension (Docket)—I.C.C.
I.&S.	Docket Investigation and Suspension Docket.
I.B.	Inbound, in bond.
I.C. Rep.	Interstate Commerce Report.

I.C.A.O.	International Civil Aviation Organization.
I.C.C.	Interstate Commerce Commission.
I.C.C. Rep.	Interstate Commerce Commission Report.
I.C.C. Spec'n.	Interstate Commerce Commission Specification.
I.C.E.M.	Intergovernmental Committee for European Migration.
I.C.H.C.C.	International Cargo Handling Coordination Committee.
i.e. (Latin, id est)	That is.
I.F.A.	Illinois Freight Association.
I.F.C.	Illinois Freight Committee.
I.H.	Ice haulage.
I.L	Interior (inside) length, interline.
I.M.R.&T.	Indiana Motor Rate & Tariff Bureau.
I.P.	Identity preserved.
I.P.A.	Including particular average.
I.P.D.	Individual package delivery.
i.q.	(Latin, idem quod) The same as.
I.R.C.	Irregular route carrier.
I.R.D.	Internal Revenue Department
I.R.O.	Internal Revenue Officer.
I.R.S.	Internal Revenue Service.
I.T.	Immediate transportation, in transit.
I.W.	Interior (inside) width.
IAS.	Indicated air speed.
IATA	International Air Transport Association.
ib., ibid	(Latin, ibidem) In the same place.
ID	Inside diameter.
id.	(Latin, idem) The same.
Id.	Load.
ILA	International Longshoremen's Association.
ILWU	International Longshoremen's and Warehousemen's Union.
imp.	Import, imperfect.
impl.	Implement.
in loc.	(Latin, in loco) In its place, at the place referred to.
In re	(Latin) In regard to.
in situ	(Latin) In its original situation.
in sum.	(Latin, in summa) In the summary.
in trans.	(Latin, in transitu) In passage (movement).
in.	Inch, inches.
inc.	Incorporated.
incl.	Inclusive, including.
ind.	Index.

indiv.	Individual.
inf.	(Latin, infra) Beneath, below or hereinafter.
Inf. L	Inflammable liquid.
Inf. S.	Inflammable solid.
init	Initial.
ins., insp.	Inspector.
ins., insur.	Insurance.
inst (Instant)	This month.
int	Interest, intermediate, interior, interchange.
Int Rev.	Internal Revenue.
int'l., intn'l.	International.
inter.	Interstate.
intra	Intrastate.
inv.	Invoice.
invest	Investment.
Ipo	Initial public offering.
IS.	Interstate.
isl.	Island.
ISO	Independent system operators of electricity.
ISP	Internet service provider.
it	Item.
itin.	Itinerary.
ITS	Intelligence transportation systems.
Iv.	Leave.
J-A	Joint agent.
J.	Judge, justice.
J.EA	Joint export agent.
j/a	Joint account.
jct, jctn., junc.	Junction.
jct pt	Junction point.
JIT	Just in time.
JIT II	Just in time II.
jt agt	Joint agent.
jt, jnt	Joint.
jtr.	Joint rate.
K	Kilogram (kilo).
K.D.F.	Knocked down flat.
KD.	Knocked down.
KD.CL	Knocked down carload.
KD.LCL	Knocked down less than carload.
kg, kilQ, kilog.	Kilogram (metric system).
kg., kgs.	Keg(s).
kl., kilol.	Kiloliter (metric system).
km., kilom.	Kilometer (metric system).

KPI's	Key performance indicators.
kr.	Kroner.
kv.	Kilovolt.
kw.	Kilowatt.
Ky., Ken.	Kentucky.
L	Lake, length, loaded, pound sterling.
L to S	Lighterage to shipside.
L&D	Loss and damage.
L&R	Lake and rail.
L. Lmt	Load limit.
l.c.l.	Less than carload, less than containerload.
L.W.M.	Low water mark.
L/C	Letter of credit.
LA	Letter of Authority, Local agent.
Lab.	Labrador.
LASH	Lighter Aboard Ship.
lat	Latitude.
lb., lbs.	(Latin, libra) Pound(s).
Lat	Latin.
Lbl. gds.	Label goods (stored).
Lbr.	Lumber.
LCA	Lake Carriers Association.
lcl.	Local.
LD. Agt	Agent for long-distance movers (Hh.G.).
Ld.	Limited.
LF.T.B.	Louisville Freight Tariff Bureau.
LFA	Local Freight Agent.
Lg.	Landing, loading.
Lge.	Lighterage.
LHAR.	London, Hull, Antwerp or Rotterdam.
lic	License.
liq.	Liquid, liquor.
LIS	Logistics information system.
LL, Lg. Lmts.	Lighterage limits.
LNG	Liquid natural gas.
log.	Logistics.
lon., long.	Longitude.
LOOP	Louisiana Offshore Oil Port.
LORAN	Long range aid to navigation
Lr.	Lira.
LR.	Lloyd's Register.
LS.	Legal scroll.
LSA	Livestock agent.
Lsd.	(Latin, libra, solida, denarii) Pounds, shillings, pence.

Lt wt	Light weight.
lt. tn.	Long ton.
LT., tn.	Long ton.
LT.L	Less than truckload.
Ltd.	British limited liab. company.
Ltr.	Lighter.
MF.T.	Motor Freight Terminal.
m.	Month, mile.
M. (Latin, mille)	A thousand, (meridian) Noon.
M.C.	Marked capacity, motor carrier.
M.C.B.	Master Car Builder.
M.C.B.R.	Master Car Builders' Rules.
M.C.C.	Motor Carrier Cases (I.C.C.)
M.C.R.B.	Motor Carrier Rate Bureau.
M.F.	Motor freight.
M.F.B M.	Thousand feet, board measurement.
M.F.L.	Motor Freight Line.
M.L.C.	Multi-level rail car.
M.M.	Master mechanic.
M.O.	Money order.
M.P.	Milepost.
M.S.T.	Mountain Standard Time.
M.T.	Metric ton.
M.T.D.	Manager, Traffic (or Transportation) Department.
M.T.M.T.S.	Military Traffic Management and Terminal Services.
M.W.M.F.B.	Middlewest Motor Freight Bureau.
M/D	Months (after) date.
M/S	Months after sight.
M/V	Motor vessel.
MA Form A	Document necessary for exporting into Canada.
MAC	Military Airlift Command, Middle Atlantic Conference.
MARAD	Maritime Administration.
mat hdlg.	Material handling.
max.	Maximum.
MBF	One thousand board feet.
mdse.	Merchandise.
mem., memo.	Memorandum.
Memo. B/L	Memorandum Bill of Lading.
Messrs.	Gentlemen, sirs.
mfd, mird.	Manufactured.
mfg	Manufacturing, manufacture.
mfr.	Manufacturer.

min.	Minimum, minute.
min. wt	Minimum weight.
misc., miscl.	Miscellaneous.
mk	Mark.
mkd.	Marked.
mkd. wt	Marked weight.
MM	Two thousand.
mm.	Millimeter.
mo., mos.	Month(s).
MRO	Maintenance, repair, and operating supplies.
MRP	Materials requirements planning.
MS., MSS.	Manuscript, manuscripts.
mt	Mount, mountain.
mties.	Empties.
mty.	Empty.
mxd	Mixed.
N.	North, note.
n.a.	Not applicable.
N.A.M.B.O.	National Association of Motor Bus Operators.
N.A.P.M.	National Association of Purchasing Management.
n.aa	Not always afloat.
N.B.	Northbound, New Brunswick.
N.D.T.A.	National Defense Transportation Association.
N.E.	Northeast, New England.
n.e.	Nonessential.
N.E.F.A.	New England Freight Association.
N.E.M.R.B.	New England Motor Rate Bureau.
N.ES.	Not elsewhere specified.
N.ET.R./F.T.C.	New England Territory Railroads/Freight Traffic Committee.
N.F.A.	National Freight Association.
N.F.T.B.	Niagara Frontier Tariff Bureau.
N.M.F.C.	National Motor Freight Classification.
N.Nstd.	Not nested.
N.O.E.	Not elsewhere enumerated.
N.O.F.T.B.	New Orleans Freight Tariff Bureau.
N.O.H.P.	Not otherwise herein provided.
N.O.I.	Not otherwise indexed.
N.O.I.B.N.	Not otherwise indexed by name.
N.O.S.	Not otherwise specified.
N.R.A.B.	National Railroad Adjustment Board.
N.S.	Not Specified.
N.S.P.F.	Not specifically provided for.
N.T.	Net ton, Northern Territory (Australia).

N.T.P.	National Transportation Policy.
n.w.	Naked weight.
N.W.	Northwest, Northwestern.
N.W.R.	Northwestern Region.
N.W.T.	Northwest Territory.
NA	North America.
NAC.	North Atlantic Coast.
NAFTA	North American Free Trade Agreement.
naut	Nautical.
nav., navig	Navigation.
NDA	Non-disclosure agreement.
net wt.	Net weight.
Neth.	Netherlands.
NIC	Newly industrialized country.
NICS	Newly industrialized countries.
no., nox.	Number(s).
nr.	Near.
nstd	Nested.
ntfy.	Notify.
NVOCC	Non-Vessel Operating Common Carrier.
O&R	Ocean and rail.
O.&R.	Ocean and rail.
O.C.	Official classification.
O.C.C.	Official Classification Committee.
O.D.T.	Office of Defense Transportation.
o.e.	Omissions excepted.
O.M.	Old measurement.
O.M.I.A.	Operating, maintenance, interest and adaptability.
O.R.	Owner's risk.
O.R.B.	Owner's risk of breakage.
O.R.C.	Owner's risk of chafing.
O.R.D.	Owner's risk of damage.
O.R.Det.	Owner's risk of deterioration.
O.R.F.	Owner's risk of fire (or freezing).
O.R.L.	Owner's risk of leakage.
O.R.S.	Owner's risk of shifting.
O.R.W.	Owner's risk of becoming wet.
O.S.	Ordinary seaman.
O.S.&D.	Over, short and damage.
O/C	Overcharge, Open Charter.
O/N	Order notify.
OCTG	Oil country tubular goods.
OD	Outside diameter.
ODS	Operating differential subsidy.

OEM	Original equipment manufacturer.
OO	Owner-operator.
Oper. Exec.	Operating Executive.
Opr.	Operator.
Oswo	Oh, shucks, we're out.
OT	Open top trailer.
OTIF	On time and in full.
OTIFNE	On time, in full, no exceptions.
OTR	Over the road.
OWB	Over without bill.
oxd m.	Oxidizing material.
oz, ozs.	Ounce(s).
P	Perishable.
P&D	Pickup and Delivery (service).
P&I Club	Protection and indemnity insurance (ship).
P&L	Profit and loss.
p.	Page.
P.B.	Privately bonded.
P.C.	Per cent.
P.C.F.B.	Pacific Coast Freight Bureau.
P.D.	(Latin, per diem) By the day, property damage.
P.H.P.	Packing house products.
P.I.	Publication instructions.
P.L.	Public Law.
P.L.&P.D.	Public liability and property damage.
p.m.	(Latin, post meridiem) After noon.
P.M.	Postmaster, paymaster.
P.O.	Post Office; purchase order.
P.O.D.	Post Office Department, pay on delivery.
P.O.O.	Post Office Order.
p.p.	Picked ports.
P.P.	Prepay, prepaid, parcel post.
p.p.i.	Policy, proof of interest.
P.P.O.	Prepaid order.
P.R.A.	Public Roads Administration.
P.S.	(Latin, post scriptum) Postscript.
P.S.C.	Public Service Commission.
P.S.T.	Pacific Standard Time.
P.T., P.Tel.	Postal telegraph.
P.T.C.	Postal telegraph code.
P.T.M.	Passenger traffic manager.
P.U.	Pickup.
P.U.&D.	Pickup and delivery.
P.U.C.	Public Utilities Commission.

P.W.	Packed weight.
P/C	Prices current.
P/N	Please note.
PA	Particular average, purchasing agent, passenger agent, per annum.
Pa, Penna	Pennsylvania.
Pac.	Pacific.
palts	Pallets.
Pan Am.	Pan American.
par.	Paragraph.
Para	Paraguay.
pass.	Passenger.
PAY.E.	Pay as you enter.
payt	Payment.
pc., pcs.	Piece, pieces.
pd	Paid.
pen.	Peninsula.
per	By the, according to.
per an. (Latin, per annum)	By the year.
per ct (Latin, per centum)	By the hundred, percentage.
persh.	Perishable.
pf., pfd	Preferred.
pk., pka	Peck(s).
pkg, pkgs	Package(s).
pkt	Packet.
pl.	Place, plural.
pltf	Plaintiff.
PMA	Pacific Maritime Association.
pntd	Painted.
POC	Purchase order cost.
pod	Purchase order draft.
Pol.	Poland.
popl, popl.	Population.
POS	Point of sale.
POU	Point of use.
pp.	Pages.
PPd, ppd	Prepaid, postpaid.
pr.	Price, pair.
pra	Progressive.
pre.	Prefix.
pres., pres't	President.
prev.	Previous.
priv.	Private.
prod	Product.

prop., propl	Proportional.
prop., propr.	Proprietor.
propa	Proportion.
prov.	Province.
prox	Proximo, next (month).
ps.	Pieces.
PT 20	Per 20 foot trailer or container.
PT 40	Per 40 foot trailer or container.
pt.	Port, point, pint, part.
Pty	"Proprietary" privately owned company in British Commonwealth.
PWC	Pacific Westbound Conference.
pyn–	Payment.
Q, Qu.	Question.
Q.F.	Quick freeze.
QC.P.	Overland Common Points.
QED	(Latin, quod erat demonstrandum) Which was to be proved.
qr.	Quire, quarter.
qt.	Quart, quantity.
qta	Quarts.
qtr.	Quarter.
quar.	Quarterly.
R&C	Rail and canal.
R&L	Rail and lake.
R&M	Repair and maintenance.
R&O	Rail and ocean.
R&T	Rail and truck.
R&W	Rail and water.
r,v., rwy.	Railway.
R-W-R	Rail-Water-Rail.
R. Rod	Road.
R.25	Rule Twenty-five (Consolidated classification).
R.26	Rule Twenty-six (Consolidated classification).
R.D.	Regional director, rural delivery (P.O.).
R.E.R.	Railway Equipment Register.
R.F.T.B.	Richmond Freight Tariff Bureau.
R.IT.	Refining in transit.
R.L&R.	Rail, lake and rail.
R.M.C.	Regulated motor carriers.
R.P.O.	Railway Post Office.
R.R.	Railroad.
R.R.C.	Regular route carrier.
R.S.	Right side.

R.S. or L	Rated same or lower.
R.U.I.	Railroad Unemployment Insurance.
R/C	Reconsigned, recovered.
R/D	Refer to drawer.
RAOA	Railway Accounting Officers Association.
RC&L	Rail, canal and lake.
rc'd, rec'd	Received.
RC	Relief claim, release clause.
RCRA	Resource Conservation and Recovery Act.
rd	Road.
rdo.	Radio.
re (in re) (Latin)	Referring to, in regard to.
RE agt	Real estate agent.
re-exp.	Reexport.
re-imp.	Reimport.
rec.	Receipt.
recap	Recapitulation.
recon, recong	Reconsign.
red	Reduction.
refg, refrig.	Refrigerating, refrigeration.
refgr.	Refrigerator.
refrig'd.	Refrigerated.
reg.	Regulation.
regd.	Registered.
rel.	Released.
rep.	Report, republic, representative.
ret	Reference.
ret., retd.	Returned.
Rfgn.	Refrigeration (charges).
RFP	Request for proposal.
RFR	Radio frequency.
RICA	Revised Interstate Commerce Act.
riv.	River.
RJ	Road junction.
RO/RO	Roll-on/roll-off.
ROCE	Return on capital employed.
R.P.M.	Revolutions per minute.
rpt., rep.	Report.
Rs.	Rupees.
RTA	Refer to Acceptor.
rtd.	Returned.
rte.	Route.
RTX	Real time.
S&C	Shipper and Carrier.

S.	State, south.
S.A.	Sociedad Anonima (Spanish sp. Countries), Société Anonyme (Fr.)
S.A.	Società Anomima—Italy companies
S.B.	Southbound, shipping board, steamboat, separately binned.
S.C.	Special circular, Southern Classification, surcharge.
S.C.&S.	Strapped, corded and sealed.
S.C.C.	State Corporation Commission, Southern Classification Committee.
S.D.	Single deck, side door.
S.D.D.	Store door delivery.
S.E.	Southeast, Southeastern.
S.E.M.V.F.A.	Southeastern Mississippi Valley Freight Association.
S.E.F.A.	Southeastern Freight Association.
S.F.I.B.	Southern Freight Inspection Bureau.
S.I.T.	Stopping in transit, storage in transit.
S.L&C.	Shipper's load and count.
S.L&T.	Shipper's load and tally.
S.M.C.R.	Southern Motor Carrier's Rate Conference.
S.O.	Seller's option, ship's option, shipping order.
S.O.S.	A distress signal.
S.P.	Supra protest.
s.p.a.	Subject to particular average.
S.P.L.C.	Standard Point Location Code.
S.R.	Shipping receipt, Southern Region.
S.R.&C.C.	Strikes, riots and civil commotions.
S.R.O.	Special rate order.
S.S.	Shipside.
S.T.	Stopping (or storage) in transit, Superintendent of transportation.
s.t.	Shipping ticket.
S.T.C.	Single trip container.
S.T.C.C.	Standard Transportation Commodity Code.
S.U LC.L	Set up in less than carload.
S.U.	Set up.
S.U.CL	Set up carload.
s.v.	Sailing vessel.
S.W.	Southwest, Southwestern, stenciled weight.
S.W.F.T.B.	Southwestern Freight Tariff Bureau.
S.W.M.F.B.	Southwestern Motor Freight Bureau.
S.W.R.	Southwestern Region.
S.W.T.	Southwestern Territory.
S.W.T.C.	Southwestern Tariff Committee.

S/B	Statement of billing.
S/D	Sea damaged, statement of differences.
S/N	Shipping note.
S/S	Steamship.
SAC	South Atlantic Coast.
SC, SCS.	Scale, scales.
SCD	Special Commodities Division.
sch.	Schooner.
scl.	Scale.
sdg.	Siding.
sec	Section, second.
sec, secy.	Secretary.
sect	Section.
SED	Shippers export declaration.
sh.tn.	Short ton (2,000 lbs.).
shpt	Shipment.
shtg.	Shortage.
sid.	Sailed, sealed.
stds.	Standards.
SKU	Stock keeping unit.
so., Sou.	South, Southern.
SOLE	Society of Logistics Engineers.
Sou. Class'n	Southern Classification.
sp. gr.	Specific gravity.
sp. iron	Special iron.
SPC	Statistical process control.
spec.	Specification.
spgs.	Springs.
spt	Seaport.
sq.	Square.
ss.	Sworn statement.
SS.&C.	Same sea and country (or Coast).
St	Saint.
st., sts.	Street, streets.
ST.	Short ton.
sta	Stationer, station.
sta agt	Station agent.
stat	Statistician.
stats.	Statutes.
ster., stg.	Sterling.
steve.	Stevedore.
stg., stge., stor.	Storage.
stge. trk	Storage track.
str.	Steamer, straight.

str. kpr.	Storekeeper.
Sup. Ct Rep.	Supreme Court Reporter.
sup., supl., suppl.	Supplement.
supra	Above.
supt	Superintendent.
Supt Car Ser.	Superintendent Car Service.
supvr.	Supervisor.
swg., swt	Switching.
sys., syst	System.
T&R	Truck and rail.
T-C.F.B.	Trans-Continental Freight Bureau.
T-C.W.&I.B.	Trans-Continental Weighing–Inspection Bureau.
T.	Terminal, temperature.
T. Commr.	Traffic commissioner.
T.B.	Traffic (or Tariff) Bureau.
T.C.	Traffic counselor (consultant), traffic or transportation commissioner.
T.D. or T. Dir.	Traffic director.
T.EA ER	Traffic Executives Association Eastern Railroads.
T.I.P.	"Taking the inbound pilot" (term in ship charter).
T.L.	Truckload.
T.L.A.	Trunk Line Association.
T.I.R.	International Road Transport.
T.M.	Traffic Manager, trainmaster.
T.N.	Tariff number.
T.O.F.C.	Trailer-on-flat-car.
T.R.&W.	Truck, rail and water.
T.RF.	Transportation Research Forum, Transportation Research Foundation.
T.S. area	Total storage area.
T.T.B.	Texas Tariff Bureau.
TA or T. Aud.	Traffic auditor.
TA, T.	AgL Tax agent, temporary authority.
TAA	Transportation Association of America.
TAC	Total acquisition cost.
tb.	Trial balance.
TC	Tariff (or traffic) circular.
tc, tcs.	Tierce, tierces.
tc.&s.	Free of capture and seizure.
TCO	Total cost of ownership.
td.	Free discharge.
tel., telg.	Telegram, telegraph.
ter. terr.	Territory.
term, term'l.	Terminal.

tk	Truck.
tkt	Ticket.
tl.o.	Total loss only.
tnge.	Tonnage.
tot	Total.
TOVALOP	The Tanker Owner's Voluntary Agreement concerning Liability for Oil Pollution.
Tpd	Tons per day of fuel that a vessel consumes.
traf.	Traffic.
tran.	Transit.
trans. priv.	Transit privileges.
transfd	Transferred.
trans, transp.	Transportation.
treas.	Treasurer.
trf.	Tariff.
trfr.	Transfer.
trk	Track.
trk stge.	Track storage.
trm	Terminal.
TT or TWX	Teletype communication system.
ttr., trnfr	Transfer.
U.F.C.	Uniform Freight Classification.
U.K./Cont (B.H.)	United Kingdom or Continent (Bordeaux/Hamburg Range).
U.K./Cont (H.H.)	United Kingdom or Continent (Havre/Hamburg Range).
U.K./Cont (G.H.)	United Kingdom or Continent (Gibraltar/Hamburg Range).
U.K.F.O.	United Kingdom for Orders—the vessel is to proceed to the U.K. for Orders.
U.LD.	Unit Load Device.
U.S. CA	U.S. Code Annotated.
U.S.A.	United States of America.
U.S.C.	United States Customs.
U.S.I.R.B.	United States Internal Revenue Bonded.
U.S.M.	United States Mail
U.S.M.C.	U.S. Maritime Commission.
U.S.N.D.	United States Navy Department.
U.S.N.H.	United States North of Cape Hatteras.
U.S.R.A.	United States Railroad Administration.
U.S.S.	United States Ship.
U.S.S.B.	United States Shipping Board.
U.S.S.G.	United States Standard Gauge.
U.S.S.H.	United States South of Cape Hatteras.

U.S.T.D.	United States Treasury Department.
U.S.W.A.B.	United States Warehouse Act Bonded.
U/A	Underwriting account.
U/C	Undercharge.
U/W	Underwriter.
UCC	Uniform Commercial Code.
UCC	Uniform Code Council, ANSI
ULCC	Ultra large crude carrier.
ULD	Unit load device.
unimtd.	Unlimited.
Unrep. Op.	Unreported Opinion (I.C.C.).
UPC	Uniform product code.
Urg.	Uruguay.
utt, ulto.	(Latin, ultimo) Last (month).
V	Five or fifth.
v., vs.	(Latin, versus) Against or in opposition.
V.C.	Visible capacity.
v.d.	Various dates.
V.P., V. Pres.	Vice President.
V.S.	Visible Supply.
val.	Value.
ves.	Vessel.
via	(Latin) By way of.
viz	(Latin) Namely, to wit.
vol.	Volume.
W&F	Water and feed.
W&I	Weighing and inspection.
W&IB	Weighing and Inspection Bureau.
W&R	Water and rail.
W.	West, western, width, weight.
w.a	With average.
w.b.	Water ballast.
W.B.	Westbound.
W.B./E.I.	West Britain/East Ireland.
W.C.	Western classification.
W.C.C.	Western Classification Committee.
W.D.F.	Waterfront dock facilities.
W.F.T.B.	Western Freight Tariff Bureau.
W.I.	West Indies.
W.O.	Wait Order.
W.PA	With particular average.
W.T.L.	Western Trunk Line.
W.T.L.A.	Western Trunk Line Association.
W.T.L.C.	Western Trunk Line Committee.

W.U.	Western Union.
w.w.	Weather working.
W.W.&I.B.	Western Weighing and Inspection Bureau.
W/B	Waybill.
W/M, W or M	Weight or measurement.
W/R	Was received.
W/W	Warehouse warrant.
Wash.	Washington.
wdt.	Width.
WERC	Warehouse Education and Research Council.
West'n	Western.
West'n. Class'n.	Western classification.
whf.	Wharf.
whfg.	Wharfage.
whm.	Weighmaster.
whse.	Warehouse.
wk	Week, work.
wkds.	Weekdays.
wrfg.	Wharfage.
wt	Weight.
WTO	World Trade Organization.
WVA	West Virginia.
X CAR	From car.
X.	Extra.
Xg. Xing.	Crossing.
y.	Yard.
Y/A	York-Antwerp Rules (Marine Insurance).
Y2K	Year 2000.
yd, yds.	Yard, yards.
ydg	Yarding.
yr., yrs.	Year(s).
Z	Zone, zero, zinc.
Zn	Zinc.
ZORF	Zone of Rate Freedom.

1990 INCO TERMS

Ex works (EXW)—at named place

Free Carrier (FCA)—at named place

Free Alongside Ship (FAS)—at named port of outbound shipment

Free on Board (FOB)—at named port of outbound shipment

Cost and Freight (CFR)—to named port of destination

Cost, Insurance and Freight (CIF)—to named port of destination

Carriage Paid To (CPT)—to named place of destination

Delivered at Frontier (DAF)—at named place

Delivered Ex Ship (DES)—to named port of destination

Delivered Ex Quay (Duty Paid) (DEQ)—to named port of destination

Delivered Duty Unpaid (DDU)—to named place of destination

Delivered Duty Paid (DDP)—to named place of destination

KEY WORD TRANSLATIONS:

English	Italian	French
Airline	linea area	compagnie
Airport	aeroporto	aéroport
Bank	banca	banque
Container	recipiente	récipient
Currency	moneta	monétaire
Customer	cliente	client(e)
Customs Duties	tariffa doganale	droits de douane
Delivery	consegna	livraison
Distribution	distribuzione	distribution
Export	esportazione	exportation
Import	importazione	importation
Inventory	inventario	inventaire
Handling (as in materials handling)	maneggio	manutention
Manufacturing	manifatturiero	fabrication
Order (to place an order)	ordinare (verb)	commander
Package	pacco	paquet
Payment	pagamento	paiement
Pipeline	condotto di petrolio	conduite
Port		
Purchase (or purchasing)	acquistare	acquisition
Railroad	ferrovia	chemin de fer
Receiving	ricettazione	réception
Service	servizio	service
Ship (the vessel, not the act of)	nave	navire marchand
Transport/Transportation	trasporto	transport
Truck	carro	camion
Warehouse	magazzino	magasin

DICTIONARY TERMS—Spanish★

English	Spanish
Airline	línea aérea
Airport	aeropuerto
Bank	banco
Container	contenedor
Currency	moneda
Customer	cliente
Customs Duties	derechos de aduana
Delivery	entrega
Distribution	distribución
Export	exportación
Import	importación
Inventory	inventario
Handling (as in materials handling)	manejo
Manufacturing	fabricación
Order (to place an order)	un pedido (noun), pedir (verb)
Package	paquete
Payment	pago
Pipeline	oleoducto (for oil)
Port	puerto
Purchase (or purchasing)	compra
Railroad	ferrocarril
Receiving	recepción
Service	servicio
Ship (the vessel, not the act of)	barco/buque
Transport/Transportation	transporte
Truck	camión
Warehouse	almacén

★ These terms were provided by Janet L. Cavinato, BP-Amoco Corporation.

DICTIONARY TERMS—German★

English	German
Airline	die Fluglinie
Airport	der Flughafen
Bank	die Bank
Container	der Container
Currency	der Kurantgeld or der Zahlungsmittel
Customer	der Kunde
Customs Duties	die Zollgebuhr
Delivery	die Ablieferung
Distribution	der Vertrieb
Export	der Export
Import	der Import
Inventory	der Warenbestand
Handling (as materials handling)	die Behandlung
Manufacturing	die Produktion
Order	*v.* bestellen *n.* der Auftrag
Package	die Verpackung
Payment	die Bezahlung
Pipeline	die Rohrleitung
Port	der Hafen
Purchase (or purchasing)	*v.* einkaufen *n.* der Einkauf
Railroad	die Eisenbahn
Receiving	der Empfang
Service	der Dienst
Ship	das Schiff
Transport/Transportation	der Verkehr
Truck	das Landkraftwagen
Warehouse	das Lagerhaus

★ These terms were provided by Dr. Richard R. Young, The Pennsylvania State University and the Acquisition Research & Development Center.

OFFICIAL 2-LETTER POSTAL CODES

U.S. and CANADA

Alabama	AL	Montana	MT
Alaska	AK	Nebraska	NE
Arizona	AZ	Nevada	NV
Arkansas	AR	New Hampshire	NH
California	CA	New Jersey	NJ
Colorado	CO	New Mexico	NM
Connecticut	CT	New York	NY
Delaware	DE	North Carolina	NC
Dist. of Columbia	DC	North Dakota	ND
Florida	FL	Ohio	OH
Georgia	GA	Oklahoma	OK
Hawaii	HI	Oregon	OR
Idaho	ID	Pennsylvania	PA
Illinois	IL	Rhode Island	RI
Indiana	IN	South Carolina	SC
Iowa	IA	South Dakota	SD
Kansas	KS	Tennessee	TN
Kentucky	KY	Texas	TX
Louisiana	LA	Utah	UT
Maine	ME	Vermont	VT
Maryland	MD	Virginia	VA
Massachusetts	MA	Washington	WA
Michigan	MI	West Virginia	WV
Minnesota	MN	Wisconsin	WI
Mississippi	MS	Wyoming	WY

CANADA

Alberta	AB
British Columbia	BC
Manitoba	MB
Ontario	ON
Prince Edward Island	PEI
Quebec	PQ
New Brunswick	NB
Newfoundland	NFLD
Northwest Territories	NWT
Nova Scotia	NS
Saskatchewan	SK
Yukon	YT

INTERNET COUNTRY CODES

Afghanistan	AF	Chile	CL	
Albania	AL	China, People's Republic of	CN	
Algeria	DZ	Christmas Island	CX	
American Samoa	AS	Cocos Island	CC	
Andorra	AD	Colombia	CO	
Angola	AO	Comoros	KM	
Anguilla	AI	Congo	CG	
Antarctica	AQ	Cook Islands	CK	
Antigua and Barbuda	AG	Costa Rica	CR	
Argentina	AR	Côte D'Ivoire (Ivory Coast)	CI	
Armenia	AM	Croatia	HR	
Aruba	AW	Cuba	CU	
Australia	AU	Cyprus	CY	
Austria	AT	Czech Republic	CZ	
Azerbaijan	AZ	Denmark	DK	
Bahamas	BS	Djibouti	DJ	
Bahrain	BH	Dominica	DM	
Bangladesh	BD	Dominican Republic	DO	
Barbados	BB	East Timor	TP	
Belarus	BY	Ecuador	EC	
Belgium	BE	Egypt	EG	
Belize	BZ	El Salvador	SV	
Benin	BJ	Equatorial Guinea	GQ	
Bermuda	BM	Eritrea	ER	
Bhutan	BT	Estonia	EE	
Bolivia	BO	Ethiopia	ET	
Bosnia and Herzegovina	BA	Falkland Islands	FK	
Botswana	BW	Faroe Islands	FO	
Brazil	BR	Fiji	FJ	
Brunei Darussalam	BN	Finland	FI	
Bulgaria	BG	France	FR	
Burkina Faso	BF	France, Metropolitan	FX	
Burundi	BI	French Guiana	GF	
Cambodia	KH	French Polynesia	PF	
Cameroon	CM	Gabon	GA	
Canada	CA	Gambia	GM	
Cape Verde	CV	Georgia (Republic of Georgia)	GE	
Cayman Islands	KY	Germany	DE	
Central African Republic	CF	Ghana	GH	
Chad Republic	TD	Gibraltar	GI	

Greece	GR	Mali	ML
Greenland	GL	Malta	MT
Grenada	GD	Marshall Islands	MH
Guadeloupe	GP	Martinique	MQ
Guam	GU	Mauritania	MR
Guatemala	GT	Mauritius	MU
Guinea	GN	Mayotte Island	YT
Guinea-Bissau	GW	Mexico	MX
Guyana	GY	Micronesia	FM
Haiti	HT	Moldova, Republic of	MD
Honduras	HN	Monaco	MC
Hong Kong	HK	Mongolia	MN
Hungary	HU	Montserrat	MS
Iceland	IS	Morocco	MA
India	IN	Mozambique	MZ
Indonesia	ID	Myanmar	MN
Iran, Islamic Republic of	IR	Namibia	NA
Iraq	IQ	Nauru	NR
Ireland	IE	Nepal	NP
Israel	IL	Netherlands	NL
Italy	IT	Netherlands Antilles	AN
Jamaica	JM	New Caledonia	NC
Japan	JP	New Zealand	NZ
Jordan	JO	Nicaragua	NI
Kazakhstan	KZ	Niger Republic	NE
Kiribati	KI	Niue	NU
Korea (North)	KP	Norfolk Island	NF
Korea, Republic of	KR	Norway	NO
Kuwait	KW	Oman	OM
Kyrgyzstan	KG	Pakistan	PK
Lao People's Democratic Republic	LA	Palau	PW
Latvia	LV	Panama	PA
Lebanon	LB	Papua New Guinea	PG
Lesotho	LS	Paraguay	PY
Liberia	LR	Peru	PE
Libya and Jamahiriya	LY	Philippines	PH
Liechtenstein	LI	Pitcairn	PN
Lithuania	LT	Poland	PL
Luxembourg	LU	Portugal	PT
Macau	MO	Puerto Rico	PR
Macedonia	MK	Qatar	QA
Madagascar	MG	Reunion Island	RE
Malaysia	MY	Romania	RO
Maldives	MV	Russian Federation	RU

Rwanda	RW	Tajikistan, Republic of	TJ
Saint Kitts and Nevis	KN	Tanzania	TZ
Samoa	WS	Thailand	TH
San Marino	SM	Togo	TG
Sao Tome and Principe	ST	Tokelau	TK
St. Helena	SH	Tonga	TO
St. Lucia	LC	Trinidad and Tobago	TT
St. Pierre and Miqueion	PM	Tunisia	TN
St. Vincent and the Grenadines	VC	Turkey	TR
Saudi Arabia	SA	Turkmenistan	TM
Senegal Republic	SN	Turks and Caicos Islands	TC
Seychelles Islands	SC	Tuvalu	TV
Sierra Leone	SL	Uganda	UG
Singapore	SG	Ukraine	UA
Slovakia	SK	United Arab Emirates	AE
Slovenia	SI	United Kingdom	UK
Solomon Islands	SB	United States	US
Somalia	SO	Uruguay	UY
South Africa	ZA	Uzbekistan	UZ
South Georgia/Sandwich Islands	GS	Vanuatu	VU
Spain	ES	Vatican City	VA
Sri Lanka	LK	Venezuela	VE
Sudan	SD	Vietnam	VN
Surinam	SR	Wallis and Futuna Islands	WF
Svalbard/Jan Mayen Islands	SJ	Western Samoa	WS
Swaziland	SZ	Yemen, Republic of	YE
Sweden	SE	Yugoslavia	YU
Switzerland	CH	Zaire	ZA
Syrian Arab Republic	SY	Zambia	ZM
Taiwan, Republic of	TW	Zimbabwe	ZW

STANDARD TIME DIFFERENCES   United States Cities

At 12 o'clock noon Eastern Standard Time the standard time in U.S. cities is as follows:

Akron, OH	12.00 noon	Memphis, TN	11.00 a.m.
Albuquerque, NM	10.00 a.m.	Miami, FL	12.00 noon
Atlanta, GA	12.00 noon	Milwaukee, WI	11.00 a.m.
Baltimore, MD	12.00 noon	Minneapolis, MN	11.00 a.m.
Birmingham, AL	11.00 a.m.	Newark, NJ	12.00 noon
Bismarck, ND	11.00 a.m.	New York, NY	12.00 noon
Boise, ID	10.00 a.m.	New Orleans, LA	11.00 a.m.
Boston, MA	12.00 noon	Norfolk, VA	12.00 noon
Buffalo, NY	12.00 noon	Okla. City, OK	11.00 a.m.
Butte, MT	10.00 a.m.	Omaha, NE	11.00 a.m.
Charleston, SC	12.00 noon	Philadelphia, PA	12.00 noon
Charleston, WV	12.00 noon	Phoenix, AZ	10.00 a.m.
Cheyenne, WY	10.00 a.m.	Pierre, SD	11.00 a.m.
Chicago, IL	11.00 a.m.	Pittsburgh, PA	12.00 noon
Cincinnati, OH	12.00 noon	Portland, ME	12.00 noon
Cleveland, OH	12.00 noon	Portland, OR	9.00 a.m.
Columbus, OH	12.00 noon	Providence, RI	12.00 noon
Dallas, TX	11.00 a.m.	Reno, NV	9.00 a.m.
Denver, CO	10.00 a.m.	Richmond, VA	12.00 noon
Des Moines, IA	11.00 a.m.	Rochester, NY	12.00 noon
Detroit, MI	12.00 noon	Santa Fe, NM	10.00 a.m.
Duluth, MN	11.00 a.m.	Sioux Falls, SD	11.00 a.m.
Fort Worth, TX	11.00 a.m.	Spokane, WA	9.00 a.m.
Galveston, TX	11.00 a.m.	St. Paul, MN	11.00 a.m.
Grand Rapids, MI	12.00 noon	St. Louis, MO	11.00 a.m.
Hartford, CT	12.00 noon	Salt Lake City, UT	10.00 a.m.
Helena, MT	10.00 a.m.	San Francisco, CA	9.00 a.m.
Honolulu, HI	7.00 a.m.	Savannah, GA	12.00 noon
Houston, TX	11.00 a.m.	Seattle, WA	9.00 a.m.
Indianapolis, IN	12.00 noon	Tacoma, WA	9.00 a.m.
Jacksonville, FL	12.00 noon	Tampa, FL	12.00 noon
Juneau, AK	7.00 a.m.	Toledo, OH	12.00 noon
Kansis City, MO	11.00 a.m.	Topeka, KS	11.00 a.m.
Knoxville, TN	12.00 noon	Tulsa, OK	11.00 a.m.
Lincoln, NE	11.00 a.m.	Washington, DC	12.00 noon
Little Rock, AR	11.00 a.m.	Wichita, KS	11.00 a.m.
Los Angeles, CA	9.00 a.m.	Wilmington, DE	12.00 noon
Louisville, KY	12.00 noon		

Times by City
— London —

At 12 o'clock noon Greenwich Mean Time, the standard time in foreign cities is as follows:

Alexandria	2.00 p.m.	Lima	7.00 a.m.
Amsterdam	1.00 p.m.	Lisbon	12.00 noon
Athens	2.00 p.m.	Liverpool	12.00 noon
Auckland	12.00 mid.	London	12.00 noon
Baghdad	3.00 p.m.	Madrid	1.00 p.m.
Bangkok	7.00 p.m.	Manila	8.00 p.m.
Belfast	12.00 noon	Melbourne	10.00 p.m.
Berlin	1.00 p.m.	Mexico City	6.00 a.m.
Bogota	8.00 a.m.	Montevideo	9.00 a.m.
Bombay	5.30 p.m.	Montreal	7.00 a.m.
Bremen	1.00 p.m.	Moscow	3.00 p.m.
Brussels	1.00 p.m.	New York	7.00 a.m.
Bucharest	2.00 p.m.	Oslo	1.00 p.m.
Budapest	1.00 p.m.	Paris	1.00 p.m.
Buenos Aires	9.00 a.m.	Rio de Janeiro	9.00 a.m.
Calcutta	5.30 p.m.	Rome	1.00 p.m.
Cape Town	2.00 p.m.	San Francisco	4.00 a.m.
Caracas	8.00 a.m.	Santiago (Chile)	8.00 a.m.
Copenhagen	1.00 p.m.	Shanghai	8.00 p.m.
Dawson (Yukon)	4.00 a.m.	Singapore	8.00 p.m.
Djakarta	7.00 p.m.	St. Petersburg	3.00 p.m.
Dublin	12.00 noon	Sydney (Australia)	10.00 p.m.
Gdansk	1.00 p.m.	Teheran	3.30 p.m.
Geneva	1.00 p.m.	Tel Aviv	2.00 p.m.
Halifax	8.00 a.m.	Tokyo	9.00 p.m.
Havana	7.00 a.m.	Vancouver	4.00 a.m.
Honolulu	2.00 a.m.	Vienna	1.00 p.m.
Hong Kong	8.00 p.m.	Warsaw	1.00 p.m.
Istanbul	2.00 p.m.	Wellington (N.Z.)	12.00 mid.
Jerusalem	2.00 p.m.	Winnipeg	6.00 a.m.
Johannesburg	2.00 p.m.	Yokohama	9.00 p.m.
Le Havre	1.00 p.m.	Zurich	1.00 p.m.

Times by City
— New York —

At 12 o'clock noon Eastern Standard Time, the standard time in foreign cities is as follows:

Alexandria	7.00 p.m.	Lima	12.00 noon
Amsterdam	6.00 p.m.	Lisbon	5.00 p.m.
Athens	7.00 p.m.	Liverpool	5.00 p.m.
Auckland	5.00 a.m.★	London	5.00 p.m.
Baghdad	8.00 p.m.	Madrid	6.00 p.m.
Bangkok	12.00 mid.★	Manila	1.00 a.m.★
Belfast	5.00 p.m.	Melbourne	3.00 a.m.★
Berlin	6.00 p.m.	Mexico City	11.00 a.m.
Bogota	12.00 noon	Montevideo	2.00 p.m.
Bombay	10.30 p.m.	Montreal	12.00 noon
Bremen	6.00 p.m.	Moscow	8.00 p.m.
Brussels	6.00 p.m.	Oslo	6.00 a.m.
Bucharest	7.00 p.m.	Paris	6.00 p.m.
Budapest	6.00 p.m.	Rio deJaneiro	2.00 p.m.
Buenos Aires	1.00 p.m.	Rome	6.00 p.m.
Calcutta	10.30 p.m.	St. Petersburg	8.00 p.m.
Cape Town	7.00 p.m.	San Francisco	9.00 a.m.
Caracas	1.00 p.m.	Santiago (Chile)	1.00 p.m.
Copenhagen	6.00 p.m.	Singapore	1.00 a.m.★
Dawson (Yukon)	9.00 a.m.	Sydney (Australia)	3.00 a.m.★
Djakarta	1.00 a.m.★	Teheran	8.30 p.m.
Dublin	5.00 p.m.	Tel Aviv	7.00 p.m.
Gdansk	6.00 p.m.	Tokyo	2.00 a.m.★
Geneva	6.00 p.m.	Vancouver	9.00 a.m.
Halifax	1.00 p.m.	Vienna	6.00 p.m.
Havana	12.00 noon	Warsaw	6.00 p.m.
Hong Kong	1.00 a.m.★	Wellington (N.Z.)	5.00 a.m.★
Istanbul	8.00 p.m.	Winnipeg	11.00 a.m.
Jerusalem	7.00 p.m.	Yokohama	2.00 a.m.★
Johannesburg	7.00 p.m.	Zurich	6.00 p.m.
Le Havre	6.00 p.m.		

★ Indicates morning of the next day

Times by City
— Singapore —

At 12 o'clock noon, Singapore, the standard time in foreign cities is as follows:

Alexandria	6.00 a.m.	Lima	11.00 p.m.
Amsterdam	5.00 a.m.	Lisbon	4.00 a.m.
Athens	6.00 a.m.	Liverpool	4.00 a.m.
Auckland	4.00 p.m.	London	4.00 a.m.
Baghdad	7.00 a.m.	Madrid	5.00 a.m.
Bangkok	11.00 a.m.	Manila	12.00 noon
Belfast	4.00 a.m.	Melbourne	2.00 p.m.
Berlin	5.00 a.m.	Mexico City	10.00 p.m.
Bogota	12.00 mid.	Montevideo	1.00 a.m.
Bombay	10.30 a.m.	Montreal	11.00 p.m.
Bremen	5.00 a.m.	Moscow	7.00 a.m.
Brussels	5.00 a.m.	New York	11.00 p.m.
Bucharest	6.00 a.m.	Oslo	5.00 a.m.
Budapest	5.00 a.m.	Paris	5.00 a.m.
Buenos Aires	1.00 a.m.	Rio deJaneiro	1.00 a.m.
Calcutta	10.30 a.m.	Rome	5.00 a.m.
Cape Town	6.00 a.m.	San Francisco	8.00 p.m.
Caracas	12.00 mid.	Santiago (Chile)	12.00 mid.
Copenhagen	5.00 a.m.	Shanghai	12.00 noon
Dawson (Yukon)	8.00 p.m.	Singapore	12.00 noon
Djakarta	11.00 a.m.	St. Petersburg	7.00 a.m.
Dublin	4.00 a.m.	Sydney (Australia)	2.00 p.m.
Gdansk	5.00 a.m.	Teheran	7.30 a.m.
Geneva	5.00 a.m.	Tel Aviv	6.00 a.m.
Halifax	12.00 mid.	Tokyo	1.00 p.m.
Havana	11.00 p.m.	Vancouver	8.00 p.m.
Honolulu	6.00 a.m.	Vienna	5.00 a.m.
Hong Kong	12.00 noon	Warsaw	5.00 a.m.
Istanbul	6.00 a.m.	Wellington (N.Z.)	4.00 p.m.
Jerusalem	6.00 a.m.	Winnipeg	10.00 p.m.
Johannesburg	6.00 a.m.	Yokohama	1.00 p.m.
Le Havre	5.00 a.m.	Zurich	5.00 a.m.

METRIC CONVERSION FACTORS

AREA

When you know	Multiply by	To Find
square inches	6.4516	square centimeters
square feet	0.0929030	square meters
square yards	0.836127	square meters
square miles	2.58888	square kilometers
square centimeters	0.15500	square inches
square meters	10.7639	square feet
square meters	1.19599	square yards
square kilometers	0.386138	square miles

LENGTH/DISTANCE

When you know	Multiply by	To Find
inches	2.540000	centimeters
feet	0.304800	meters
yards	0.914400	meters
miles	1.60934	kilometers
centimeters	0.393701	inches
meters	3.380840	feet
meters	1.093610	yards
kilometers	0.621371	miles
statute miles	0.868978	nautical miles
nautical mfles	1.150777	statute miles

MASS/WEIGHT

When you know	Multiply by	To Find
pounds	0.453592	kilograms
short tons (2,000 lbs.)	0.907029	metric tons
long tons (2,240 lbs.)	1.016046	metric tons
kilograms	2.20462	pounds
metric tons	1.10250	short tons
metric tons	0.984205	long tons

VOLUME

When you know	Multiply by	To Find
cubic inches	16.3871	cubic centimeters
cubic feet	0.0283168	cubic meters
cubic yards	0.764555	cubic meters

gallons	3.78541	liters
cubic centimeters	0.0610237	cubic inches
cubic meters	35.3147	cubic feet
cubic meters	1.30795	cubic yards
liters	1.05669	quarts (liquid)
liters	0.264172	gallons

TEMPERATURE

When you know	Calculate by	To Find
Fahrenheit (F°)	Subtract 32 then multiply by 5/9	Celsius
Celsius (°C)	Multiply by 9/5 then add 32	Fahrenheit